Oct

Paul R. Hanna
STANFORD UNIVERSITY

Rose E. Sabaroff
HARVARD UNIVERSITY

Gordon F. Davies
CALIFORNIA STATE COLLEGE AT HAYWARD

Charles R. Farrar
STANISLAUS STATE COLLEGE

GEOGRAPHY IN THE TEACHING OF SOCIAL STUDIES

Concepts and Skills

HOUGHTON MIFFLIN COMPANY · BOSTON

New York · Atlanta · Geneva, Ill. · Dallas · Palo Alto

Illustrations by Nathan Goldstein

Preface

During the past quarter century there has been a slowly developing inverse relationship between the accelerating importance of geography in our daily lives, on the one hand, and a decreasing emphasis on geographic education in our schools and colleges, on the other hand. It would appear that as direct life experiences and the mass media focus our attention more and more on the significance of the location and spatial distribution of social, economic, and political facts and events, we pay less and less attention to preparing our young through formal curriculum to comprehend the structure of relationships that exist between the natural conditions of one's environment (one's habitat) and the human activities carried on therein, and to develop the skills with which to deal rationally with matters that have geographic aspects.

Increasing Cruciality of Geographic Knowledge

A few examples of our increasing awareness of natural phenomena might help to make the point clear. For instance, the more than twenty nations that make up the western hemisphere are struggling to create social technology that will contribute to peace, order, prosperity, and the dignity of man throughout the Americas. We have developed over this century a series of associations of nations (e.g., the Pan-American Union, the Organization of American States, the Alliance for Progress) to work toward these goals. Too often limited or inaccurate knowledge of the diversities in such natural characteristics as soil, flora and fauna, minerals, climate, and terrain throughout this vast space of the Americas has prevented us from anticipating or understanding the responses of the peoples who inhabit places that are strange to us in the United States. This lack of knowledge about our natural environment has been the cause of many mistakes and subsequent frustrations to the progress universally desired.

Copper and petroleum reserves face possible depletion in the United States, so we arrange to increase copper imports from Peru and Chile and to increase oil imports from petroleum reserves of northern nations of South America. Bananas and coffee, not grown commercially in continental United States, are supplied from Central America and Brazil. As voting and consuming citizens and as public and private officials representing the United

States, we are not as aware of or as sensitive to the effects of these economic activities on the social and political lives of our neighbors to the south as we might be if we were better grounded in geographic education. Central to any social decision or action is a more accurate and extensive concept of the diversity of existing natural environments and the cultural adaptations within a land mass stretching from pole to pole.

One might use the conflicts in Asia as other examples in which failure to know or comprehend geographic realities leads to questionable international policy and the threat of escalation of wars. One must understand the amounts and spatial distribution of physical and biotic resources in these lands to see the roots of poverty, disease, and despair that lead to violence. One must know the projected population figures in India, China, Japan, and Indonesia in order to think soundly about the demographic pressure on resource bases that will keep this portion of the human family in constant turmoil, unless the world community, informed of the geographic conditions, takes steps to redirect the natural chain of events associated historically with people-land pressures.

A third illustration in our own national community: Climatic factors give us limited and unequal distribution of water resources. Modern industrial processes in the factory and on the farm, coupled with population mobility and explosion, threaten to cause serious water shortages and subsequent reversals in our economic growth. The people, as consumers of water and as voters who support local and national plans for water management, must know far more than they do about the hard facts of water source, distribution, and management in order to avert hardship and even catastrophe of flood or drought. We must understand that replacing sod and forest with pavement and depleting underground water supplies can bring disaster unless comprehensive water development plans are activated.

One could continue at length to recite the new problems of man's social and economic development as related to the natural world which sets many of the limits of human survival. But the proposition is so generally accepted that it needs no further elaboration: geographic knowledge and skill are increasingly important for survival and progress in today's world.

Need for Increased Geographical Education
in the School Curriculum

We have suggested that there has been a marked lessening of attention to geographic education in the schools and colleges during the very period in which survival and progress demand greater competence in this discipline. Attention was sharply drawn to the neglect of geographic education when the United States faced the possibility of defeat in the Pacific theater at the opening of World War II. Our military leaders and civilian officials were appallingly deficient in a knowledge of geography. For several decades prior, the time devoted to geography had been declining steadily in schools and colleges. During the war, an effort was made to compensate for this deficiency by giving more time to the study of geography in the Army Specialized Training Program for all new inductees. But the spurt of interest in the geographic curriculum in the military training program was short-lived and had little impact on the curriculum of the elementary and secondary schools and the colleges.

It is difficult to understand and foolhardy to condone this decline of geography in the curriculum of the schools and colleges. When leading institutions like Harvard and Stanford Universities abandoned their geography departments, the tumbling dominoes effect was pronounced. In the elementary schools, geography was almost forgotten in many state and local school systems. The newer elementary school social studies programs were too often planned and taught by those who had little preparation in geography and therefore undervalued this component in what was meant to be a multidisciplinary and coordinated program. In high school, geography (hardly ever a required subject) became an unpopular elective. The situation across the nation by midcentury was critical.

Throughout this unfortunate period of fading geographic education, some organizations and individuals maintained their efforts to bring geography back into the schools and colleges. Fortunately, the massive impact of the National Science Foundation on developing school curriculum based both on substantive content from the disciplines and on psychologically sound instructional method is bringing to these embattled proponents of geographic education the financial support and national concern that is turning the tide. Across the nation, the geographers are busy assisting their scholarly associations and school systems to build geography back into the curriculum. Once again it is pedagogically respectable to advocate equipping our children and youth with the concepts and skills that are the stuff of geography.

How This Volume Is Organized

The authors of this book are hopeful that it will contribute to the sound growth of geographic education currently under way in the elementary school. We take our stand for a coordinated, multidisciplinary design for the social studies program in which geography, history, economics, political science, anthropology, sociology, and social psychology will each have its basic concepts and methods of inquiry deliberately built into the teaching-learning strategies. The design around which we have organized our research and have written this professional text is widely known and used in this and other nations. Part II describes this design in detail.

We choose to open the volume with a presentation of background materials: (1) the significant geographic content and map skills drawn from the literature of cartography and geography and (2) the biopsychological considerations that must enter into the selection and organization of teaching-learning sequences. We believe that any curriculum reform must be rooted firmly in the disciplines from which content is drawn and must square its practices or methodologies with the best theories of learning and pupil maturation. These basic considerations are presented briefly in Part I.

Part II, as indicated earlier, is a presentation of the skeleton or design used to select and program the geographic concepts and skills to be learned.

Part III, the bulk of the volume, presents for teachers the concepts and skills in geography that can be taught and learned while exploring each of the eleven expanding communities of men and the ways in which societies carry on the basic human activities. Years of research have gone into the identification of these pupil experiences out of which, over the elementary school years, should emerge a sound knowledge of the geographic bases of human societies.

The Appendixes present in ready reference form many of the aids a teacher needs to carry out a program of geographic education, regardless of the particular design adopted for the social studies in his school system.

Contents

PART THREE · *A Program of Teaching-Learning Activities
in Geographic Content and Skills*

GEOGRAPHY IN
THE TEACHING OF
SOCIAL STUDIES

Concepts and Skills

PART ONE

Background

AN OVERVIEW The two chapters of Part One present a synthesis of background literature on (1) geographic content and skills and (2) the biopsychological conditions and strategies for teaching and learning geographic understanding and behavior.

Chapter One reviews the domain of geography and cartography. The literature of these two disciplines is examined to identify the major principles, concepts, structures, and methods of inquiry. For instance, Gopsill, a British geographer, suggests that his discipline is characterized by three stages of inquiry: (1) observing or seeking information; (2) recording what has been found; and (3) reasoning about these observations and drawing relevant conclusions from them. Thralls, an American, lists four skills that are relevant to the work of both the geographer and the cartographer: (1) ability actually to see in the mind's eye the landscape that the map symbols represent; (2) ability to understand the distinctive types of information that can best be expressed on maps; (3)

ability to draw inferences from the facts revealed on the map; and (4) ability to translate into map language information secured in field work, statistics, and other reading material.

In Chapter One, also, the three most significant objectives in the geographic strand of the social studies program are presented. These objectives are developed in depth under the categories of geographic abilities, which then become the criteria for the selection and sequential arrangement of geographic content and skills in Part Three, the principal section of this book.

In Chapter Two, important guiding principles are extracted from the literature of biology and psychology. They should be understood and applied as the curriculum designer and the classroom teacher pursue their related objectives. These teaching-learning principles are organized around four broad areas: (1) child growth and readiness for learning; (2) children's interests as related to motivation and learning; (3) the nature and development of concepts and generalizations; and (4) the transfer of learning. In the discussion of each of these categories, its significance and application to geographic content and skills is kept constantly in view.

The best theories drawn from biopsychology strongly support a carefully planned and developmental sequence of learning experiences. Starting with the most crucial and elemental geographic content and skills, learning experiences are systematically deepened and expanded as the capacity of the children to learn matures. A corollary thesis states that the conceptual system of geographic content and skills is not found in the biopsychological disciplines, but must emerge from the disciplines of geography and cartography directly; the psychological sciences only give us clues as to what learning strategies work under what conditions. The geography component in the social studies program is therefore rooted primarily in the foundations of substantive geographic content, and the procedural guides emerging from psychology are the supporting foundation.

But both content (from geography) and method (from psychology) are essential to a good school program. The essence of "goodness" resides in the proper mixing of content and method. Chapter Three, in Part Two, proposes such a combination in the form of a multidisciplinary social studies program in which geographic content and skills can be best presented and learned.

chapter one

GEOGRAPHIC CONTENT AND MAP SKILLS

Implications for a Coordinated Social Studies Program

The purpose of this chapter is to analyze the literature of the fields of geography and cartography in order to establish the essential content and skills to be utilized in a program of map making, map reading, and geographic interpretation for the elementary school grades. Since all learning takes place through some content or subject matter, sound curriculum planning demands that careful consideration be given to the selection of significant and valid content.

Since we propose to teach geographic concepts and map skills within the context of a multidisciplinary social studies program, we must take care to insure the preservation of the unique features and techniques of cartography and geography. A useful parallel from a field of science is given by Taba:

> . . . if the "essence" of a chemical formula is in its exact application, this exactitude must not be violated, irrespective of whether that formula is learned in a systematic chemistry course or in connection with analyzing cosmetics. It is on this score that hasty innovations in combining subjects and in using projects, problems, and activities which combine ideas and facts from different subjects have sinned most often. The ideas and knowledge in these new projects have often been diluted to the point where they lost their educative value.[1]

Similarly, under no circumstances should basic geographic concepts and principles be violated even though they are being taught within a coordinated social studies program. The general objectives for the proposed components of geographic concepts and of map making, map reading, and geographic interpretation will be spelled out in detail and the skills that are needed to achieve the objectives will be described. At each grade level the geographic concepts and map skills* will be developed to the extent that children's abilities, maturity, and experiences allow, and to the extent that the skills have relevance to the areal or cultural community under analysis.

Our point of view, developed and supported by the findings of specific research studies reported elsewhere in this volume, is that growth of intellectual skills and of the ability to classify, interpret, apply, and analyze is a gradual and continuous process, fed on experience. We assume, then, that even first-grade pupils can identify and solve problems when the problems are within their background of experience. Included in this point of view is the recognition of the difficulty of considering mental "growth" independent of learning. Educationally, it means providing specific learning experiences and arranged teaching strategies which permit interpretation and explanation in keeping with children's experiential background.[2]

A study by Haupt is especially pertinent since it does in a limited experimental way what our social studies program is trying to do on a much broader scale. Haupt set himself to test the proposition that development is continuous and that the same objective can be used throughout the elementary grades. He concluded from his findings:

> The same objective can be used to select elements of learning for presentation throughout a range of grade levels. All of these contributory elements may not be learned on every grade level but some of them will be learned on each grade level. The learning depends upon the complexity of the elements. The complexity of the elements depends upon (1) the number of concepts associated and (2) the number and immediacy of the experiences which are involved in the concepts associated.[3]

The assumption underlying this gradation of content as a method of *teaching for analysis and for interpretation in terms of an objective* is that young children are capable of making inferences and generalizing when involved in experiences within the range of complexity and concreteness that they can handle. Our attempt to develop skills in map making and geographic interpretation in the elementary grades is based on such an approach to curriculum development: teaching for interpretation and understanding in terms of objectives.

What, then, will be the geographic and the cartographic objectives and content for an elementary school program? This chapter attempts to

---

* Where applicable in the classroom the work with map skills should include globe skills.

(Numbered references appear at the end of the chapter.)

provide some answers to this general question of content and skill as found in the literature of the geographer and of the cartographer.

The two chapters which follow will attend to (1) the biopsychological conditions of teaching and learning and (2) the coordinated social studies framework or design we have created to give structure to the development of the geographic content and skills identified in this chapter.

The central purpose of our geographic content and skill program is the development of a system of procedures and of the basic tools which will foster a child's ability to observe, to analyze, to interpret, and to understand man's response to his physical and cultural environment. Two of the most valuable tools in this process of thinking and behaving geographically are the map and the globe. These tools are used to help organize geographic information and to show the areal distribution and relative density of both cultural and physical phenomena.

An examination of the literature in geography and cartography suggests several guides in the orientation of systematic programming in the development of a geographic point of view. The cartographer Raisz says the process of revealing the earth's pattern has three phases: "The surveyor measures the land, the cartographer collects the measurements and renders them on a map, and the geographer interprets the facts thus displayed."[4]

Gopsill describes the geographer's method of working as follows:

1. to observe or to seek information
2. to record what has been found
3. to reason about these observations and to draw relevant conclusions from them[5]

He further says that the teacher's function is "to direct this process— to make the sources available and to show children how to use them; to instruct in the most appropriate method of recording; and finally, to direct the interpretation, to point out obvious relationships and the conclusions which may be drawn from them, and so to train children to make their own."

James states that geography makes three kinds of contributions to understanding:

1. extends the findings of the systematic sciences by observing the differences between the theoretical operation of a process and the actual operation as modified by the conditions of the total environment of a particular place;
2. provides a method of testing the validity of concepts developed by the systematic sciences; and

3. provides a realistic analysis of the conditions of a particular place and so aids in the clarification of the issue involved in all kinds of policy decisions.[6]

The following objectives of map instruction are given by Thralls:

1. ability actually to see in the mind's eye the landscape that the map symbols represent
2. ability to understand the distinctive types of information that can best be expressed on maps
3. ability to draw inferences from the facts revealed on the map
4. ability to translate into map language information secured from field work, statistics, and other reading material.[7]

Educational Objectives

Many other geographers, cartographers, and educators interested in the teaching of geography in the elementary grades have developed lists of skills, understandings, attitudes, or objectives that they believe can be realized. We have analyzed these suggestions and conclude by selecting three objectives of geographic instruction for development in the elementary school coordinated social studies program:

1. *The ability to observe, collect, and reorganize data gained from firsthand and vicarious experiences and to represent them on maps with appropriate symbols.* This means the development of (a) the ability to observe critically and systematically and to gather information accurately from a variety of sources; (b) the ability to formulate bases for grouping data; (c) cartographic skills in the creation or use of symbols for map documentation, in the application of scale to the reduction of area and distance, in the use of simple systems of projection as related to comparative shape and area, in the elements of map makeup, and in the orientation of a map with regard to space and direction.

The value of appropriate techniques and systematic procedures is underscored by Bowman:

> The purpose in employing a technique is to focus the attention upon selected objectives. This tends to confine observations and conclusions to the requirements of a given problem. The investigator does not wander off into all sorts of questions that are not pertinent, or make vague declarations and untested easy generalizations that have no basis in intensive and systematic inquiry.[8]

2. *The ability to read and comprehend data recorded on maps and globes and to differentiate, classify, and translate these symbolic data*

into conceptual patterns of landscape. This means the development of (a) reading skills that enable one to obtain information from many kinds of maps; (b) the ability to translate the symbolic representations of the physical and cultural phenomena on maps into systematic patterns of landscape features; (c) competence in recognizing essentials and differentiating them from the irrelevant aspects of the map.

One dimension of these map-reading skills is stated by Lobeck:

> Map reading is what all of us do when we want to find out where a place is on the map, or the distance between places, or their relative positions, or any other simple geographical fact. Map reading is what boy scouts do when they use maps out of doors to keep from getting lost. Map reading is what the motorist does when he uses a road map to find the best route for his journey.[9]

An awareness of the importance of seeing what the symbol represents in terms of landscape features is pointed out by Thralls:

> A blue or black line, representing a river, must be translated or seen as a real river flowing between its banks. . . . Reading or interpretation of a map depends on this ability to visualize the landscape represented by the map symbol.[10]

Firsthand experiences in the immediate environment are fundamental to map reading. Kohn makes the following observation in his discussion of recognizing landscape features outdoors:

> The first step in teaching children to read the language of maps is to provide either real or vicarious contacts with the physical and the man-made features for which the symbols stand. Because incorrect ideas are often more harmful than total ignorance and extremely difficult to erase from memory, teachers should not assume that pupils know the landscape features which map symbols represent. As in teaching any skill, the child's introduction to map symbols, therefore, should begin with reality itself.[11]

3. *The ability to analyze and interpret the locations and distributions that are portrayed on maps and globes and to reason about things geographic.* This means the development of (a) the ability to interpret data recorded on maps and globes and to make comparisons and inferences concerning two or more ideas gained from maps; (b) the abilities and skills to make realistic geographic analyses of relationships, densities, and correlations of phenomena both cultural and physical; (c) the ability to form generalizations by interpreting the data and using the known facts or principles to explain phenomena that are new or to predict consequences from the known or described situation or conditions.

Map-reading skills are much broader than merely naming landscape features on a map. Teaching and learning experiences must provide opportunities for systematic examination of the assumptions about relationships between cultural and physical phenomena. These mental processes are at the core of geographic reasoning. The idea is to discover and interpret the significance of any likeness or any difference among places and to assign probable causes or consequences.

The implications of what we have just said for a teaching-learning sequence are illustrated by the following description of a study of traffic in an urban area:

> The traffic census may be considered as an example. The pupils record the numbers of vehicles of different types and their direction of movement at certain places and at different times of the day. Such activity requires the making of an accurate record, and the portrayal of the information in a suitable chart. . . . But the real geographical significance of the work comes from a discussion of the conclusions which may be drawn from the evidence; the types of traffic which preponderate, the nature of the loads as far as they may be determined, and the direction of the loaded vehicles, comparison between traffic on different roads or on the same road at different times, and so on.[12]

Map interpretation is not limited to topographical features; it includes the human and economic activities of a community as well. For example:

> A study of the settlements themselves has much to tell. Often the reason for their positions cannot be discovered by scrutiny of the map, but sometimes they are sufficiently obvious or can at least be inferred. There are those which stand at a natural meeting place, at a crossing of a river or in a strategic position. In some districts it can be seen how the settlements and indeed individual farms seek out the fold of dry valleys for shelter. In the low lying flood plains the little villages cluster on the tops of modest undulations, on a patch of glacial gravel perhaps, as a refuge from the winter floods. . . . The shapes of the villages reflect their situations. In the high valleys they tend to string themselves marginally along a single road. . . . In the plains the villages are compact and tightly grouped.[13]

Maps and globes have an important part in the coordinated social studies program; they are basic tools to anyone seeking to gain an understanding of the geographic distribution and densities of life on our earth. The school has the obligation to provide the experiences needed in developing skills, abilities, and understandings in map making, reading, and interpreting, and in developing a geographic point of view.

In summary, the following objectives have been selected as the bases of a developmental program in map making and geographic interpretation for the elementary school social studies: (1) the ability to observe, collect, and reorganize data gained from firsthand and vicarious experiences and to represent them on maps with appropriate symbols, (2) the ability to read and comprehend data recorded on maps and globes and to differentiate, classify, and translate these symbolic data into conceptual patterns of landscape, and (3) the ability to analyze and interpret the locations and distributions that are portrayed on maps and globes and to reason about things geographic. These three objectives are to be developed at each grade level to the extent and degree of exactness compatible with the level of development and previous experiences of pupils. We will describe ten map and globe skills that will be used to achieve the three objectives.

Let us briefly examine these educational objectives for their implicit cognitive dimensions before going into more detailed descriptions of related geographic content and map skills. Bloom's *Taxonomy of Educational Objectives*[14] provides the teacher with useful terminology for conducting fruitful dialogue concerning the improvement of teaching-learning experiences designed to build the pupil's intellectual abilities and skills.

In particular let us consider *knowledge, translation,* and *interpretation.* The reader should note that our three broad objectives require the social studies curriculum to develop, extend, and refine these central cognitive abilities and skills. *Knowledge,* as Bloom notes, refers to intellectual abilities and skills requisite to "organizing and reorganizing material to achieve a particular purpose." Our first objective stresses observing, collecting, and reorganizing. In order to achieve the social studies aims, pupils must gain knowledge of "specifics," "terminology," "specific facts," "ways and means of dealing with specifics," "conventions," "trends and sequences," "classification and categories," "criteria," "methodology," "universals and abstraction in a field," "principles and generalizations," and "theories and structures."[15]

Bloom states, "*Translation* is judged on the basis of faithfulness and accuracy, that is on the extent to which the material in the original communication is preserved although the form of the communication has been altered."[16] Comprehension of the nature of map reading (our second objective) places emphasis upon translation abilities and skills. Bloom suggests that *interpretation* seeks "a new view of the material" while extrapolation "goes beyond the given data" and application sets out for use general rules, methods, principles, and theories.[17] Map interpreting and reasoning geographically (our third objective) call for these abilities and skills of interpretation, extrapolation, and application.

The maturational rather than the mastery approach to skill development has implications for the organization of the map program. Selected map skills and geographic understandings provide the thread of continuity throughout the elementary grades, and mastery of a skill is not expected at any particular grade level. As one geography educator puts it, "Many map skills can be introduced to children when they are young, but these skills need to be reintroduced, maintained and developed in the junior and senior high school and at the beginning college level if they are to become lasting."[18]

Geographic Understanding and Map Skills To Be Developed

The following groups of map skills and geographic abilities have been selected for sequential development within the context of the coordinated social studies program:

1. The ability to observe systematically and to identify and note the location and distribution and density of features of the landscape.
2. The ability to orient self and to note directions in space and on maps and globes.
3. The ability to locate places, distributions, and densities on maps and globes.
4. The ability to use scale and to judge or measure distance in space and on maps and globes.
5. The ability to use and understand symbols and to visualize the realities for which they stand.
6. The ability to use cartographic principles of map composition and graphic expression.
7. The ability to recognize and express relative location.
8. The ability to use and understand basic map projections.
9. The ability to understand and relate areal distributions.
10. The ability to use and understand the globe as a model of the earth.

Each of the above skills and abilities is highly complex and interrelated with all others. The complexity of map making and geographic interpretation becomes apparent when we consider this statement by Renner:

If a map be examined, it will be found that sound is absent, as are also motion, perspective, and dimensional depth. Likewise color as a natural attribute is lacking, although color is often employed for arbitrary conventional purposes—a circumstance which is highly confusing. Position and locus are present but in such manner as to necessitate teaching the geometric elements of the map and its geometrical orientation in nature. Form is present but is so highly conventionalized as to require special training in reading and interpretation. Size is entirely fictitious, but may be deduced if the mathematics of scale and ratio be taught.[19]

It is essential for the curriculum builder to plan for the gradual and systematic introduction of the teaching-learning experiences involving the ten groups of skills. "An important task in planning the program of skill development," Carpenter and Spieseke point out, "is the analysis of complex abilities into manageable parts for instructional purposes and the arrangement of them for emphasis in the proper sequential order with reference to the maturity of the learner."[20] Detailed descriptions and applications of the ten groups of skills follow.

1. *The ability to observe systematically and to identify and note the location and distribution and density of features of the landscape.* The importance of developing in children skills in observing and describing the natural and cultural features of the immediate landscape cannot be overestimated. "Learning how to study the landscape," Thralls says, "is essential in functional geographic education because the landscape is the basic source of all geographic knowledge."[21] Field trips to observe geographic features of the local environment provide opportunities for direct learning experiences in which children are "taught from the first to understand that geography deals with real life and that knowledge learned from it has genuine significance."[22]

Attention is called to both natural and cultural phenomena that relate to the basic human activities within the geographic region or community emphasis on which the group is focused. Natural phenomena that influence human activities should be noted: movement of the sun across the sky; changing seasons as they affect plants, animals, human activities; the influences of daily changes of weather. Too, attention should be drawn to variations in the local terrain; thus the basis for understanding regional geography is laid. In addition, plants, animals, and various science experiments and demonstrations may be observed in the classroom.

These concrete experiences are the initial ingredients out of which the child's first concepts are formed. From the observation of features in the local landscape comes an understanding of the arrangement of cultural and physical features, and mental images are formed which help the pupils visualize similar landscape features in other geographical areas. These images of actual landscape features enable them to see through the map symbols to the realities for which they stand.

Experiences in observing at home, at school, and in the local neighborhood are a part of the readiness program in the primary school grades. Later school grades offer many opportunities to extend observational skills beyond the immediate sensorimotor environment. Trips provide a chance to look at physical features of the immediate communities: hills, lakes, seacoast, rivers, ridges, knolls, valleys, a mountain range, and so on. The cultural features of the area may be observed from such vantage points as the tower of a nearby airport, a tall building in the downtown section of the town or city, or a high hill or mountain. Field trips should be well planned in advance and the children directed to focus their observations on specific features.

Children are guided to look beyond the surface manifestation, to find out not only *what* a thing is, but *how* it works, *why* it is where it is, whether it could be otherwise. When exploration is purposeful, attention is called and held to relationships that might otherwise be overlooked. Children must often probe the details beneath the surface to find the answers to their questions. Also, if children are looking with the intention of reproducing or locating what they see on a map, they are required to be more precise in observing size, relative position of objects, and relative distance between them, or in noting the relation of an object or phenomenon to its surroundings. Systematic observation is the foundation on which all other map skills are built.

Mapping of data obtained from observation should become a regular activity so that children can learn to translate real landscape features into map symbols. When reading the maps they have made, they have visual images to associate with the symbols, and from the beginning they understand a map as a representation of the earth or a portion of the earth on a plane or a flat surface. They see how maps help them to organize information and show the areal distribution and density of observable phenomena, both cultural and physical. They discover that maps serve a number of functions, provided that both the field trips and the mapping activities are purposeful.

Significant learnings come in answers to questions such as: Where are the basic human activities of production and exchange being carried on in our communities? Does their location have any relationship to transportation facilities? Systematic provision should be made for interpreting the significance of the observed and recorded data in relation to the map-making activities.

2. *The ability to orient self and to note directions in space and on maps and globes.* The ability to orient oneself and to acquire a sense of direction is one of the prime requisites of mapping. Since this skill is not inborn but learned, children need experiences which will make the language of direction meaningful.

In the primary grades a readiness program provides activities in which children learn to relate themselves and the maps they make of the home, school, neighborhood, and local communities to the cardinal directions. Children gradually become oriented in familiar surroundings. At first, they only recognize that something is "over there." Presently they can point from school in the direction of familiar places. Eventually, when they have learned something about cardinal directions from exercises with sun behavior, the use of cardinal directions should be encouraged in speech. Directions should be used in play on large floor maps; symbols can be placed on the children's own maps to show their real places in space and in relation to each other. All such maps should be on a horizontal surface and oriented with outdoor space. Children can be guided to orient the school with regard to directions in space. It might be best to emphasize E-W or N-S until one set of relationships is well established, and then to work on the other pair. Children should constantly check where they are in relation to school or some other familiar landmark. They should be helped to develop an understanding of "up" as away from the center of the earth and "down" as toward the center of the earth. North is toward the North Pole; South is toward the South Pole. Latitude can eventually be introduced, but at the primary level the concept should be developed as distances north and south from the equator. The use of the compass can also be introduced at this level.

The middle grades program of teaching-learning experiences should provide opportunities for children to extend meanings and abilities in reading directions on maps and globes and to develop proficiency in orienting them with outdoor space. Unless a pupil learns to orient maps, they can be of very little help to him in finding his way in a strange place, for instance. By the end of the middle grades, most children should be able to orient themselves in space, orient maps, and read directions from both large- and small-scale maps.

There are many classroom activities which children may carry on to further their understandings of the cardinal directions and to develop the ability to express the direction one place is from another in terms of eight points of the compass. Field trips provide opportunities to orient unfamiliar locations with the position of the sun and the pupil-prepared guide maps. The practice of orienting classroom wall maps and desk maps should be continued throughout the middle grades.

As children learn to understand cardinal directions on the map and the earth's grid system, the concepts of true north and magnetic north may be introduced in conjunction with the use of the compass. The phenomena of magnetic influences can be explored in both social studies and science classes. Sometime during the upper elementary grades children should learn how to use the North Star as a nighttime marker for finding north. With considerably more work sun position can be helpful for determining east and west as well as north and south.

Many teaching-learning experiences should be provided to help children develop the ability to perceive relationships of land masses and major bodies of water on first the globe and then world maps in terms of direction. We should always remember, however, that only the globe gives the true direction one place is from another for all points of the compass.

The junior high school map program* must continue the training begun in the primary and middle grades, for many children are normally "slow" at building concepts of direction. As the growing child enters upon systematic study of the more remote communities of men, correct habits of orienting small-scale and world maps must be well established. Relative location and direction studies (where various map projections may be used) are likely to be frustrating and/or miseducative if the pupil has not mastered the directional lines of latitude and longitude or still retains incorrect concepts of "up" and "down" when north-south directions are meant. The junior high school map program will include many opportunities to extend and refine the pupil's knowledge of the orientation of self to map and the reading of direction from maps and globes, especially if he is given the opportunity to discover relationships through his own mathematically based problem solving.

3. *The ability to locate places, distributions, and densities on maps and globes.* The question "Where is it?" is almost a daily occurrence for most of us. Albeit the communities close at hand provide familiar landscape features as reference points, most of us experience difficulty in describing the location of a place definitely and accurately. Location becomes even more difficult in the larger communities.

Robinson's analysis of the concept of location suggests that this concept is much more complex than is generally thought.[23] First of all, it is necessary to understand the concepts of direction and distance. Second, "All spatial locations are relative, and they must, therefore, be established in relation to some reference or starting point." From such a designated point the location of every place can be stated in terms of a defined direction and distance from it. For example, we describe the location of the library as three blocks east of the post office, that of the fire station as two blocks north of the post office, and so on. A reference point like this serves very well in the small neighborhood community; however, as we move into the larger communities of the county, state, nation, and beyond, it is wholly inadequate. We have the same problem on maps and globes; as Robinson points out, "On a limitless plane surface or on a motionless surface, there is no natural reference point; that is, every point is the same as every other point except for relative location." The significance of the problem can be demonstrated to children. For instance, if children are asked to relocate or describe the location of a dot on a ball, they quickly see the difficulty of doing so.

---

* In this volume we have used the term *junior high school* to denote Grades 7, 8, and 9, although we are aware that many school systems across the nation refer to Grades 7 and 8 as the *upper grades*. It is our purpose here to be of service also to the teachers who work in school systems where the latter grouping is employed. We thus suggest that the reader think of *junior high school* as more or less synonymous with *upper grades*.

Coordinate systems are used extensively in describing locations of places, whether in the local community or on the high seas. The use of a simple grid to describe location has common usage in the everyday activities of children. The primary school child can describe the location of his cubbyhole or bin in a classroom cabinet as the third bin, bottom row. A coordinate system is regularly used in children's workbook exercises. Grid lines are laid out on a football field so that everyone knows where the ball is at all times. These activities provide the readiness experiences for the construction of simple rectangular grid systems on the maps of the local community. The streets and avenues of the city or the network of county roads serve as a kind of grid for describing the location of place, and the streets or roads have a numbering system. We need to be sure the cardinal directions are always indicated on these maps.

Simplified mathematic grid systems may now be introduced for sequential development. It is suggested that a rectangular drawing of a classroom cabinet be made on the blackboard with letters assigned to the horizontal row of bins and numerals assigned to the vertical row of bins. In describing location, the letters indicate horizontal directions and the numerals indicate vertical directions. If we designate the upper left-hand corner as the point of origin for lettering and numbering, the third bin, bottom row, can now be identified as C-3, and so on. A similar rectangular grid drawn on a sheet of acetate may be superimposed on maps of the local community and the state community; the lines of the grid need not coincide with the pattern of streets and avenues or roads (see Figure 1). Again, we must be sure to include

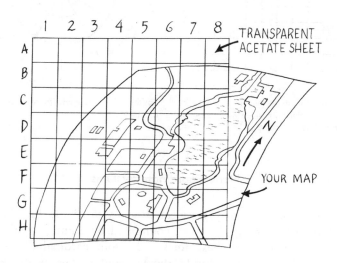

Figure 1

Superimposing a Grid

the cardinal directions on the map. Later on these lines may be referred to as the east-west lines and the north-south lines.

The commercial road maps of the pupils' local and state communities should be examined and their grid system used when finding locations. The class may want to draw in the vertical and horizontal lines connecting the numerals and letters. Activities such as these help children to see that the grid lines on any map are not a part of the features of the earth's actual landscape since it is easy for them to get this false impression from the commercial classroom maps that always show the lines of latitude and longitude. At this stage of teaching there is no need to refer to the grid systems as lines of latitude and longitude; continue to refer to them as the east-west and north-south lines.

The mathematical Cartesian plane coordinate system[24] is comparatively easy for children to understand. The base lines of a plane coordinate system may be placed in various locations of the network; for instance, by establishing a "point of origin" at the intersection of two conveniently located perpendicular axes, an arbitrary system of location on a plane surface may be developed (Figure 2). If we use a square,

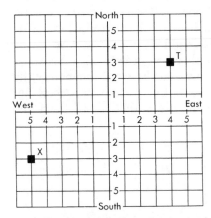

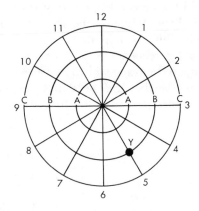

Position T corresponds to the ordered pair of points (4 East–3 North); Position X corresponds to the ordered pair of points (3 South–5 West).

Position Y corresponds to the ordered pair of points 5B.

Figure 2

Plane Coordinate Systems

the axes or base lines may be located so as to divide the figure into four equal parts. The grid is then completed by adding equally spaced lines parallel to the two base lines. The four cardinal directions are added so that we again refer to the horizontal lines as the east-west lines and the vertical lines as the north-south lines. Each of the north-south and the east-west lines is named with a numeral beginning from the point of origin. Thus, we can state the position of any point on the plane with reference to the point of origin by indicating the perpendicular distance from each axis, or each base line, to the point. This grid of rectangular coordinates drawn on a large-sized sheet of transparent acetate should then be superimposed on a map of the neighborhood community and the state community. The point of origin can be placed on any well-known local landmark such as the post office or the school; on the state map, the neighborhood community can be the point of origin. The map and its grid system should be placed on the floor or a table so that the designated cardinal directions are always correctly oriented in space. By giving the number of the east-west line and the north-south line you can locate any place on the map.

Children should also be introduced to a circular system of polar coordinates. Here again, only one point or place in the plane corresponds to every ordered pair of numbers or letters (Figure 2).

Having learned to locate on maps with the use of systems of rectangular and polar coordinates (the Cartesian grid), children are ready to learn to develop a similar spherical grid system for locating places on the globe. We have two natural reference points on the globe: the poles. The polar points can be placed on a large project globe. Next the east-west base line (a circle) is drawn equidistant from the two poles. This line the children will recognize as the equator. It divides the sphere into two equal parts or hemispheres. A set of lines (circles) equally spaced and running in the same east-west direction are then drawn to complete this one set of lines. From the base line, the equator, any part of the globe toward the North Pole will be north and any part toward the South Pole will be south.

A set of north-south lines will complete the grid. These lines will go from the North Pole to the South Pole. Since there are no natural earth features that determine where the base line should be located, the class may decide to draw it through the point representing the approximate location of their local community on the globe. Equally spaced marks are described along the length of the equator, which are then connected with the North and South Poles. Thus the entire surface of the globe has been covered by the grid network. Number names (1, 2, etc.) are given to all the lines beginning from the point of origin; to the east-west lines north of the equator is added the name North, and to those south of the equator the name South. To the north-south lines are added the names East and West. As with the plane grid system, by giving the number and cardinal direction name of the north-south line and the east-west line, we can locate any place on the globe. We need not use the terms *latitude* and *longitude* at this stage of development. Later on the term *parallel* will be associated with these east-west circles and the term *meridian* with the north-south circles. (See Figure 3.)

The concept of the prime north-south line, or prime meridian, is not a difficult one once children understand the spherical grid system developed above. Since all meridians are equal, any one can be chosen

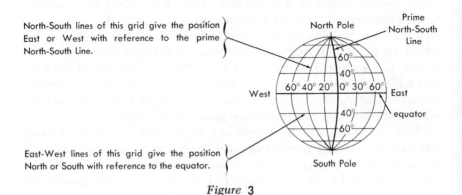

North-South lines of this grid give the position East or West with reference to the prime North-South Line.

North Pole

Prime North-South Line

West

East

60° 40° 20° 0° 30° 60°

equator

East-West lines of this grid give the position North or South with reference to the equator.

South Pole

Figure 3

A System of Coordinates Drawn on a Sphere

as prime meridian. On the grid system the class developed for this project, the north-south line drawn through the location of the local community was designated as the prime north-south line. This is precisely what happened in the past; some nations chose the north-south line drawn through their national capital as the prime meridian, and a great deal of confusion resulted. The class can discuss the disadvantages of having many different prime meridians.[25] The teacher can then point out that the parallels of latitudes North and South are reckoned from the equator, and the meridians of longitudes East and West from Greenwich, England, up to 180 degrees. Children need this information before they can understand the numbering system used on commercial classroom globes.

In the junior high school we may refine terminology and develop with pupils the mathematics of exact location. Kohn states that examining and measuring experiences with globes should clarify these latitude facts for the junior high school pupil:

1. All places located along the same line of latitude are the same distance from the equator. All lines of latitude are parallel to each other and hence are known as "parallels."
2. All places located along the same line of latitude or parallel are the same distance from the equator and are due east and west from each other. All lines or parallels are true east-west lines.

3. The equator is designated as 0 degrees latitude, and latitude is measured north and south from the equator. The degrees of latitude are indicated on each parallel drawn on the globe.[26]

A useful device for remembering acceptable mathematical equivalents for low, middle, and high latitudes is found in the fact that the earth tilts as much as 23½° from the plane of its orbit around the sun—once 23½° North and six months later 23½° South. So we call the belts lying between the equator and 23½° South of the equator and between the equator and 23½° North of the equator the *low* latitudes. The *middle* latitudes are between 23½° North and 66½° North, and between 23½° South and 66½° South. The 66½° is reckoned by subtracting the 23½° from 90° at the poles, leaving 66½°. The *high* latitudes are the areas north of 66½° North to the North Pole and south of 66½° South to the South Pole. Some geographers prefer the 0°–30°, 30°–60°, and 60°–90° division for low, middle, and high latitudes.

A similar but more extensive list of understandings was compiled by Kohn for longitude followed by an emphasis on much practice in relating these coordinates because he felt pupils should learn to express in this way the exact location of any places they are studying. Of course, this coordinate system and its mathematical relationships should be "problemed-out" by pupils so that it may be understood rather than merely memorized. Latitude must be well understood first to avoid confusion later.

This discussion of the concept of location gives us some idea of its complex nature. Explicit provisions must be made in arranging the teaching-learning activities so as to provide for the continuity and sequential development of the concept in the elementary grades. Teachers who depend upon incidental pupil experiences or begin with the mature abstractions of the cartographer will not provide the needed foundational learnings that are necessary in the acquisition of place-locational skills.

4. *The ability to use scale and to judge or measure distance in space and on maps and globes.* The difficulty in making a "life-sized" picture of large objects such as a house, the schoolyard, or the state in which we live is readily apparent to children. First of all, getting a piece of paper as large as the schoolyard, for example, would be extremely difficult, and secondly, nothing would be gained by making it that large. It would be easier to work with the actual landscape than with a map of this size. Thus if we are to make a practical picture or map of the schoolyard, we must devise some means of reducing its size to fit our paper, at the same time keeping its dimensions in correct scale. If dimensions are not kept in strict proportion, the map has severe limitations; for instance, it would be of little help in determining whether

the area is large enough for several baseball diamonds unless the actual measurements were made over again. However, on a map drawn to scale the actual ground distances can be calculated directly from the map without difficulty if the scale units of length of line on the map to distance on the ground are given. The process of making a reduced-sized picture or map of an object, be it a house or a part of the earth's surface pattern such as the schoolyard, describes the essential elements of the concept of scale.

The importance of the earth-map relationship cannot be minimized in the development of map-making and map-reading skills. "The fact that the earth is so large that it is impossible to draw a map at actual size, and it therefore must be mapped at sizes smaller than but in direct proportion to the actual size of the earth, is seldom realized or understood."[27] Scale may be defined as the relationship between distance measured on the map and the corresponding distance on the earth's surface and is expressed as a ratio between a linear unit on the map and a stated number of the same units on the ground.[28] Since the relationship between the map and the territory it represents is beyond recognition, it is precisely at this point that we have one of the major problems of map reading. Kohn states the problem well:

> . . . even relatively small parts of the earth's surface are beyond the range of the child's sensory experience. Hence, their graphic representation on maps in a reduced form is an abstraction because it cannot be directly related to any such experience. This is one of the major problems of map reading. Because the reduction of areas on maps is difficult for the child to comprehend, map scales are correspondingly hard. Yet he must learn to read the map by scale and to understand the degree of reduction.[29]

While an understanding of scale is essential to making and reading maps, it is probably one of the most complex and abstract concepts to be developed in the elementary school map program.

Scale becomes important very early. Dramatic play on floor maps, even block play, depends on a rough idea of scale. Primary children can be helped to understand that they are representing relative distance on a floor map as they decide the position of each object or symbol. They can understand that the map they make is a representation of a larger area they have seen, that they use scale to approximate the distance between places on a simple map of a small area, and that they place features on the map by use of the same scale.

Children can learn to approximate distance by use of a scale chosen in relation to the landscape or area they wish to represent. For example, a given size wooden block on their three-dimensional map can stand for a city block or an acre or a square mile out in the country. They may reproduce a room or store and use crude scale to get approximate sizes. They can learn to place features fairly accurately on a map by use of some kind of scale to measure appropriate distances. As they represent the same area on different-sized maps, the concept of scale is being developed. As they locate the same place on maps of different sizes, the concept of scale grows.

Pupils can easily compare relative distance between places on the same map: "The store is nearer to home than to school." "The park is halfway between school and the superhighway." "The barn is halfway between the house and the river." Later such relative distances can be replaced by a scale based on more exact measurements: so many blocks to the store; so many feet, yards, or miles to the river. Finally, the children may be able to analyze the scale of a map (not of their own making) and use it to compute distances. Large maps of small areas should be studied first and then placed in the context of a map of a larger area which includes the smaller areas.

Children can be helped to understand the principle of scale by being taken to look down at a landscape from a height and carefully noting what happens to the size of objects as they get higher and higher above them. They may make estimates of the size of a given feature first seen from a height, then measure it when they come down. This might help them see why features must be smaller as more and more area is represented on a map.

In working with globes, children can learn that different-sized globes represent the same earth. On a globe of any size the poles can be located; the equator can be located halfway between the poles; and the concept of latitude can be developed as distance north or south from the equator toward the poles.

Children in the middle school grades should continue to have opportunities for many experiences with actual landscapes to help them develop a sense of distance, a basic concept in understanding scale. For example, they can compare the distances between places in their neighborhood community and then check their estimates by making actual measurements. Children must appreciate the fact that the map represents on paper a certain amount of space on the ground. Such organized concrete experiences with the local environment are the initial ingredients out of which the concept of scale is formed. We should recognize that some of these first concept formations exist in varying degrees of perfection though they are often not well enough organized for children to verbalize them in adult terms.

Hence, distances in each of the expanding communities of men should continue to be interpreted as concretely as possible. This discussion suggests that the process of developing spatial concepts is a prolonged and gradual one extending from the many early experiences with concrete objects in the local environment to the larger communities of men

—the state, the nation, and the world. Careful advanced planning of the teaching-learning experiences insures a measure of continuity from one grade emphasis to the next. Likewise, systematic provisions should be made for the repeated study of the concept of scale in each new context on which pupils are focusing, thus enhancing the opportunities to enlarge and deepen meanings and associations.

Scale is usually expressed on maps in one of three ways: by the graphic scale, by the inch-to-mile statement, or by the numerical scale or the representative fraction (see Figure 4). The ability to make linear

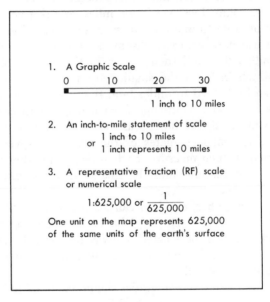

Figure 4

Ways of Expressing Scale

measurements is fundamental in the use of any of the methods. Children entering the middle school grades are ready for many kinds of experiences in computing and expressing distances in terms of the simple linear measurements of inches, feet, yards, and miles. The program should provide opportunities again for measuring various classroom objects such as desk and table tops, the floor, and the bulletin boards. Pupils can be helped to discover that using a scale of 1:1 indicates that the map is as large as the object's surface itself; that a scale of 1:2 says that one inch or one foot on the map represents two inches or two feet of the object; and so on. Mapping an object in three or four different scales helps make it clear that an object may be reduced to any size, and that regardless of what scale is used, the map still represents the same amount of territory. The scale alone tells the amount of territory a map represents; hence its importance in reading maps.

Mapping activities should not be postponed until children have learned to use and read scale. A carefully designed sequence of teaching-learning experiences in making maps, guided by a teacher who understands the principles involved, will provide a developmental approach to learning the skills. The following understandings concerning scale will have been sequentially developed by the end of the middle grades map-making and map-interpreting program:

> Scale is the relation of distance on the map to the distance it represents on the ground.
> The scale of a map is large or small in relation to the object it represents.
> The use of a large scale for a map enables the mapper to show many details about a small area.
> The use of a small scale for a map enables the mapper to show a large area but fewer details.
> Scale on the globe may be used to measure the distance between any two points on the earth's surface.
> The scale on one part of a map may be different from the scale on another part (an inset map, for instance).

Most of the pupils in the junior high school will be learning the mathematics necessary to translate scale and compute area, but it still remains difficult to comprehend area reduction on a global scale. In junior high school small-scale and large-scale maps should be understood in terms of their verbal aspects, in terms of cartographic challenges, and in terms of the mathematics inherently a part of their design or interpretation.[30]

By this time graphic scale (map key graduated line) should be fairly well mastered, but the verbal statement form (inches to the mile) will probably need much additional work as the junior high school pupil seeks to cope with small-scale maps of the world. Converting representative fractions to statement of scale or graphic scale offers pupils the opportunity to try out their knowledge of fractions and mathematics in general.* Those who are ready for algebra may find this work with ratios stimulating and tending to help fix scale abstractions in their thinking. The conversion tables they might produce would provide helpful aids for their peers with lesser mathematical aptitude. Useful maps are accurate maps; correct scale should be required of all maps

---

* Note that there are 63,360 inches in one mile. However, for convenience, most commercially prepared school maps use an RF of 1:62,500. This RF means that one inch on the map represents approximately one mile of the earth's surfaces. An RF of 1:1,000,000 converted to an inch-to-mile statement means that one inch represents approximately 16 miles.

produced by teachers or pupils at all grade levels above the primary.

5. *The ability to use and understand symbols and to visualize the realities for which they stand.* When we think of the map as a symbol for the earth's surface rather than as a picture, we are taking the first step toward realizing its abstractness and complexity. Whittemore says, "A map is itself a symbol and it is interpreted through the use of other symbols. 'City' is expressed on a map by a dot, 'river' by a line, 'between five and ten inches of rain' by a color. Such map symbols are not so numerous as word symbols, but in many ways they are more complex."[31] Many of the symbols placed on maps and globes stand for concepts such as boundary lines of a city or state which are not visible at all.

The only resemblance the map has to nature is its relative shape and distance; in every other way it is symbolic. Symbols are used to represent both physical and cultural elements of our earth environment. It is with regard to this process of representation that many pupils have difficulty associating the various symbols on maps and globes with actual objects or ideas. The fact that the language of maps is highly symbolic and requires arbitrary associations with the realities which they represent is only one aspect of the difficulty. The effective use of maps is also dependent upon the ability of pupils to understand the ideas behind a combination of symbols since the map employs a complex scheme of conventions.

Facility in using and reading the symbolic language of maps involves a set of ideas and skills acquired through a gradual, well-ordered development which begins with the most simple conceptions and builds to the more difficult. Such a program should lead the pupil to understand "that a map symbol does not stand for a word but for something real (though not necessarily visible) on the earth."[32] Learning to use and read map symbols calls for more than the rote memorization of a number of arbitrary associations. Map symbols ought to suggest the corresponding reality, and they will do so only if the teaching-learning sequence is such that children do not encounter the abstract symbol first. Parker stresses this notion:

> Children should not be allowed to get their first ideas of the appearance of a given kind of feature from the map. . . . Introducing symbols of features children have not seen in real or pictured landscapes is one of the chief causes of failures to learn to read maps—that is, to read *through* them to the *realities* the map symbols represent.[33]

The prime concern in symbolization is that the children see through the map symbols to the physical and cultural elements which they represent. One way to achieve this is to begin with a study of the local landscape. Children can reproduce the immediate landscape in their floor scheme maps, roughly laying out streets, streams, etc. Toys, blocks, and other props can be used as symbols. When they then decide which symbol they will use to represent a house, school, street, road, or river that they have seen, they *naturally* picture in their minds the reality being represented. Hence, making a map *following* observation of the landscape is one way of insuring that the feature symbolized has a true image behind it and is not first encountered as an abstract symbol, with all the concomitant misconceptions made possible by a premature use of the abstraction.

The symbols selected for primary pupils to learn will depend on the particular landscape they are exploring in their home, school, neighborhood, or local community. They will also depend on the content area of the coordinated social studies being investigated. As pupils use these symbols, certain concepts need to be developed. When they are using lines for streams on their own maps, it might be well to find a map on which they can locate the source, mouth, tributaries, etc., of the same stream. It is important to help them interpret "upstream" and "downstream." By using three-dimensional models and pictorial maps, children can learn to interpret degree of slope, relief, and relation of slope to the flow of a stream. In addition, if the concept of river is related to each of the basic human activities, the meaning can continue to grow with each new experience. However, as Parker points out,

> People do not study maps to understand maps. They study maps to understand the earth and its inhabitants. . . . Every map symbol stands for something real. . . . A student has truly learned the meaning of a symbol only when he understands the real thing it stands for. With every new map symbol . . . the student gets a new understanding of the earth and of relationships between the earth and man.[34]

For example, what does the symbol that stands for street, or road, or highway, mean? Roads of different widths, lengths, and surfaces serve different purposes, from a small country road serving two or three farms to a cross-continental freeway; observing step-by-step construction of a road might develop other understandings relative to the tremendous work and cost required to surface and maintain roads. Pupils might then begin to realize why some places have few roads with crude surfaces—as in lightly traveled farming areas, in mountainous regions, or in jungle areas. They might also be helped to realize how roads or lack of them help or hinder development of an area.

Unless the child has the concept that is expressed by the map symbol, the symbol is meaningless. However, this does not mean that a concept must be completely developed before maps representing that concept can be used. Concepts continue to grow. With each related experience new depth of meaning is added to a symbol and the reality for which it stands.

The middle grades program should build on the primary readiness program. The teaching-learning experiences should be designed to provide opportunities for continued activities in mapping the local landscape and its many physical and cultural features. Thus the ability to associate real places and features with the conventional map symbols continues to be developed toward the point where children can begin to think in terms of abstract symbols. In fact, this process of symbolization is probably a very helpful step in concept acquisition, for children must focus on the specific features of the object and then decide on an abstract symbol that will best represent it on a map. Children may begin to represent distribution patterns of resources, vegetation, rainfall, length of growing season, and other natural features with which they are familiar. They should learn to use a key referring to these features.

Symbols, as we have emphasized, should not be taught apart from the development of the concept of the object. Symbolizing a geographical element, either physical or cultural, is not an adjunct to but an integral part of conceptualization. Furthermore, it provides an excellent way of checking the accuracy of children's concepts.

The middle grades and junior high school social studies program takes children into larger or more distant communities having landscape features that are not indigenous to the lesser and more immediate communities. Here visual aids such as pictures, motion pictures, filmstrips, and other materials should be used to provide sensory data for building concepts. While pictures are a valuable source of geographic information, children also need guidance in how to read information from them. (See "Aids for Teaching," Appendix A.)

Learning how to read maps made by others should parallel mapmaking activities. One of the objectives of a map program is to develop the ability to read maps for information. The elementary school makes use of a number of maps: large wall maps, atlases, globes, and maps in the social studies textbooks that are specially prepared to accompany the textual material. Not only do children find some of these maps difficult to read and interpret, but they get many false impressions from them about the earth's surface. For example, the use of one color for representing elevations of 1000 feet or less often covers a variety of relief sufficiently great to include plains and areas of hill terrain, yet tends to convey to a child a false notion of equal elevation. Desert areas of this elevation are often misread as having vegetation because maps usually show elevations of 1000 feet or less in a green color regardless of surface cover. John Carroll makes an excellent case for providing careful instruction and guidance in order to avoid confusion in reading more complex maps.[35]

Although children should always refer to the key for interpreting the color symbols, the following color conventions may be introduced and used:

1. Cultural features are shown in black and red.
2. Water features are shown in blue.
3. Relief features are shown in green for elevations of less than 1000 feet and in shades of brown for higher elevations.
4. Vegetation features on vegetation maps are shown in green.

By using these well-established color conventions for all classroom mapping activities children will have less difficulty in reading these map symbols on maps prepared by others.

The following principles should serve as guides in developing children's abilities to use symbols:

Map symbols can be recognized with the aid of the key.

The symbol and not the name indicates the location.

The vertical scale for relief symbols is exaggerated in relation to the horizontal scale.

The symbols representing roads, streets, rivers, and so on are greatly exaggerated on most maps.

Map symbols may represent ideas and facts that are visible or invisible on the surface of the earth.

The size and use of symbols depends on the scale of the map.

A variety of symbols may be used to depict the spatial distributions of the basic human activities.

A map is a systematic arrangement of symbols representing the earth's surface.

The importance of places often may be denoted either by the size of the symbol or by the size of the lettering which gives its name.

6. *The ability to use cartographic principles of map composition and graphic expression.* Maps that are attractive in appearance and easily understandable not only are interesting and inviting to read but also can go far in stimulating geographic thinking. Appealing maps are the result of the application of map-making techniques based on fundamental cartographic principles of map composition; they don't just happen. As Bauer points out, "Just how well or how truly a map represents an area and its features is a matter of size (scale), detail, choice of projection and—last but not least—of the experience, skill and reliability of its designer, the cartographer."[36] In planning map-making activities for children we should keep in mind that statistical material as well as geographical data lend themselves to cartographic and diagrammatic treatment. And finally, map making should not be thought of as a mechanical process, for mapping can be a highly creative art. In far

too many instances, however, mapping activities deteriorate to "seat-work" copying and coloring. It is no wonder so many children soon view making maps as a very dull classroom chore.

The following general principles for map making are particularly pertinent:

1. Children learn their maps by making them and not merely by looking at maps that have been made by others.
2. There should be emphasis on the fact that each map is drawn for a specific purpose, which appears in the title. Only information which is relevant to this purpose should be shown upon it.
3. Maps should be drawn on the assumption that they are to be *read* after they have been made. The meaning of the map language should be made clear in the key, and pupils should be trained to regard the key as an integral part of the map and essential to the interpretation of it.
4. A map should not be overloaded with detail so that it becomes a confused jumble.
5. Children should be taught from the beginning that neat execution makes for legibility and good map use.[37]

In addition, scale and direction should always be noted. One common criticism of elementary school maps is that they try to show far too much detail. It is the map maker's responsibility to see that his map is easy for others to read. Class discussion focused on maps illustrating principles of good map composition should be a regular part of the program.

Pupils should view a map as being incomplete until they have given it a title, provided a legend or key, stated the scale, indicated direction, and added the necessary lettering. The title is an important part of the map for it tells the reader its special purpose along with helping the map maker to decide what should be shown.

To be read, a map must have a legend telling what each symbol stands for and explaining any special abbreviations. Other information, such as the scale used, the date the map was made, and the name of the map maker, can be conveniently listed in the title. A direction indicator for the reader to orient the map should appear in a space where it is easy to find. The legend should be placed in the lower left-hand corner of the map, unless circumstances dictate otherwise.

Lettering is an important part of the map albeit it is not part of the conventionalized picture of the earth's surface. Children must keep in mind those features of the map, such as the grid lines, the political units, and the boundary lines, which are not visible in the real landscape. Legibility is the main aspect of lettering, yet the application of lettering is one of the most difficult problems in cartography. Legible lettering requires practice and skill. Although the pupils may use the manuscript alphabet they learned in the primary grades, opportunities to learn some of the basic principles of cartographic lettering should be provided. Some of the following conventions may be adopted: The names of cities are usually to the right of the city symbol; wherever feasible, the names of rivers should be written parallel to their courses; other words are usually printed horizontally; major features of the landscape such as the oceans, mountain ranges, and all features that extend over a large area are named with capital letters.

The legend should go in the lower left-hand corner. To give the map sheet balance, empty spaces may be filled up with the title or with insets, or a picture may be drawn to enliven the map. These additions allow for the expression of individuality and some personalization of the map. A neatly drawn border, decorative if desired, provides an effective frame for the map.

Probably no single map element intrigues children more than does the use of color. While color holds many implications for cartographers, basic concepts about the physical properties of light and their use in cartography are too complicated for younger elementary school children. However, children should receive guidance from their teacher about the judicious use of color on the maps they make. For example, they should be helped to see that the fewer the color choices, the more obvious the effect; that the use of contrasting colors makes a map or diagram easier to interpret; and that color inspires various emotional responses. The conventional color symbols can be appropriately used in mapping activities—green for vegetation, blue for water features, and red and black for cultural elements. The value of conventional symbols should be brought out.

A final comment concerning a significant psychological aspect of designing a map has to do with selecting a means for calling attention to whatever is deemed important. The child needs to learn to select the "important" for mapping and to call attention to it by the way he designs and arranges his data. To the cartographer this is the problem of visual significance. Robinson suggests five facts which the cartographer considers when seeking to call the map reader's attention to certain selected phenomena or relationships:

1. The degree to which an item departs from its expected appearance. The more it departs, the more visually interesting it is.
2. The relative complexity of its delineation. The more complex the item is, the more visually interesting it is.
3. The relative size of an item. The larger an item is, the more visually important it is.
4. The relative brightness of an item. The brighter or lighter an item is contrasted with its surroundings, the more visually interesting it is.

5. The position of an item with respect to the other components of the map. The nearer to the visual center of a presentation an item is, the more significant it is visually.[38]

7. *The ability to recognize and express relative location.* The ability merely to identify and locate the earth's major physical and cultural features on either globe or map has little significance in terms of geographic understandings. What counts is a comprehension of the *functional significance* of the locative factor and the skills of correctly evaluating and expressing the functional significance of a place.

Undoubtedly, the most important factor in developing an understanding of the concept of place relationship is a recognition of the existence of many variations in the earth's topography and resources. The influence of these variations cannot be ignored, for geographical forces and conditions indirectly or directly affect most phases of human activity. For example, the mountainous terrain influences the modes of transportation of goods and services in certain South American countries as well as the relative location of such other cultural features as villages and cities. "Learning to understand relative location," Kohn points out, "is basically a process of learning first to read exact locations as shown by maps and globes and then of interpreting the interrelatedness of these exact locations."[39]

Meyer suggests the following basic questions for the analysis of place relationships:

Where is the place in terms of latitude, coast line, and type of climate?
Where is it in terms of elevation, relief, landform, water bodies?
Where is it in terms of neighboring peoples, cities, and countries?
Where is it in terms of types of soil, vegetation, mineral resources?
Where is it in terms of dominant types of agriculture, of manufacturing, and of other land use forms?
Where is it in terms of transportation and commerce?[40]

A most valuable tool in making such an analysis is the map.

Kohn mentions five factors that determine the relative location of one area in respect to another:

1. The distance between any two or more places;
2. The character of the terrain separating any two places in terms of the time needed to travel from one to another;
3. Natural waterways that make it possible to penetrate deeply into one section of the world, while mountain barriers impede travel to another;
4. Arbitrary political, social and economic systems that form invisible barriers between various areas of the earth, thus making them inaccessible to each other;

5. The degree to which modern technology has made possible the use of modern means of transportation in the area.[41]

Then, too, the significance of location often has historical dimensions which should not be overlooked. For instance, the advent of new tools and technics in transportation and production of goods has caused major shifts in population centers in many of the national and state communities. The location of county and state seats of government often can be accounted for only in terms of historical knowledge. Sudden changes in ways and methods of carrying on the basic human activities must always be considered; with the building of rapid transit and modern highway systems, isolated areas may all at once find themselves only short distances from large metropolitan centers. The significance of physical factors does not remain constant. Airplanes now connect cities once separated by mountains, deserts, or oceans. Furthermore, the obvious relationships between the human activities, such as the production of goods, and the physical features of a region are not always apparent. Both physical forces and men are changing the surface patterns of the earth; we must select our maps with care for older maps do not tell us the latest story.

Thus, in location analysis, there are dynamic interrelationships between physical and cultural factors that cannot be disregarded. An understanding of the concept of relative location is dependent not only upon the skill of map reading but also upon a repertory of social studies concepts and generalizations as well. The focus in the developmental program of geographic generalizations and map skills must always be on the total coordinated social studies program.

Maps themselves are vehicles for learning interspatial relationships and for understanding physical conditions and cultural features that affect ways in which the basic human activities are carried on within the many communities of men. In fact, the ability to recognize and to express relative location is one of the most vital skills in a map program.

8. *The ability to use and understand basic map projections.* Fundamental to the development of the concept of map projection is an understanding of the spherical nature of our earth. The earth's surface is not flat even though the sensory data we collect from our daily experiences with the local landscape suggest that it is. Understanding the globe as a symbol or model of the earth is essential to the conceptual development of map projection.

Projection is an extremely difficult concept to verbalize, yet well chosen demonstrations with spherical objects can provide concrete experiences illustrating some of the properties of sphericity. Some notion of map projection can be conveyed even to very young pupils. For example, if a large ball showing land masses of one color and water bodies of another color is cut into gores toward the "equator," the children can see what happens to the size or shape when an attempt is made to flatten the cut ball. Any attempt to keep a land mass in "one piece" makes the ball puff up again. With a little experimentation, children will discover that some ways of flattening the globe minimize the distortion in one way or another. The main generalization they must arrive at is that all map projections are distortions of the earth's surface due to picturing a spheroid upon a flat surface. Different projections distort either size or shape of land or water bodies in different ways. This more advanced concept may be pursued with a group that seems able to grasp it from their experimentation. Those who are able to go this far may also understand that we choose to use the projection that distorts least for a given purpose.[42]

In making or reading maps of small areas of the earth's surface the problem of distortion can be ignored for all practical purposes. Children can find out that they can copy a small island or state without distortion by laying a piece of tracing paper on a fairly large globe. They soon find out, however, that it is impossible to use this method to copy a map of a large area such as the United States without crinkling the paper.

Beyond the primary school grades the significance of map projections cannot be ignored because children have many uses in their social studies and other subjects for maps showing large areas of the earth's surface. The fourth-grade class that wants to compare the sizes of its state and Alaska and uses a Mercator projection to do so will not arrive at a sound conclusion. This does not mean that the projection is at fault; it simply cannot be used to compare areas of land in widely separated latitudes. While we are not concerned, then, about the choice of projections when dealing with small areas such as the neighborhood community, we must be concerned with choice of projection when we deal with the larger areas explored in the expanding community emphases of the middle grades and junior high school.

Various methods of overcoming the problem of representing the curved surface of the globe on a flat piece of paper may be demonstrated:

> . . . envelop the globe with a cylinder or cone, or . . . lay a tangent plane against it, and project a part of the grid system of the globe from its center or from some other convenient point upon the cylinder, cone, or plane. The cylinder, or cone, is then cut open and laid out flat, and we have a projection system which has been derived from the actual process of projecting.[43]

To perform this demonstration, all that is needed in the way of a globe is a translucent hemisphere with a bold outline map of North and South America drawn on it along with a grid system. The images of the map outline and the grid system are thrown forward upon the surface of the cylinder or cone or plane much as the movie projector throws the picture on a screen. (See Figure 5.) While there are many ways in which the

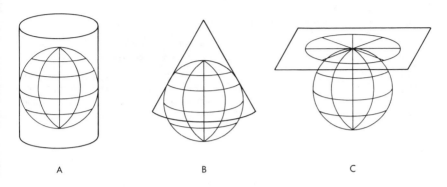

A   B   C

A related to a cylinder; B to a cone; and C to a plane

Figure 5

Projections: Cylindrical, Conical, and Azimuthal

earth's grid system can be constructed, the shadow-casting method serves as an excellent illustration of the basic principle involved in map projection. In actual practice in commercial work, the shadow-casting method is not used by cartographers.

For demonstrating how a flat map can be made from a globe, a map projection device is an invaluable teaching aid. It consists of a transparent globe and a transparent cone, cylinder, and flat disk. Each map projection—conical, cylindrical, and azimuthal—is explained by the transparent map that may be projected by a light located in the center of the transparent globe. The cylindrical and conical maps may be unsnapped to be seen as flat maps. (Details about this device and other aids can be found in "Aids for Teaching," Appendix A.)

An examination of map projections upon a cylinder by this method shows some interesting results; while the polar areas are greatly distorted, the equatorial regions are true to shape. The grid system appears as straight lines. The North Pole is no longer a single point. (See Figure 6.) Varying the location of the source of the projecting light produces different distortions for the polar regions. If the light is located in the center of the globe, the east-west lines become widely separated— Canada, Alaska, and Greenland are extremely exaggerated in shape and the North Pole now seems to be a line equal in length to the equator. Also, a very tall cylinder of paper is needed to catch the shadows for this region. When the source of light is moved to a point at some dis-

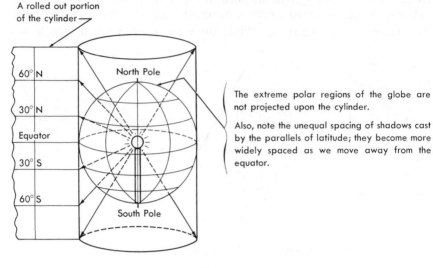

A rolled out portion of the cylinder

60° N

30° N

Equator

30° S

60° S

North Pole

South Pole

The extreme polar regions of the globe are not projected upon the cylinder.

Also, note the unequal spacing of shadows cast by the parallels of latitude; they become more widely spaced as we move away from the equator.

Figure 6

Projection of a Globe Upon a Cylinder

tance from the hemisphere, these polar regions are tightly compressed. In either case, the grid system appears as straight lines, a feature shared with the Mercator projection.

The Mercator projection is a balancing of the two extremes described as a two-way stretching process in which the shapes of land masses retain some semblance of their true selves. However, the areas in the higher latitudes are made to look larger. How the two-way stretching process retains the general shape of objects can be simply demonstrated by drawing various geometrical shapes on thin sheets of rubber and then pulling in two directions. A small sheet of dental dam, a semi-transparent rubber sheet, is an excellent material to use and is readily available through local dental supply outlets. (See "Yellow Pages" of your local telephone directory for addresses.)

Children should compare the area of Greenland and South America on the Mercator projection and then check their results with the globe. Since we cannot have complete accuracy in all four properties of shape, area, distance, and direction in a single flat map projection, the globe should be a constant companion to all maps of large areas on the entire earth. (See "Aids for Teaching," Appendix A, for specific reference to such visual aids as the film *Global Concepts*.)

Azimuthal projections have become popular maps. In the polar case, for instance, these projections "emphasize vividly the strategic importance of high latitudes in controlling great-circle air routes between nations of the Northern Hemisphere."[44] The polar case is an excellent map projection for showing the hemispheric relationships of the North American community to the Atlantic community and to the Pacific community.

The map grid for an azimuthal projection is comparatively easy to make in the polar case (Figure 7). Radiating from the North or South

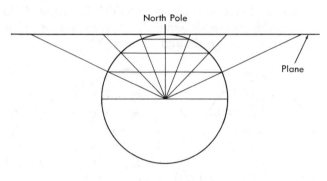

North Pole

Plane

Figure 7

Polar Case, Gnomonic Azimuthal Projection

Pole at the center of the grid networks are the straight north-south lines or the meridians. The east-west lines or parallels may be equally spaced circles, in which case the result is an azimuthal equidistant projection. (See page 19 for a discussion of a system of circular coordinates.) In the Gnomonic azimuthal, all great-circle routes are straight lines, and hence this projection is most useful for plotting radio waves or air routes in a global setting.

Another basic map projection is the conic group. A selected part of the earth's surface may be projected to a tangent cone set upon a globe. The cone can then be cut open and laid out flat. Conventional conic projections have straight-line meridians and circular parallels. Modified conic projections such as Albers' projection with two standard parallels, one in the upper part of the map and one in the lower, provide equality of area, small scale error, and reasonably good conformity (shape). Conic projections are particularly well adapted to represent land areas in the middle latitudes with large dimensions in an east-west direction, such as the United States, the USSR, and Europe. Most atlas and government maps of the United States are based on the Albers Conic Projection.

Teachers, unfortunately, seldom like to use classroom maps that are not conformal (the shape as shown on the globe) and for this reason readily accept a Mercator or closely related projection. However, for purposes of comparing relative areas of land masses, areal equivalence is needed, and the equal-area projections do not preserve the property of shape. No single map projection can be both conformal and equivalent at the same time. Interrupted map projections make it possible to display the earth's land areas better, in addition to providing better shapes for the continents, than do the typical equal-area projections. Interrupted equal-area world map projections choose several central meridians, usually one for each major world land mass, and a grid system is constructed around each one. Goode's Interrupted Homolosine Projection, a readily available equivalent projection, is recommended when areal comparisons are desired (Figure 8).

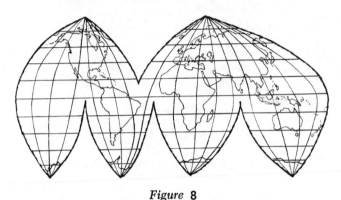

Figure 8

Interrupted Equal-Area World Map Projection

Since premature use of projections could become miseducative with elementary school children, globes should be in continuous classroom use, and an effort should be made to help pupils obtain an adequate grasp of the global grid system. Kohn lists the concepts concerning the global grid system that seem within the achievement range of upper elementary pupils:

1. Parallels of latitude between the Equator and either pole are all of different lengths. They decrease in length with increase of latitude. At the Equator they divide the earth into two hemispheres. The 60 degree line of latitude is only one-half the length of the Equator.
2. The North and South Poles are points.
3. All the lines of latitude of the global grid are parallel to each other.
4. Meridians of the earth all are of equal length. Each pair of meridians are great circles which divide the earth into hemispheres.
5. All meridians converge at the North and South Poles and bisect or cut across not only the Equator but also every line of latitude.
6. Degrees of latitude are of equal length, or are equally spaced on the globe.
7. Degrees of longitude decrease in length with distance from the Equator and are reduced to zero at the poles.[45]

The various kinds of manipulative experiences alluded to in this section on map projections should be thought of as a readiness program for more detailed instruction later. Again, we are not primarily concerned with the complete mastery of the concepts and skills involved. While the degree to which these concepts can be developed in the junior high school is probably somewhat limited, this does not minimize the importance of having children acquire true impressions about the shape, area, direction, and distance of the land masses of the earth in their global setting from the maps and globes they read. Sequential teaching-learning experiences should help them understand the concepts involved in map projection and appreciate the basic problems of projecting a spherical surface upon a plane surface.

9. *The ability to understand and relate areal distributions.* Maps are used not only to plot the specific location of cultural and physical elements of the earth's landscape but also to show the patterns of areal distribution of any one of the elements. Distribution maps are among the most important maps we use today. They may show the pattern of distribution in the state community of a single element, as, for instance, vegetation such as forest or grasslands. Important fishing grounds, soils, or coal deposits of a continent may be shown on a map so that the facts can be grasped quickly and easily. The commonly used symbols for qualitative distributions are small pictorial symbols: simulated trees for forests, grass bunches for swamps, and so on. Only after these symbols have been used and mastered should older children learn to employ the abstract color symbols, commonly known as color patches. Maps of this type show the variations in distribution of an element over a region without taking into account the amount and density of distribution.

The importance of the concept of quantity became an early consideration in cartography for, as Robinson points out, "When man became conscious of the variety of phenomena on the earth it was only natural that he should also have been interested in variations in amount from place to place."[46] Maps of quantitative areal distributions show the variations in the value, amount, or density of the distributions.

Variations in quantity may be plotted in a number of ways, using lines connecting places of equal value, called isopleths (rainfall, temperature, and elevation); shadings of areas of equal densities or concentrations, called chorepleths; and dots, with each dot of equal size representing the same amount of units of a thing. These quantitative maps present data expressible as numbers, such as the number of inches of rainfall, the temperature ranges, or the number of people per square mile in a state or nation. All quantitative maps fall into one of two classes: (1) representations of a single category of data where the values are observed and expressed on the map in absolute terms and (2) representations that show derived values such as averages, percentages, and densities. The three general classes of relationships in the second group of maps are (1) measures of central tendency—for example, averages which are obtained from weather observations over a period of time; (2) proportions or percentages, in which some element of data is singled out and compared to the whole, such as the average number of cloudy days per month; and (3) the density or concentration of the element, such as the number of things per square mile (Figure 9).

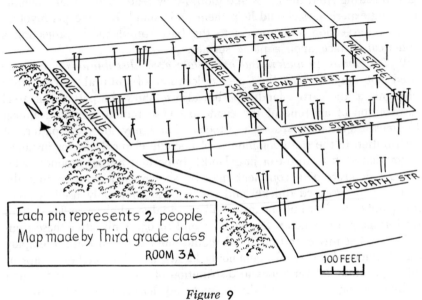

Figure 9

Density Map

Involved in making and reading these maps is an understanding of numerical concepts. All of the concepts are introduced in the middle school arithmetic program except that of percentages; however, fractions may be used to express proportions at this level, and percentages left to junior high school.

Data for any one of the three general classes of relationships may be derived from observations and measurements that are made in the pupils' home, school, neighborhood, or local communities. For instance, children can take a census of the neighborhood area and then calculate the density per block. Thus 100 people in a ten-block area can be considered a density of ten people per block. The children can make dot or pin maps of the number of automobiles in various sections of their neighborhood community. The dots may be spaced evenly throughout the total area; however, if there is a concentration of cars in particular sections the dots may be run together to give the impression of heavy distribution. Meaningful map-making and map-reading experiences such as the above should be carried on before children are expected to read the maps of others, such as those in atlases. Quantitative maps are complex and difficult to read and understand without an adequate background of map skills and geographic understandings.

Each of the basic human activities has a pattern of distribution as well. For example, primary children can record the distribution of mail-box drops, fire alarm boxes and fire hydrants, traffic lights, parks, motion-picture theaters, branch libraries, drug stores, etc., in their immediate communities. They can also try to discover how the natural environment in their zone of contact influences their food, clothing, shelter, transportation, communication, recreation, etc. Whether the population is dense or sparse, whether the community in question is an agricultural or a manufacturing center, the amount and kind of transportation and communication—all are influenced by the natural environment and the uses to which the people have put it.

The influence of technology should be noted in relation to each of the basic human activities being emphasized at that grade level.

Some relations are more difficult to understand than others. It is not hard to see that on flat land the roads are straight and in hilly areas roads are curved. It is easier to grasp agricultural land use than to understand why manufacturing communities developed where they did, especially today when sources of raw materials are often remote. One suggestion is to *study effects before causes.* We might add, study effects and look for *many* causes. Often one sees the statement, even in textbooks: "Cotton is grown in the southeastern United States *because* the soil and climate are just right." It is important, instead, to help children observe where cotton is grown and then try to discover the *many causes,* and realize that *people,* not environment alone, make the *choice.* The people make a choice within the limits of their environment and the state of their technology. The question to investigate further is why the people made this particular choice. Such an approach helps children develop the ability to raise questions and look to many sources for answers rather than try to guess *the* cause for a given effect on the basis of only the limited data they already possess. It is in analyzing the natural-cultural relations that maps most often become a question-raising instrument rather than just a source of information.

10. *The ability to use and understand the globe as a model of the earth.* Globes have an important place in the map-making and map-interpreting program of the elementary school grades since they are true representations of the earth. Raisz appraises the educational value of the globe as follows:

The globe is the highest achievement of cartography. It enables man to step outside his planet and see its wonderful pattern as from the heavens. We can see the relationships of oceans, of continents, and of the polar regions; we can see unusual views and unusual relationships. It is with good reason that in the most progressive schools they use globes in the very earliest stages of geographical education. It is on a globe that such fundamental concepts as day and night, summer and winter, planetary winds, time zones, tides, etc., can best be understood.[47]

Since the globe is spherical like the earth it shows the distances and directions between points correctly and reveals the comparative size of continents and oceans. Exact areas are shown true to scale. The map that is on the globe's curved surface is a more accurate representation of the earth's surface than can be shown on a flat map. The superiority of the globe as an instructional aid in developing concepts concerning the earth on which we live cannot be overestimated.

Globes should be available informally for children to handle and to ask questions about even in first grade. Children can be told that the globe shows the shape of the earth; we live on the earth; the position of our own home can be noted on it. The globe is a part of the readiness program to enlarge children's horizons. It is useful if only to demonstrate that there are other places with other people, and that it is their earth too. Even very young children can become familiar with the shape of land and water bodies.

As for the technical aspects represented on the globe, primary grade children may learn the name and location of the poles, the equator, and the idea of north and south as distances from the equator toward the North Pole and the South Pole. To the extent that their interests are aroused, they may learn our own continent and adjacent oceans, then the names and shapes of other continents and oceans. On a slate globe that shows only land and water bodies, children can gradually add the names of continents and oceans. They may name and locate important nations and cities talked about in a social studies or other content period. Names and places should have some relevance to ongoing concerns. Probably only continent names should remain on the globe so as not to confuse smaller land subdivisions with continent names.

Where globes have been made available in the primary grades, the pupils often become fascinated with them, spending much of their free time thoughtfully gazing at them, rotating them, and often asking very good questions. Barton describes an experiment with globes in a second-grade classroom. Most of the pupils' questions were political-locational in nature: "My uncle is in Texas. Where is Texas?" "Is this Illinois?" "Where is England?" "What does the blue show?" One boy, after four days of seemingly aimless examination, generalized, "The water never ends."[48]

The use of the globe should continue throughout the grades as a carefully planned series of experiences in order to provide development of geographic understanding and skills. It should be recognized that globes cannot be made large enough to have much interest from the point of view of the details of the earth's surface. Furthermore, only half of the world can be seen at one time. Globes present some classroom management problems for the teacher in that they are too small for more than a handful of children to view in a single group, and they cannot be stored as conveniently for ready use as maps can be. However, the larger items such as the land and water masses and basic concepts concerning the earth as a spheroid can be taught to larger groups of children without any difficulty. The globe is an essential instructional aid in a program of teaching-learning experiences directed at helping children develop a geographic point of view.

The following geographical concepts and understandings concerning the globe as a model of the earth are suggested for sequential development in the elementary school map-making and geographic interpretation program:

> The globe is a spherically shaped model of the earth.
> The shape of the earth is round in every direction.
> The globe shows the earth's natural features such as the land and water masses, and some globes show some of the cultural features.
> A system of grid lines is drawn on the surface of the globe—north-south lines and east-west lines.
> The grid system provides the means of locating places on the globe's surface.
> North and south are definite points on the globe (the North and South Poles), whereas east and west are not definite points.
> The cardinal directions are read along the grid lines of the globe.
> A great circle divides the globe into two equal parts.
> Global distances are measured along great-circle routes.
> The shortest distance between two points is along the great circle.
> The earth turns (rotates) on its axis.
> The turning or rotation of the earth gives us day and night.
> The earth revolving around the sun gives us the seasons.
> The map of the world on the curved surface of the globe is the only exact map we have.
> The surface of any spheroidal object cannot be flattened without breaking and stretching parts of it. This is called distortion.
> The transfer or projection of any large area of the globe's map to the flat surface of a map results in some distortion.

The teaching-learning experiences designed to develop the above basic concepts concerning the nature of the world in which we live should be directed toward developing the following generalizations about the globe as a model of the earth: The globe shows the true *shape* of the earth; it shows the correct *distances* and *directions* between points; we can determine the exact *location* of any feature; it shows the exact *area* true to scale; and it shows *distances* and *routes* of great circles. It is important that a program of teaching-learning experiences be structured so that these generalizations are full of meaning and are susceptible to functional use by children.

The unique properties of the globe require that consideration be given to sequential arrangement of map skills in the school program. Children should have a thorough understanding of basic concepts concerning the globe as a model of the earth before the concept of projection is introduced. Globes should be used throughout the elementary school grades, and if they are constantly used in conjunction with flat maps, children will experience little difficulty in using both of them together.

To summarize, this chapter has attempted to set forth the views of geographers and cartographers concerning the major geographic objectives for an elementary school program and to identify and describe in some detail the basic skills and geographic understandings that must be developed if maps and globes are to be used effectively in a coordinated social studies program. As has been stressed throughout the chapter, achieving growth in these ten groups of geographic concepts and map skills is a slow, sequential, and cumulative process. Teachers at every grade level have responsibilities for organizing learning experiences that enable the learner not only to acquire the essential skills and understandings but to maintain them at successively higher levels. A detailed program of map-making, map-reading, and geographic interpretation activities to develop these skills and understandings at the primary, middle, and junior high grade levels is outlined in the chapters that follow.

REFERENCES

1. Hilda Taba, "General Techniques of Curriculum Planning," *Curriculum Reconstruction*, Forty-fourth Yearbook, National Society for the Study of Education, Part I (Chicago: University of Chicago Press, 1945), p. 90.
2. Hilda Taba, "Teaching Strategy and Learning," *California Journal for Instructional Improvement*, 6:3–11 (December, 1963).
3. George W. Haupt, *An Experimental Application of a Philosophy of Science Teaching in an Elementary School*, Contributions to Education, No. 633 (New York: Bureau of Publications, Teachers College, Columbia University, 1935), p. 102.
4. Erwin Raisz, *General Cartography* (New York: McGraw-Hill Book Co., Inc., 2nd ed., 1948), p. xi.
5. G. H. Gopsill, *The Teaching of Geography* (New York: St. Martin's Press, 1958), p. 18.
6. Preston E. James, *A Geography of Man* (Boston: Ginn & Company, 2nd ed., 1959), p. iv.
7. Zoe A. Thralls, *The Teaching of Geography* (New York: Appleton-Century-Crofts, Inc., 1958), pp. 24–25.

8. Isaiah Bowman, *Geography in Relation to the Social Sciences* (New York: Charles Scribner's Sons, 1934), p. 111.

9. Armin K. Lobeck, *Things Maps Don't Tell Us* (New York: The Macmillan Co., 1956), p. x.

10. Thralls, *op. cit.*, p. 24.

11. Clyde Kohn, "Interpreting Maps and Globes," *Skills in Social Studies*, Twenty-fourth Yearbook, National Council for the Social Studies (Washington: NCSS, 1953), pp. 166–167.

12. E. W. H. Briault, and D. W. Shave, *Geography In and Out of School* (London: George G. Harrap & Co. Ltd., 1960), p. 64.

13. Gopsill, *op. cit.*, pp. 57–58.

14. B. S. Bloom (ed.), *Taxonomy of Educational Objectives: Handbook I, Cognitive Domain* (New York: David McKay Co., Inc., 1956).

15. *Ibid.*, pp. 201–204.

16. *Ibid.*, p. 204.

17. *Ibid.*, pp. 204–205.

18. Kohn, *op. cit.*, p. 146.

19. George T. Renner, "The Map in Modern Education," *Teachers College Record*, 40:707 (May, 1939).

20. Helen M. Carpenter and Alice W. Spieseke, "Skills Needed for Democratic Citizenship," *Skills in Social Studies*, Twenty-fourth Yearbook, National Council for the Social Studies (Washington: NCSS, 1953), p. 10.

21. Thralls, *op. cit.*, p. 140.

22. Gopsill, *op. cit.*, p. 23.

23. Arthur H. Robinson, *Elements of Cartography* (New York: John Wiley & Sons, Inc., 2nd ed., 1960), pp. 18–22.

24. For a basic discussion of cartesian coordinates see a reference such as William L. Schaaf, *Basic Concepts of Elementary Mathematics* (New York: John Wiley & Sons, Inc., 2nd ed., 1965), p. 103.

25. Erwin Raisz, *Principles of Cartography* (New York: McGraw-Hill Book Co., Inc., 1962), pp. 146–149.

26. Clyde Kohn, "Maps as Instructional Aids in the Social Studies," *Audio-Visual Materials and Methods in the Social Studies*, Eighteenth Yearbook, National Council for the Social Studies (Washington: NCSS, 1947), pp. 158–159.

27. Clarence B. Odell, "The Use of Maps, Globes, and Pictures in the Classroom," *New Viewpoints in Geography*, Twenty-ninth Yearbook, National Council for the Social Studies (Washington: NCSS, 1959), p. 202.

28. J. Riley Staats and George E. Harding, *Elements of World Geography* (New York: D. Van Nostrand Co., Inc., 2nd ed., 1953), p. 19.

29. Kohn, "Interpreting Maps and Globes," p. 151.

30. For a basic reference the reader should refer to scale drawings in Schaaf, *op. cit.*, pp. 321–326.

31. Katheryne T. Whittemore, "Map-Reading Readiness," *Childhood Education*, 14:114 (November, 1937).

32. Ruby M. Harris, *Map and Globe Usage* (Chicago: Rand McNally & Co., 1959), p. 4.

33. Edith P. Parker, *Seeing Our World Through Maps* (Chicago Heights, Ill.: Weber, Costello Co., 1942), p. 6.

34. *Ibid.*, p. iv.

35. John B. Carroll, "Words, Meanings and Concepts," *Harvard Educational Review*, Spring, 1964, pp. 178–202.

36. Hubert A. Bauer, *Cartography* (Cambridge, Mass.: Bellman Publishing Co., 1945), p. 5.

37. Gopsill, *op. cit.*, p. 68.
38. Robinson, *op. cit.*, p. 223.
39. Kohn, "Interpreting Maps and Globes," p. 223.
40. Alfred H. Meyer, "Geography in the Teacher Education Program," *Geographic Approaches to Social Education*, Nineteenth Yearbook, National Council for the Social Studies (Washington: NCSS, 1948), p. 284.
41. Kohn, "Interpreting Maps and Globes," p. 162.
42. Raisz, *Principles of Cartography*, p. 189.
43. Raisz, *General Cartography*, p. 63.
44. Staats and Harding, *op. cit.*, p. 26.
45. Kohn, "Maps as Instructional Aids in the Social Studies," p. 160.
46. Robinson, *op. cit.*, p. 142.
47. Raisz, *General Cartography*, pp. 265–266.
48. Thomas F. Barton, "Geographic Instruction in the Primary Grades," *Geographic Approaches to Social Education*, Nineteenth Yearbook, National Council for the Social Studies (Washington: NCSS, 1948), pp. 214–215.

chapter two

BIOPSYCHOLOGICAL
CONSIDERATIONS

Commonly accepted as one of the bases of curriculum building is a knowledge of the contributions made by the biopsychological sciences. Certainly if we are to be at all scientific in curriculum planning, we must base curriculum not only on what we want children to learn but also on what they are *able* to learn. Although there is still much about child development and the learning process that is not known or that is in dispute, an impressive body of studies is accumulating which, when analyzed, gives us valuable cues as to what we may expect from children.

The purpose of this chapter is to analyze the biopsychological literature in the fields of learning theory and child growth and development in order to set forth those principles or generalizations which seem best able to guide us in programming a series of teaching-learning experiences designed to develop geographic understandings and map skills in a coordinated social studies program for the elementary school. Several broad areas will be explored: (1) child growth and readiness for learning, (2) children's interests as related to motivation and learning, (3) the nature and development of concepts and generalizations, and (4) the transfer of learning. These areas are not mutually exclusive; considerable overlapping exists. However, a synthesis of the pertinent studies in these areas can be useful in our selection of experiences that will have maximum value for elementary school children who are becoming young geographers.

Child Growth and Readiness for Learning

A review of the literature reveals that much psychological and educational research has been concerned with the developmental behavior of

47

children. The research has yielded a number of general principles of child development that have implications for curriculum planning.

Olson and Hughes suggest seven general principles of growth and development that have implications for educational policy:

1. Children differ in rate and level of growth.
2. Growth tends to be unified.
3. Children differ in the pattern of growth.
4. Growth with time is a highly individual matter.
5. Growth has stability and continuity and makes demands for nurture.
6. Membership in a given family influences the pattern of growth.
7. Children viewed as wholes are more alike than when viewed as parts.[1]

Millard outlines four general principles of growth and development that account for the variation in developmental patterns:

1. Growth is qualitative as well as quantitative.
2. Growth is continuous in reference to beginning and end points of cycles.
3. Growth patterns are individual in reference to:
   a. present status
   b. rate of all kinds of growth and learning
   c. variations within a pattern
   d. maximums or ceilings
   e. timing of sequence in a given individual's pattern
4. Growth is modifiable.[2]

Millard points out that while the principle of modification has common acceptance, the manner in which modification may be brought about most effectively is often misunderstood.

> Attempts at modification, usually considered as change in status of the child in a particular skill, through pressure, excessive drill, and extensive practice periods, are usually ineffective or downright harmful when measured in terms of permanent learning. . . . In the ideal situation modification results with the greatest permanent benefits by continuous work on improvement of the total culture surrounding the child.[3]

If growth is qualitative as well as quantitative, continuous, individual in its variations, yet modifiable, an important implication for curriculum development would be that curriculum, though planned, must be left open ended. We cannot know in advance the upper limits of children's capabilities; therefore we may continue to offer opportunity for increasingly complex experience as long as we check to make sure we are not going beyond what the children can handle without developing erroneous concepts.

It is the total environment of the child that supplies the context within which growth occurs. Since there are differences among children of the same age group, we can expect different reactions to the school environment. Olson and Hughes caution that the child is not a passive recipient of stimulation; he makes demands of the environment for nurture according to his maturity level.

> He reacts selectively to the surroundings that are supplied and creates his own world of experience within them. He tends to reject the experiences for which he is not ready. Teachers may make full use of "seeking" behavior by providing a school environment in which children find suitable experiences of a wide variety in kind and difficulty. No narrowly conceived curriculum of fixed content can attain this goal.[4]

We may say, then, that development is a product of maturation and nurture. Environmental stimulation and the seeking behavior of children are interactive processes. Achievement in school subjects results from maturation *and* the available experiences. In fact, as an expression of growth it does not occur without the nurture of experiences provided by the school.

> The idea that the study of the content of educational experience and the preparation of improved textbooks can help the educational process is sound. The idea that such material can provide uniform experience suitable to all in a class, or that they will make children alike, is unsound.[5]

This study of content of educational experiences clearly involves a description of the educational goals.

> It is important that persons charged with nurturing the early learning of a child should agree sooner or later on the kinds of things that should be learned. Otherwise, the child may be subjected to opposing objectives and methods.[6]

There need be no conflict between child development considerations and the prescribing of learning experiences concerned with fostering desired behavior. In fact, if we are to expect growth in subject matter areas of the curriculum, appropriate learning experiences must be organized and provided for children.

Perhaps, in general, the need for experiences commensurate with growth is known, but the teaching of geographic concepts and the use of maps has largely been neglected. It has too often been assumed by school teachers that maps are self-explanatory, and that once a child is old enough to read, he can simply look at a map and "read" it. Further, unless adults regard the abilities to think and behave geographically and to use maps as worthwhile and necessary accomplishments, the child may well be at a stage where he could benefit from such instruction and yet be deprived of it. The knowledge that individual children make differential gains when all are exposed to an experience should not lead us to the false conclusion that sequential curriculum experiences are unimportant. If a geographical viewpoint is considered essential to successful living in the world today, children must have the experiences necessary to produce this viewpoint. Such experiences, in keeping with the children's potential to benefit, must be carefully planned in the curriculum.

We hold that biopsychological factors of learning are best served when the broad framework of the curriculum is planned in advance by a team of (1) scholars in the content discipline, (2) theorists in learning, and (3) specialists in curriculum designing. For the coordinated social studies program this team must include (1) a geographer (in addition to a historian, an economist, a political scientist, an anthropologist, and a sociologist to represent all the important social sciences), (2) a psychologist, and (3) a curriculum planner. The design produced will consist of the sequence of the major themes or emphases to be covered and the activities which will put the meat on the sequential coordinates of the program. Such a planned-in-advance design will keep pupils moving in an orderly fashion through a series of experiences extending over all the elementary school years.

Biopsychological conditions are also closely related to the daily planning by teacher and pupil within the guidelines provided by those who plan in advance. The advanced planning must be flexible enough to allow for wide variations among individual pupils, differences in teacher preparation and interest, and all the other factors that are crucial in generating pupil and teacher motivation, involvement, and understanding. A good advance design offers hundreds of options to pupils and teacher. It will, in fact, suggest far more possibilities for worthwhile and exciting things to do than the best teacher could suggest if left to his own resources, or the most alert pupil would generate by himself. But choices from among the rich possibilities must be made. We call this phase of curriculum development "planning in process." "Planning in process" means focusing on that essential set of working conditions in which teacher and pupils (1) study the emphasis intended in the broad curriculum design for next sequential development, (2) examine their individual interests and goals, (3) select and plan a course of action that is the resultant of the first and the second sets of factors, and (4) feel free to evaluate and replan as they proceed to undergo the experiences selected in (3).

Cook points out that *itemized* goals are not achieved in a given order, once and for all time, nor should all instruction be organized around them.[7] Pupils should have a large share of responsibility for setting immediate goals. Olson notes that if children participate in planning classroom experiences, they have an opportunity to bring into school more of their own current interests and problems.[8] This participation by the pupils in selecting and organizing the immediate teaching-learning experiences (planning in process) provides a safeguard against unrealistically imposed instructional programs. Thus Cook and Olson both lend support to our hypothesis that overall "planning in advance" of the broad developmental design is a prelude to daily pupil-teacher choice and plan.

The major task of the school is to arrange experiences that match the capacities of children with the expectancies of the culture as expressed in the curriculum planned in advance. With added maturity, children learn specific subject matter in much less time, require less practice, and are able to apply what they learn to problems. Does this not suggest the postponement of all such experiences to later grades? The ease of acquisition of skills and concepts is not the only criterion for the ordering of content and the teaching-learning experiences. Postponing all geographic and map experiences to junior high school grades would deprive younger pupils of the use of one of the most fundamental tools in the social studies program. The school has the responsibility of organizing appropriate readiness programs to insure a gradual development of understanding so that children are not suddenly plunged into teaching-learning experiences in geography at a specific time in the middle grades or junior high school.

The maturational rather than the mastery approach to learning has implications for the curriculum scheme organized around basic concepts, such as is proposed in this volume. Mastery of a concept is not expected at any particular grade level. Rather, the curriculum is so organized that provisions are systematically made for repeated study of the concepts and generalizations in subsequent grades in new contexts, thus enhancing the opportunity for children to acquire new meanings and associations. These concepts, understandings, and skills are used in our organization of the social studies program within the context of the expanding communities of men.* Thus at each grade level each of the skills and understandings will be developed to the extent that children's abilities, maturity, and previous experiences allow, and to the extent that the skills have relevance to the community emphasis assigned to the particular grade.

Motivation, Learning, and the Interests of Children

That children must be motivated to learn is an accepted psychological principle. Consequently, stress in curriculum development is placed

* See Chapter Three.

upon children's interests as a base from which to initiate the learning process. However, children's interests should not be perceived as being innate; rather, they are behavior tendencies that are the products, in large measure, of previous experiences. The random experiences and interests that children bring to school are mostly unselected and un-guided and are influenced by the general social and cultural context.

There are significant educational responsibilities in the appraisal and cultivation of interests. Jersild cautions,

> A child's expression of interest may represent anything ranging from a momentary caprice to a profound and strong disposition to lean toward one line of action in preference to certain others. . . . What seems to represent the interests of the group may be something determined primarily by a few rather aggressive pupils who assert their wishes and have their way. The bias of the teacher very readily also comes into the picture. . . .[9]

Horn says that in stressing the importance of interests we should recog-nize that:

> interests arise out of values; that is, out of a sense of pertinence to funda-mental needs. It is not the purpose of the school to interest the child in the sense of entertaining him, but to utilize and develop interests in those things that are most universally significant in life outside the school. Students in school where this more fundamental view is taken . . . develop a more crit-ical sense of values and superior power to evaluate. Their interests become intelligent.[10]

The role of children's interests in planning teaching-learning experiences is indicated by Witty:

> It appears to be the responsibility of the teacher to utilize interests as a starting point in the introduction of many activities, but teachers must recog-nize that many interests are transitory or actually unworthy of extension, and hence need re-direction or replacement. Therefore, every teacher should aim to modify old patterns and create new interests.[11]

Most of the studies in the area of children's interests have been of the descriptive, survey type. Elementary school children have responded to questions about their reading interests, the school subjects they like or dislike, and the kinds of play activities they enjoy. A summary of the findings of a few such studies follows.

Cowan made a detailed analysis of the research on children's interests for factors which would give clues in organizing the sequence of ele-mentary school social studies. With respect to reading interests, he found that the younger children enjoyed stories about other children and familiar experiences; they liked tales of fantasy, fun, and humor; they enjoyed reading about acts of kindness or bravery. Children in the intermediate grades were more interested in realistic tales—action stories of adventure, sportsmanship, the work of inventors; they were interested, too, in learning about how inventions worked and how to make things. Cowan concludes with this statement:

> Most all interests dovetail and are predicated by our culture; however, the age level in which they become dominant is tied up with the psychosociological factors of maturation such as: personal and social development; ego-centrism versus altruism; leadership and isolation; transient and stable group structure and its concomitant standards; variations between sexes; and adult-child relationships. Thus if interests are learned, they can be strengthened or redirected in the degree to which they can serve basic individual and societal needs . . . it remains for the school to assume the directing explorations that widen interests of children, if the result is to be an adjusted, well rounded, creative and enthusiastic citizenry.[12]

The influence of social convention, tradition, and group pressures with regard not only to the time of onset of particular interests and activities but also to the point at which they stop is a matter of common observation. Longitudinal and cross-sectional studies of groups of children show broad age trends. The factor of chance comes more into play as children grow older and their abilities and potentialities expand. Their choices of interests come to depend more and more upon the example set by others, both children and adults, and the way in which the experiences are presented. Interests are developed in the intricate network of contacts the child has with other persons, with his own performance, and with both the natural and the cultural environment. Primary children have more interests in common than do children in the middle grades or junior high school because interests become differentiated as children progress through the grades.

> As the environment of the child broadens to include his school, his neighborhood, his [local] community, and finally the whole world, new opportunities are opened up for the acquisition of other interests. That is why many of the interests of childhood are abandoned and are replaced by other interests as the child emerges from childhood into adolescence, and then into maturity.[13]

A desirable curriculum design provides an ever expanding range of experiences so that children are stimulated and have opportunities to cultivate new interests.

The play interests of children are important to the curriculum design for the primary grades. Mitchell, who worked with children for over forty years in an experimental school and in the public schools of New York, reported on the *process* of play as well as its content. Children are interested in "playing out," a kind of rethinking and re-enacting, the relations of people and things they see in their environment.

> What is characteristic of the educational process in this early play stage seems to us to hold true always. There is not only an "intake" but an active "outgo." The chief program for geographic intake in these early years lies in trips—explorations of the environment. Provision for outgo, equally important, is made within the classroom through "adaptable materials." . . .[14]

> The children explored the immediate world around them and observed the work that different people were doing. . . . Scattered facts gathered in their research (trips, discussion) fell into organized relationships through their constructive play. The outgo was play. But it was thinking, too. With their blocks, toy animals, trucks and ferries the children were making new discoveries about the inter-relationships of work.[15]

> The media through which children find their most fluent, most satisfactory expression, change as they mature. Blocks disappear about seven when the children wish a more permanent medium in order to carry on longer-span, more consecutive play or thinking.[16]

Mitchell emphasized that children learn with all their senses; learning is never purely intellectual. They are interested in tasting, smelling, seeing, hearing, touching, feeling, and then actively dramatizing this "intake" in their play. In developing methods for teaching geographic understandings and map skills, especially in the primary grades, the importance of the process of play must be taken into consideration.

Baker investigated children's contributions during free discussion periods in Grades 2, 4, and 6.[17] His studies reveal the content of children's interests, the place of the local environment in the curriculum, and the role of real and vicarious experiences. At least 70 to 80 per cent of the children's contributions were devoted to social matters—to people, their activities, their problems (both individual and group), their institutions, their needs and achievements. Eighty-four per cent of the contributions made in discussion by second-grade children dealt with matters in their immediate surroundings. In fourth grade the percentage was 55; in the sixth grade, 27. As children progress through the grades, it appears that less attention is given voluntarily to the immediate environment. A very similar pattern appears in the importance of personal presence. In Grade 2, 83 per cent of the contributions were concerned with events at which the children were personally present and in which they were involved. In Grade 4, the figure had decreased to 52 per cent and by Grade 6 it was down to 25 per cent. Contributions from vicarious sources increase with age although actual experience accounts for 25 per cent of the contributions even at the sixth-grade level. Children in all grades studied gave considerable attention to their own trips, a circumstance that offers a valuable clue to method. As to content, second-grade children directed most of their discussion to their own play and recreation, to their family and home activities, while children in fourth grade gave their attention to trips, books, radio, movies, and metropolitan current happenings. Sixth-graders were more concerned with national and world happenings as well as with metropolitan current events.

Hill made a study of the ideals urban children selected.[18] Among the six- to eight-year-olds, over 50 per cent idealized characters from their immediate environment. Nine-year-olds chose 45 per cent of their ideal characters from their immediate environment. Twelve-year-olds chose only 30 per cent from the immediate environment. Hill's findings support those of Baker in showing a steady decrease in interest in the immediate environment with age. Hill found that from the age of twelve on there was little change. Girls at each age, however, chose more from the immediate environment than did boys. The influence of ideals by historic and public characters increases steadily from age eight to age fifteen (from 32 to 64 per cent).

Probably one of the most extensive studies of children's interests was made by Jersild and Tasch, who surveyed over two thousand elementary school children in the Midwest and New York from Grades 1 through 12.[19] A summary of their findings has particular relevance to the present study.

1. At all grade levels children are preoccupied with people and personal relations.
2. There are strong elements of self-interest and self-reference in ideas about life and the world at large.
3. There are many variations among interests of children in different schools and in different classes.
4. Children's interests to a large degree are learned. What a child likes to do is influenced by what he has had an opportunity to learn to like to do and provided he has the ability to make use of it. Their interests demonstrate what children have learned rather than what they could learn to like to learn. Since children's interests reflect the past more than they provide a guide to the future, interests must be carefully interpreted in order to determine their true significance for education.
5. There is a decline in educational morale with age. As children grow older they tend to make less mention of things that the school uniquely offers—such as the opportunity of learning ideas and skills.
6. Topics in the social studies were mentioned more unfavorably than not.
7. The range of children's out-of-school interests is restricted compared with children's potentialities. The amount of time children spend in cer-

tain activities does not seem to represent deep interest but, rather, it indicates the lack of anything better to do.

8. There is a need for the school and the community to deal together with the fact that the typical child learns to utilize and to enjoy only a few of his many talents.

Jersild and Tasch underscore the importance of making provision in the educational program for a variety of interests in order to take account of the fact that children differ in their makeup. Interests, then, not only serve as aids or guides to the learning process but are also forms of experiences through which the child discovers and realizes his own resources. This study makes clear the extent to which interests are the result of particular experiences. The gap between the interests that children acquire and those they might acquire thus suggests that the school has a responsibility to plan a sequential series of experiences out of which new interests and purposes will emerge.

Since interests are learned, they can be strengthened or redirected in the degree to which they serve the needs of the individual and the society. The organization of the school curriculum can both cultivate the present interests of children and stimulate in them whole new purposes. Effective guidance and the use of appropriate classroom techniques to motivate children may ultimately be more influential than any reliance upon a categorically outlined series of expressed interests or the reactions of children to various kinds of research measuring instruments.

The Nature and Development of Concepts and Generalizations

Children are not born with concepts; they acquire their first ones informally and in a hit-or-miss way during their preschool years. Thus they come to school with a store of concepts depending on the range and kinds of experiences their particular environment offers. In addition, the child entering school has already developed a system of concepts and characteristic ways of perceiving and organizing stimuli from his environment. Concepts are complex affairs that change with additional experiences and new knowledge. The elementary school years represent a period of rapid increase in the number of concepts formed and improvement in their quality.

As educators, we expect the pupil to gain social knowledge both through his real experiences and through vicarious experiences with the abstractions and constructs of the social sciences. Obviously, in terms of citizenship behavior, the real task is not to "know" the constructs and "facts" but to generate meaningful concepts and generalizations upon which one can act. Robinson states,

> The knowledge and understanding which an individual brings to bear in determining his attitudes, his ideals, his thinking on public questions and his social conduct are derived from two kinds of experience, real and vicarious. The world in which he lives is far too large for him to acquire, solely through direct personal experiences, all the insight needed to make him a competent member of society. Vicarious experience, made possible by the communicative arts, must contribute to his social education by helping to bridge the gaps between the world of today and the world of the past and between the world about him and the large world of which he is a part.[20]

Concepts are the structural steel of thinking. The clarity and breadth of a child's concepts are among the best predictors of school progress; his concepts in a large measure determine what he knows and what he does. Concept formation is related to the total development of his personality.

How can we define a concept? McDonald says that a concept is a classification or systematic organization of stimuli or events which have common characteristics.[21] Brownell and Hendrickson give this illustration:

> The concept "river" is appropriately applied to a given object, but it is not properly restricted to that one object. Rather, "river" applies to a class or group of objects which have certain qualities in common. Hence, the child who uses "river" only in connection with a single particular object has no concept of "river"; or at least his concept is too incomplete to be of much value.[22]

Not only are concepts complex, but their many dimensions need to be fully considered in organizing any curriculum scheme for teaching them. The following discussion by Brownell and Hendrickson is particularly pertinent to the area of geography:

> Some of the dimensions of conceptual development are: from concrete to abstract, from vague to clear, from inexact to definite. When development takes any of these forms, a given concept "stays" within its particular group or system of ideas, the while it undergoes changes of the kinds just mentioned. The concept, "river" for example, belongs to the system of ideas, "bodies of moving water," and it gets its first or core meaning from this class idea. But with experience, changes occur through differentiation among members of the class. Distinctions unnoted at first become important. "River" is seen to have characteristics which are peculiar to it and which separate

it from other "bodies of moving water," such as "geyser," "canal." The process of learning is, as stated, one of differentiation. "River" remains within its general class (it is still a "body of moving water"); but the concept gains in clarity, specificity, and abstractness, and its meaning is increased in these senses.[23]

From this analysis it becomes apparent that concept development is no simple matter to be accomplished in short order for such complex map concepts as latitude, longitude, scale, projection, prime meridian, and the cardinal directions. However, if the fundamental aim of education is to produce an intelligent citizenry, we must concern ourselves with both factual knowledge and the skills and understandings which will enhance the effective use of knowledge. Concept formation becomes a major concern.

Too few studies in the psychological literature have investigated how children develop concepts; rather, most of the literature has concentrated on what children understand. The psychological process of concept acquisition has been studied indirectly by observing behavior and the products of learning processes. Too often the assumption is made that children have learned a concept when they can repeat a verbal definition.

> When verbal materials are presented to students without adequate prior perception of the information involved in them, and without provision for the process of concept formation in the class, the activity is forced into memorization of symbols with little or no meaning. It becomes uninteresting and unprofitable, and cannot carry over into life and behavior.[24]

Buswell has described the various stages of concept development:

> In the beginning stages of understanding the learner is always concerned with the concrete aspects of experience. As learning proceeds, these concretes are related into larger patterns which make possible more meaningful experience. With more and more experience the relationships in the field emerge with greater clearness; they take form into organized patterns that fit into a broad, systematic relationship. As the pattern of understanding takes form the learner begins to develop mature interest in the field as contrasted to his original interest in individual concrete situations.[25]

There is general consensus that the child's early repertory and knowledge of concepts is probably a direct function of the kinds and degrees of concrete experiences he has had. However, later on concepts and generalizations may be formed in various ways. Vicarious experiences afforded by reading books, seeing TV and motion pictures, and communicating with other people are means of acquiring concepts.

McDonald offers five generalizations that are pertinent to an understanding of the complex process of concept formation:

1. Concepts cannot be learned without some relevant experience with the phenomena which are to be conceptualized.
2. To acquire a concept a person must abstract or infer from sensory data and his experience.
3. The kinds of concepts children develop will be limited by the kinds of experiences that are available to them.
4. Concepts are learned both through organized experiences and from casual, everyday experience.
5. The child's interpretations of new concepts will be influenced strongly by the concepts he has already developed, both formally and informally.[26]

One of the best and most recent statements on concepts and their formation is that of John B. Carroll of Harvard. He defines concepts as "the abstracted and often cognitively structured classes of 'mental' experience learned by organisms in the course of their life histories." He says that with humans, "their concepts will show a high degree of similarity; and through language learning, many concepts (classes of experience) will acquire names, that is, words or phrases in a particular language."

Carroll sets two conditions for the formation of a concept: (1) "that the individual must have a series of experiences that are in one or more respects similar; the constellation of 'respects' in which they are similar constitutes the concept that underlies them"; and (2) "the series of experiences embodying the concept must be preceded, interspersed, or followed by other experiences that constitute negative instances of the concept." The more complex the concept to be acquired the greater is the need for programming the alternating sequences "of positive and negative instances in order to insure adequate learning of the concept."[27]

Carroll has some potent suggestions on the mix of school and out-of-school experiences in learning concepts:

It would be relatively rare to find a concept taught in school by the procedure of showing a student a series of positive and negative instances, labeled as such, and asking him to induce the nature of the concept with no further aid. Such instances could be found, of course; perhaps they would exemplify a pure "discovery method," and perhaps there should be more use of this method than is the case. . . . Even if a teaching procedure incorporates "discovery" elements, it is likely to be combined with deductive elements . . . not every concept is learned *solely* in a formalized, prearranged school setting. The school environment is in many ways continuous with the out-of-school environment; concepts are learned partly in school, partly out of school.[28]

Carroll joins two processes which are too often seen as antithetical: "What is actually going on in most school learning of concepts is a process that combines in some way deductive and inductive features." He then proceeds to illustrate with several examples, one of which treats the formation of the concept *longitude*. He first questions the theory that concepts related to the earth's sphericity are not easily taught in the middle grades. He says of the modern child who knows about space capsules orbiting the earth,

> Though it may still be difficult to get a child to see how the flatness of his immediate environment is only apparent and that the immediate environment corresponds to just a small area on the globe, it can certainly be done, well before Grade VI, through suitable demonstrational techniques. Having established the sphericity of the earth, one should be able to [teach latitude and longitude as concepts involved in specifying locations on the globe]. Their introduction should properly be preceded by simpler cases in which one *uses a system of coordinates to specify location—e.g., equally spaced and numbered horizontal and vertical lines drawn on a blackboard with a game to locate letters placed at intersection of lines,* a map of one's town or city in which marginal coordinates are given to help locate given streets or places of interest, and finally a Mercator projection map of the world with coordinates of latitude and longitude. Children exposed to the "new math" with its number lines and coordinates should have no trouble with this. Then let us show children by easy stages how a Mercator projection corresponds to the surface of the Earth (certainly an actual globe marked off with latitude and longitude should be used), then how it is necessary to select a particular line (that passes through the Greenwich Observatory) as the vertical coordinate from which to measure, and how the circumference of the earth is marked off in degrees—180° West and 180° East from the Greenwich meridian.
>
> The object is to build for the child a vivid experience of the framework or cognitive structure within which the concept of longitude is defined. The further complications introduced by the use of other kinds of world projections or by the use of regional or even local maps could then be explored. Easily-obtained U.S. Geological Survey maps of one's locality would concretize the meanings of further concepts, e.g., the division of degrees into minutes and seconds, and the fact that a degree of longitude will gradually shrink in length as one moves northward from the equator.[29]

From this analysis of the processes of concept development it becomes obvious that no one including the teacher can "give" the child his concepts. He must construct them out of his own experiences or interactions with the environment. The school's responsibility lies in supplying some of the ingredients out of which concepts are formed. For example, if children are to acquire concepts that contribute to the development of a geographical point of view, the school must present relevant experiences, both concrete and vicarious, appropriate to that end. This process is influenced by the character of the child's school environment, including the teaching-learning experiences and the teaching methods used. Field trips, maps, motion pictures, books, charts, and verbal descriptions are provided on the assumption that each of these experiences is contributing to the development of a particular concept or generalization.

Disciplined perception is obviously an essential and integral aspect of thinking. The individual reflects about and with his accumulated facts; facts tend to produce newly perceived relationships; hence, refinements in concepts take place. What we perceive we tend to "put to memory" if we further perceive potential value in remembering. However, memorized facts in and of themselves do not constitute knowledge (skills and understandings). Too frequently pupils are encouraged by poorly conceived teaching-learning experiences to "cram" facts, and with such crippled educational purpose their perceptualization and conceptualization tend to become limited. Perceiving and conceptualizing must be thought of as components of thinking rather than as separate entities.

If our goal is to train children to see accurately and to think about what they see, then the following material on perception cannot be overlooked. The similarity between the comments and problems of psychology and geographic education is no surprise, for both disciplines are involved with analyzing the adjustment of the individual to his environment. Krech and Crutchfield introduce their psychology students to the problems of perception in much the same way that the geography teacher must approach the task of helping pupils to develop the ability to "think geographically" and to solve problems of relative location in differing cultural environments:

> Each man lives in his own world. . . . And what he perceives, feels, thinks about and imagines depends upon the physical and social environments in which he lives and upon his own biological nature, particularly the way his brain and nervous system work. . . . How the person *behaves* depends upon this world of his own. To understand his behavior we must first ask: What is the specific nature of his world? We are then in a position to ask: Why is it? What is it? How did it come about? What effects does it have on his actions? In brief, we ask the standard questions in the scientist's catechism as he approaches any problem: What? How? Why?[30]

The geographer stresses one other question: "Where?" However, the significance of "where" can only be discovered by first asking, "What? How? Why?"

If "where" is a central question in geography it is because geography is concerned with space and the distribution of phenomena in space.

> Our world is spatial, but space without content is perceptually meaningless. As we look about us, we see that our space is inhabited by *objects* that

are located somewhere in space, are separated from their surroundings, and possess various perceptual properties that distinguish them from other objects. Some of these perceptual properties are simple, e.g. size, shape, texture, color; others are complex.[31]

How better to characterize the task of reading a map? The map reader must translate a two-dimensional abstraction into a visualization of three-dimensional reality. He must use firsthand and then later vicarious experiences to train his sense organs so that he may cope adequately with the map's abstract messages from distant places. The map itself illustrates the simple perceptual problems of size, shape, texture (contour lines and shading), and color, and the complex problems of synthesizing the many clues and facts into meaningful generalizations.

The school is concerned with the guidance of the learner toward culturally approved and/or scientifically accurate impressions primarily because the human intellect has no innate "guidance system" which systematically selects with validity and reliability the correct synthesis of all that is perceived. For example, training the child to identify correctly all map symbols and conventions must be followed by educational experiences for "synthesizing out" meanings that are useful to both him and society.

When an individual is able to perceive a relationship between two or more concepts, the resulting product is a generalization. Generalizations, as well as concepts, are ways of organizing and interpreting experience.

When are children able to generalize? It is a common assumption that children in the primary grades are unable to generalize. However, an interesting study of elementary school children's ability to deal with concepts and generalizations was conducted by Haupt, who explored the psychological basis for proposing a plan of rational gradation and sequence of science content from Grade 1 through Grade 6.[32]

The purpose of his study was to test the proposition that concept development is a continuous process; that children have the mental ability to deal with the "objective" or "large generalization" type of aim in a teaching situation. Two steps were involved: (1) selecting an objective and (2) determining teaching-learning experiences, the interpretation of which would contribute to an understanding of the chosen objective. The science generalization chosen as the teaching objective was "Green plants convert the energy of light into the energy of food and fuel." The detailed description of the procedures and learning experiences will not be described here.

The data of Haupt's study give abundant evidence that even first-grade children are able to generalize. Several examples will be given in illustration: The first-graders observed that plants turn toward the window and then generalized, "Plants turn to the window to get light because light makes them strong," or "Plants bend to the window to get light because they must stay green." In the second grade the pupils observed that plants turn toward the window to get light and explained, "Plants get yellow and die in the dark because they have no light to make food." The fourth-grader, observing first that plants turn toward the sun, made this generalization: "If you put a plant in the dark it will not have green in its leaves because the little machines that make food for the plant stop working." In the sixth grade the children observed that plants turn toward the light and explained, "The chlorophyll (or green color) in the leaves acts like a machine, and through the energy of the sun makes food which is stored in the stem and leaves of the plant."

As one can see, children on every grade level were able to generalize although the generalizations made by the younger children were less complete or complex than those made by the pupils in the later grades.

Haupt points out these implications among others for curriculum development:

> The same objective can be used to select elements of learning for presentation through a range of grade levels. All of these contributory elements may not be learned on every grade level. The learning depends upon the complexity of the elements. The complexity of the elements depends upon (1) the number of concepts associated and (2) the number and immediacy of the experiences which are involved in the concepts associated. Thus, since the same objective can be used to select a progressively complex array of elements and since some portion of the array can be learned on every grade level, gradation by use of the objective type of aim is not only possible but to be recommended. . . .[33]

On the basis of the Haupt study and others, it may be said that there is no one point in the elementary school at which scientific experiments, demonstrations, and causal explanations should be introduced into the curriculum for the first time. Young children are capable of reasoning and generalizing when they are involved in experiences within the range of complexity that they can handle. Generally, as children grow older the age-progression curves in concept growth and development show gradual improvement and expansion so that older children can be expected to handle more complex concepts and abstract content. In other words, the methods and materials that might be appropriate for younger children will not necessarily be the same as those that might be used at the middle level or junior high school. Nevertheless, the same objective could be used, although the elements selected would become progressively more complex. In the Haupt study the prime objective selected was "Green plants convert the energy of light into the energy of food and fuel." The learning which took place on the lower grade levels, though elementary, was worthwhile in itself and at the same time contributed to the major objective.

This developmental and sequential approach has been used in our effort to foster map skills and geographic understandings in the elementary grades. General objectives have been selected which will be instrumental in developing concepts and skills considered basic to map interpretation. Pupil experiences for each of the concepts and skills will be proposed at each grade level, but the complexity will gradually increase.

Probably the most vital relationships the individual may draw from his perceptions of his environment are those of causality. "Thinking geographically" demands of the individual the ability to discern and reject spurious cause-effect relationship. Deutsche investigated the nature and growth of children's concepts of causal relations.[34] Over 700 children in Grades 3 through 8 were asked to give written explanations of a number of science experiments that were demonstrated before the class. Deutsche found in her analysis of the data that no answer was typical of a single age and that in many cases a single kind of answer was given by children over the whole age range.

Such information reminds educators not to set overly ambitious goals for some pupils but to expect other pupils to make great gains. Many educators see the great variation in responses as an encouraging sign of the creative potential of each individual. Deutsche drew forth the implication that maturation alone would not produce the kinds of thinkers our society needs, that specific teaching and guidance must be offered pupils to improve their understanding of causality.

Learning good perceptual habits, then, means more than increasing perceptual speed or span. Obviously, perception is a matter of habits and of total behavior patterns. Selection in what children perceive is apparently due to a combination of their past experiences and their purposes and needs. The teacher cannot be "scientific" in the sense of taking human error out of experience but must concentrate on helping children and adolescents to understand how their purposes, needs, and predispositions influence what they perceive.

Although perceptualization is dependent upon experience, modern life with its secondary relationships has become so complex that much that affects the child must be experienced indirectly through abstract symbols and verbalized ideas. Quillen clarifies why the school must seek to guide the child's categorizing and meaningful conceptualizing:

> The content employed in critical thinking is highly perceptual, based on the sense of sight, sound, touch, taste and smell. This perceptual content is acquired largely not through a formal educative institution such as the school, but as a result of the direct experiences of children and adults in their im-

mediate environment. In the mass associations and organizations of an urban-machine culture, relationships are largely impersonal and anonymous. The content of critical thinking tends to be conceptual, based on the manipulation of verbal symbols, often abstract and loaded with emotional charges of considerable potency.

Conceptualization, unlike perceptualization, cannot safely be left to the exigencies of direct experience. . . .[35]

Since the specific concepts of space are of significance in geographic behavior, we will now proceed to discuss them.

Lord, in a study of spatial orientation of children, administered four tests involving directions in space, cities in space, the arrangement of places by the conventional system of fixed directions, and maintenance of orientation in travel.[36] The results of the tests showed that many children have two frames of reference—a conventional map frame for distance places and a "direct experience" frame for relatively nearby places. Children found it difficult to describe the location of a place by cardinal directions. They were fairly accurate, however, in pointing to the relative location of a nearby city.

The implication for education is the need to provide out-of-door exercises, observations, and drills with regard to compass directions. Lacking the foundational experiences necessary to make directions in space meaningful, children need to develop a close relationship between the arrangement of cardinal directions and self.

Howe's studies of children's knowledge of directions offer specific guidance for developing such concepts.[37] Thirteen hundred children, in kindergarten through sixth grade, were involved in the first study. Four tests were given: (1) outdoors, point north; (2) outdoors, point east; (3) in classroom, point north; (4) in classroom, point east on a wall map. This last test was given from third to sixth grade only. Howe concluded,

1. Children do not know directions as well as commonly supposed.
2. Children do not acquire this knowledge incidentally outside of school since in kindergarten to second grade, more wrong than right answers were given.
3. Children in grades three to six were more right than wrong, but there were many errors. This would tend to show that children have not been taught directions systematically, thoroughly and accurately.
4. Children seem to have acquired the wrong associations in determining directions. Thinking is in terms of local objects rather than natural phenomena.[38]

Howe later undertook a study to see if children *could* be taught directions in space "systematically, thoroughly and accurately." Nine teachers and 274 children in Grades 1 through 3 were involved. Ten weeks of intensive instruction were given, with the skills to be taught carefully laid out in a sequence. At the end of the training period the children were tested, with the following results: first grade, 50 per cent correct; second grade, 75 per cent right; third grade, 88 per cent correct. Ninety per cent of the answers were based on deduction from sun position. From this second study Howe concludes,

1. Children can systematically and accurately acquire a clear concept of directions in space.
2. Children should be taught directions outside of the classroom in order to exclude the probability of association with local objects.
3. Though it may in some instances be desirable to begin instruction in the latter part of grade two, evidence points to the third grade as the most favorable period of comprehension.[39]

Preston conducted a study of children's concepts of time and space in third grade and found that spatial concepts were very confused. Children lacked the three-dimensional experiences that should have come before work with two-dimensional maps was begun. They had not had opportunities for developing the concept of a bird's-eye view upon which a map is based. They could not draw a book lying upon the floor, which is a simple version of this concept. Yet the emphasis of their geography was upon a two-dimensional map which had obviously been introduced prematurely. The emptiness of learning the abstract too soon is also illustrated by the finding that the children could verbalize 93,000,000 miles to the sun but could not estimate the required distance from a fireplug for parking.

To remedy this purely verbal mouthing of information, Preston suggests that children be taken on trips from which they can look down at a landscape and get a bird's-eye view; that they draw informal sketches, diagrams of how they walk to school; that they construct floor plans. In addition, he offers the following suggestions:

> Abundant opportunities should be provided for the consolidation of geographical experiences through the manipulation of blocks, and through pencils, paints, and other media. Through estimating and measuring their own speeds and distances, children may gain important insight into the relationship between time and space and the magnitude of various units of distance. . . . Making homemade compasses, and experimenting, testing, and playing with them should be standard school experiences.[40]

Apparently even young children can systematically and accurately acquire spatial concepts if they are exposed to suitable experiences. These foundational experiences should be active ones in space, as we have suggested, supplemented by verbal (reading, looking at pictures, and talking) experiences. All are necessary if the later, more abstract, learnings are to be successful.

The world of today's child is filled with a vast array of things and events both concrete and abstract. The school, dedicated to the building of geographic knowledge and skill, is responsible for assisting the child in his selection and development of those concepts and skills which are most meaningful and useful.

Transfer of Learning and Curriculum Organization

The problem of the transfer of learning has been a topic of major interest to educators and psychologists for a long time. Certainly those of us concerned with the process of education assume that classroom experiences will enable the child to deal more effectively with outside experiences that he will have now or in the future.

What is meant by transfer of learning? McDonald uses the term to describe the systematic use of previous learnings to facilitate and enhance new learnings.[41]

While there is general agreement about the importance of transfer in education, experimental studies have not yielded the kind of conclusive evidence that is most serviceable for curriculum planning. In a recent review of the research literature Stephens discusses the following general principles that seem to cover a fairly wide range of situations and have some application to curriculum development in the geographic strand of the coordinated social studies program:[42]

1. Bring out the features to be transferred. The element to be transferred—facts, methods, general principles, or attitudes—should be brought into clear focus for the learner.
2. Develop meaningful generalizations.
3. Provide a variety of experiences. Whenever it is a principle or generalization that is to be transferred, it is most important to use a variety of experiences to develop the generalizations.
4. Practice should be provided in applications to other fields. The element to be transferred should be applied to fields outside the subject matter of the lesson.
5. Provide practice in transfer. A student who has had an experience of successful transfer learns the process of transfer. Transfer itself may be made to transfer.

Other research makes it clear that, to assure the maximum possibility of transfer, the school curriculum should contain activities and problems which are similar to those the pupil meets in life out of school. It is important, too, that the educator have clearly in mind what he wants children to learn; he should then select for presentation experiences that are related to these objectives.

Summary

One of the fundamental hypotheses underlying this volume and its proposals for geographic content and map skills is that curriculum designing has two major stages: (1) aspects of the curriculum that are carefully planned in advance and (2) aspects that are planned just prior to and during the educative experience. This would serve to resolve the current issue in education as to whether curricula should be determined by primarily psychological considerations or sociological considerations, or, as it is sometimes expressed, by children's needs or adult planning. The curriculum proposed herein suggests that it is not an either-or proposition; it assumes that the two-factor process of curriculum development serves both psychological and sociological purposes of education.

> It would preserve the advantages of both systematic organization of content and excellent motivation through life situations. It would break down the present wasteful strife between curriculum groups whose views are actually supplementary rather than fundamentally opposed. It would recognize the requirements of a sound psychology of learning in properly relating concretes and generalizations, parts and wholes, and in viewing learning as a continuous process of reorganizing experience.[43]

Some of the implications of organization in the learning process have been discussed in the preceding sections of this chapter. Now let us briefly concern ourselves with some further applications of the biopsychological nature of learning and curriculum organization.

Blair cites a number of experimental studies supporting the hypothesis that learning proceeds more rapidly and is retained longer when that which is learned possesses meaning, organization, and structure.[44] Since isolated, incidental experiences are not likely to change behavior or result in the kind of retention which we are after, organization of the learning experiences becomes a critical phase of curriculum development.

Several psychological generalizations are of sufficient breadth and importance to furnish an initial working guide to curriculum construction:

> First, a curriculum must be such that it will motivate vigorous, active, "doing" responses from the learner. Second, a curriculum must so emphasize organization that the successive experiences of the learner will be con-

tinuously related and interrelated into larger and more significant patterns—into increasing hierarchies of understandings. Responses must not be left as isolated entities.[45]

To insure a measure of continuity from one grade to the next requires advanced planning. This planning is broad in scope so as to give the classroom teacher leeway in tailoring a program of teaching-learning experiences appropriate to the experiential background of the children in her particular class.

A carefully organized sequence of geographic concepts and map skills with established goals and objectives would do much to upgrade the quality of geographic experiences in the coordinated social studies program of the elementary school. Such a sequence rests on a theory of curriculum organization that recognizes the need for advanced planning as well as in-process planning with the pupils, if the total overall scheme is to be consistent with the general principles of learning discussed in this chapter.

An analysis of the literature on the content areas of cartography and geography is necessary in order to determine the fundamental geographic concepts and map skills. This analysis was made in the first chapter. In the present chapter we have attempted to analyze child growth and development and learning theory for principles which have important implications for the nature of curriculum content and organization. These major principles are briefly summarized in the following paragraphs.

The findings from the field of child growth and development show that the developmental patterns of children vary. Therefore, each segment of the curriculum should provide flexibility of requirements and be sufficiently broad to match a variety of combinations of abilities. Grade levels do not signify definitive stages of educational achievement; hence teaching-learning experiences should be adapted to fit a range of maturity levels.

Interests are learned and tend to be related to abilities and skills. The school is in a position to provide experiences that will develop a broader range of interests in each child. However, research evidence does not provide clear-cut information on which to make decisions about sequential placement of content. Such guidance must come from the nature and structure of the content fields.

The development of a conceptual system is a function of the kinds and degrees of concrete and vicarious experiences to which the child has been exposed. It is a gradual, continuous, and cumulative process. Studies show that children at all grade levels are able to reason and deal with concepts. Since there is little experimental evidence on what kinds of experiences facilitate the development of a particular conceptual system, the curriculum builder and teacher must construct hypotheses when they organize a series of teaching-learning experiences.

Evidence from research in the field of transfer of learning yields no conclusive principles for the curriculum builder, although it is an accepted principle that transfer is facilitated when new and previous learnings are similar and when previous learning has been generalized.

Organization of the learning experiences is a critical phase of curriculum development. Experimental evidence supports the hypothesis that learning proceeds more rapidly and is retained longer when the subject matter possesses meaning, structure, and organization.

Chapter Three will develop a design for the sequential development of geographic content and map skills, combining what was noted about geography and cartography in Chapter One with what was said about the biopsychological conditions of learning in Chapter Two.

REFERENCES

1. Willard C. Olson and Byron O. Hughes, "Concepts of Growth: Their Significance For Teachers" (1944), in Arthur P. Coladarci (ed.), *Educational Psychology* (New York: Dryden Press, 1955), pp. 65–81.

2. Cecil V. Millard, *Child Growth and Development* (Boston: D. C. Heath & Company, rev. ed., 1958), pp. 10–17.

3. *Ibid.*, p. 17.

4. Olson and Hughes, *op. cit.*, p. 78.

5. Willard C. Olson, *Child Development* (Boston: D. C. Heath & Company, 2nd ed., 1959), p. 145.

6. *Ibid.*, p. 381.

7. Walter W. Cook, "Individual Differences and Curriculum Practice" (1948), in Coladarci (ed.), *op. cit.*, pp. 330–338.

8. Olson, *op. cit.*, p. 388

9. Arthur T. Jersild, *et al.*, *Child Development and the Curriculum* (New York: Bureau of Publications, Teachers College, Columbia University, 1946), p. 164.

10. Ernest Horn, *Methods of Instruction in the Social Studies* (New York: Charles Scribner's Sons, 1937), p. 134.

11. Paul Witty, "Some Recent Research in Child Development," *Childhood Education,* 19:399 (May, 1943).

12. A. William Cowan, "Elementary School Social Studies: A Research Guide to Sequence," unpublished Ed.D. dissertation, Stanford University, School of Education, 1950.

13. Elizabeth B. Hurlock, *Child Development* (New York: McGraw-Hill Book Co., Inc., 3rd ed., 1956), p. 440.

14. Lucy S. Mitchell, *Young Geographers* (New York: The John Day Company, Inc., 1934), p. 22.

15. Lucy S. Mitchell, *Research on the Child's Level* (New York: 69 Bank Street Publications, no date).

16. *Ibid.*, p. 32.

17. Harold V. Baker, *Children's Contributions in Elementary School General Discussion,* Child Development Monographs, No. 29 (New York: Bureau of Publications, Teachers College, Columbia University, 1942), pp. 117–130.

18. David S. Hill, "Personification of Ideals by Urban Children," *Journal of Social Psychology*, 1:379–392 (1930).

19. Arthur T. Jersild and Ruth J. Tasch, *Children's Interests and What They Suggest for Education* (New York: Bureau of Publications, Teachers College, Columbia University, 1949).

20. Ruth M. Robinson, "Reading and Listening Skills," *Skills in the Social Studies*, Twenty-fourth Yearbook, National Council for the Social Studies (Washington: NCSS, 1953), p. 105.

21. Frederick J. McDonald, *Educational Psychology* (San Francisco: Wadsworth Publishing Co., 1959), p. 134.

22. W. A. Brownell and G. Hendrickson, "How Children Learn Information, Concepts, and Generalizations," *Learning and Instruction*, Forty-ninth Yearbook, Part I, National Society for the Study of Education (Chicago: University of Chicago Press, 1950), p. 106.

23. *Ibid.*, p. 107.

24. Asahel D. Woodruff, *Basic Concepts of Teaching* (San Francisco:Chandler Publishing Co., concise ed., 1961), p. 110.

25. G. T. Buswell, "Organization and Sequence of the Curriculum," *The Psychology of Learning*, Forty-first Yearbook, Part II, National Society for the Study of Education (Chicago: University of Chicago Press, 1942), p. 455.

26. McDonald, *op. cit.*, pp. 136–143.

27. John B. Carroll, "Words, Meanings and Concepts," *Harvard Educational Review*, Spring, 1964, pp. 178–202.

28. *Ibid.*, p. 191.

29. *Ibid.*, pp. 197–198.

30. David Krech and Richard S. Crutchfield, *Elements of Psychology* (New York: Alfred A. Knopf, Inc., 1959), p. 4.

31. *Ibid.*, p. 18.

32. George W. Haupt, *An Experimental Application of a Philosophy of Science Teaching in an Elementary School*, Contributions to Education, No. 633 (New York: Bureau of Publications, Teachers College, Columbia University, 1935).

33. *Ibid.*, p. 102.

34. Jean M. Deutsche, *The Development of Children's Concepts of Causal Relations* (Minneapolis: University of Minnesota Press, 1937), p. 93.

35. I. James Quillen, "What Are the Basic Concepts to Be Developed in Children?" *Childhood Education*, 23:405 (1947).

36. Francis E. Lord, "A Study of Spatial Orientation of Children," *Journal of Educational Research*, 34:503–504 (March, 1941).

37. George F. Howe, "A Study of Children's Knowledge of Directions," *Journal of Geography*, 30:298–304 (October, 1931).

38. *Ibid.*, pp. 303–304.

39. George F. Howe, "Teaching Directions in Space," *Journal of Geography*, 31:209–210 (May, 1932).

40. Ralph C. Preston, "Implications of Children's Concepts of Time and Space," *Social Studies*, 36:219 (May, 1945).

41. McDonald, *op. cit.*, p. 290.

42. J. M. Stephens, "Transfer of Learning," in Chester W. Harris (ed.), *Encyclopedia of Educational Research* (New York: The Macmillan Co., 1960), pp. 1534–1543.

43. Buswell, *op. cit.*, p. 457.

44. Glenn M. Blair, "How Learning Theory Is Related to Curriculum Organization" (1948), in Coladarci (ed.), *op. cit.*, pp. 14–16.

45. Buswell, *op. cit.*, p. 454.

PART TWO

Designing a Coordinated

Social Studies Program with

Special Attention to Geography

AN OVERVIEW   Part Two presents a multidisciplinary design for the social studies program of the elementary school. This design is developed in detail, for the reason that each chapter in Part Three elaborates upon one component of it. Unless one comprehends the rationale of the entire design, he will miss the crucial role of each link in the sequence which develops from year to year. Although there are several alternative schemes that could serve as well, limitations of space confine us to elaborating upon one framework for teaching-learning activities to develop geographic content and skills. It is assumed also that most readers prefer authors to take one position consistently rather than try to be eclectic.

However, the reader can adapt much of what is laid out in detail in Part Three to practically any design—be it geography as a separate subject or a markedly different plan for a social studies program. No reader need feel bound to accept the particular multidisciplinary design presented in Part Two. But in any social science education endeavor an understanding of the framework as presented here will greatly enhance the utility of the hundreds of teaching-learning activities developed in the several chapters of Part Three.

It should be clearly understood that the design sketched in Part Two is not confined to teaching-learning activities in geography alone. The design is multidisciplinary, encompassing the full range of human association: past (history) as well as present (economics, political science, sociology, and anthropology in addition to geography). The subject matter is developmental pupil experiences in geography.

This design is built around two sets of coordinates: (1) the expanding communities of men from the family through eleven ever-enlarging areas and associations such as neighborhood, state, nation, and world communities; and (2) nine clusters or categories of basic human activities in which men in all societies engage, such as producing and exchanging goods and services, or organizing and governing. Chapter Three describes these two sets of coordinates and then superimposes the one set over the other to form the total design for our social studies program.

chapter three

THE DESIGN

There are several designs or patterns available or imaginable for the social studies program of the elementary school. Some people advocate a separate subject pattern in which each of the disciplines—history, geography, economics, political science, sociology, and anthropology—is treated separately in the curriculum. Others propose that the pattern not be planned in advance but allowed to emerge as youngsters and the teacher weave a design out of the strong stimuli that come from living in an exciting world. Still others contend that one of the several separate disciplines mentioned above ought to be the core of the social studies program, with the other disciplines enriching and rounding out the story of man-to-man relations as seen through the particular subject chosen for this central role.

The present authors have elected to use a multidisciplinary approach to designing the social studies program. This approach is not new, having been researched and tested in schools for almost forty years. Within the last decade more and more schools have adopted it, and the majority of the recently devised courses of study issued by states, counties, and local school districts attest to this trend.

This volume focuses on the geographic concepts and map skills that are desirable in the multidisciplinary social studies program. First the design is sketched in broad strokes, then geography and cartography are used to fill in the details, to make more meaningful the spatial distribution of the phenomena of human relationships that are classified as history, or economics, or any other of the social sciences.

One could conceive of a series of professional texts paralleling this book, each one in the series focusing on one of the component social sciences out of which we fashion our social studies program. One volume might be titled *Economic Content and Processes in the Teaching of the Social Studies;* another, *Political Science Content and Processes in the*

Teaching of the Social Studies; and so on until each separate discipline had been searched for the high-priority content and methods of inquiry which should become integral parts of a multidisciplinary design for the social studies program.

This chapter will present in detail the particular coordinated design we have developed over the past twenty-five years. It is used as the framework for selecting and structuring the geographic content and map skills discussed in Part Three.

There is great merit, we believe, in providing *all* children *first* with experiences that will help them discover the structure of the relationships that are the warp and woof of the culture in which they live and are participants. We advocate in the beginning school grades a multidisciplinary study of people living in societies which we call communities. All people live simultaneously in every one of these communities: the family, the neighborhood, the local community, the state, the region, and the nation. And beyond the borders of the national community are multinational regional communities: the inter-American, the Atlantic, the Pacific.

We propose to move gradually and systematically from the lesser and more intimate communities to the larger and more inclusive communities as the child progresses through the elementary school and expands his activities both geographically and culturally. By careful programming we can guide pupils to discover, through observation and inquiry, the economic, geographic, historic, social, anthropological, and political science generalizations and tools of research underlying each of the enlarging communities of which he is a member. From the beginning of our program, we deal with those component subject matters out of which the life of any community, of whatever scale, is composed. But in studying any one community, we emphasize the unity of the societal configuration, drawing the separate disciplines out of context only momentarily for a closer look. We contend that the child is helped psychologically if he starts his examination of human communities by studying and generalizing about total cultural patterns of intimate scale rather than by concentrating on the separate threads of geography, history, economics, political science, anthropolgy, and sociology, one after another, each in its own separate class period or in its own school grade.

We hasten to declare as forcefully as possible that the preceding paragraph *does not* argue for the rejection or even the neglect in the elementary school social studies program of content and method as isolated and structured by the scholars in geography, history, or the several social sciences. On the contrary, the elementary school curriculum has been starved in the past because the program was not infused with sufficient content and methods of inquiry from these basic disciplines. We are determined that the foundational social sciences, history, and geography must have a much more carefully programmed place in the coordinated program than has generally been true in the past.

A Social Studies Design

The following sketch is our proposed design for the multidisciplinary social studies program of the elementary school. The reader should keep in mind that there are and properly should be alternative approaches to designing the social studies program. Our model is but one of such available, and our program for developing geographic content and map skills is not limited to those who use our model for structuring the social studies program.

We begin to construct the model by showing a preschool child standing in the middle of his vast and dimly lit world. He is keenly aware that around him exists an exciting world of people, objects, institutions, and events. But for the most part these external forms and functions, bombarding his senses by the thousands during his waking hours, threaten him fully as much as they excite him for the simple reason that he has had little opportunity to observe these sensory inputs systematically and to relate them in any organized manner to himself and his personal universe. Formal schooling is the prime social technology modern man has invented to help the child discover the order and the rationale of this external world. The school curriculum must guide him, over time, in sorting out and organizing the sensory data to achieve a mature understanding of and adult behavior in all communities of which he is a member.

Where shall we find the help needed for this bewildered child and his perhaps equally bewildered teacher? We believe the proper resolution to the welter and confusion can be found in a judicious use of the high-priority generalizations and methods of inquiry which our colleagues in the social sciences, history, and geography have extracted and structured for us in their several disciplines.

We select *history* as one highly luminous source. We deliberately cause the bright light of historical method and cause-effect relationships generated by historical research to illuminate all of the dark spaces between the child and his ultimate world.

But the child's external world consists not just of events of the past; it is not history alone. The real world exists in the present. It is made up of physical and cultural objects that are distributed over space and have distributional relationships. So we add the sunlight of *geography* to our model to help the pupil and the teacher find their way intelligently over earth's landscapes.

We are not content to leave the elementary child with either a fused history-geography course or two separate courses, one history and another geography. The man-to-man relations go far beyond these two disciplines. Since ours is a multidisciplinary and coordinated approach, our model must have light flooding from the several social sciences.

Political science sheds its significant light on the processes of decision making in the private and public sectors and helps the child to see the ways men in communities organize to create and direct the power essential to keep a community, of whatever size, viable.

Men strive to satisfy unlimited wants with limited resources. *Economics* reveals the mechanisms by which goods and services are produced, exchanged, and consumed to satisfy human needs and aspirations. The recent inclusion of content from economics in the elementary school brings a chorus of favorable comment from citizens who want their children to be literate about the material basis of our civilization.

Because they have been nurtured within a particular culture, men have assimilated values, ways of thinking, and customs that profoundly affect the interaction of individuals and groups. *Anthropology* helps us to understand the values, customs, and institutions of our communities and provides significant tools both for preserving and for changing them.

And lastly, from *sociology* come important generalizations and methods of inquiry into a host of man-to-man relations that must be understood and controlled if we are to survive. Certainly school pupils can learn the elementary concepts of population explosion, urban congestion, racial tension, automation, welfare, etc.

Sequence of Emphases: Expanding Communities of Men

Our design for the social studies has two dimensions: *sequence* and *scope*. We will first discuss the *sequence* of themes or emphasis that form one set of coordinates of our design.

The logic of the sequence of emphases emerges from the fact that everyone lives simultaneously within a set or system of enlarging but interdependent communities of men. Between the individual child at the center of Figure 10 and his ultimate world (the outer band) lie a number of communities of varying size and scale. It is the responsibility of the school to help each child become aware of each community in the set and develop competency to participate effectively in it.

At this point a generic definition of the term *community* is in order. *A community is any group or society of people who live in a definable geographic space; who possess sufficient historic values and customs in common to hold the community together; who face common problems; who have devised solutions (mechanisms, institutions, laws, customs) to these problems that are workable and somewhat unique to the people who inhabit the terrain of that community; who have developed means*

Emphasis No. 1 — The Family Community
Emphasis No. 2 — The School Community
Emphasis No. 3 — The Neighborhood Community
Emphasis No. 4 — The Local Communities: County, City, and Metropolis
Emphasis No. 5 — The State Community
Emphasis No. 6 — The Region-of-States Community
Emphasis No. 7 — The United States National Community

Figure 10

Sequence Coordinates: Expanding Communities of Men

of communication throughout the community space; and who acknowl-
edge that they belong, have membership in the community. We shall
consistently use a modifier (such as family, state, or nation) to designate
which community we are emphasizing at any moment in our design
sequence.

Our multidisciplinary social studies program in the primary grades
starts by emphasizing the oldest, the smallest, the most intimate, and
the most crucial grouping of men—the *family community*. In Figure 10
this innermost concentric band of the model represents the child's family—his father, mother, sisters and brothers, and other blood relatives
who constitute a household. In the mind's eye of each reader will flow
a series of flash pictures of terrains occupied by a family—perhaps a farm
and its house, a shack in the woods, a slum tenement in a city, a single
dwelling in a tree-shaded town or suburb, a modern high-rise apartment;
or the flash pictures may be of more remote family terrains—a grass hut

on a tropical isle, a steeply pitched roof of a mountain shelter, a palace of some potentate, or the river sampan dwelling of a family of over-crowded Asia. With these pictures of the family community space, ac-companying pictures of the wide variety in types of families and their activities could fill the inner vision for some time. No other community of men equals the family in the number and significance of daily human relationships for the child. Throughout his entire life the family will remain central in the satisfaction of his personal needs.

The family community, however, is not the sole human group to which the child belongs. Because the family in our time is not equipped to provide all of the formal education needed, the child at five or six years of age normally becomes a member of a *larger-than-family* community: the *school.* In Figure 10 the school community is represented by the concentric band 2. Here the beginning school child meets many chil-dren—some of his age, but most older. His school community consists of administrative personnel, teachers, and pupils. One can imagine schools of different historic periods, with different purposes and cur-riculum, etc.

The school community is obviously somewhat different in purpose and composition from the other communities in our sequential design, but, for reasons which should be clear later, it is designated as the next larger band in this model. The spatial terrain or arena in which the school operates can be illustrated by a picture of an old brick building in a crowded city, a new school in a suburban development, or the tradi-tional "little red schoolhouse" of yesterday.

Because a family finds that it cannot be completely self-sufficient, it is natural for it to join informally with other families to form a *neigh-borhood community.* This next larger concentric band shown on the illustration as band 3 represents the loosely cohesive community of families who live usually close or fairly close together, who have some relatively common identifying features, and who are, by virtue of their neighborly efforts, more self-sufficient than the separate families com-prising the neighborhood could be. The geographic arena of the neigh-borhood is usually a well-recognized portion of a county or city with rather distinctive boundaries such as a stream, a wide thoroughfare, or those set by zoning regulations. In addition to an elementary school, the neighborhood terrain usually has churches, stores and shops, public and private recreation facilities, a branch library, and substations for mail, police, fire, and similar services. These man-made features of the neighborhood landscape are there to extend and enrich the efforts of the individual families to provide for their needs.

Once again the model expands. No neighborhood community is self-sufficient, and most such communities are far from being able to survive in isolation from other neighborhoods. Consequently, neighborhoods join with neighborhoods to form *local communities* called, for example, county, township, city, suburbia, and metropolis. We mention only a very few cultural phenomena that serve the needs of several associated neighborhoods: the city hall and the county courthouse, the city water system, the city market, the city transportation system, the city newspapers and radio and TV stations, the county medical associations, the county library, the metropolitan recreation district, the metropolitan water district, or the metropolitan law enforcement association. As the impact of modern science and technology mounts, as more and more neighborhoods come within the dynamic influence and boundaries of the expanding metropolis, the common problems of local communities will demand a larger proportion of our time, energy, and money. This complex of local communities, lying between the larger state community and the lesser neighborhood communities, is represented by concentric band 4 in our model of expanding communities of men.

Beyond the local communities in this design, the elementary school pupil next focuses his study on his *state community*, shown in the illustration as band 5. The geographic, historic, and political dimensions of a child's state are well defined but generally under-taught in the school curriculum. Historically the state community came into being when the several local communities in a former territory needed services which few or none could perform successfully alone. The public and private institutions and organizations that operate throughout the state try to furnish the lesser communities with those services that are beyond individual capabilities of local, neighborhood, and family communities, or than can be supplied more effectively by the state community because of its larger resources.

Ordinarily, the citizen thinking about the set of interdependent communities moves directly from the state to the nation. This jump unfortunately misses an increasingly crucial community that lies between: the *region of states*. The U.S. Bureau of the Census recognized the growing number of common concerns of the solutions by regions and, beginning with the 1950 census, gathered, summarized, and presented all data by four regions: the South, the West, the North Central, and the Northeast. In the illustrative design under discussion, the pupil moves from an emphasis on his state to an emphasis on his region of states. From there he progresses to a study of the three other regions that make up the national community. The region-of-states community is shown on Figure 10 as concentric band 6.

Note here that flexibility is both possible and desirable. For a class of pupils living in the North Central region of states, that region would be the logical one to study in depth first. For a child on the Pacific coast, the West comes first. The remaining three regions could follow in any order.

The outer band in this subset of communities is the *United States national community,* shown as band 7 in our illustration. Within this nation, about 200 million citizens today benefit from the foresight of our forefathers, who, following the War of Independence, wrote in the Preamble to the Constitution,

> We the people of the United States, in order to form a more perfect Union, establish justice, insure domestic tranquility, provide a common defense, promote the general welfare, and secure the blessings of liberty to ourselves and our posterity, do ordain and establish this Constitution of the United States.

The public and private efforts of the many during two centuries to bring about this national dream have been successful, perhaps beyond the fondest hopes of the founding fathers.

The national community emphasis completes the first subset of expanding communities. Family through nation, this subset is a highly interdependent system of interlocking communities, always expanding in size and complexity. It is necessary and desirable for the lesser communities to join with other lesser communities of similar scale in forming a larger community whose united effort allows it to carry on activities not possible within the resources of any lesser community working in isolation. One can better understand each of the interlocking communities by studying the system: the family community in the United States can be comprehended much better by knowing the cultural complex we speak of as the national personality; or one's own state can be grasped much better if he knows the composite characteristics of the typical families, of the neighborhoods, and of the local communities that have come together to form the particular state under study.

Scope of Foci: Basic Human Activities

Temporarily remove from the center stage of the mind's eye the partially completed sequence dimension of our multidisciplinary social studies program and store it for later use. We move on to a brief discussion of the second set of coordinates of our design—*the scope,* organized into nine categories of basic human activities. Figure 11 lists the categories and represents them as a pie-segmented "Wheel of Basic Human Activities." Universally, men living in groups in times past, present, and future carry on these same activities, though in differing ways. There are numerous systems for cataloging or clustering them; no single classification scheme is wholly satisfactory. The main purpose

Producing, Exchanging, Distributing, and Consuming Goods and Services
Transporting People, Goods, and Services
Communicating Information, Ideals, and Feelings
Providing Education
Providing Recreation
Protecting and Conserving Life, Health, Property, and Resources
Organizing and Governing
Expressing and Satisfying Aesthetic and Spiritual Needs
Creating New Tools, Technics, and Institutions

Figure 11

Scope Coordinates: The Wheel of Basic Human Activities

of grouping is to provide teacher and pupil with some logical and orderly way to observe and organize the kaleidoscopic world. Whether the categories number six or sixteen is of lesser consequence than the assurance that any specific group activity of men can be classified in one or more of these categories.

Examine the scope dimensions of our illustrative model. Each pie-shaped segment represents a category of basic human endeavor. One might start almost anywhere on the wheel's circumference to list a cluster of basic human activities. As a first cluster, we arbitrarily identify the basic human activities of *producing, exchanging, distributing, and consuming goods and services.* The mind's eye sees a rapid succession of pictures: primitive men hunting and fishing; modern men with mechanical power and machines producing crops on the land and in the sea; men in simple cottage shops or in complex and automated factories shaping raw materials into finished goods and services; colorful primitive marketplaces or the interior of a supermarket; some people starving and other people consuming the abundant food, clothing, and other goods available in a modern economy. These kaleidoscopic pictures are for the moment universals and not classified by time, by place, or by any one of the several communities of men. Refinements of classification will be illustrated later in our presentation. We now proceed to fill in appropriate headings for the other eight segments of the wheel.

Closely allied with producing, exchanging, distributing, and consuming is the second cluster in our grid: *transporting people, goods, and services.* The boundaries of this segment are *not* solid lines separating this basic human activity from the cluster on either side; the fluidity of the boundaries is illustrated by dotted lines. Each category is partially found within several or all of the other segments. We are attempting here to *focus* on a cluster of activities that can be identified as distinct although not disassociated from the other clusters. The transporting activities probably bring to mind a flood of pictures of animal or mechanical means and of institutional arrangements that could be classified as historic, as contemporary, or as possibilities for the future.

A third cluster we shall call *communicating information, ideals, and feelings.* The reader is invited to create pictures in his own mind to illustrate this activity found in any community regardless of time and place.

A fourth category is labeled *providing education.* The range of appropriate pictures would include such diversity as an ancient caveman teaching his offspring to stalk and kill wild game; a child of the frontier learning lessons from his hornbook; the modern mass education invention we call the school; a possible world learning center where programmed instruction might be beamed to the pupils of the future via a worldwide network of communications satellites.

A fifth cluster centers around *providing recreation.* All communities of men through all time have played and amused and refreshed themselves. True, some communities with encouragement from a luxuriant environment have placed a higher value on this basic human activity than have other communities in which a barren environment "forced" men to work long and hard to survive, leaving little time for recreation. But all men need and desire recreation.

We next highlight a sixth cluster: *protecting and conserving life, health, property, and resources.* Housing, medicine, defense, and law are just a few illustrations of the provisions men make to satisfy the universal needs in this category.

For a seventh group of activities we use the phrase *organizing and governing*. Both public and private sectors of any community need to organize, manage, direct, administer, and govern. These activities, which we might call decision making and enforcement, range from the relatively simple agreements within a family to avoid conflict over the use of the telephone to the highly complex machinery of national governments and of the United Nations for regulating the uses of outer space.

Next we focus on a cluster entitled *expressing and satisfying aesthetic and spiritual needs*. The universal desire of men to associate with others in pursuit of beauty, or in spiritual satisfaction, has been and continues to be one of the deepest motivations in a community of any scale.

And finally we come to *creating new tools, technics, and institutions*. Men in societies are forever inventing better theories and solutions, be it a new molecule, a spaceship, or a substitute for force in settling disputes.

Thus Figure 11 is a complete catalog of the basic human activities— the *scope*. It is complete to the extent that we can find a segment in the scheme into which can easily be fitted any group activity that is past history, contemporary life, or conceivable in a possible future.

We now refer again to that subset of our model, Figure 10, which represents seven expanding communities of man (family through nation)—the *sequence*.

So far we have detailed two dimensions of the coordinated social studies design: (1) the expanding communities *sequence* and (2) the basic human activities *scope*. Now we can superimpose one dimension on the other and have a composite—the complete social studies design: the segments of basic human activities intersect the concentric bands of the communities of men (see Figure 12). Each of the seven bands we have discussed cuts through all nine pie segments. Each of the nine segments is present in all seven bands: each community of men carries on all of the basic human activities.

Sequence of Emphases Beyond the United States
National Community

But our suggested design for sequence of the elementary school social studies is, to this point in our statement, incomplete. We have now to conclude our particular logic of expanding communities of men by moving beyond the national community. Modern science and technology make obsolete the once defensible notion that the nation is the outer

Figure 12

Basic Human Activities Superimposed on Expanding Communities of Men

limit of the set of expanding communities. Today we know that nations cannot exist as islands: some multinational values, institutions, laws, customs, and mechanisms are even now appearing, while others wait for the time when men shall find it desirable and possible to welcome larger-than-national communities.

What criteria may be employed for introducing pupils to their broad sub-world communities? We are caught between the equally attractive objectives of breadth and depth. Somehow a happy balance must be struck. Depth or breadth per se is neither good nor bad. Useful breadth, for example, is not attained by exposure to or memorization of representative statistics.

Kenworthy suggests that criteria for selecting individual nations for study "in depth" usually include (1) world powers; (2) nations of the "future"; (3) nations from which our ancestors came; (4) representatives of different cultural groups; (5) nations against which there is prejudice; (6) representative nations of different types of economic development; (7) availability of references and resources for pupils;

(8) teacher competency and interests; and (9) degree of difficulty for the ability of pupils.[1]

Such a listing highlights the philosophical differences and the purposive void in much that is current in the social studies. Obviously, there is need to focus upon topics and strategies for achieving mutually agreed-upon major social objectives through the curriculum. Study of the emerging sub-world communities seems to offer such a strategy and purpose.

Implicit in the rationale for study of physical, political, and cultural regions of world communities of men is the focus upon selected nations in interaction—past, present, and future. The appropriate depth of study in the history, economic structure, political institutions, etc., of these associated nations must be determined in view of the pupil's needs for understanding present and future world community developments.

Young adolescents, generally speaking, will not profit greatly from being taught "all about the world." Effective geographic study turns to region-of-nations analysis, then selects representative problems and interrelationships to illustrate generalizations about the basic human activities that are carried on more effectively in the emerging expanded communities.

James, in outlining new viewpoints in geography, pointed out the usefulness of building regional concepts concerning land masses, climates, resources, and culture areas. Children must come to realize that the commonalities of a region may be based upon any or all of these factors in various combinations.

> . . . there are no completely homogeneous areas on the face of the earth. Every region is identified by selecting some criterion or combination of criteria and by overlooking those features considered to be irrelevant. . . . A region, like any generalization, is good if it illuminates the features or processes being studied; a region is bad if it obscures what is being studied.[2]

The selection of teaching-learning experiences in a social studies program must reflect the nature of the region selected for study. Logically, also, it must serve to enhance the development of the essential geographic, historic, and social science aspects which this particular physical-cultural environment best illustrates.

As children repeatedly use maps to compare and contrast sub-world regional communities, their ability to visualize physical and cultural commonalities should grow—and likewise their ability to conceptualize the generalization "cultural region." Of course, meaningful generalizations are more readily derived from experiences and inductive thinking than from passive verbalization and memorization.

Regions are derived by way of at least four types of delimitational factors.

1. Land masses serve as delimitations of regions of nations in the broader sense. However, the arbitrary splitting of the world's largest land mass into Asia and Europe is an example of how land masses alone are not an adequate basis for differentiation.

2. Climates tend to differentiate people's common interests in the broader sense, but many of the world's national communities have wide climatic ranges.

3. Resources also aid to distinguish or delimit areas of the world. However, it is man's recognition and use of resources that we notice on the cultural map; hence cultural communities may be characterized in part by the uses made of available resources. (America's rich resources meant very little to the primitive Indian cultures of yesteryear.)

4. While physical land mass, climate, and resources constitute important elements of a region of nations, the more important facet of the man-land equation remains the cultural development of the area's inhabitants. James suggests that

> . . . although the meaning of . . . things changes as human culture changes, the basic patterns remain the same. A region of aridity is still arid, even when technology makes it habitable . . . there is need for a basic regional framework which brings out the fundamental patterns of the physical and biotic features. But the meaning of these features is a function of the culture. A regional system that is based on the physical and biotic features must be matched with a system of cultural areas.[3]

The educator should recognize that cultural areas are identified so as to illuminate subject matter and selected concepts and generalizations. The people in cultural-area communities generally have similar customs, ways of looking at life, institutions, laws, and means of communication, and common problems, as well as a particular definable spatial area within which they feel more or less at home. The pupil must not be expected to master "college level" regional concepts but rather penetrate to such depth and breadth as is appropriate to our social studies purposes and his capacity (which is expandable) and experiential background. It might even be suggested that a "region of nations" is a core of activities or interrelationships in the "eye of the beholder," since complete agreement as to criteria for defining cultural areas cannot be expected.

Thus, in identifying regions of nations for study by young adolescents, it seems strategic to combine criteria and settle on three emerging sub-world communities: the United States and inter-American, the United States and Atlantic, and the United States and Pacific. This is not to say, however, that the various verbal, pictorial, and map-reading teaching-learning experiences should neglect to point out that our three region-of-nations communities are comprised of smaller component associations. It follows, then, that while children are being guided to recognize certain common problems and interrelationships of nations within the broad Atlantic community, for instance, they also begin building concepts concerning the nature of such "sub-communities" as Europe, North Africa, the Middle East, Anglo-America, Africa south of the Sahara, etc.

Finally, beyond the three emerging region-of-nations communities, we complete our sequence by emphasizing the worldwide community of man.

The study of the emerging inter-American, Atlantic, Pacific, and world communities must be built upon an adequate foundation of facts concerning these physical and cultural environments. Hence, the introduction to region-of-nations communities logically consists of familiarization with concrete facts much akin to the pupil's prior experiences in the middle grade emphases. The readiness of the young learner for "formal operations" is largely determined by the nature and extent of prior concrete orientation. It seems obvious that if the pupil is to achieve both a "sense" and factual cognizance of the great sub-world communities of men he must be able to proceed logically and intuitively. Happily, such intellectual capacity is maturing in pupils of this age. Bruner reports,

> . . . the child's intellectual activity seems to be based upon an ability to operate on hypothetical propositions rather than being constrained to what he has experienced or what is before him. The child can now think of possible variables and even deduce potential relationships that can later be verified by experiment or observation.[4]

Such assertions are not to be interpreted as a cue to offer pupils social science materials couched in adult "packages of logic." The challenge to the social studies teacher and those who develop instructional materials is that much is yet to be learned about the nature and range of logical operations enjoyed by pupils.

However, the coordinated social studies framework selected for this volume is centrally concerned with guiding pupils through logically arranged sequences of teaching-learning experiences. Through employment of the spiral system, the pupil is systematically returned, at maturationally appropriate intervals, to reinforce previous learnings and to extend and refine skills and understanding. By employing this framework we help remind ourselves to respect the nature, limitations, and capacities of the child. It is proposed that the pupil's growing repertoire of map skills and understandings be employed and augmented in the task of conceptualizing and appreciating the role of community in human existence. The development of a "sense of community," then, becomes a worthwhile social studies objective.

Community Awareness as an Objective

Many of the newer social studies programs are seeking to foster region-of-nations communities and world community awareness, which has been characterized as follows:

> . . . it is learning to appreciate and respect the individual wherever he is. It is learning to know peoples of other countries or other cultures—whether in their classrooms or in another continent—as human beings. It is finding out the kind of homes they live in, what they eat, what they wear, how they work and play. It is learning something about the songs they sing, the pictures they paint, and the books they write. It is becoming familiar with the names and something of the lives and deeds of the men and women they honor. It is helping children see the similarities and the differences in people's lives and customs, and the reason for them. It is helping children realize how the lives of these people are all interwoven with our own. Finally, and most important of all, international understanding is helping children gain some idea of the imponderables—the way people of other countries feel about their problems, what they think about certain questions, and why they think and feel as they do.[5]

Major supranational problems differ from less-than-national community problems mainly in degree for all include conservation methods, population explosion control, public health, interclass and intergroup struggles, economic abundance or shortage, problems of organization, etc. Related to these matters are goals sought by most of mankind, which include renunciation of war as an instrument of national policy; recognition of the inherent dangers of nations' demanding unrestricted pursuit of self-interest; recognition of the necessity for strong and binding international law and government and its requisite police powers, courts, and voluntary international cooperation; world-wide implementation of the democratic way of life; and freer movements of goods, peoples, and ideas.

It is unlikely that adequate solutions to these pressing problems of mankind will be derived from uncoordinated local efforts, regardless of how well intentioned they may be, for as Phenix summarized,

> It is not enough, in the present age, to promote justice in the local community and in state and nation. Events and peoples beyond our borders can no longer be regarded simply as subjects for inquiry by the adventurous and the curious. The world has become a neighborhood.[6]

The world community has an elusive meaning; its referent is affected constantly by social changes which alter both its material and spiritual components. The word *community*, according to Lindeman, originally "designated a geographical area with definite boundaries, occupied by residents engaged in interrelated economic activities and constituting a politically self-governing unit."[7] Essential attributes included structure, area, interrelated economic institutions, and independent frameworks of government. Such factual criteria now are recognized as seriously deficient unless concurrent attention is given to existent psychological ramifications. A community is defined by human interrelationships or mutual expectations and responsibilities that are outgrowths of membership and referent group identifications.

Helping the pupil achieve a sense of community must be a fundamental goal of the social studies program. In our present urbanized and technological society, community is an abstraction that is exceedingly difficult to teach. The primary community has given way to a host of secondary social relationships. *Where* the child lives no longer provides obvious clues concerning the people and institutions upon which he is dependent and to whom he owes loyalty and gratitude. The child thus deprived of concrete illustrations of his real communities must be guided so that he may become cognizant of his many categories of "needs" and then correctly apprise himself of his many interdependent worlds.

At some point in the pupil's introduction to the many communities of men there must come an awakening to the fact that human needs are not always satisfied adequately by existent man-to-thing, man-to-man, and man-to-spirit structures and processes. As the physical world grows relatively smaller owing to technological developments, concurrently the individual's experiential worlds grow larger and more demanding of quality of citizenship behaviors. The maturing pupil begins to recognize that, along with all of mankind, he must join in the search for additional sense of community. That is, the individual's more immediate communities are rapidly changing while his more extended communities are still emerging and are to a large degree in the realm of "the possible" as perceived through mankind's mutual appreciation of ultimate needs and available means for achieving social satisfactions. The phrases starting with the modifiers Inter-American, Atlantic, Pacific, and World and ending with the generic word *community* denote both reality and ideal.

Pupils must recognize that members in any community, of whatever scale, are going to disagree, may strike out in opposite directions, and inevitably experience conflicts of interest. Yet, regardless of innate and/or learned response patterns which tend to negate harmony, members of emerging communities do have common needs, aspirations, and institutions which are woven into the patterns of their basic human activities. As they gain educated maturity, they must develop the insight to meet members of other communities as friends—friends who seek to understand one another. Recognizing their common ground, then, generally should lead to cognizance of the need for taking common action. True "community" responses are not coerced but entered upon willingly. Thus defined, "community" may well epitomize enlightened self-interest.

Today's social studies program must seek to help pupils attain a sense of community (psychological) in addition to an appreciation (intellectual) of the fact of worldwide interdependence among all nations. Building a sense of community beyond nation constitutes a major undertaking in that men everywhere seem more readily able to recognize the "fact" of competition (a childish level of egocentricism rather than a mature level of enlightened self-interest) for the world's somewhat limited supply of goods and services. Competition between members of a community or between communities can be a healthy stimulus; competition between peoples who fail to recognize the fundamental human community, which is all of mankind, constitutes a disastrous undertaking, especially when men are equipped with the destructive potentials of modern science.

It is not enough, then, that pupils become alert to the necessity of achieving citizenship through taking active and responsible roles in their more immediate communities. The social studies framework of the expanding communities of men, especially those emerging beyond narrow national boundaries, must be recognized as a curricular device for guiding pupils through maturationally appropriate and systematic redefinitions of the concept and sense of *who we are* and *where we live.* Map skills and understandings and geographically related concepts of relative location, areal extent, areal association, and areal interaction are recognized as major contributors to these ends.

Beyond the national concentric band (7 in our design) we recognize three region-of-nations communities as shown in Figure 12: the inter-American community, the Atlantic community, and the Pacific community. Arbitrarily we next depict *the emerging United States and inter-American community* as emphasis 8 in our sequence. A map of this geopolitical terrain would include all the Americas: North, Central, and South.

Band 8 is shown as an ellipse stretching from pole to pole. With half a billion human members, this emerging community of men has in common more than 10,000 years of Indian history, almost 500 years of European cultural overlay, and over 100 years of struggle to win independence from European colonialism. These half-billion Americans are creating public and private networks of communication, production and exchange, education, etc., that knit and bind them together into a recognizable community of men. In the lifetime of youngsters now in school it will become an increasingly important instrument for the satisfaction of human needs and aspirations.

The United States national community is a member of a second region of nations: *the emerging United States and Atlantic community.* This elliptic band (9 in our design), represents all the lands and people who live around the shores of the Atlantic Ocean: the Americas, Europe, the Middle East, and Africa. In the past the Atlantic Ocean was considered a strategic defense boundary by each nation washed by its waters. In the nuclear power age the same Atlantic Ocean is but the inner sea of an emerging Atlantic community. The outer territorial limits of the community are certainly not fixed; they are controversial and will probably always be less definite than the borders of a national community. But the centripetal forces pulling the outlying nations more closely into an Atlantic community are slowly but surely intensifying and predictably will overbalance such centrifugal forces as currently operate to keep England out of the Common Market, attempt to weaken NATO, or isolate South Africa from its Western cultural heritage.

Western culture, infused with elements of great historical cultures of the Middle East, permeates the vast Atlantic community terrain. The industrial and scientific revolutions have deposited over this arena a cohesive cement that makes the former unrelated units more and more parts of a new whole. NATO, CENTO, OECD, EURATOM, and the Afro-Anglo-American Association of Teacher Education are just the beginning of a long list of institutions and agencies created since World War II to serve an emerging Atlantic community. Posterity has a right to expect that the social studies program in the elementary schools will lay the groundwork of values, understanding, and competencies required in building an Atlantic community in the decades ahead. Today's schools should not impose tomorrow's uncertain answers on school children; but schools should equip tomorrow's citizens with the raw materials and the skills with which they may one day fashion multinational establishments to match soaring aspirations.

We speak of a third region of nations, named after the great Pacific Ocean that washes the shores of most of the nations of *the emerging United States and Pacific community.* This enormous area with its constantly changing boundaries is represented in our model by band 10. In a space covering more than two-thirds of the surface of the earth live more than 1.8 billion people—almost two out of every three humans alive today. Lands of the Occidental and the Oriental Pacific lie far apart, and only in our time has this huge, loosely knit aggregate been regarded potentially as a region of the globe.

The possibility of a Pacific community arises out of the common frustrations and aspirations of Americans, Asians, Australians, and Oceanians. Many young nations in this emerging community are busily engaged in glorifying nationalism. But at the same time, science and technology are shrinking or shattering the ancient barriers of water, mountains, distance, language, and cultural differences. Material advances force larger-than-national concerns and ultimately encourage mutual understanding and respect for the diverse cultures and aims of the Pacific partners. Underneath the noisy and often bitter conflicts of ideologies there quietly grow new roots of cooperation: the Pacific Science Congress, the Asian Games, the East-West Center, the Colombo Plan, and hundreds of private corporations that cross national boundaries to build economic establishments to serve an emerging Pacific community.

In the first illustration presented in this chapter, we placed the child in the center and the world band far out. It is now time for closure in the sequence coordinates of our design, so we return to the outer band, which has the only solid line in the model. *The emerging world community,* No. 11 in our sequential emphases, is not by definition a part of any larger community of men—at least not yet. Perhaps science fiction writers are prophetic and our children one day will need to join with inhabitants of other planets for self-defense in a war between solar systems. But we are content to end the set of our expanding communities at earth's limits.

The world community is even less an actuality than the three smaller region-of-nations communities, notwithstanding the fact that the territorial boundaries of this last community are far more definable than those of the three sub-world regions. Conflicts divide the world into armed camps, and the threat of reckless use of nuclear, bacteriological, or chemical warfare darkens the future. The great uncertainty of our time lies with the USSR and China. The Communist powers continue to subvert and threaten the neutrals and the free nations.

Yet man's ageless yearning for world peace, fraternity, and plenty gains hope anew in the successes of ecumenical conferences, increasing tourism, multilingual capability, the International Red Cross, the International Bank, the International Court of Justice, and scores of other public and private mechanisms created to solve problems beyond the capacity of single nations or regions of nations. One can hope and strive to help the United Nations and its specialized agencies survive and prosper in pursuit of these causes.

The emerging world community has a rich historical content of bold dreams. It has made courageous attempts to bring unity to a splintered and quarreling world: Alexander the Great dreamed, acted, and came close to success; the Holy Roman Empire gave peace and prosperity to a large portion of the Western world; the literature and the arts of most of the world's cultures contain a common theme of man's universal brotherhood. While man's reach for universals has exceeded his grasp in the past, perhaps the time is approaching when the human family will be forced to accentuate the positive values of humanity as a prelude to creating worldwide conditions which will satisfy the generic definition of community cited earlier in this chapter. The schools of the world must prepare tomorrow's citizens to grapple successfully with problems of such universal magnitude. The social studies program carries a major responsibility for this objective.

By superimposing the wheel of nine basic human activities over the full set of eleven communities of men, we create in Figure 12 (page 86) a finished social studies program design for the elementary schools.

Illustrating the Sequence through One Basic Human Activity

We will reserve for later chapters detailed elaboration of possible teaching-learning experiences youngsters may undergo within this design with special attention to the relevant geographic content and map skills. But we illustrate how the model works by rushing you through one of the nine clusters of the basic human activities to demonstrate how it helps to focus on learning experiences in each of the eleven communities.

Selected for illustration is that segment of the wheel of basic human activities labeled *protecting and conserving life, health, property, and resources.* In Figure 12 examine first the intersection of the band representing the *family* community with the segment called *protecting, etc.* In the mind's eye flash pictures of the family protected by its sheltering house; the family caring for the newly born; the family conserving its property by covering plants against the cold or watering plants against dehydration; caring for pets; children picking up toys so adults can walk without danger of tripping. One can think of scores of other ways Mary's family or John's family today protects and conserves; how these activities were handled by past generations of the families; how the ways of protecting may change in the future. Focusing on this small segment (protecting) of the band (family) helps to start the train of ideas relevant to this series of possible teaching-learning experiences.

Now that the pattern has been established, move rapidly through the ever expanding communities. The next larger community, the *school,* protects and conserves against weather, fire, emergency, etc. The school conserves its supplies and equipment through orderly routines, locked storage rooms and closed cabinets, janitorial services, etc. The school traffic policeman, nurse, physician, and dentist are conspicuous personnel assigned responsibilities for protecting and conserving.

Again, expand the size of the community by moving into the intersection of protecting and the next larger band, *the neighborhood.* Obviously each family alone could not afford to maintain peace and order or to provide fire protection and the hundreds of other services needed; so the solutions are partly found in a loose aggregate of families—a neighborhood. The reader has probably already flashed a dozen pictures through his inner vision of ways that a neighborhood protects and conserves through police, health clinics, neighborhood protective and improvement associations, rules regulating the riding of bicycles, etc.

Once more increase the community arena by moving into the next larger band, the *local* communities. A metropolitan water and air pollution prevention commission, a city law enforcement agency, a county medical society are illustrations of protecting and conserving in local communities.

Move again outward. The *state* community provides courts, state highway safety patrols, a state game and fish commission, a state association of insurance underwriters, and many more mechanisms and services, both through governmental channels and through private initiative, to protect and conserve life, health, property, and resources within the state terrain.

Again change scale and note that a *region-of-states* community could, among many things, build a great dam to conserve its water and soil resources and save life and property from floods. Conservation in a river basin that cuts through several states is more properly the responsibility of the region of states than it is of the individual lesser state or local communities. Many examples of protection in a region of states can be cited.

We come next to the *national* community. The readiness of our national defenses to ward off possible attacks is a dramatic example of protecting. Surely here is a problem of such size and complexity that it is properly placed by the lesser communities in the hands of the larger and inclusive national community for solution. We might suggest that the FBI, the Coast Guard, the Department of Health, the conservation agencies in many federal departments, the American Automobile Association, the cancer research effort of private and government agencies— these and many more fall within the cluster of protecting and conserving in the national community.

Moving beyond the national community to an emerging *United States and inter-American* community, we suggest that the OAS (Organization of American States) is one of the newer inventions of a multinational nature to protect this hemisphere against aggression. The Alliance for Progress is an all-American effort to conserve and use the vast resources of the Americas to bring forth a larger measure of the good life for all. Many equally striking examples could be given.

Another region-of-nations community, an emerging *United States and Atlantic* community, focuses our attention on a unique invention called NATO (North Atlantic Treaty Organization), which protects its member nations. The Atlantic community has already developed scores of scientific and social technologies that contribute to the health and welfare of the peoples of this arena.

In a third multinational complex, an emerging *United States and Pacific* community, the SEATO military alliance (South East Asia Treaty Organization) exists to protect the lives and property of certain member nations. We might cite as another example the Pacific Science Congress, which is researching to conquer disease and malnutrition in this vast arena. The yearly *World Almanac,* the pages of the telephone directory, etc., list scores of newly formed agencies that protect in the Pacific.

We conclude this series of quick glimpses into possible teaching-learning experiences of protecting and conserving by focusing on the World Health Organization, the purpose of which is to make the entire *earth* a more healthful place in which to dwell. The world community protects the fish of the oceans, the birds of the airways; in many ways it works to protect and conserve on a global scale.

To provide closure in our model, we simply suggest that we could have used all the other eight segments of the basic human activities to demonstrate the infinite possibilities of this design.

Illustrating the Scope through One Community of Men

We next rapidly demonstrate the linkage of all nine basic human activities as they are used to guide the study of one of the expanding communities: *the nation.* Think first of *producing, exchanging, distributing, and consuming goods and services* and direct inner vision to a national network of farms, factories, mines, forests, fisheries, etc., laid over a map of the U.S.A. Then focus on the national networks of commerce, finance, etc., that pass the finished goods and services to ultimate consumers. These and scores more of pictures would not exhaust a study of the manner in which our nation carries on its economic activities.

Look at the next segment intersection of the national community band entitled *transporting* and imagine a federal interstate highway system superimposed on a U.S.A. map. Air, water, or rail networks could be used just as well to illustrate the national effort to supply these services through the public and the private sectors.

Examine briefly the intersection of the national community and the problems of *communicating* and think of the federal postal service. Imagine the confusion if mail services were carried on by fifty competing state systems! Nationwide telephone, radio, and TV networks; the press wire services; and many other activities can be grouped within a study of national enterprises in communicating.

Again shift focus, to the national effort to *provide education,* both as an item of personal consumption and as an investment on behalf of national goals. Federal financial support to state land-grant universities and to states for supplementing local revenues to run schools, federal scholarships for study, private national associations of educational professionals, national educational TV, and a host of other operations proclaim the national determination to provide education.

Next consider the segment of the national band labeled *providing recreation*. The network of national parks is one type of national effort in this category. The national sports leagues, national associations of tourist agencies, national radio networks are additional examples of providing recreation.

The famous cartoon character Smokey the Bear represents one way the public and private interests of our nation try to *protect and conserve* the natural beauty and our wilderness areas from fire and destruction. The President's emphasis on conservation, supported by many nongovernmental efforts, is typical of activities in this cluster.

For the intersection of *organizing and governing* in the national community band, we suggest the national Capitol. Political organizations and business administration furnish many good ideas for pictures of this cluster of activities carried on at the national community level.

The national community *expresses and satisfies aesthetic and religious needs*. The spirit of our nation is found in great national religious organizations, in the beauty of the landscape, in the national art treasures, in national music, dance, theater, etc.

And finally, the national community *creates new tools, technics, and institutions,* as is illustrated by the Comsat network but could just as well be represented by a nuclear reactor, a national cancer research laboratory, a marine experimental ship, or Project English to improve performance in school language arts.

Multidisciplinary Attack on Community Study

The series of pictures relevant to the national community which we have been suggesting illustrates the means by which we use the design (as summarized in Figure 12) as a skeleton or frame on which to fasten the generalizations, methods of inquiry, and structures of history, geography, and the social sciences. The United States national community exists in physical space on planet earth. Knowledge of the distribution of physical and cultural features over the nation is indispensable to understanding national problems and successes. The light of geography shining on the clusters of basic human activities (the scope and the design) will help to explain why the distributions are as they are and how transportation, production, consumption, protection, recreation, and so on are interrelated not only with each other but also with earth's physical features.

But the national community exists in time as well as in space. History highlights another indispensable structuring of knowledge which the pupil must master about his nation. How have the available tools, mechanical power, and social technologies affected the geography and changed the character of the ways each of the basic human activities has been carried on in this arena from the time of the first Indians right up through the present? And what may we speculate about our creative efforts to provide new solutions for tomorrow? Clearly, history gives us instruments for reconstructing the long story of development of a community over time, and even projecting the future with broad brushstrokes. History and geography are essential and related components for the study of every community, of whatever scale, in a modern multidisciplinary social studies program.

But we cannot end our floodlighting of the national community with light from only geography and history. A community must organize to make and carry out decisions on behalf of that community. *Political science* shows us how the national efforts of both government and private sectors solve the problems of organizing and governing and helps us to understand the rationale behind the diverse solutions.

It is clear that many of the categories of basic human activities of our design are aspects of the science of *economics*. So this discipline becomes an important component of a coordinated social studies program. Such national activities as producing, exchanging, consuming, transporting, or communicating are understood and mastered better as one gains knowledge and skill in the elements of economics. But we raise a basic question: Can one tell where economics ends and political science begins? Or where geography and history may be found in pure form unrelated to economics and political science? The reasonable framework for the social studies program of the elementary school is a multidisciplinary design that uses all the scholarship we can obtain to throw its coordinated light on the study of each expanding community.

Any study of the national community is incomplete without the structured generalizations and methods of inquiry of *anthropology*. The same must be said for the discipline of *sociology*. Both are increasingly crucial to a minimal understanding of any community by a modern man.

We now leave our demonstration of how the multidisciplinary approach assures coverage of the national community—one of the eleven expanding communities of men. It is a simple maneuver to bring back the complete model for all eleven communities, overlaid with the wheel of nine clusters of basic human activities, and show in Figure 13 the glow of the six disciplines bathing the entire design. In their combined floodlights the social studies landscape gleams and sparkles.

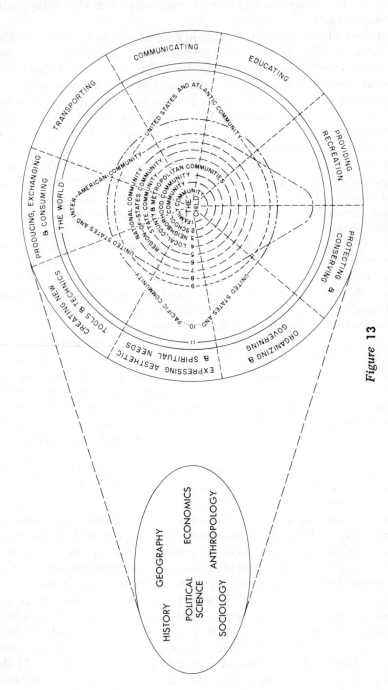

Figure 13

The Social Studies Design Illuminated by Six Social Science Disciplines

Suggested Assignment of Community Emphases to Grades

The logic of this coordinated social studies design suggests that the pupil study each larger community in sequence. In the kindergarten and first grade, he might start with emphasis on his own family and on his own school. As he studies each of these lesser communities, he learns what phases of life are properly the concern of himself as a member of these small intimate groups. He also learns that families (his and others) need to join together to provide for the satisfaction of many needs through neighborhood apparatuses. Consequently, he moves naturally to the third emphasis in the sequential design, his neighborhood community, which exists to provide services not available to families or to his school working alone.

This particular social studies design may assign the study of the child's neighborhood to the second grade. However, assignment of the community to be emphasized to a particular grade is relatively unimportant; *following the sequence* from the lesser community to the next larger is the governing principle.

The sequence typically followed in schools adopting such a structure is to complete the sequence of eleven community emphases by the end of Grade 6 or the elementary school years. It may be more defensible to stretch out the time for covering the eleven communities through the junior high school years. Any design must be flexible enough to accommodate differences in pupil ability or differences in the expectations of patrons and professionals at the local or state community level.

Another principle essential to this particular design: the pupils constantly move inward and outward among the several communities of the set. As each community is studied, children should be helped to see that many problems they examine thrust them inevitably into larger communities for solution. There is always a forward look, anticipating the several communities that lie ahead for deeper study in later grades. But at the same time there must always be a review and a deepening of insights concerning the lesser communities previously emphasized in the sequence. A child is not through studying the family at the end of the first grade! Provision is made in each expanding community in the set for (1) a fuller meaning of the lesser communities previously studied and (2) building readiness for the examination of the larger communities to follow.

There is still another characteristic of this design. When youngsters are studying their own state, for instance, they will naturally be comparing and contrasting other states in our nation. To the extent that there exist, or can be created, meaningful bridges to a state or its equivalent in Mexico, Japan, or Switzerland, these exciting and enriching experiences should be made a part of the work. But the teacher has the obligation to prevent the program from jumping wildly hither and yon. The teacher *must* be responsible for bringing youngsters back from these useful side excursions to the major arena in the sequence to be emphasized in a particular grade.

Many of us believe it is desirable to plan the design of the coordinated social studies program as a Kindergarten-through-Grade 12 continuum, where sequence and not grading are of major importance. Assuming that some strategy of "studying how men carry on the basic human activities in a system of expanding communities of men" has been rounded out in the elementary or the junior high school, we contend that adolescents in the senior high school will be more ready to pursue profitably a program of separate study of each of the several social science disciplines, geography, and history. The final proof of such a contention has yet to be fully documented; but a multidisciplinary and coordinated design for the elementary school social studies program makes sense to an increasing number of school systems throughout the United States.

This volume is written to assist the professional educator in focusing the powerful floodlight of geographic content and map skills on the elementary school social studies program. In the chapters of Part Three, each of the eleven expanding communities of men is emphasized in turn; each community is observed as carrying on the nine categories of basic human activities; and within each category of activity, relevant geographic content and map skills are suggested. The teacher and his class still face the task of making choices among the wealth of possibilities, which are far more numerous than any class can undertake. The chief benefit of this volume is to be found in providing carefully planned developmental experiences from the beginning grades on into the junior high school that will assure the inclusion of meaningful and significant geographic content and map skills in the coordinated social studies program.

REFERENCES

1. Leonard S. Kenworthy, *Studying Asia in Elementary Schools,* World Affairs Materials (Brooklyn: Brooklyn College, 1962), p. 4.
2. Preston E. James, "New Viewpoints in Geography," *New Viewpoints in the Social Sciences,* Twenty-eighth Yearbook, National Council for the Social Studies (Washington: NCSS, 1958), p. 49.
3. *Ibid.,* p. 56.
4. Jerome S. Bruner, "Learning and Thinking," *Harvard Educational Review,* 29:184–185 (1959).
5. Delia Goetz, *World Understanding Begins with Children,* Bulletin No. 17 (Washington: Government Printing Office, 1955), p. 6.
6. P. H. Phenix, *Education and the Common Good* (New York: The Macmillan Co., 1961), p. 218.
7. E. C. Lindeman, "Community," *Encyclopedia of the Social Studies* (New York: The Macmillan Co., 1950), Vol. III–IV, p. 102.

PART THREE

A Program of Teaching-Learning

Activities in Geographic Content

and Skills

AN OVERVIEW   In Part Three we come to the main course of our offering. In this longest section, the several related elements
of the social studies program are combined and the
composite is translated into specific suggestions for teachers who wish
to strengthen the program in geographic content and skills.

The chapters in this part are organized into three main divisions: The
Beginning Grades Emphases, The Middle Grades Emphases, and The
Junior High School Emphases. Within each of these divisions several of
the expanding communities of men are presented. Each succeeding chapter treats one (sometimes more than one), of the eleven communities.
The chapter title will cue the reader to the emphasis or emphases treated.
Within each chapter, the work is organized around the basic human
activities. For instance, in the Middle Grades, the *state* community is
emphasized in one chapter. Within this arena, the geographic content
and skills are presented as they relate to each of the nine clusters of

103

human activities that form the second set of coordinates of our design. In many chapters a parallel column format is used so that the column labeled "Objectives" appears beside the column labeled "Pupil Experiences," enabling the teacher to think concretely about the possible range of experiences which might develop in the learner the geographic content and skill under consideration for a particular community and for a specific basic human activity of that community. A glance at the text on pages 111–124 will illustrate how most of these chapters in Part Three are constructed.

In such an offering of teaching-learning experiences for pupils completeness is not possible. Many volumes would be required to accomplish the task in all of the conceivable situations that involve geographic content and skills. But comprehensive coverage has been systematically attempted to indicate the possible range of the progressively maturing experiences within this design. The creative classroom teacher will think of many parallel experiences that he can initiate with his pupils.

Once again, the authors stress the importance (with any small portion or any chapter of Part Three) of the reader's being familiar with the rationale of the overall design as presented in Part Two. There is built into these eleven expanding communities a developmental sequence that can be ignored only at the risk of failure to help the pupil to build a strong geographic competence. We expect that relatively few in-service teachers will pursue all of the chapters in Part Three; they are more likely to read and be influenced by those chapters which deal with pupils of the age groups and/or community emphases assigned to them by the school in which they teach. But the authors hope that whatever portions of Part Three are used will be understood against a background of the total design as given in Part Two. Most or all of the several chapters dealing with the eleven expanding communities in Part Three will probably be studied by pre-service teachers. These teachers in training are urged to refer again and again to Parts One and Two as the background and the rationale for the more specific and practical suggestions that make up Part Three.

chapter four

THE BEGINNING GRADES
EMPHASES

/ 1. *The Family Community*
/ 2. *The School Community*

General Introduction to Family and School Communities

Three major objectives have been identified for development in the elementary school program in map making and map interpretation: (1) the ability to reorganize data gained from firsthand and vicarious experiences and to represent them on maps with appropriate symbols, (2) the ability to read data recorded on maps and globes and to translate these data into conceptual distributions and locations that are represented on maps and globes, and (3) the ability to reason about things geographic.

These objectives are then further broken down into groups of skills which describe in behavioral terms what a pupil might be expected to do in order to achieve them. We suggested earlier that both objectives and skills would undergo some modifications in order better to meet the needs of pupils at particular educational levels. For this reason we have chosen to add a fourth objective for primary pupils—one that is inherent in the first objective mentioned above but that needs particular emphasis as part of a readiness program for younger pupils—the ability to observe thoughtfully.

As we approach the grade-by-grade allocation of pupil experiences by which these skills and generalizations are to be developed and objectives achieved progressively over time, we are immediately confronted with the problem of sequence. Others who have faced this problem have concluded that it is not possible to make a definitive list of skills and concepts to be covered at each grade level because of the range of ability and previous experience found in each grade, but that skills and concepts can be graded in order of difficulty so that they can be taught at successive levels. However, experiment also bears out the idea that grading skills and concepts as well as materials becomes essentially a problem of presentation. Thus we are faced with three questions: (1) What map skills and geographic understandings can most profitably be begun and developed in the light of child development and the learning abilities of six- and seven-year-olds with whom we are concerned at this level? (2) Within what context shall the objectives be presented at this level? (3) What shall be the sequence of pupil experiences? Closely related to the last question is the one of methodology to be used in planning the sequence of pupil experiences.

The next four sections of this chapter will endeavor to cope with these vital questions. First, we will analyze studies in child development and in the learning abilities of six- and seven-year-olds, in order to obtain cues to developing a program in map making and map interpretation at this level. Second, we will describe the nature of a "community" and clarify the place of the family community and of the school community in our coordinated social studies framework. We can then apply the overall objectives and skills for this particular age group, acting in the arenas of family and school.

As people interact in a community, regardless of its size or location, the very processes of interaction result in the basic human activities: protecting and conserving; producing, exchanging, and consuming; transporting; communicating; expressing aesthetic and spiritual impulses; providing recreation; providing education; organizing and governing; and creating tools and technics. Although the emphasis placed on each such cluster of activities may vary from community to community, the activities are carried on in every community to the extent necessary to meet the purposes of the members of that community. Therefore, in the third following section, we will use the basic human activities as a checklist. Here we will analyze the major objectives for developing map skills and geographic understandings in relation to each basic human activity and suggest pupil experiences within the context of that activity as it is carried on in the family community and the school community.

Having analyzed the many possibilities for map experiences in relation to the basic human activities within family and school, in the final section we will coordinate this information into a detailed sequence of pupil experiences. This sequence may then serve as a guide for the classroom teacher who is working to develop desirable map skills and geographic understandings that are within the children's capabilities.

The final section in each community emphasis should be regarded by the classroom teacher as a working hypothesis, to be used flexibly and corrected as need be.

Child Development and the Learning Process

At every grade level the teacher is faced with both an age range and an experience range. Lack of maturity or lack of opportunity for certain experiences makes some children younger than their chronological age; others are more advanced than their chronological years would suggest. A kindergarten or a first-grade teacher, or the first-year teacher in a non-graded organization, then, must consider what children are like from five to seven years of age. Here we are especially concerned with map skills and geographic understandings to be developed within the social studies framework. What cues can we glean from studies of children in this age group? Gesell has been especially helpful here.[1] He describes five as a nodal age—the time of consolidating gains made up to that point. The five-year-old lives largely in a here-and-now world. His father and mother, his seat at the table, his clothes, his cap, his tricycle, the backyard, the kitchen, his bed, the drugstore and grocery store around the corner, or the barn and granary in the country, are his world. He is interested in his home and in every part of the world he discovers as he comes into contact with it. He plays house. He tries to reorganize his ideas of the world around him. As Gesell says, "He must make the familiar more familiar to himself; the familiar world is still new."[2] The child is trying to identify with his present immediate environment, with which his relations are very personal. He tends to be realistic; he depends on concrete experience; he is first-personal. His questions show how he is seeking to interpret his world: "What is it for?" "What is it made of?" "How does this work?" "Why does the bus come around this way?" He is exploring, and *asking* for *instruction:* "How do you do it?"

Even the five-year-old is oriented within his space range. He likes to do errands around the house. He can cross streets with traffic lights and find his way to school. He likes to go on excursions. He can point out simple routes which he takes. He likes to trace a journey on maps and make simple maps indicating the route he takes to school, etc. He can indicate specific landmarks.

By the time he is six, the environment is expanding. He is now interested not only in specific places but in *relationships* between home, neighborhood, and an expanding community, including school. Home interests now include people, keeping house, pets, animals, outdoors, amusements, sources of food, preparation of food, clothing, books, holidays. School interests now include materials, equipment, library, various rooms, playgrounds. He has an orientation to the schoolroom: he is oriented to the room as a whole and to his position in it. He has some interest in what the rest of the school is like and enjoys exploring the school with his group. We often fail to realize what a completely new and intriguing world the school community is for the six-year-old.

He likes to visit in his own neighborhood; he knows the names of some streets and the location of some major points of interest. He may be able to tell points of a compass from a familiar starting point. While he may be able to name nearby streets, he tends to travel on a specific route so as not to get lost. The child still relates everything to himself, but he is interested in the sun, the moon, the whole world.

At seven, the child is capable of greater understanding of relationships. School and home are both important. His community interests include the grocer, the policeman, and the fireman, as he comes into contact with them. He is interested in the earth's crust, stones, heat, fire, and sun. His spatial orientation is improving. He can go from his classroom to another familiar room but wants specific directions. His major space orientation is within his own space experience and range, but he is becoming aware that there are places other than just "right here." However, even at seven he knows right and left primarily in relation to his own body.

Mitchell points out that children learn about things largely through firsthand experiences where they can find answers to their curiosities through exercising their senses and muscles.[3] She emphasizes that the chief program for geographic "intake" in these early years lies in trips— explorations of the immediate environment. However, provision must also be made for an active "outgo." The children must have adaptable materials in the classroom with which they can reorganize and relate for themselves what they have observed. Mitchell charts the stages in development of children's geographic thinking.[4] Following is a summary:

> *Interest drives.*—As children observe in their immediate environment, they begin to notice the function of moving objects; for example, a train is related to the track, to the station, to carrying of passengers and freight, etc. A train is for something. At 7, children are beginning to be aware of the more distant, but it must still be connected closely with the here and now.
>
> *Orientation.*—Familiar places can be crudely placed in space relations. Rough block-building maps can be made of the house environment, the school environment, the immediate street environment. Later, children can draw rough maps of the same with crayons.
>
> *Tools and children's methods of expressions.*—Dramatic play is much elaborated. There is increasing possibility for cooperative play. Symbols are used in dramatic play as props to represent the realities observed previously. Toward age 7, symbols can begin to represent general ideas, but they are still closely tied with direct images.

Curriculum implications.—What can be done through trips and mapping? Motor memories are still dominant. Children should take many trips in the immediate environment that make use of all senses and muscles. They should take a trip to a high building to see many things in their space relation. They should look at airplane views and draw perspective maps. In their dramatic play they can lay down a strip of blue oilcloth for rivers and on the floor chalk in streets. In three-dimensional models they can begin to learn about the concept of erosion, rivers and drainage. They can be helped to relate the growth of living things as they are conditioned by earth forces.

In trying to set up a sequence of school experiences in maps and globes for children, we face this problem: psychology alone cannot give us all the necessary information and cues. The significance of a child's behavior depends upon the position of that behavior in a sequence—what growth preceded, what growth is likely to follow. Also important are the experiences which the culture values and provides for the child in that growth sequence. The development of a geographical point of view is gradual and continuous. Now is the time for children to experience some of the factors and forces at work in their immediate environment. Now is the time to start with the simplest of concepts and guide the pupil's growth to larger and more complex ideas. Failure to provide accurate guidance at this point may well dull his interest or teach him inadvertently to be a careless or superficial observer rather than one who searches for underlying relationships.

Scope and Sequence of the Social Studies Framework

The first step in drawing up a curriculum design is to state objectives. This chapter opened with a statement of our objectives in developing map skills and geographic understandings with primary children. The second step is to define the *scope*, the content within which these objectives will be realized, the *what* of the curriculum. For our purposes the range of content has been grouped into nine categories of basic human activities. Wherever men live and work together, these activities emerge. They become an excellent checklist against which to test the comprehensiveness of the map experiences suggested.

The third step is concerned with the *sequence*, the continuity and order of experiences to be provided from year to year, the *when* of the curriculum. The sequence of emphases used here is based on the expanding communities of men.

The world of the child can be thought of as a set of horizons that widens as he grows up. The world for the baby is the area surrounding his crib, and the population of that world is his family. Later his world becomes the family house and yard, and the population of this world is the family and all who service and visit the home. Still later the world becomes the urban block or the rural township in which the home is located; its population naturally increases to include the neighbors. After the child bursts the bounds of the block or the township, his world expands rapidly as he comes into contact with more people living in larger and larger arenas. In this way his set of interlocking communities grows steadily outward.

What do we mean by a "community"? A community may be defined as a consciously assembled group of people living in a defined geographic space within which the processes of human interaction result in the development of basic human activities appropriate in kind and intensity to meet the problems and purposes of the members of the community. A community need not be self-sufficient, nor need it be politically organized, but those who comprise a community have a sense of belonging to it. In contemporary society individuals live within several communities of different scale simultaneously. Thus a child in kindergarten or first grade* is already consciously a member of family and school communities.

The family community functions as a biological group required for procreation and for rearing of the young. It exists within a definable area such as the home and yard, an apartment, the farm boundaries. It engages in each of the basic human activities for the mutual benefit of its members. Parents protect the health and lives of their children. The family produces, exchanges, and consumes many goods and services although numerous economic functions have been removed from the home to larger communities. The family often transports itself. Members communicate with each other almost constantly. Many forms of aesthetic and spiritual impulses may be expressed. Recreation is engaged in. The activity of educating is evident in innumerable forms—from the infant learning to eat, walk, or talk, to conversation at the dinner table revolving around a multitude of topics. The family organizes in different ways for different purposes. Clearly the family in some degree engages in each of the basic human activities. It is the oldest and the most significant of all the communities in which the individual has membership.

In the kindergarten and first grade, we are concerned also with the community of the school, to which the child now begins to give major attention and will continue to do so until late adolescence. Next to the home or family community, the school is considered the most influential in its effect on the early childhood years.

---

* In a non-graded school setting, kindergarten or first-grade designations hereafter refer to the beginning school years (five to seven years of age).

The school is a community: it is a consciously assembled group of people living within a defined geographic space, the school building and grounds. The school also engages in every cluster of human activities. Protection is provided by nurse, safety patrol, and the fire drill. Many activities revolve around producing and distributing though they are of a less economic nature. Consuming of food takes place in the hot lunch program or in the milk break. Children engage in some sort of transportation to and from school and on school trips. Communication with the school is essential to the life of this community. Pupils express aesthetic impulses in art forms and learn spiritual values in holiday celebrations, flag salutes, etc. Playtime provides recreation. And finally, the school provides education, its major function.

Additional possibilities for worthwhile map experiences and geographic concepts will emerge from checking the basic human activities as they occur in the pupils' own family communities and in their own school community. Of course, the child—through books, radio, television, cars, buses, trains and planes, and other means of communication and transportation—will soon be aware that there are other communities than the family and the school. But the *emphasis* will be on the family and the school communities because it is with these arenas that the child has direct contact. Geographers agree that what is most needed in the early years is to help children build *clear images* of the immediate environment and *accurate concepts* in relation to their firsthand experiences. These will serve them later as a foundation for map experiences in studying larger communities where they cannot experience direct, firsthand sensory data.

Analysis in Terms of the Basic Human Activities

This chapter is concerned with six- and seven-year-olds within their communities of immediate contact: family and school. Let us now analyze each of the basic human activities as they function within these communities at a level at which it touches the life of the child.

In the first column on the succeeding pages are listed four major objectives, modified and reordered for our present purposes from the three given at the beginning of the chapter: (1) the ability to observe thoughtfully, (2) the ability to reason about things geographic, (3) the ability to map in some form what has been observed, and (4) the ability to read through symbols of maps to the landscape or realities represented.

The second column contains possible pupil experiences that are pertinent to the basic human activity under consideration and that may be used to develop map skills and geographic understandings. No one-to-one relationship exists between the first and second columns. The *sequence* of experiences in the second column should help to achieve the objectives of the first column. The experiences are not exhaustive; they are merely suggestive. Teacher and pupils should engage in many other experiences proposed by their social studies units. The type of *process* suggested here is important. It is hoped that the teacher will find this approach a useful one: set up objectives and then think through the pupil experiences that are possible to achieve these objectives using the basic human activities as a checklist.

THE FAMILY COMMUNITY (EMPHASIS 1) AND THE
SCHOOL COMMUNITY (EMPHASIS 2)

*Basic Human Activity: Protecting and Conserving
Life, Health, Property, and Resources*

OBJECTIVES	PUPIL EXPERIENCES
1. *Ability to observe thoughtfully.* Observe home and school as communities in which protecting and conserving are carried on. Question who is involved. Where? With what? Why?	1. *Firsthand experiences.* Walk around the school and the classroom to observe distribution of protecting and conserving functions and associated features. Children can then be asked to do the same at home. Observe the means of (1) protecting from injury; (2) protecting from weather by the use of clothing; (3) protecting or conserving clothing, furniture, supplies, etc.; (4) conserving energy: rest, using energy constructively.
2. *Ability to reason about things geographic.* Analyze examples of protecting and conserving in home, in school, on school grounds, to note (1) relative location of these features; (2) relation of location to function;	2. *Reorganized experience.* a. *Discussion.* Analyze how the distribution of features relates to function, as in the kitchen at home. Could the arrangement be different? Would a change improve it or make it worse? Analyze maintenance function in the school. Analyze safety pre-

(3) relative distance and direction (bounding areas).

3. *Ability to map in some form* what has been observed.

Discover use of symbols (three-dimensional, pictorial, semipictorial)
(1) to show relative location;
(2) to show relative distance and direction;
(3) to make representations in different sizes (crude use of scale);
(4) to communicate what is portrayed by other than verbal means (use of legend).

4. *Ability to read through symbols* of maps to the landscape or realities represented. Ability to read teacher-made map of school or school grounds and simple floor plan of school or classroom. Ability to read such symbols as those representing a building, walls, windows, doors, and special features concerned with protecting and conserving such as the nurse's room, fire bell, fire extinguisher, fire alarm boxes, etc.

cautions for a home.

b. *Dramatic play.* Children set up props showing relative location of layout at home, or a room at home or at school. Play out conserving and protecting functions previously observed or discussed.

c. *Mapping.* Use above acquired information to
(1) build school or home with blocks or other materials, locate protecting and conserving features, analyze routes used in carrying out some of these functions, e.g., the exit for fire drill;
(2) draw pictures;
(3) diagram pictorially—and semipictorially—in large scale and in smaller scale
(a) classroom, school, school and yards, school and adjacent streets and roads;
(b) rooms at home: bedroom, kitchen, playroom, study, bathroom; home, home and yard, home and adjacent streets or roads.

3. *Using and interpreting maps made by others.*

Children and teacher might build a simple model of the school building and agree on symbols pertinent to protecting and conserving. Teacher might draw a map on the floor or on large paper with the children observing, discussing, and determining the symbols to be used. Teacher might then present a diagram of school or classroom and request that children locate and interpret the familiar symbols.

Basic Human Activity: Producing, Exchanging, Distributing, and Consuming Goods and Services

OBJECTIVES	PUPIL EXPERIENCES

1. *Ability to observe thoughtfully.*

Observe family and school as communities

in which producing goods and services occurs:

of food, clothing, shelter, laundry, art products, landscaping, maintenance—and how the home and school organize for these functions;

in which distributing and exchanging occur:

of food, other supplies, utilities, services, etc.;

in which consuming occurs:

of food, other supplies, utilities, services, etc.

2. *Ability to reason about things geographic.*

Analyze examples of producing, distributing, and consuming in the home, at school, on the school grounds, to note:

(1) relative location of features;

(2) relation of location to function (land use, functional layout);

(3) relative distance and direction of features (bounding areas).

1. *Firsthand experiences.*

Walk around school to observe location of producing, exchanging, distributing, and consuming functions. Children may be requested to do the same at home. At home mother cooks, sews, washes; father paints, gardens, repairs house—these are producing goods and/or services functions.

Trucks and various people deliver foods. Heat, light, water are brought to the home. The milkman may bring milk; the newsboy may bring the paper. These are all exchanging and distributing functions.

In the home, water, electricity, and heat are used. Food is consumed. Clothing wears out. The house and car need repairs. These are all consuming functions.

In the rural area the producing function is much clearer. Some of the exchange and distribution is away from the home. Similar consuming occurs in both urban and rural family communities.

2. *Reorganized experience.*

a. *Discussion.* Question who produces, exchanges, distributes, consumes? Where? With what? Why are these features so located? What advantage? What disadvantage?

b. *Dramatic play.* Dramatize those functions observed wherein adults produce and distribute what all consume. Have children engage in real activities which they can be guided to recognize as producing, exchanging, distributing, and consum-

3. *Ability to map in some form* what has been observed.

Discover use of symbols (three-dimensional, pictorial, semipictorial)

(1) to show relative location;

(2) to show relative distance and direction;

(3) to make representations in different sizes (crude use of scale);

(4) to communicate what is portrayed by other than verbal means (use of legend).

4. *Ability to read through symbols* of maps to the landscape or realities represented. Ability to read teacher-made maps showing location of features involved in producing, exchanging, distributing, and consuming: cafeteria, supply room, utilities, maintenance, etc.

ing. Children produce many products and services at school; children can be made responsible to get and distribute supplies, milk, etc.

c. *Mapping.* Build with blocks, draw with crayons, portray in some map form the producing, exchanging, distributing, and consuming areas in school and home. Have children show on their maps the route for delivery of supplies to supply room and thereafter to classrooms, the delivery of supplies to the office, to the nurse, or to building maintenance. Show route to cafeteria, etc. Determine what symbols will be used to represent the necessary features.

3. *Using and interpreting maps made by others.*

Children may make a base map of the school on a large table. Children can add three-dimensional symbols of producing, exchanging, distributing, and consuming features. These three-dimensional symbols may then be replaced with pictorial symbols, then semipictorial or abstract symbols. A flannel map may also serve as base. Eventually, the teacher presents a completed map and the children locate features, read symbols, and interpret. A simplified blueprint of the school or home layout may be used. A pictorial representation of a school and grounds is sometimes available for comparable map interpretation experiences.

Basic Human Activity: Transporting People and Goods

OBJECTIVES

PUPIL EXPERIENCES

1. *Ability to observe thoughtfully.*

1. *Firsthand experiences.*

Observe family and school as communities which transport people and goods. Question who is involved. From where? To where? With what? Why?

Observe the kind of transportation available in family and school communities: walking, tricycle, bicycle, wagon, roller skates, baby carriage, family car, school bus. Also trucks deliver a wide variety of supplies to home and school. On a farm, additional modes of transportation are available: horses, tractors, and trucks carry products and move people around the farm.

2. *Ability to reason about things geographic.*

Analyze the examples of transporting seen in connection with family and school communities, to note

(1) relation of time to distance when using different means of transportation;

(2) relation of function to technology: power involved in walking, riding tricycle, riding in car;

(3) how physical factors influence means of transportation. Transportation problems in a crowded city with multi-storied apartment buildings are different from those on a ranch. Hills, water bodies, mountains affect transportation.

2. *Reorganized experience.*

a. *Discussion.* Discuss the different purposes served by the different means of transportation noted at home and at school. Bring children to the point where they recognize what a wheel does for transporting weights, even when hand or foot powered, and what is added when the vehicle is driven by mechanical power. Who uses the various transportation means that come to home and to school? What costs and abilities are involved? How does time necessary to cover distance vary with means used: for example, walking to school, as compared with coming in the family car or by the school bus?

b. *Dramatic play.* Dramatize the transporting activities observed within their own family communities and within the school. Duplicate traffic signs found within the school building or the apartment and through dramatic play practice reacting reasonably to these traffic directions.

3. *Ability to map in some form* what has been observed. Ability to make crude street or road maps (three-dimensional, pictorial, semipictorial) of city block or rural township in which home and school are located, oriented with outdoor space.

c. *Mapping.* Build a simple model of school or home with blocks, depicting farm boundaries, streets and roads, water bodies, and other features that are used in transportation or that form obstacles to transportation

Discover symbols that can be used to represent sidewalks, streets, roads, water bodies within the area, and means of depicting aids or obstacles to transportation; gates, hallways, fences, doors, bridges, tunnels, elevators, stairways, pedestrian paths, etc.

4. *Ability to read through symbols of maps to the landscape or realities represented.* Ability to read teacher-made map of streets and roads bounding the city block or rural township in which the school and home are located. Ability to recognize features that are aids or obstacles to transportation for the family or for the school community.

within the communities being studied. For example, stairs in a school provide means of transportation by foot but are an obstacle for wheeled vehicles. Draw a pictorial or semipictorial map depicting transportation observed in family and school communities. Draw a large base map on which to push wheeled toys. Later, make a smaller-scale map and use pictorial or semipictorial symbols.

3. *Using and interpreting maps made by others.*

Children may use a base map of the school block or township made by the teacher on a large table to which they add three-dimensional symbols of transportation, later replaced by pictorial and semipictorial symbols. Eventually the teacher presents a completed map on which the children locate and interpret symbols related to transportation. In addition to streets and roads, oriented with outdoor space, there may be a traffic light, bus stop, etc.

Basic Human Activity: Communicating Facts, Ideas, and Feelings

OBJECTIVES

1. *Ability to observe thoughtfully.*
   Observe home and school as communities in which ideas, thoughts, and feelings are communicated. Question who is involved. From where? To where? With what? Why?

2. *Ability to reason about things geographic.*
   Analyze examples of communi-

PUPIL EXPERIENCES

1. *Firsthand experiences.*
   Observe channels of communication in school and family. Observe means of communication and features necessary: mailbox; newspaper stand or delivery box; electric outlets necessary to plug in radio, television, and telephone; telephone poles and telephone wires; television aerials.

2. *Reorganized experience.*
   a. *Discussion.* Discuss how members of a family and of a school

cating in family and school communities, to note
(1) relation of time to distance when using different means of communication;
(2) relation of function to technology: what power makes possible the various means of communicating such as talking in person compared to writing, or telephoning, or listening to radio?

3. *Ability to map in some form* what has been observed. Ability to locate on a map (three-dimensional, pictorial, or semipictorial) features concerned with communicating.

Discover or invent symbols to represent mailbox; newspaper box; electrical outlets for radio, television, intercommunication system, telephone; telephone poles and wires; television aerials.

4. *Ability to read through symbols* of maps to the realities thus represented. Ability to read maps provided by teacher of a typical home or of the school which depict symbols representing features of communication.

communicate. Discuss features of communication observable in home and school and what is necessary to make them operate. Discuss how technology has speeded up communication even in the home and school communities.

b. *Dramatic play.* Dramatize the route a messenger from the principal might take to deliver a message to all the classrooms. Use a rough floor plan of the school. Urge the children not to violate walls but to enter and exit only through door symbols. Dramatize how one might phone for a doctor or notify the fire department by use of a fire alarm box. Actually write and mail letters that communicate. Dramatize a program for radio or television. Have the children role-play a staff meeting, a teacher teaching, mother scolding, etc.

c. *Mapping.* Make maps in various forms (three-dimensional, pictorial, semipictorial) on which channels for communication and symbols representing means of communication within a home or within a school appear.

3. *Using and interpreting maps made by others.*

Teacher may provide a base map of the school and the immediate area in which it is located and use symbols depicting features of communication with which the children are familiar from their own map-making experiences. Telephone posts and wires may appear which the children have previously observed firsthand. A base map can be made of the school, to which children as a group add communicating features. Children can be given smaller base maps on which they then add these features for themselves. They can also draw routes that a messenger may take in carrying a message in response to the teacher's directions. Similar map interpretation experiences can be provided for the family community.

Basic Human Activity: Expressing Aesthetic and Spiritual Impulses

OBJECTIVES	PUPIL EXPERIENCES
1. *Ability to observe thoughtfully.*	1. *Firsthand experiences.*

1. *Ability to observe thoughtfully.*

Observe home and school as communities in which aesthetic and spiritual impulses may find expression.

2. *Ability to reason about things geographic.*

Analyze examples of aesthetic and spiritual expression in family and school communities:
(1) relative location of some of the natural and man-made beauty;
(2) relation of beauty to natural features.

1. *Firsthand experiences.*

Observe natural and man-made beauty. Observe gardens, landscaping, trees, grass, or lack thereof in family and school communities. Observe color, lighting, furnishings, and their maintenance in the immediate environment. Observe art work and exhibits. Notice the architecture of school and home.

2. *Reorganized experience.*
a. *Discussion.* Discuss what man has added to natural beauty. How has man destroyed natural beauty? Discuss what makes a product an aesthetic expression. How can one's writing, the map one makes, the painting or object in clay or wood become more of an aesthetic or spiritual expression?
b. *Dramatic play.* Express the beauties, or lack thereof, in one's environment by bringing into play all the senses: smell, sight, taste, sound, feel. Act out cutting the grass and the freshness of its smell, climbing and rolling down a hill. In a farm commu-

3. *Ability to map in some form* what has been observed.

Discover or invent symbols (three-dimensional, pictorial, semi-pictorial)

(1) to show relative location;

(2) to show extent;

(3) to communicate by legend which are areas of greenery, places of worship, places of creative expression, etc.

4. *Ability to read through symbols* of maps to the landscape or realities thus represented. Ability to read teacher-provided maps of typical homes and of the school which depict symbols of natural and man-made beauty. Ability, with help of the teacher, to understand some of the simplest symbols of an architectural or landscaping plan.

nity there is the smell of hay, horses and other animals, the barn; the taste of fresh milk, an apple off a tree, etc.

c. *Mapping.* Build with blocks, draw with crayons and other art media, portray in some form the immediate environment. Show the distribution of greenery and landscaping in relation to school and home as buildings. A three-dimensional model of the school building and its grounds in a sand table or table exhibit may be a worthwhile project.

3. *Using and interpreting maps made by others.*

Teacher may be able to secure architect's drawings and layout of school and grounds to show children. Some children may be able to secure such drawings of their own homes or those of others to bring to school for interpretation.

Basic Human Activity: Providing Recreation

OBJECTIVES

1. *Ability to observe thoughtfully.*

Observe home and school as communities in which recreational activities occur. Analyze placement of playground equipment and play areas in school and in home.

2. *Ability to reason about things geographic.*

Analyze recreational areas and facilities in family and school communities as to

(1) relative location;

(2) relation of location to function;

(3) relation to physical and cultural features;

(4) distribution.

PUPIL EXPERIENCES

1. *Firsthand experiences.*

Observe location of playground equipment and play areas and facilities, or lack of them, within school and home.

2. *Reorganized experience.*

a. *Discussion.* Discuss location of playground equipment and the reason for its placement. What are the advantages and disadvantages? Was some other arrangement possible? Discuss recreational facilities in family community. Discuss difference between indoor and outdoor

3. *Ability to map in some form* what has been observed.

Discover or invent symbols (three-dimensional, pictorial, semi-pictorial)

(1) to show relative location;

(2) to show extent;

(3) to communicate by legend or color symbols.

4. *Ability to read through symbols* of maps to the landscape or realities thus represented. Ability to read teacher-provided maps of typical homes and the school and understand symbols representing recreational areas and features.

play. Discuss means of transportation used for recreational purposes.

b. *Dramatic play.* Express recreational activities in terms of all the senses: sight, taste, smell, sound, feel. Enlarge concepts of what may be included as recreation in school and family communities. Dramatization itself can be recreational.

c. *Mapping.* Build with blocks, draw with crayons and other art media, portray on floor maps or on table model the distribution of recreational areas and facilities in school and home communities. Develop symbols to represent recreational features.

3. *Using and interpreting maps made by others.*

Teacher may present a base map of school and surroundings to which children add three-dimensional, pictorial, or semipictorial symbols of playground equipment and other recreational features. Teacher may then present a map with symbols already added which children are to interpret. Similar map interpretation experiences may be devised concerning the home environment and recreational activities.

Basic Human Activity: Providing Education

OBJECTIVES

1. *Ability to observe thoughtfully.*

Observe home and school as communities in which educational activities occur.

PUPIL EXPERIENCES

1. *Firsthand experiences.*

Walk through the school. Observe all the different rooms and functions that provide means of education. Note features of the home that provide education: library or magazine stand, radio and TV, baby's playpen, etc.

2. *Ability to reason about things geographic.*
   (1) Where do educational activities occur in school and home?
   (2) What facilities and organization are necessary in order to provide this function?

3. *Ability to map in some form* what has been observed.

   Discover or invent symbols (three-dimensional, pictorial, semipictorial) to represent the school itself and the specific educational features to be portrayed. Same for the home.

4. *Ability to read through symbols* of maps to the realities thus represented. Ability to read floor plan of the school and understand some of the interrelations of functions. Similar abilities for the home.

2. *Reorganized experience.*
   a. *Discussion.* Analyze how the school as a whole is organized and functions in order to provide education: role of principal, staff (teaching, secretarial, custodial); need to order textbooks, supplies; purpose of library; importance of the building, grounds, utilities, maintenance; value of parent-teacher organizations; need for extracurricular functions, etc. Discuss educational functions of the home.
   b. *Dramatic play.* Dramatize the roles of the various school personnel and their functions. Provide the setting in which these functions occur. Dramatize situations at home that are educational.
   c. *Mapping.* Build a simple three-dimensional model of each floor of school building, including storage, maintenance, utility areas, etc. Draw pictures and semipictorial representations of educational functions of school and related features.

3. *Using and interpreting maps made by others.*

   Study a blueprint or teacher-made floor plan of each floor of school building and grounds. Interpret what takes place educationally in each room by the map symbols contained thereon. Initiate similar experiences with blueprints of homes, farms, or apartments.

Basic Human Activity: Organizing and Governing

OBJECTIVES

PUPIL EXPERIENCES

1. *Ability to observe thoughtfully.*
   Observe family and school as communities in which organizing

1. *Firsthand experiences.*
   Visit principal's office; observe secretary at work; visit nurse; visit

and governing functions occur. Question who is involved and where and why.

2. *Ability to reason about things geographic.*

Analyze examples of organizing and governing in family and school, to note

(1) who is involved;
(2) where it takes place;
(3) relation of location to function.

3. *Ability to map in some form* what has been observed.

Discover or invent symbols (three-dimensional, pictorial, semi-pictorial)

(1) to show location of organizing and governing functions;
(2) to show location of features that help make it possible.

4. *Ability to read through symbols* of maps to the realities thus represented. Ability to locate on a teacher-made floor plan of the school and grounds where organizing and governing take place and channels for effective functioning.

maintenance areas. Perhaps children may even be able to visit briefly at a parent-teacher meeting. They might also visit the school band and orchestra, a meeting of the traffic squad of the school, or a meeting of the student governing body if one exists.

Ask children to observe the home and see if they can discover organizing and governing functions.

2. *Reorganized experience.*

a. *Discussion.* Analyze organizing and governing functions observed above.

b. *Dramatic play.* Act out different ways in which people can work together toward the solution of a problem. (Pick a problem that really needs democratic group interaction.) Help children to see how a leader functions democratically, yet gives leadership. Help children see how "bossiness" often defeats its purpose. Organize to carry forth some functions necessary for classroom efficiency. Have children decide what room jobs are necessary and then have each accept a job. Act out jobs that they could do at home.

c. *Mapping.* Map the layout of the school and locate where major organizing and governing functions occur. Show the routes by which some of these functions are made effective. Draw pictures of groups observed organizing as mentioned above.

3. *Using and interpreting maps made by others.*

Using a simplified blueprint or teacher's floor plan of school, children locate areas and features used in organizing and governing: principal's office, maintenance, organ-

Similar abilities for the family and organizing and governing.

ized groups of various kinds that operate in the school.

Basic Human Activity: Creating Tools and Technics

OBJECTIVES

PUPIL EXPERIENCES

1. *Ability to observe thoughtfully.*

Observe family and school as communities in which tools and technics are used and developed. Question who uses and who invents. When? For what purpose? What happens when a new piece of equipment appears?

1. *Firsthand experiences.*

Note the usual use made of tools and technics in school:

use of pencils, pencil sharpener, crayons, paint, clay, scissors in the classroom; various uses of electric and gas power, incinerator, availability of running water, fire-fighting equipment in the school; machines and equipment in the office.

Ask children to observe the home and see what tools and technics are used. It is particularly important to note the changes that occur when a new piece of equipment is introduced at school or home, e.g., a school intercom system, a vacuum cleaner at home, etc.

2. *Ability to reason about things geographic.*

Analyze examples of the use and creation of tools and technics in home, at school. Where are they used? What effect on time and product occurs with the introduction of a new tool or technic? How may a new tool or technic affect the distribution of the activity over space?

2. *Reorganized experience.*

a. *Discussion.* Discuss who uses tools and technics. For what purpose? What happens when a power mower appears? An automatic snowplow? A post digger? A dishwasher? Contrast time spent and ease of operation with the same functions carried on manually. On a farm, new equipment often brings about a dramatic change. Ask children to observe if they ever try to find a better way of doing something. What new tools or technics have they to offer to improve living at home or at school?

b. *Dramatic play.* Dramatize child functions where a tool makes a difference: trying to sharpen a pencil without a pencil sharpener; trying to tear along an outline without a scissors; trying to comb hair without a comb; trying to sweep the floor without a broom. Dramatize adult functions where a change in tool makes a difference: a hand saw versus an electric saw; dishwashing by hand versus a dishwasher, etc. Include different placement of activities when new tool is invented or introduced.

3. *Ability to map in some form* what has been observed. Discover or invent symbols (three-dimensional, pictorial, semipictorial):
   (1) to show relative location;
   (2) to show relative distance and direction;
   (3) to make representations in different sizes (crude use of scale);
   (4) to communicate what is portrayed by other than verbal means (use of legend).

c. *Mapping.* Build with blocks, draw with crayons, portray in some map form the location and distribution of tools and equipment in schools and home. Develop symbols to represent equipment depicted. Then map the new distribution of activities that could follow the introduction of a new tool or technic, e.g., a new hand truck at school or a new arrangement of playground space.

4. *Ability to read through symbols* of maps to the realities represented. Ability to read teacher-made maps showing location of equipment in school maintenance area, cafeteria, office, etc., and to anticipate how these locations are changed as new tools are invented or introduced into home and school.

3. *Using and interpreting maps made by others.*

Teacher may provide a base map of the classroom, office, cafeteria, or maintenance area of the school. Children may add three-dimensional, pictorial, or semipictorial symbols of the equipment used. If some major change or improvement takes place, it should be depicted and interpreted by redistribution of map symbols to correspond to new location of activity.

Sequence of Pupil Experiences

Having analyzed some possibilities for map experiences for six- and seven-year-olds in relation to each of the basic human activities within the family community and the school community, we now attempt to coordinate this information into an illustrative and detailed sequence of pupil experiences. The sequence is based on a review of the literature of (1) what geographers and educators think children ought to know; (2) what classroom teachers, teachers of geography, and geography specialists have tried successfully with groups of children; and (3) what studies in child development and learning theory contribute to understanding of children's abilities.

It has usually been assumed that map skills and geographic understandings in any form are too difficult to be considered as kindergarten and first-grade material. Studies that will be used as source material for support of the program to be developed in this book make no such limiting assumption. Two guidelines suggested by Anderzhon[5] are especially useful: *Do not underestimate what children can do. Do not overestimate what they know.*

ORIENTATION TO THE CLASSROOM

Observation is fundamental.

> From the first historical records of the teaching of geography, except during the Dark Ages, observation has been considered fundamental. Emphasis upon observation and sense perception led Comenius, first; then Rousseau, Pestalozzi, Ritter, and Diesterweg to make knowledge of geographic facts within the direct observation and experience of the child the basis of all geographic instruction. . . .[6]

The arena within the *direct* observation and experience of six- and seven-year-olds is the family community and the school community. The teacher, of course, is more able to give guidance to observation in the school community, so we will start our guided experiences there and then have the children relate them to their own homes.

First, then, let us get acquainted with the classroom. What about the physical room itself? Where are the windows, the door to the hall, the closet to hang one's wraps, the supply cupboards? How is the furniture arranged: children's seats, teacher's desk, library corner, science corner, painting easels? How is the lighting distributed in the room? Where is the light switch? Where is the source of heat? How is it controlled? When children first come into a new classroom, they need to become oriented to the new space. They will not do so by one glance around or by having the teacher quickly enumerate where everything is to be found. Part of the orientation will develop as they live, work, and play in the classroom.

But if this space orientation is to serve also as preparation for developing a geographical point of view, the guidance the teacher gives will help serve broader purposes. The classroom can be studied as it relates to the basic human activities carried on by all people in all communities. For example, in addition to what has already been mentioned, in relation to protecting and conserving: where and how to hang one's outer clothing could be observed and discussed; the paint aprons may be located and their use in protecting clothing discussed; care and watering of plants in the classroom is a conservation activity as well as a science learning and one that adds to the aesthetic environment of the room; the thermometer can be located, its function analyzed as protective in helping to maintain a healthful room climate. Location of supplies and construction materials relates to producing, exchanging, distributing, and consuming. Writing, listening, speaking in a group, expressing oneself in many media—all are ways of communicating. Even transporting of supplies occurs. Art and construction media, phonograph, and flag contribute to expression of aesthetic and spiritual impulses. Balls and other play equipment may be located. Such careful study of the room, including an analysis of room jobs, clear allocation of functions, even location and discussion of the calendar can help children understand how the classroom is organized for effectively carrying on its educational function.

Study of the spatial distribution of the items and activities in the classroom should be carried on in a relaxed manner over a period of time, not all at once. Location of features should be discussed in relation to a particular focus of importance at a given time. The children should be encouraged to raise questions which help make clear the relation between location and function. They should be led to question whether some changes could be made that would be an improvement.

Geography is basically a study of relations. It is desirable that certain attitudes be developed, such as the following: There are reasons for spatial location of things; this is not a haphazard world; distributional changes are possible and may bring improvement, but they do not necessarily do so. The kinds of questions children are encouraged to ask about the spatial relations of features they observe in any environment can help them develop such attitudes.

What children do with their observations involves the second part of the educational process: the outgo. Children can reproduce in blocks or other materials a simple model of the classroom and then play out the relations they have observed. Blocks cut in multiples of a given unit are a valuable and adaptive material. Guide the children in their selection of props and blocks for the floor, doors, windows, desks, cupboards, and tables. Encourage them to observe carefully the size of the objects, their relative location, the relative distance between them, and to choose their symbols in relation to the original size. Help the children place the blocks or other objects used; help them to see the need for the desks to be in proper relation to each other, to the windows, to the doors, and to the teacher's desk. Help them see that it is necessary to think of the room as though they were looking down at it and to observe the distance between objects so that they will allow comparable space on their three-dimensional map. It might even be wise to have each child climb a ladder in order to get a view of the classroom from above (see Figure 14).

Figure 14

Classroom as Viewed from Above

After the simple model is finished, each child should have an opportunity to look down at it and carefully check relative size, location, and distance of the features as compared with the classroom itself. Sketches of the floor plan of the classroom can be duplicated and each child allowed to draw in the features for himself. The teacher should be available to help. The child may also be allowed to play with the model and try rearranging features.

TRIPS AROUND THE SCHOOL

When the children are well oriented in their classroom, it is time to take a trip through the school to get acquainted with the location of other classrooms and places having supporting functions: nurse's room, cafeteria, principal's office, secretary's office, supply room, gymnasium or all-purpose room, library, heating and maintenance area, etc. The children should be helped to notice likenesses and differences, how the rooms vary to serve their different functions. They should be observing with the intention of drawing a diagram of what they have seen when they get back to the classroom. This will tend to make them pay closer attention to relative location and the route they are following. If the school has more than one floor, it may be best to observe and diagram one floor at a time. The children will be less confused and will then be better able to compare the relative location by floors afterward.

Special trips can be planned in the school building for specific purposes. For example, in a visit to the secretary the attention of the children could be directed to the location of the telephone, typewriter, duplicating machine, record files, etc. It might be prearranged that the secretary would actually do a job of importance to the group—perhaps type and duplicate an original group story that the children bring with them—while they observe the process and then receive the end product. Returning to the classroom the children could set up props and act out what they observed, the teacher guiding them as to proper placement of the equipment, etc. They might duplicate the office with blocks and other props, or make a table model. They might draw pictures or diagram what they have seen. All of these experiences are the beginnings of mapping.

Another special trip of importance could be to the heating and maintenance area of the school. If heating is through a hot-water system, children could be helped to trace the pipes, etc. Many concepts may have their inception as children are guided to observe in their school building the sources and means of distribution of power for lighting, water for the sinks and toilets, etc.

The library is a room for study. First-graders might best enjoy a trip to it late in the year when they are farther along with their reading, but there is much to learn at any time about arrangement of books, files, furniture, and facilities that can be the basis of worthwhile discussion, dramatic play, and mapping experiences.

There are always new details to be observed in the school building—the location of fire alarm box, the fire bell, fire extinguisher, the route taken during a fire drill; display areas, bulletin boards, new exhibits; the setup for orchestra or band rehearsals; the stage being set for a play in rehearsal by some older group; some change or improvement being made in the school. All such activities have locational aspects relating to a given function and lend themselves to mapping. If the school is a community, as we claim, then the kindergarten and first-grade children become more and more a part of this community as they relate themselves to functions in the school outside their own classroom. If the first grade selects the school as a unit of study, no doubt display space could be obtained for a simple three-dimensional model of school and grounds, or for pictures, diagrams, etc., as a culmination. Each child could provide some form of map expression suitable to his ability and level of understanding.

We have been describing a relatively large elementary school. In a smaller school the same functions still generally appear, but in a telescoped form. Yet similar analysis of relation of location to function can be made, even if all the functions occur within one or two rooms.

Now that the child is oriented in the classroom and school building, it is time to take a trip around the school grounds and relate the school building to the surrounding space. Have the children locate the play areas and play equipment, walks, parking areas, trees, shrubs, and grassy areas. Guide them in seeing where and why each of these features is located in relation to the school building and to each other. Help them identify parts of the school from the outside as they walk around it.

If they can't identify everything from the outside on the first trip, let those things remain questions to be answered. Back in the classroom after a trip around the school, the children can reproduce what they have seen with props. Discussion and dramatic play may help them clarify relationships or give them an opportunity to ask questions about specific relationships that should be checked on the next trip.

The children could map the school and grounds right on their play area. Teacher and pupils could outline the grounds with white chalk, string, or masking tape, and the children could add what they had seen and also act as props themselves. The teacher should encourage some feeling for scale, relative location, direction, and distance. As the teacher goes from child to child, questions can be raised: Which way does the school face? If we make our school this size, how big should the sandbox be? Where should we place the bike and the auto parking area? Why there? Where are the trees? What is next to this grassy area? Where are the walks and paths? Why?

The children should be given opportunities to compare the inside and outside of the school building until they are so well oriented that they can identify features with ease from either position. They should now draw a pictorial representation of the school and its grounds. Give them chalk, crayons, a large sheet of paper, and a place in the classroom to work uninterruptedly. Chace had a group of first-graders make such drawings and relates, ". . . they realized that they were attempting to reproduce something they had actually seen and they tried to make their drawings recognizable. Many succeeded. The most common inaccuracy was in the coloring."[7] Chace does not explain why the children felt they had more freedom to depart from reality in the use of colors. We might speculate that they did not consider the coloring as part of the problem. (See Figure 15.)

Figure 15

The School on Its Grounds

Mapping Experiences

Early mapping experiences, following upon visits through and around school, were largely with dramatic play using three-dimensional objects, blocks, and some pictorial representation of the functions observed. With such a background, the children become ready for more abstract diagramming. Start with the first floor of the school. Draw it in the sand of the playground with sticks. Discuss the correct number and proper location of doors and windows. Have the children decide what symbols to use to represent doors, windows, etc. Orient the school as it is in outdoor space. The children can play out various functions on this floor plan. They can be teacher and pupils, guests visiting between rooms, etc. It is interesting to see the children open "windows," knock on "doors." Most children will not walk through "walls."

In the classroom the children can draw the same plan on the floor with chalk. They can now work for more accuracy. The diagram should be properly oriented, relative to the room. The children can now be introduced to the use of a legend.

As the children become more able, they can reproduce the floor plans of the school on paper (Figure 16). From the outdoor representation in the sand, to the floor plan, to the plan on paper, they are improving in accuracy and learning about scale. Even though they may not know the meaning of large scale and small scale or even the word *scale,* they are learning that this same school building can be represented in various sizes of diagrams. Gradually more symbols can be added—chairs, tables, etc. All should agree on the symbols to be used. Children can get ideas from each other. The teacher should make sure the orientation is always correct (north on map lined up with north in the out-of-doors) and should show them how to communicate their symbols with a legend. It is important to place the legend properly from the start. Put it in the *lower left corner* and show symbols and colors used. The name of the map and the "cartographers" can be placed in the lower right corner. Geographers agree that accepted practice should be used from the very beginning, thus avoiding learning that would later have to be corrected.

Having gone through this sequence under the teacher's direct guidance, children can be encouraged to do a similar sequence of mapping exercises about their homes. They can study the various rooms and their functions, analyze the relation of each room to the whole house, analyze the layout in any particular room. They can discuss their discoveries at school and compare differences in different houses. They may try to understand why certain things were located where they were and how function might be improved if they were relocated. The teacher, however, should be careful to keep the discussion on the level of analysis of function and location and not let one child start telling

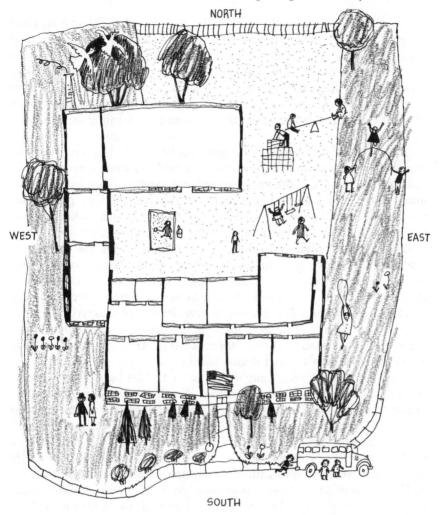

Figure 16

Plan of Interior of School on Its Grounds

another how his house or kitchen is "laid out all wrong." Also, the teacher should emphasize the need for having as much information as possible to explain why rooms and equipment were located as they were before one decides that a layout was improperly done. Maybe at the time the house was built, different conditions were effective, different tools and technics were in use. This is all good geographical thinking.

How the basic human activities are carried on in the home can be discussed as they relate to functions of rooms, room distribution, room layout, etc. Such discussion need not require long periods of sitting and talking. Much of it can be induced by the children's interest in these activities as it is reflected at sharing time. Some of it will appear in their dramatic play and can be guided into more fruitful learning by a few questions from the teacher. Such thinking can be encouraged in block building or in longer-lasting three-dimensional representations. A floor plan of a house may be a very difficult undertaking for a child, but with blocks he can accomplish much the same kind of learning in a medium he can handle.

Other activities relating to the home can be initiated in the classroom, where the teacher is able to give guidance and aid when necessary. The children can bring a dollhouse to school and together draw its plan. The group might visit a house being built and discover the floor plan before the outside walls and partitions shut it away from view. What technics are being used in its construction? The teacher might be able to get a blueprint of a building in progress and simplify it for the children to study as they watch the building going up, or the teacher might bring any simplified blueprint to class (Figure 17). Some of the children might enjoy copying it; others will like to look at it and recognize doors, windows, and so on. The class may also draw a plan for the home of "The Three Bears" with bedroom (three beds), living room (three chairs), kitchen (table, stools, three bowls). They might even build a "set" from their plans and dramatize the story.

A trip around the block might be planned. The basic human activities may again be used as a checklist. Watch for fire alarm boxes, fire hydrants, sewers, traffic lights or stop signs, and white lines for crossing the street in relation to conserving and protecting, for example. Watering systems and care of lawns and shrubs are conserving, too. If bare earth on a slope is visible within a school block, a trip soon after a rain may impart some understanding of erosion. Children might look for mailboxes, newspaper boxes, telephone poles and wires (communication). They might be asked to note especially all the different kinds of transportation they see. On a warm sunny day in a residential neighborhood they might come back with quite a list: scooters, wagons, roller skates, tricycles, bicycles, doll carriages, baby carriages, cars, bus, trucks, etc. If necessary, remind them that walking is also transportation and see if some concept of the great service of the wheel can be developed in classroom discussion; later the benefits of mechanical power added to the wheel can be brought out.

It can be especially worthwhile to plan some walks around the block when the postman or milkman is making deliveries, when sidewalk or street repairs are in progress, when some construction is taking place, when a water main is being laid or repaired, etc. Repeated trips can be planned to watch for seasonal changes. Select a bush or tree and watch it specifically at each season. Watch also for man-made changes

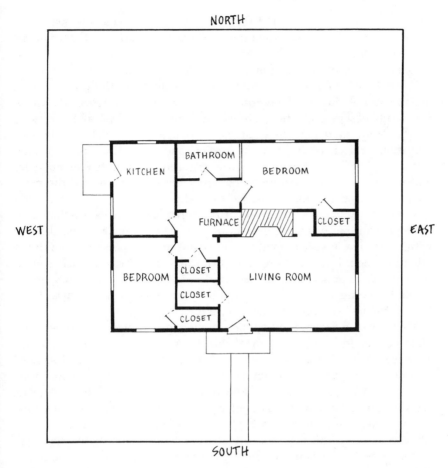

NORTH

WEST

EAST

SOUTH

KITCHEN

BATHROOM

BEDROOM

FURNACE

CLOSET

BEDROOM

CLOSET

CLOSET

LIVING ROOM

CLOSET

Figure 17

Floor Plan of a House

and improvements in a block over the period of the school year.

When the children return to the classroom, they should discuss and play out what they have seen. They should be encouraged to develop images using all of their senses. Have them describe sights, sounds, smells. Have them pretend that they are the dog they saw or the little children at play with a wagon. If something exciting in the world of adults occurred along the way, let them dramatize that. The trip might have been planned for various reasons and the specific reason would influence the reorganization of that excursion in the classroom. At least one trip should be taken around the campus limits for the purpose of checking the natural or man-made features that bound the school grounds, and the children should observe carefully with this in mind.

The bounding features should then be put on a map and the school set on the map with proper orientation. Thereafter, various other symbols may be added—for example, when a trip is made specifically to observe conserving and protecting functions on the school grounds.

For children who live in a rural area, a walk along the roads bounding the school site could be equally instructive. They too could check for means of fire protection, observe carefully the physical features of the landscape and note to what use it is being put, look for signs of irrigation or lack of it, signs of erosion and protection from erosion, watch for the various means of transportation, notice telephone poles and wires, watch for mail and newspaper boxes (perhaps see the mailman on his delivery route), notice the natural beauties and destruction of such beauty by encroachments of the spreading metropolis, etc. If by any chance a cultivated field or farm with dairy animals or chickens is within the area, a visit to analyze the layout may be possible. Children's attention should also be directed to the tools and technics being used. Visits to farms of several members of the class would permit comparison of land use and layout of the grounds, relative location of house, barn, fields, animals, equipment available, etc.

There is a difference of opinion among geographers as to whether children should be given cardinal directions for their maps at this age. However, there are several aspects of readiness for cardinal directions that might be developed. Even before children start going to school, they are aware of sun and shadows. Few of them have noticed, however, that the sun can be located at a particular place in the sky at a particular time of day. Take the children out on the playground at different times during a sunny day and call their attention to the position of the sun. Ask them, "Where is the sun early in the morning? Where is the sun at noon? Where is the sun in the late afternoon?" It is uncertain how much a first-grader can grasp concerning the cardinal points. By the end of the school year, however, a few youngsters may be able to say with some meaning, "The sun is in the eastern sky in the early morning. The sun is higher in the sky at noon. The sun is in the western sky in the late afternoon."

Children's attention should also be called to shadows. On the playground, let them observe the direction in which their shadows fall at noon and have them notice that all shadows fall in the same direction at that time (Figure 18). Go to the same place on the playground and have them observe where their shadows fall in the early morning and the late afternoon. Some children may be able to see the relation between the position of the sun in the sky and the direction in which their shadows fall on the ground. Such observations are essential for building the background needed later on for understanding directions on maps.

Figure 18

Children Observing Their Shadows

When children make maps showing the streets or roads bounding the school area, they may be given the terms *North, South, East,* and *West* to put on their maps, much as we use page numbers with children long before they understand their true meaning. The purpose here would be to familiarize the children with the terms as such. Placing the labels *North, South, East,* and *West* on the corresponding walls (or corners) of the classroom also serves this purpose.

The first step in developing an understanding of location and direction is to help children relate their bodies to space. "Which is your left hand? Which is your right hand? When you are facing another person, where is *his* left hand? Where is *his* right hand? How do we determine left and right?" Such games as "lobby-loo" are helpful. It is also helpful to use the terms *right* and *left* when talking to the children in the classroom: "The windows are to your left." "The door is to your right."

Children also need help in identifying other positions relative to themselves, as "step forward," "step back"; "in front," "behind"; "at the side";

"in the center"; "near, nearer, nearest"; "far, farther, farthest." Encourage the children to talk about the chalkboard *at the front*; the bulletin board *at the back*; radiators *to their left* side under the windows.

Many of these concepts have already been discussed in the pupil experiences suggested earlier in this chapter. Almost all are possible of firsthand observation in the family community and in the school community. Those that are not easily observable in the immediate out-of-doors can often be developed easily in classroom demonstrations. Concepts that are outside the firsthand experience of a particular group of first-graders should be omitted.

A concept difficult to understand and to portray on a map is elevation. Mitchell says that vertical orientation is more difficult for children than horizontal. Therefore, she suggests, before symbols of relief are presented, "try to get a dramatic, a motor sense, of elevation."[8] In first grade it may be best to represent elevation largely in three-dimensional symbols. Children can put chairs in a row to represent a wall or partition, leaving openings for doors, a stick across for a window, etc. Thus the third dimension is clearly an obstacle to movement. The children can then play in this structure. Children can also *talk* about directions; they can discuss *up* and *down* in relation to their own observations and activities. Encourage them to think of *up* as meaning away from the ground (away from the center of the earth) and *down* as meaning toward the ground (toward the center of the earth). Ask them to name all the things that they can think of that go up, that come down. For example, a kite flies up; a ball tossed up in the air comes down; a teeter-totter goes up and down. We climb up the steps and slide down the slide. We go up a hill and down a hill. We look up at an airplane in the air. We dig a hole down into the sand. If young children are helped to build some associations for *up* and *down*, they may avoid many later confusions.

When young children draw pictures, they use various means of showing three dimensions. They should not be pushed beyond these natural representations at this age. Two-dimensional diagramming should represent only horizontal orientation.

The making of three-dimensional models and pictorial maps should have given the children some readiness for reading and interpreting pictorial maps made by others of familiar areas. The teacher could show the class a pictorial map of a school. Together they could locate the rooms, analyze their relative location, and discuss how it compares with *their* school.

The children can also gain some experience in reading maps by interpreting the picture maps of other children in the class. And the teacher can prepare a flannel-base map of the school, its grounds, bounding streets and roads to which pictures of features nearby can be added.

Many supportive geographic concepts and appropriate symbols might be developed. Children can daily put weather symbols on the calendar. They may use pictorial symbols to represent the sun, clouds, rain or snow, or colored thumbtacks to represent the weather: yellow for sunny, gray for cloudy, blue for rain or snow. They can be taken outdoors to observe the grounds during and after a rain to see what they can discover about slope. Many natural features can be found in miniature where bare ground is exposed to actions of sun, wind, rain, running water. Children may thus observe actual illustrations of streams, tributaries, lakes, cliffs, shorelines, islands, and peninsulas in miniature. However, such school campus features are in miniature, and these features should be observed in larger size when possible so as to prevent misconceptions. When first-graders watch drainage on the playground after a rain, they are learning something of the relation of slope to the flow of water. But some of them will be learning much more, some of it correct and some perhaps erroneous.

Awareness of seasonal change should be encouraged. Attention should be called to the sequence followed as plants and trees start to get their leaves, their blossoms, their pods or fruit, and finally drop their leaves.

Children should observe the *effect* of daily changes in weather and the changing seasons. They should note the differences in clothing: they need rubber boots when it rains, warmer clothing to protect them in colder weather, lighter clothing in warmer weather. There are differences in activities in summer and in winter. When are people out planting? Raking leaves? Repairing and building homes? Discussion and dramatic play can follow observation. Children's concepts can be broadened beyond what they themselves might notice or relate by questions of the teacher in guiding discussion and play. How many children know, for example, that the reason we have a long summer vacation is that in farming areas in great-grandfather's time children were much needed to help with the work on the farm during the summer months?

Other supportive concepts can be developed through growing plants and having pets in the classroom. Children can study the effect on plants of different kinds of soil, amounts of moisture, and exposure to sun. They can observe the habits, needs, mating, etc., of pets. They can be taken on a trip to observe duck-mating season or hatching season.

We here use and modify a listing by Poole, Barton, and Baker[9] of concepts possible to develop with first-grade children:

| *Earth and Universe:* | The sun shines on the earth. |
| *Land and Landforms:* | Some land is hilly or mountainous and some land is level. |

There is soil on most of the surface of the land.
Plants grow on the land.
Streams flow across the land.
There are lakes on the land.
People travel across the land.
Soil is found on yards, farms, ranches, forests, and gardens.
Plants grow from the soil.
Food and fiber come from these plants.

Water and   Some water from rain or snow flows away and
  Water Bodies: some soaks into the ground.
                         Water forms streams and lakes.
                         The streams generally flow into the oceans.

Weather and Climate: Water falls as rain or snow.
                         Rain or snow falls from clouds.
                         The sun shines on clear days.
                         The sun warms the earth and the oceans.
                         Plants need sunshine and rain.

Plant Life: Some plants are cultivated.
                         Some plants grow naturally without cultivation.
                         Many plants grow from seeds.
                         Plants help to provide food and fiber.
                         People harvest products from plants.
                         Plants help to provide interesting scenery.

Animal Life: Some animals are domesticated.
                         Some animals live naturally in the wilderness environment.
                         Animals live and move about in different ways.
                         Animals help to provide food and skins and fiber.
                         Some animals work for man.
                         Some animals are pets.
                         Animals help to provide interesting environments.

Locational and Spatial People use transportation to overcome distance.
  Relationships: People use communication to overcome distance.

Distribution of   Most people live in family groups.
  Population: Some people live in rural environments.
                         More people live in urban environments.

Houses and Settlements: People need houses and other buildings for shelter.
                         Animals need shelter.

Production:	Different members of a family carry on specialized work.
	Man uses vehicles, machines, and tools to produce and exchange goods and services.
	Farmers raise plants and animals.
	Some people sell things in stores and markets.
Transportation and Communication:	People travel from place to place.
	People haul goods from place to place.
	People transport by automobile, bus, truck, train, boat, airplane, horse-drawn vehicle, etc.
	People communicate by means of voice, letter, telephone, telegram, etc.
Conservation:	People enjoy natural features in the environment.
	People often help to make their surroundings more beautiful and useful.
	People conserve property, resources, life, and health.
Recreation:	People have fun in their homes.
	People have fun outdoors.
	People like to play with pets.
	People like to look at animals.
	People like to look at natural scenery.
	People like to travel.

It will be noted that the methodology used for the primary grades follows a given pattern. First, the children start with the most immediate environment—in this instance the classroom. They observe carefully under guidance. This constitutes their firsthand experience. The experience is then reorganized, and relationships are clarified and developed through discussion and dramatic play using props and a base floor map (which is kept accurate within the limits of a crude scale and always properly oriented). Then mapping experiences follow: three-dimensional, pictorial, semipictorial. Always symbols are developed to represent previous observation. Eventually the teacher may present a map of school or grounds or a simplified blueprint of a floor plan which uses symbols familiar to the children.

The sequence as here developed provides many opportunities for the teacher to check the developing concepts and to correct simple errors as they first occur so that they do not become compounded in future experiences. It gives the children many opportunities to observe carefully and think out relations in a variety of ways, using all their sensorimotor mechanisms to support their thought processes. We believe that with such an approach young children will be able to develop many geographic concepts and skills previously believed to be too difficult for primary pupils. Also, such an approach provides much leeway for individual differences. There is no upper cutoff point for the more able children. Each may develop geographic concepts and skills just as far as his ability allows.

REFERENCES

1. Arnold Gesell and Frances Ilg, *The Child from Five to Ten* (New York: Harper & Row, Publishers, 1946).
2. *Ibid.*
3. Lucy S. Mitchell, *Young Geographers* (New York: The John Day Company, Inc., 1934).
4. *Ibid.*
5. Mamie L. Anderzhon and Hazel R. Newhouse, "Teaching Geography Out-of-Doors," *New Viewpoints in Geography*, Twenty-ninth Yearbook, National Council for the Social Studies (Washington: NCSS, 1959), pp. 177–199.
6. Mamie L. Anderzhon and Hazel R. Newhouse, "The Child Looks Upon the Map," *Journal of Geography*, 53:238–242 (September, 1954), p. 239.
7. Harriet Chace, "Map Skills in the First Grade," *Social Education*, 19:361–362 (December, 1955), p. 361.
8. Mitchell, *op. cit.*, p. 50.
9. Poole, Barton, and Baker, "Concept Chart," *Geographic Foundation Series* (New York: The Bobbs-Merrill Company, Inc., n.d.).

chapter five

THE BEGINNING GRADES
EMPHASES

/ *3. The Neighborhood Community*

General Introduction to the Neighborhood Community

As we focus on the neighborhood community, our pupils are probably seven- and eight-year-olds in the second grade. This emphasis will be developed in the same manner as the preceding one: First, we will describe briefly the development and learning abilities of this age group as reported in the literature; second, we will discuss the nature of the neighborhood community and its position within the social studies framework; third, we will analyze the four major objectives and pupil experiences for achieving them in the context of exploring each basic human activity; and finally, we will correlate the material so analyzed into a suggested sequence of detailed pupil experiences.

Child Development and the Learning Process

All students of child development are well aware that within any chronological age group there is a wide growth and experience range. However, general characteristics may be expected within a given age grouping, and these can guide the teacher who keeps in mind the fact that such information must be flexibly applied to any particular group.

Research shows that growth is, in gross terms, continuous. There is a development from the personal to the impersonal; from interests in the immediate environment to those further removed in time and place;

143

from a need for concrete, tangible objects to support thinking to an ability to think in increasingly abstract terms. Where does the second-grade child generally come in this continuum? Baker, in a study of children's contributions in free discussion, found that until the age of seven the child is predominantly occupied with his own personal affairs, not only in his private thought but in his discussion before a group.[1] In second grade, 61 per cent of the contributions in discussion concerned immediate, personal, active experience; 83 per cent were based on personal presence, direct contact; only 18 per cent were concerned with world or domestic news. Hill found that six- to eight-year-olds are interested in people of their immediate environment; home life, food, clothing, and familiar experiences are more readily understood and furnish the more correct concepts of primary grade children.[2] Mitchell corroborates the above findings:

> All five, six, and seven-year-old children still live largely in the here-and-now world around them, the world both of things and of human beings. They learn about things largely through firsthand experiences where they can find answers to their curiosities through exercising their own senses and muscles. Telling them about experiences of other people, in words, has comparatively little meaning for them. They have little power to "identify" with people with whom they have no personal contacts.[3]

Were Mitchell writing the above paragraph today, no doubt she would take note of the fact that modern communications bring the world of "far away in time and space" to the conscious attention of children. But TV, radio, and motion-picture sensory data are still vicarious for the child who sits passively before the screen with no opportunity to interact with the described situations. So in essence Mitchell is probably more correct in her reliance on direct and personal interaction with the "here and now" than are those who advocate a primary school emphasis on people remote in time or space. The current resolution to this pedagogical dilemma gives priority to the family, school, and neighborhood communities of the child's environment, but also relates the sensory data of the wider world coming through modern mass media to the here and now for purposes of comparison and contrast.

The cues given by Baker and Mitchell are very pertinent to developing a curriculum in map making and interpretation for this age. The sequence herein considered starts with firsthand experiences in the child's here and now which is the neighborhood community (and includes his family and his school), encourages use of all the sensorimotor mechanisms, and progresses toward the abstract only as the child becomes increasingly competent both through his growth and through planned exercises. Provision is made for a constant check on correct concept and skill development.

Many of the experiences planned depend on the ability of children to play and work together, on their becoming increasingly able to observe carefully and reproduce in some realistic form what they have seen on trips. What support does the literature give us for such a program?

Gesell points out that second-grade children are earnest, assiduous, and somewhat channelized.[4] They have a new "holding-on" quality. They take kindly to drill as individuals and in small groups. They want to be correct. They have a growing interest in form and performance. Learning takes place through projects and excursions. Centers of interest help them organize knowledge. Even the weather calendar can become an organizing interest.

In relation to space, Gesell says seven-year-olds are similar to six-year-olds but are able to develop deeper meanings and more understandings of the relationships they observe in the neighborhood community.[5] School and home are still important. There is a growing interest in the earth itself—its crust, stones—heat from fire, power from water, the sun, geology. With regard to immediate space orientation, the seven-year-old can go from his homeroom in school to another familiar room but wants specific directions. Interest in various parts of *his* neighborhood community is definitely expanding. He is becoming aware that there are other places than "just right here," but distance still has to be closely connected with the here and now. He still knows right and left primarily in relation to his own body.

At eight, there is a definite expansion in understanding of space and in freedom to move about in it. There is a deeper understanding of wider community relationships. The child is expansive and evaluative, adventurous, willing to try new things and new places. He can go to the city on a bus if he is put on it and met by someone. He can return home by bus; he can travel by bus on a prearranged route. He walks quite a distance in his own neighborhood. He is willing to try new ways since he now feels confident enough to do so. He is eager for trips to museums, zoos, and similar places of interest. He has a fairly clear notion of how the different parts of the community relate to each other. He can now distinguish right and left on the person of others as well as himself. He has achieved a new objectivity.

The Ohio State University study of *How Children Develop* also offers much for our planning for discussion, dramatic play, and mapping experiences.[6] In an analysis of research in the whole child development field, it reports as follows:

At 7:   Children can understand simple oral reasoning problems, tell time, measure in inches, write numbers, and understand the meaning of some symbols.

From 6 to 9:   They can solve simple everyday problems of living, such as writing and mailing a letter, going to the store and making purchases.

From 6 to 8:   Most children participate willingly in activities of the group. They can play together in groups of 7 or 8 for quite a long period of time.

From 7 to 8:   Children engage in many group cooperative activities: dramatic presentations of stories, conducting roadside stands, making boats, caring for pets, on which several children work together over a considerable period of time.

From 6 to 9:   Children interpret books and stories in terms of their own experiences.

There is a general trend toward realism and objectivity. Children ask, "How big is the biggest ocean liner?" "How high can an airplane fly?"

They try to reproduce in their drawings and paintings what they see. It is usually recognizable. They are making the transition to the realistic stage.

As previously suggested, there is disagreement in the literature as to just when children should be taught cardinal directions. Howe's study of children's knowledge of directions revealed that children do not know directions as well as is commonly supposed. Howe found, however, through a ten-week intensive program with children in Grades 1 through 3, that children *can be taught* directions by studying sun position. He was successful with 50 per cent of the first-graders, 75 per cent of the second-graders, and 88 per cent of the third-graders. He concludes that, "though it may in some instances be desirable to begin instruction in the latter part of grade 2, the evidence points to the 3rd grade as the most favorable period of comprehension."[7] Gesell reports a marked improvement in understanding of orientation in regard to cardinal points of the compass at age seven.[8] The concept of cardinal directions seems to be one whose full meaning matures slowly over a long period of time. The classroom teacher through experimentation must determine the pupils' degree of readiness for experiences of this kind. However, directions in relation to local landmarks should be within the understanding of most seven- and eight-year-olds.

We reported studies of children's reasoning in an earlier chapter. This research in relation to seven- and eight-year-olds can be summarized as follows: Children still live very much in a here-and-now world. They still need personal contact in order to identify with something. However, verbal processes are growing, and they are developing increasing ability to symbolize and reason if the problems are within their experiences. By this we mean that though symbols of general ideas are taking form, they are still closely tied up with direct images. The trend is toward realism and objectivity. They are interested in how things function.

Scope and Sequence of the Social Studies Framework

The *sequence* of social studies experiences within which we are operating is based on the expanding communities of men. In the kindergarten and first grade we were concerned with providing geographic concepts and map experiences within the arena of the family community and the school community. In the second grade we will focus on the neighborhood community, to be followed by the next larger arena, the local communities (city, county, or metropolitan area), in the third grade.

The studies in child development of seven- and eight-year-olds give evidence of the child's growing feeling of familiarity with, and spirit of inquiry into, the neighborhood community. Occasionally he enjoys a trip to the museum, downtown area, or the county fair in the local community, the next expanding circle in geographic and cultural space. In stories, radio, and TV he may go far beyond the boundaries of the neighborhood or local communities; however, the major focus and area of direct contact will be concentrated in his own neighborhood.

For our purposes the neighborhood community may be defined as the group of families within an area served by a single elementary school and including the nearest gas stations, markets, post office, churches, and other service agencies necessary to meet immediate needs at this level. In an urban community this area is usually within walking distance of both home and school. The neighborhood is not self-sufficient but depends on the local, state, national, and even the world community to provide solutions for many of its problems. Nevertheless, the basic human activities can be observed in some form at the neighborhood level. Members of the neighborhood community may, and often do, organize to improve their education, recreation, transportation facilities, etc., although the neighborhood itself is not organized as a political unit.

The nearest rural equivalent to the urban neighborhood might be the township, including the school and nearest service institutions with which it has contact, or the village at the crossroads with its church, service station, small cluster of dwellings, and the immediate farm families who send their children to a common school. There is no exact correspondence to the urban neighborhood community. Geographically the township is much larger, usually six miles square, as determined by the public land system of the United States. It often has an administrative government function not found in the urban neighborhood community. The village, on the other hand, is often much smaller. For want of a better term, we will refer to the rural township as representing the neighborhood focus. For us it will include those families with children in the same school and those service institutions in closest proximity to them.

Analysis in Terms of the Basic Human Activities

We can see how the neighborhood community expands beyond the school and the home communities and enlarges the pupil's relationships with all the basic human activities. Within it lie many firsthand experiences which can become the basis for developing map skills and geographic understandings.

In the urban neighborhood, the branch fire station offers protection and will even send a fireman and a ladder to rescue a frightened kitten trapped in a neighborhood tree. The child can buy a loaf of bread for his mother at the corner grocer or take his shoes to the cobbler to be repaired. In rural districts, the school bus provides transportation to the school, and the milk truck comes for its daily pickup. In urban and rural neighborhoods alike, communicating is face to face or via telephone; the daily news and entertainment are brought into homes through newspapers, radio, and television. There is the local church and there are places of amusement. The township may be organized as a local unit of the government; the neighborhood has its "Improvement Club," which works to obtain a needed mailbox or a traffic light or arranges for each family to plant a tree and beautify the area.

The following section analyzes our four basic objectives in terms of each of the basic human activities and offers suggestions for rich firsthand experiences that will contribute to the further development of map skills and geographic understandings within the new arena, the neighborhood community.

THE NEIGHBORHOOD COMMUNITY (EMPHASIS 3)

*Basic Human Activity: Protecting and Conserving
Life, Health, Property, and Resources*

OBJECTIVES	PUPIL EXPERIENCES
1. *Ability to observe thoughtfully.* Observe the neighborhood to find protecting and conserving functions. Question who is involved.	1. *Firsthand experiences.* Observe location and distribution of protecting and conserving activities and associated features in the

Where? With what? Why?

2. *Ability to reason about things geographic.*

Analyze examples of protecting and conserving in the neighborhood. Note
(1) relative location of these features;
(2) relation of location to function;
(3) relative direction (bounding areas);
(4) protective relation of people to each other, to plants, animals, land, property.

3. *Ability to map in some form* what

neighborhood, such as traffic lights, stop streets, white lines for crossing; police station, police phones; firehouse, fire hydrants, fire alarm boxes; medical clinic; hospital; pet hospital; reservoir. Observe natural landscape and precautions, if any, to preserve it.

2. *Reorganized experience.*

a. *Discussion.* Analyze: Who protects and conserves? Where? With what? Why? How does distribution of features relate to function? Where is the fire station located in relation to homes? Are stations distributed in such a way as to give homes best protection? Are more stations needed? How is painting and repairing of homes, fences, buildings protecting?

b. *Dramatic play.* Dramatize protecting and conserving functions of the neighborhood. Examples:
(1) What route would a fire truck take to get to school most quickly? What hydrants would be used? How?
(2) How would an ambulance come from the nearest hospital? Would it come from the nearest hospital or is there a special emergency hospital that must be called? For what kind of reasons might it come? What would it do?
(3) How do we protect plants, animals, soil, natural landscape? Where do we plant trees and seeds? How do we care for plants and animals?
(4) How do we paint and repair for protection?

c. *Mapping.* During a trip in the

has been observed.

Agree on use of symbols to represent above protective features such as streets and roads, water bodies, etc., included in the area. Color symbols may be used to show distribution of police protection, fire coverage, areas of natural landscape. Show

(1) location (accurate as to blocks or in miles);

(2) relative distance and direction from landmarks;

(3) representations in different sizes (crude use of scale);

(4) legend to communicate.

4. *Ability to read through symbols* of maps to the landscape or realities thus represented. Ability to read a simplified map of the neighborhood prepared by the teacher, using only familiar symbols of protecting and conserving life, health, property, and resources.

neighborhood to note particular conserving and protecting features, some children should make a careful count of blocks, others make sure to note all cross streets, and others note landmarks passed to arrive at the given place. The intention should be that on return to the classroom the trip will be mapped. Re-enact the route in dramatic play using props, and with teacher's guidance make a floor plan, being accurate as to relative location and approximate distances. The same can be done with blocks. Reproduce sketch on large paper, then on smaller paper, with increasing accuracy. This crude street map of the neighborhood should be accurate as to blocks (or miles in the country). It can be placed on a large table and oriented with outdoor space. Three-dimensional symbols of protecting and conserving activities can be added. These can be replaced with pictorial and finally with semipictorial symbols.

3. *Using and interpreting maps made by others.*

The teacher can prepare a neighborhood map enlarged from a city or county map and using the conventional symbols, but only those representing features the children have seen, discussed, re-enacted, and mapped themselves. Since all features will have been seen previously, the children should be able to associate imagery of the realities represented with the symbol used.

If the children seem able, they may get a street or road map of city or county and locate features outside the neighborhood that are important to protecting and conserving functions in the neighborhood. They should note location of these larger community features relative to those in the neighborhood, such as the metropolitan water supply system.

Basic Human Activity: Producing, Exchanging, Distributing, and Consuming Goods and Services

OBJECTIVES	PUPIL EXPERIENCES
1. *Ability to observe thoughtfully.* Observe the neighborhood as a community in which producing, exchanging, distributing, consuming occur.	1. *Firsthand experiences.* On the way to school keep alert for producing, exchanging, distributing, consuming activities. On various trips notice distribution of features concerned with these functions. (1) Locate producing features: milk bottling plant, newspaper plant, shoe repair shop, factories. In rural areas there often seems to be much more producing: crops, animals, milk, eggs, etc. (2) Locate exchanging and distributing features: Trucks distribute goods and services to stores, homes, factories. Observe how light, heat, water, sewage disposal are piped or wired to home. Mailman and newsboy distribute letters and news to homes. (3) Locate consuming features: Water, heat, electricity are consumed in homes, schools, stores, factories, farms, etc. Food is consumed at home, at school, in restaurants. Buildings themselves, cars, clothing are consumed in the sense that they wear out and have to be repaired or replaced.
2. *Ability to reason about things geographic.*	2. *Reorganized experience.* a. *Discussion.* Analyze: Who pro-

Analyze distribution of producing, exchanging, distributing, consuming functions and features in the neighborhood. Notice
(1) relative location of features;
(2) relation of location to function (land use);
(3) relation of land use to land form—often much easier to see in rural areas;
(4) relative time needed to produce and distribute by hand power as compared to machine power.

duces, distributes, consumes? Where? With what? Why? How does distribution of features relate to functions? What helps determine relative location of features? Of what importance does land form seem to be? Does there seem to be a pattern? Might the distribution be better if it were different? What role do children play in producing, exchanging, distributing, consuming? Parents? Teachers? Others in the neighborhood?

b. *Dramatic play.* Dramatize producing, exchanging, distributing, consuming activities of the neighborhood. Examples: bottling, distribution, and consumption of milk. Compare home and commercial laundering; compare baking at home and baking in small neighborhood bakery or in a large bread plant. In a rural area children may dramatize in order to analyze in a new way many of the activities they have previously taken for granted at home. They may compare differences and likenesses between farms and city in producing, consuming, and exchanging activities. Stories might help. Urban children might be helped to dramatize the difference also.

3. *Ability to map in some form* what has been observed.

Agree on symbols to make crude street or road map of the neighborhood. It should be accurate as to number of blocks or miles, approximate location of producing, exchanging, distributing, consuming features. Features should be added gradually. Symbols will be needed to represent streets, roads, water bodies, and cultural features. Color

c. *Mapping.* Take a trip in the neighborhood to observe specific producing, exchanging, distributing, consuming functions and features; look at pictures before or after, depicting the same, similar, or contrasting functions; look at pictures when direct observation cannot be made. Get information from reading also. Map in following order of difficulty:

may be used to differentiate land use.

4. *Ability to read through symbols of maps to landscape or realities thus represented.* Ability to read a simplified map prepared by the teacher, using the conventional symbols, but only for those features seen and discussed by the class. As the children are able, they may be helped to locate the neighborhood on a simple street or road map of city or county.

(1) Tangible: Re-enact using props to depict relative location of the various steps in a production process. Example: large bakery. Also, show route of the process. On a farm show the ground plan or the layout of the milking barn in a dairy operation. Show the route taken by trucks coming to the neighborhood markets, and then to school, restaurant, or homes. On a farm show the produce leaving the farm. The route of products could be re-enacted on a base map of the township.

(2) Pictorial: Draw pictures of what has been seen or discussed, roughly accurate as to relative location and distance.

(3) Semipictorial: Draw large sketch on floor or large paper or oilcloth, with teacher guidance, using agreed-on symbols to depict features.

3. *Using and interpreting maps made by others.*

Present a simplified map of the neighborhood drawn by the teacher. This can be made by projecting the neighborhood or township from a larger map. Have children locate the familiar features. As the children are able, they may begin noting producing, exchanging, distributing, and consuming features on the larger city or county map to discover lines of transportation flow involved. Then note relation to the neighborhood or township emphasis.

Basic Human Activity: Transporting People and Goods

OBJECTIVES

1. *Ability to observe thoughtfully.*
   Observe the neighborhood as a community which makes use of transporting functions. Question who is involved. From where? To where? With what? Why?

2. *Ability to reason about things geographic.*
   Analyze examples of transporting seen in the neighborhood and between home and school. Note
   (1) relation of time to distance when using different means of transportation;
   (2) distance in terms of blocks or miles;
   (3) relation of function to technology: effect of power on transportation;
   (4) effect of distance caused by obstacles that prevent a direct route: hills, cultural features, water bodies. How do bridges, tunnels, overpasses, canals, cab stands, bus stops help to overcome geographic factors in neighborhood?

PUPIL EXPERIENCES

1. *Firsthand experiences.*
   Observe roads and streets and the kind of transportation that occurs on the route from home to school and in the neighborhood. Locate water bodies, hills, mountains, man-made transportation facilities, and obstructions to transportation. Notice trucks, buses, cars, bicycles, wagons, and other means of transportation. Notice how house and building numbers get larger away from starting points. Notice the plan of numbering or naming streets and avenues.

2. *Reorganized experience.*
   a. *Discussion.* Discuss how roads and streets differ in width, surfacing, and use. Which have bus routes? Which have trucks on them? Which have streetcars? Where are the railroad tracks? What seems important in determining function? In what relative direction do streets or roads run? Where do these streets or roads go? Discuss the time it takes to walk to school, to go shopping, to get to the mailbox.. Is it faster to ride a bike, roller-skate, ride a horse, or walk? How does that compare in time to going in an automobile or truck or boat or helicopter? What obstacles prevent a direct route? What must be done to overcome these obstacles? What is the relation of time and distance and means of transportation used?
   b. *Dramatic play.* Dramatize various methods of transportation in the neighborhood. Who uses? When and for what different

3. *Ability to map in some form* what
   has been observed. Ability to
   (1) make crude street or road
       maps (three-dimensional, pic-
       torial, semipictorial) of urban
       neighborhood or rural town-
       ship, oriented with outdoor
       space, accurate as to number
       of blocks or miles (in crude
       scale), and correct as to direc-
       tion in which bounding streets
       or roads run;
   (2) use symbols representing
       streets, roads, water bodies in-
       cluded in the area;
   (3) with symbols, differentiate
       main arteries, bus routes, truck
       routes, streets with streetcar
       tracks, railroads;
   (4) employ some means of depict-
       ing physical obstacles if they
       occur.

purposes? How are time and
distance determining factors?
c. *Mapping.*
   (1) Take a walk in the neigh-
       borhood to observe layout
       of streets or roads, bus
       routes, streetcar tracks,
       trucks, railroad tracks.
       Notice direction of heavier
       traffic and variation in
       width and surface of
       streets, roads, or canals
       carrying different kinds of
       traffic.
   (2) Begin measurement—feet,
       yards; pace off distances in
       schoolroom, schoolyard,
       around the block or sur-
       rounding roads. Estimate
       and check blocks in a mile,
       time necessary to walk a
       block and/or a mile and to
       drive the same distances.
   (3) Make a model in blocks on
       a table of street or road lay-
       out in the neighborhood
       and put on cars, trucks,
       buses, trains where they
       normally occur; also place
       people walking, riding bikes
       or wagons, pushing baby
       carriages, etc. Add traffic
       controls (traffic lights, rail-
       road signals, etc.).
   (4) Draw a rough sketch with
       pictorial symbols of means
       and routes of transporta-
       tion seen in the neighbor-
       hood. Obstacles that affect
       direction of traffic should be
       included. Agree on sym-
       bols to represent natural
       and man-made features
       that are pertinent. Agree
       on rough scale to represent
       a block or a mile.

4. *Ability to read through symbols* of
   maps to the landscape or realities

3. *Using and interpreting maps made
   by others.*

thus represented. Ability to read teacher-made maps of neighborhood or rural township depicting transporting features in familiar symbols. Eventually children should be able to locate the neighborhood or township on a commercial map of city or county.

Read a simplified street or road map of the neighborhood or township, drawn by the teacher by enlarging part of a city or county map. Transporting features should be depicted in conventional symbols, which should be familiar now. Finally, children should be able to locate their neighborhood or township on a commercial county map. Children should be helped to notice the extension of important arteries of transportation to get an idea of where neighborhood streets and roads might take them.

Basic Human Activity: Communicating Facts, Ideas, and Feelings

OBJECTIVES

PUPIL EXPERIENCES

1. *Ability to observe thoughtfully.*
   Observe neighborhood as a community in which communicating activities occur. Question who is involved. From where? To where? With what? Why?

1. *Firsthand experiences.*
   Observe distribution of communicating activities and associated features between home and school and in the neighborhood. Locate telephone exchange building, telephone poles and wires, roadside telephone booths; television aerials; mailboxes, branch post office; newspaper office, newspaper stands or boxes; fire alarm boxes; street signs; etc. Is there any pattern of distribution?

2. *Ability to reason about things geographic.*
   Analyze examples of communicating in the neighborhood, to note
   (1) communication is a means of overcoming distance;
   (2) relation of means of communication used to time it takes;
   (3) calendar and clock as means of communicating time information;
   (4) relative location of features of communication.

2. *Reorganized experience.*
   a. *Discussion.* Discuss relative amount of time it takes to communicate by letter, telephone, newspaper, radio, TV, in relation to distance. Study calendar as a means of recording time—time of week, month, season, year. Study the clock as a means of learning time of day. What problems in location do radio and TV stations face? What problems do telephone wires create?

b. *Dramatic play.* Dramatize the operation of various forms of neighborhood communication, their maintenance, and their repair. Be a mailman delivering mail or a newsboy delivering his papers. Dramatize finding a location for a radio or TV station that will insure good broadcasting. Dramatize a situation in which the time element of a given means of communication is important. Act out what to do if the telephone is dead in an emergency.

3. *Ability to map in some form* what has been observed. Ability to locate on maps of some form (three-dimensional, pictorial, or semipictorial) features concerned with communication.

Agree on· symbols to represent newspaper office, telephone exchange building, telephone poles and wires, TV stations, radio stations, mail drops, branch post office, library branch, motion-picture theaters, etc.

c. *Mapping.*
   (1) Have large base map of neighborhood (teacher-made) after having worked through early stages with children.
   (2) Together locate the pertinent feature under discussion—one medium at a time.
   (3) Have identical desk-size base maps for each child (teacher-made) on which children then gradually add pertinent features. Agree on symbols. Use conventionalized symbols when possible.
   (4) Show route of local postman on map.
   (5) Show paper boy's neighborhood route.

4. *Ability to read through symbols* of maps to the realities thus represented. Ability to read teacher-made maps of neighborhood or rural township depicting communicating activities in familiar symbols.

Eventually children should be able to locate the neighborhood or township on a commercial map of city or county.

3. *Using and interpreting maps made by others.*

Read a simplified street or road map of neighborhood drawn by teacher and bearing familiar communicating features. If conventional symbols are not yet in use, they should gradually be learned and used. Locate the neighborhood on a city or county map. Note extension of communicating features as they influence communication within the neighborhood. For example, if there is no radio or TV station, no newspaper plant or telephone exchange in the immediate neighborhood, it would be worthwhile to visit some of these places, locate them on the map, and give some attention to the fact that the neighborhood is too small a community to afford such large and expensive communication facilities but that they are provided by the next larger—the local communities —to be studied next in the sequence of expanding communities. Analyze their location in relation to serving the neighborhood.

Basic Human Activity: Expressing Aesthetic and Spiritual Impulses

OBJECTIVES	PUPIL EXPERIENCES
1. *Ability to observe thoughtfully.*	1. *Firsthand experiences.*

1. *Ability to observe thoughtfully.*

Observe the neighborhood as a community in which aesthetic and spiritual impulses find expression.

1. *Firsthand experiences.*

Observe aesthetic and spiritual features in the neighborhood. Distinguish between natural areas of beauty and man-made additions or improvements. Locate parks, gardens, landscaped areas. In what ways has man enhanced or destroyed the landscape? Locate churches and other places of worship in the neighborhood. Note the architecture, religious denominations. Notice where they are located in relation to residences. Is there a pattern of distribution?

2. *Ability to reason about things geographic.*

Analyze examples of aesthetic and spiritual expression in the neighborhood. Note
(1) size and location of areas of natural beauty, location of places of worship;
(2) pattern of distribution;

2. *Reorganized experience.*
   a. *Discussion.* Analyze size and location of natural areas of beauty. How are they being preserved or destroyed? Where are the largest areas? Where are there none? Where are the parks and whom do they serve? Which areas are neglected?

(3) distance from home;

(4) time it takes to get there.

3. *Ability to map in some form* what has been observed (three-dimensional, pictorial, semipictorial).

Agree on symbols to show extent and location of churches, museums, libraries, music halls, art galleries, parks and gardens, etc.

Why? Where are the churches and other places of worship? Whom do they serve? Discuss natural beauties observed in terms of all the senses—smell, sight, taste, sound, feel. What can children do to help beautify?

b. *Dramatic play.* Dramatize a visit to a place of beauty. Show how it smells, sounds, feels, as well as how it looks. Roll in the grass or climb a hill. Act out the route to get there; illustrate how long it takes. Are you tired? Is there much space or is it crowded? Dramatize planting and caring for lawns, flowers, bushes, trees.

c. *Mapping.* Estimate extent of areas of natural beauty in terms of city blocks or portion of rural neighborhood. Check by taking trips. Estimate distance in terms of time to walk or ride. Estimate distance to get to areas of beauty in terms of city blocks or miles. Reproduce places of beauty in a sand table or other three-dimensional model. Draw pictures or get pictures of nearby places of beauty. Agree on pictorial symbols for trees, parks, water bodies, and place these symbols on a large base map of the neighborhood, or display pictures around map and draw a string from each picture to the location on the map. Draw semipictorial representations on a large base map with the help of the teacher. Draw the same on desk-sized base map. Note relative location of landscaping, lawns, water bodies, natural vegetation, parks. Locate churches, opera house, museum, or other cultural features wherein aesthetic and spiritual impulses are

4. *Ability to read through symbols* of maps to the landscape or realities thus represented. Ability to read teacher-made maps of the neighborhood with familiar and then with conventional symbols.

Locate park areas. Locate church, museum, music hall, water bodies on map of city or county.

expressed. Note location of these features in relation to home and to school.

3. *Using and interpreting maps made by others.*

Read simplified street or road map of neighborhood made by teacher showing parks and other aesthetic features and churches. What helps determine their location? Locate neighborhood or rural township on city or county map. Note other large parks, opera house, art museum, and other aesthetic or spiritual features whose symbols are familiar. The focus is on the neighborhood, and these other features in the larger community should be located and discussed as they relate to and serve the neighborhood. For example, what features are lacking in the neighborhood that are available in the next larger community?

Basic Human Activity: Providing Recreation

<table>
<tr><th>OBJECTIVES</th><th>PUPIL EXPERIENCES</th></tr>
</table>

1. *Ability to observe thoughtfully.*

Observe the neighborhood as a community in which recreational activities occur. Analyze distribution of recreational features. Where located? Why there?

2. *Ability to reason about things geographic.*

Analyze recreational areas and facilities in the neighborhood as to

(1) relative location;

(2) relation of location to function;

(3) relation to physical and cultural features;

(4) distribution;

(5) distance from home and school.

1. *Firsthand experiences.*

Observe distribution of features of recreation (natural and cultural) and their location relative to residential, commercial, or farming areas.

2. *Reorganized experience.*

a. *Discussion.* Where are recreational features? What kind are there? Whom do they serve? Are they operated by public or private parties? Are they equally accessible to all? Are any neighborhood areas unduly neglected? How far are they in terms of time and blocks or miles? How spacious or cramped are these features? Do the physical features of the landscape influence location? Does land use influence location and/or space available for recreational features?

b. *Dramatic play.* Dramatize routes to get to features of recreation. Are they near or far in terms of time, blocks, or miles? Are they on direct routes or are they difficult to get to? What means of transportation are needed to get there? Act out what to do when there, using all senses and muscles. Who can't get there? Why? How might they feel?

3. *Ability to map in some form* what has been observed.

Discover use of symbols (three-dimensional, pictorial, semipictorial) for community center, swimming facilities, parks, play areas. Agree on color symbols—parks, green; water bodies, blue. Use legends. Commercial recreational facilities (golf course, bowling alley, motion-picture theater, playland, sports store, etc.) should be considered for mapping in appropriate symbols.

c. *Mapping.* Mapping is based on trips, pictures, reading, and discussion. A crude base map is made for dramatic play above. A table model can also be made using toy vehicles and toy figures √ to show routes to recreational areas and activities there. Pictures of places of recreation can be set around map and string drawn from each picture to its location on the map. Locate parks and other features. Draw a ground plan of the neighborhood park or play area. Agree on symbols and colors to be used. Trace routes from school or home to recreational areas. Also locate and map private recreational facilities used by families and by school.

4. *Ability to read through symbols* of maps to landscape or realities thus represented. Ability to read teacher-made maps of the neighborhood using familiar, agreed-upon symbols and then replace them with conventional symbols. Ability to locate on a map of city or county the recreational features of the neighborhood, both public and private.

3. *Using and interpreting maps made by others.*

Read simplified street or road map of the neighborhood made by teacher and showing recreational features, using agreed-on symbols, later replacing them with conventional symbols, if any. Locate the neighborhood on a city or county map. Locate familiar recreational features in neighborhood. Locate a recreational area outside the neighborhood that commonly serves the neighborhood. Look for recreational features elsewhere in the city or county.

Basic Human Activity: Providing Education

OBJECTIVES	PUPIL EXPERIENCES
1. *Ability to observe thoughtfully.* Observe the neighborhood as a community in which educational activities occur.	1. *Firsthand experiences.* Take trips to discover distribution in the neighborhood of facilities providing education: public and private schools, libraries, museums, community center. Visit other schools and compare them with your own.
2. *Ability to reason about things geographic:* (1) number and distribution of various types of schools; (2) relative distance from home to school at different educational levels; (3) ways in which physical features affect distribution of schools; (4) ways in which cultural uses of land influence location and distribution of schools.	2. *Reorganized experience.* a. *Discussion.* Are all elementary schools alike? How do they vary? What might be some of the reasons? Where are they located? How far do children have to travel to get to them? Compare your school to the junior high and senior high as to size, number of pupils enrolled, and distance to travel. Discuss relative number of elementary, junior high, and senior high schools. Do schools seem to be distributed according to population location? Do physical features of the land affect location? Do cultural features affect location? What seems to determine location? Size? b. *Dramatic play.* Dramatize going to school. What is to be seen, heard, smelled, done along the way? Dramatize playing school. How might you feel in the junior high school?
3. *Ability to map in some form* what has been observed. Discover use of symbols (three-dimensional, pictorial, semipictorial)	c. *Mapping.* Count blocks or miles to school in terms of time to get there, blocks or miles walked. Estimate distance to get to

to represent schools, library, museums. Color symbols may be used. Use legend.

junior or senior high by comparison. Walk if possible and check distance. Draw routes to various public and private schools on large-scale base map of neighborhood. Locate library, community center, or museum (if any) in neighborhood. Draw routes to get to these places from home and school. Do the same on smaller individual base maps of the neighborhood.

4. *Ability to read through symbols of maps to the realities thus represented.* Ability to read simplified teacher-made map of the neighborhood, depicting educational features in familiar symbols, and then in conventional symbols, if any.

Locate neighborhood on city or county map. Locate own school.

3. *Using and interpreting maps made by others.*

Read simplified teacher-made map of neighborhood depicting schools, library, community center, museum, etc. Locate neighborhood on city or county map. Locate those educational features regularly used by neighborhood but not found in neighborhood. Is there any pattern of distribution of educational features that becomes apparent?

Basic Human Activity: Organizing and Governing

OBJECTIVES

PUPIL EXPERIENCES

1. *Ability to observe thoughtfully.*

Observe the neighborhood as a community in which organizing and governing activities occur. Who is involved? Where? How?

1. *Firsthand experiences.*

Take trips to neighborhood institutions and organizations, both formal and informal, where organizing and governing functions can be observed: police or fire station, hospital, supermarket, bakery, laundry, shoe repair shop, telephone exchange, post office, park or playground, church, library, community center, school. In a rural area there is organizing for cooperative buying and selling, use of farm machinery; provisions are made for fire and police protection, for getting utilities, for irrigation. The farm itself can be analyzed to clarify its organization.

2. *Ability to reason about things geographic.*

Analyze examples of organizing and governing in the neighborhood to note

(1) who is involved;

(2) location of activities;

(3) relation of location to function;

(4) purpose of the organization.

2. *Reorganized experience.*

a. *Discussion.* Analyze how the neighborhood organizes to provide many basic human functions. Who is involved? Where? How do they go about it? Which organizing and governing activities can the neighborhood not provide for itself and must therefore depend on the local community? What helps determine the layout of the firehouse, the market, the post office, the library, the farm?

b. *Dramatic play.* Act out how people in the neighborhood organize to provide the many necessary human functions. Dramatize how problems are discussed and decisions made that might affect what happens in the neighborhood. For example: How do neighbors get a policeman to guide traffic at a school crossing? How do neighbors get a mailbox where it is needed? How do neighbors get the fire department to burn the dry grass and weeds from a vacant lot? How are the school traffic patrols organized? How does the school get a stop sign or traffic light put in where it is needed? Who paints the white lines on the streets or roads for pedestrian crossings and traffic lanes?

3. *Ability to map in some form* what has been observed.

Discover use of symbols (three-dimensional, pictorial, semipictorial) to represent agencies involved in governing and organizing functions in the neighborhood. Map the layout of some of these institutions and agencies, both informal and formal.

c. *Mapping.* Make three-dimensional models of some of the places visited. Move symbols to show when the function is in operation: for example, the operational layout within the firehouse, and the changes that occur when a call comes in. Make pictorial and semipictorial representations. Draw sketches of the floor plan and routes of movement.

4. *Ability to read through symbols* of maps to the realities thus represented. Ability to locate in the neighborhood those agencies responsible for organizing and governing and to trace the spatial channels followed in carrying out these basic human activities.

3. *Using and interpreting maps made by others.*

Read floor plans made by the teacher of various institutions and agencies visited. Show routes employed when functions are operative. Locate these same organizing and governing bodies on a teacher-made map of the neighborhood. Locate the same on a city or county map. Locate also some of the outstanding organizing and governing agencies that are outside of the neighborhood, for example, the city hall or county courthouse. In many instances police and fire protection are also organized outside the neighborhood boundaries, but the neighborhood depends on them.

Basic Human Activity: Creating Tools and Technics

OBJECTIVES

1. *Ability to observe thoughtfully.*
   Observe the neighborhood as a community in which tools and technics are used and created.

PUPIL EXPERIENCES

1. *Firsthand experiences.*
   Observe any construction or repair taking place in the neighborhood: buildings, streets, or roads, trenches for supply or sewage disposal lines, telephone poles. Look to see what tools and technics are being used. Watch if the same type of job is sometimes done a different way. What accounts for the difference? Visit a large and small bakery, a large and small laundry, a large and small candy-making operation if these are available in the neighborhood. Lead the children to take note of the differences in tools and technics used. Keep on the alert for any innovation in response to a neighborhood need.

2. *Ability to reason about things geographic.*
   Analyze the effect of the tools and technics being used:
   (1) What happens when an op-

2. *Reorganized experience.*
   a. *Discussion.* Analyze the difference in a large operation as against a small one (bakery, laundry, candy factory, various

eration gets larger?

(2) What happens when more automatic tools and technics are used?

(3) What happens when a neighborhood grows rapidly and needs to organize sewage or water systems? Are these efforts creative technics to solve a neighborhood problem?

construction projects in the neighborhood). Why do larger companies have more power and/or automated machinery? What brought about its introduction? What happens when more advanced tools are used? Why aren't large machines used for small road repairs? Do you sometimes see the same job done in different ways? Why?

b. *Dramatic play.* Re-enact the situations described above. Dramatize how people feel when a change in tools and technics occurs: Mother gets a new household appliance, a trench-digging tool takes the place of a shovel, machinery replaces a hand worker cutting and wrapping candy, a large machine instead of a smaller mixer mixes the batter in a bakery, a farmer gets a tractor to replace a horse, a machine bales the hay.

3. *Ability to map in some form* what has been observed.

On a base map, add symbols for the new roads and construction that have occurred recently. Note how the new additions change the land use.

c. *Mapping.* Have the children draw contrasting floor-plan maps (three-dimensional, pictorial, semipictorial) of a large and small manufacturing or construction operation they have visited. The contrasting maps should be based on the same scale so that size and complexity can be compared.

4. *Ability to read through symbols* of maps to the realities thus represented. Ability to read a map prepared by the teacher, using conventional symbols where applicable, but only for those features of creating new tools and technics for the neighborhood seen and discussed by the class.

3. *Using and interpreting maps made by others.*

The teacher can prepare sets of contrasting maps: our neighborhood a while ago, our neighborhood today (showing new roads and other construction which is using land that previously was used differently); floor plan of a small bakery, a large bakery; etc. Children may be guided to interpret these maps to discover the impact of tools and technology.

Sequence of Pupil Experiences

Many possibilities for geographic generalizations and map experiences for seven- and eight-year-olds have been analyzed in relation to each of the basic human activities within the neighborhood community. We will now correlate this information in a detailed sequence of pupil experiences, supported by psychological studies and the literature in geographic education. The sequence of pupil experiences for this chapter lies within the pupils' neighborhood community, the new arena for seven- and eight-year-olds whose immediate zone of contact is now expanding beyond the communities of family and school. The basic human activities provide the scope.

This sequence of experiences is intended to follow the one laid down in the previous grade level. Many of the experiences suggested here are similar to those the pupils engaged in within the arenas of family and school. Pupils who have not undergone the previous experiences or who have not benefited fully from them may still develop the skills and understandings they lack. The neighborhood community, however, is larger and more complex, and the skills will be expanded as well as reinforced. Children without the earlier experiences may need some extra assistance from the teacher to fill the gaps.

Geographers agree that children should not be faced with a symbol on a map which does not bring to mind an image of the reality for which it stands. Children must be given ample opportunity to observe thoughtfully what there is to see in the immediate world around them. Geography, by its nature, does provide in rich measure opportunity for such firsthand learning experiences, especially in the early grades. The child is thus able to discover important facts through his own observation. Hence we start our sequence of pupil experiences with firsthand experiences in observation.

FIRSTHAND EXPERIENCES

Ask the children to tell what they saw on the way to school. Encourage them also to describe what they heard, smelled, and felt. They should recall the natural landscape as well as the man-made features (though they need not be aware of the difference between natural and cultural features at this point). See if they can recall how many streets or roads they crossed. Let them estimate how many blocks they walked or miles they drove and how long it took them. They might describe the landmarks they noticed, a tall building, an empty lot, a pond, a dairy farm, traffic lights—anything that stands out in their memory. If they are able to write, they might list these items. If not, the teacher should jot them down. *This initial check on observation is done without any prior preparation.*

Now ask the children *to look again* on their way to school and *see what they notice when they are specifically looking.* Have them actually count the number of streets or roads they cross, the number of blocks they walk, and check the results with their previous estimate. Let them see whether there were some important landmarks they had not previously noticed, or whether the landmarks were located just where they thought. When the child checks himself in a second experience, he develops a spirit of exploration. He is now in a better position to make discoveries for himself.

As many trips as possible should be taken in the neighborhood. They will help children discover the relation of home and school to the neighborhood. The children will become more familiar with their physical surroundings as they observe natural and cultural features. They will become more aware of human relations as they observe the connection between neighborhood workers or farmers and their own lives. They will begin to see how people interact with their environment. Trips should be carefully planned in advance so that the purpose is clear and the children are able to derive full benefit from them. A spirit of exploration should be aroused. There should be adequate preparation, but the preplanning should not attempt to do what can be best accomplished on the trip or in the discussion and other activities which follow. The trip should be taken with the intention of mapping it.

The first trip should probably be a walk around the block on which the school is located or on the roads that bound it. Observations made here are similar to those previously made between home and school. Directions should be noted in relation to the school. Attention could also be called to the familiar places to which these streets or roads lead. Relative location of features should be noted. For example, is the water hydrant in the middle of the block, nearer to one corner or to the other? Where is the wooded area or creek in relation to the school? Where is the shopping area in relation to the school? The church? (See Figure 19.) Locate children's homes if any are passed. Look for important geographical phenomena. Notice the slope of the land; note that drainage of homes, buildings, lawns is toward the street or road. Watch for variations in elevation, if any. Look for signs of erosion, if any are easily visible. Where are water bodies? Where are trees growing? Where are telephone poles and electric wires placed? Where are sewers placed? How are irrigation ditches laid out? It might be worthwhile to take the trip around the block or boundary roads of the school when the postman is making his deliveries, when road repairs are being made, when some construction is taking place, when water mains are being laid or repaired, when a telephone wire is being installed. The excursion can be repeated to observe seasonal changes in trees and flowers or crops, or after a heavy rain to learn something about drainage. It is well worth

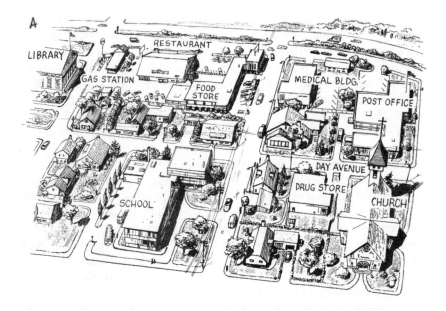

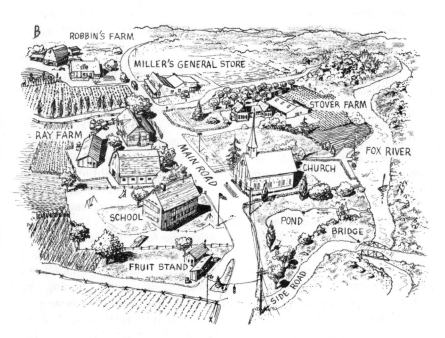

Figure 19

(A) Urban Neighborhood

(B) Rural Neighborhood

taking many walks in the same area for different purposes. A later walk may be timed, with no stops being made for observations. One such walk may be a paced walk; the counted steps from intersection to intersection and from one feature to another roughly determine the distance. The teacher or a parent might drive the children in a car or truck over the same route and clock the distance on the odometer so the children may relate the distance (the mile or part of the mile) to their actual walk. Such experiences are necessary to bring meaning to scale on a map.

Other trips might be related to the basic human activities that can be observed in the neighborhood. The class might walk to the shopping area to visit the grocery or bakery, a furniture store, a shoe repair shop, a print shop, a flower shop. They might watch the milk or produce being delivered or visit a gas station to see cars being washed, lubricated, and serviced, or to see the large underground gasoline tank being replenished. Such trips can have the purpose of seeing processes taking place or noting the great variety of stores and why they are there. Children might be encouraged to question where some of the products come from. They might observe with the intention of building a model or drawing a rough sketch of the whole shopping area; or they may be concerned with the particular layout of the supermarket or bakery, in both selling area and behind-the-scenes area.

In a rural neighborhood similar trips can be taken to the nearby village. The class might visit the farm-equipment sales and repair facilities; the feed, grain, and fertilizer store; the cooperatives. They might also observe the gasoline tank being replenished at the gas station or trucks stopping by to be serviced. Depending on the area and the size of the village, they will see various types of processing plants. There might be a railroad siding. There might be a firehouse, sheriff's office, telephone exchange, or post office. Again, the class should observe with the intention of reproducing the village facilities in their relative location or should center their attention on a particular plant layout in which they want to analyze a given function or process.

In relation to the basic human activities, the following can be investigated in the neighborhood community: (1) protecting and conserving: a visit to a police station, sheriff's office, animal shelter, firehouse, hospital, reservoir; (2) producing, exchanging, distributing, consuming: any factory, an upholsterer, a milk bottling plant, small bakery or large commercial bakery, utilities plants, processing plants, markets and shops, etc.; (3) transporting: bus terminal, taxi stand, service station, streetcar barn, railroad tracks or terminal, water bodies, boats, bridges, railroad or road construction; (4) communicating: post office, telephone exchange, radio or TV station, library, movie house; (5) expressing aesthetic and spiritual impulses: museums, churches, libraries, historic monuments, parks, places of beauty; (6) providing recreation: community center, swimming area, parks, wooded areas, playgrounds and commercial places of entertainment; (7) providing education: other schools—elementary or the junior and senior high school these children may later attend—museum, library; (8) organizing and governing: this activity is necessary for the successful operation of many of the activities listed above (it may be possible to visit meetings of neighborhood organizations, agencies, or institutions); (9) creating tools and technics: experimental and construction facilities—nurseries, laboratories, experimental farms, machine shops. Visits should also be planned to observe construction in process—roads, building, repairs.

Trips should preferably be within walking distance so that other things can be observed along the way. Direction of travel should be noted, and on later trips children might have with them very simple maps showing the route they are following. Slope of the land should be noticed, and attention given to the feel of walking up an incline compared to walking down, even when the incline is slight. The time of day and the position of the sun might be observed. The season of the year might be mentioned and any observable difference noted between this trip' and a previous one. Landmarks might be located. Again, observations should be made with the intention of reproducing them in some manner in the classroom. Any time a water body, hill, or railroad tracks and roads and streets are passed, their relative location should be noted. In the open country, crops, forest, cattle in the fields, sheep, etc., should be noted. Anything of geographical import should be utilized. However, no one trip ought to try to do too much. If enough trips are taken, new concepts are gradually added as old ones are renewed and extended.

One special trip might be to go to the top of a hill, a tall building, or a tower where the neighborhood can be seen from above. Preferably such a trip will come after several previous trips have been taken so that the children will recognize routes and places and see them in a new perspective. Another special trip might be a mile-long walk so that a mile has a tangible feel in the muscles and no longer remains a word or a symbol for scale on a map. The blocks or intersections might be tallied and the time noted so that this too could be added for concept building. One trip might be a short ride on a bus in the neighborhood to notice the exact route.

What purpose do all these trips serve? As Mitchell points out,

> The chief program for geographic intake in these early years lies in trips—explorations of the environment. Provision for outgo, equally important, is made within the classroom (after the trip) through "adaptable materials." ... (more of this later) Trips ... become the basis of the curriculum in the

younger years—(up to about 7) when children have mastered the relationships in their immediate home environment sufficiently to widen their explorations, but are not yet mature enough, experienced enough, have not yet a large
enough store of images to carry on investigations in situations which are not
immediately before them.[9]

Scarfe also emphasizes the need for contact with the immediate environment: "No geography worthy of the name is possible without constant
reference to a completely understood home region. . . . Persistent contact
with reality is necessary. . . ."[10] However, if trips are to serve more than
a passing interest, the teacher must be prepared to make good use of
them. How?

> It becomes the first task of a teacher who would base her program with
> young children on an exploration of the environment to explore the environ-
> ment herself. She must know how her community keeps house—how it gets
> its water, its coal, its electric power, its food, and who are the workers that
> make the community function. She must know where the pipes in her room
> lead to, where the coal is kept in the school, when the meters are read and by
> whom, she must know the geographic features which characterize her par-
> ticular environment and strive constantly to see how they have conditioned
> the work of which she is a part and how they have been changed by that work.
>   . . . She gathers this information in order to place the children in strategic
> positions for making explorations, in order to plan trips which will lead to
> significant discoveries, in short, in order to use her environment as a labora-
> tory. . . .[11]

The authors wish to stress a very important pedagogical principle at
this time. While the geographic experiences elaborated in the above
pages strongly focus on the environment close at hand that a child can
take in directly as sensory data, at the same time we advise using the
enriching experience of the described or vicarious types that come
through reading or listening. The modern child who is confronted by
the wide world through the mass media is stimulated to contrast and
compare his family and home with others near and far in time and space.
The modern child sees in pictures and hears by recordings the children
of classrooms of schools alike and different. No child today can be un-
aware that neighborhoods exist in almost limitless number around the
world and have persisted through time. He knows that all families live
in some kind of shelter and all produce and consume food and clothing.
Contrasting the means which neighborhoods develop for protection
or to transport goods is fascinating to youngsters and can be used
to bring new insight to bear on understanding and on behaving more
responsibly in their own family, school, and neighborhood communities.
The teacher is wise to introduce descriptive experiences that go beyond

the child's immediate environment, but we would be irresponsible as educators if we did not bring the focus back to the study of the pupil's set of expanding communities—family through neighborhood. We must prevent the side excursions of an interest in an Indian pueblo or a family in the heart of Africa or South America from becoming the major emphasis of study in the early primary grades. The child's own interlocking and interdependent communities are our chief objective here.

Obviously much can be gained in geographic generalization and mapping skills through comparisons of family, school, and neighborhood communities beyond the immediate environment. Everything that has been said or suggested for developing geographic understanding and map skills from direct sensory data of one's own communities holds with almost equal power for the communities seen or heard about through the mass media. Places near and far can be located on a globe. Maps can be drawn to show distributions of the several basic human activities that are different from the distributions found in the child's immediate environment. Books, newspapers, comics, etc., provide a rich body of data that can be mapped and thus better comprehended. Maps of other family, school, and neighborhood communities can suggest ways of using one's own environment better. The good social studies program emphasises the intensive study of the child's own communities but uses the wide range of vicarious input about other communities to enrich and sharpen geographic generalizations and mapping skills.

REORGANIZATION OF EXPERIENCE

Discussion. Now that the children have made their observations and discoveries, they must use these raw materials to build geographic concepts which will become the basis for their map making and map interpretation. Teacher and children will raise questions about what they have seen and try to understand relations.

> Most children by the time they reach the primary grades are ready for simple explanations of the natural and cultural features with which geography deals. . . . When children ask questions about the geography of the environment, they should be answered as simply and correctly as possible. Failure to give a clear, simple answer may dull their curiosity and further interest.[12]

Barton says that basic understandings are possible at the primary level. However, the children can go more deeply into the understandings that are most easily available in the immediate environment. Teachers "should make definite plans to teach the children some understandings about all the primary natural and human items. Otherwise there will be gaps in their background."[13] The teacher assumes this responsibility on the trips, in the discussion, and in guiding the dramatic play.

With young children, the teacher's role in guiding discussion is especially important. Baker, in a study of children's free discussion in Grades 2, 4, and 6, found that in the second grade there was far less "meeting of minds," inquiry, and give-and-take as compared with fourth- and sixth-grade discussion. He concludes, "To the extent that class discussion is designed to represent common intellectual endeavor in the solution of a problem . . . , if it should or could be achieved, [it] would require more adult direction and guidance at the lower grade levels. . . ."[14] Hence, when we say that children need an opportunity to have their questions answered and that discussion is a means of clarifying relations, we assume an adult's active guidance.

The earlier questions are concerned with "how" and "what." What did we see at the bakery? How did the bakery smell? How did the man at the service station fill the underground gasoline tank? What is happening to the trees and crops now that the sun is warmer and higher in the sky at noon? How did it feel to climb that long slope even though it did not seem very high? "Where" questions are very important in preparation for mapping. Teacher and class will want to decide things like: In what direction did we walk from school? Where did we make that first turn in the road? Where was the play area? Where did we cross the streetcar (or railroad) tracks? Let us suppose this last series of questions was concerned with a short walk to a play area. Teacher and children are not talking about cardinal directions or absolute distances. They are talking about relative direction—toward the play area from the school—and the relative location of features noticed along the way.

Dramatic Play. Words will not be the only way of rethinking this trip; ". . . young children live in the here-and-now world about them; they learn more through active use of their bodies and senses than through words alone; their play is a way of learning and can be developed constructively. . . ."[15] The children might learn a great deal by manipulating blocks or other adaptive materials and re-enacting their excursion.

Mapping Experiences: Three-Dimensional, Pictorial, and Semipictorial. Dramatic play in which props are used as symbols is one form of *three-dimensional mapping.* Reconstructing with blocks is another form. (See Figure 20.) Whittemore has found that children will begin early and without direction to represent places they have seen by reproducing them with blocks.[16] Older children might prefer to draw a large-scale pictorial representation on big sheets of paper scotch-taped together and placed on the floor in proper orientation. Seven-year-olds

Figure 20

Three-Dimensional Map

enjoy and learn with more permanent constructions:

> The media through which children find their most fluent, most satisfactory expression, change as they mature. Blocks disappear about seven when the children wish a more permanent medium in order to carry on longer-span, more consecutive play or thinking. This wish often gives a great impulse to carpentry work and crude "cities" or "towns" or "villages" with bench-made buildings, etc., appear in place of the block constructions. Painting and clay modelling, often in relation to houses, stores, stations, etc., are elaborated, and dramatic play, often with few words, develops.[17]

Three-dimensional reproduction can be most helpful in producing understandings of some difficult concepts: for example, an understanding of how a bridge spans a body of water or what an island really looks like. Children might set up a block at each "bank," put a board across to span an oilcloth water body, then drive their toy cars across. Many farm problems of flooding and irrigation may also be analyzed. Children may model maps in a large box or sand table. If plaster of Paris or some such material is used, they can make low areas, flood them, and discover how a lake is formed or produce a lake with an island in it. If the model is large enough, they can float tiny boats around it or bring clay animals to drink at the water's edge. Children can also make small models with putty in a cake pan (Figure 21).

Figure 21

Model in Cakepan

Drainage, a difficult concept, is equally important in rural or urban settings. Children can readily go outdoors to see the water running downhill after a rain. They can build a mound of dirt and see water drain off. Still the concept of drainage is far from complete. Older children and adults often do not thoroughly understand upstream and downstream or drainage. One additional tangible method of studying this concept is in a large sand table. Barton describes an experiment to be carried on in a sandbox (Figure 22):

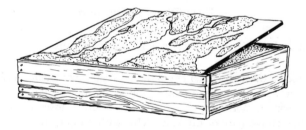

Figure 22

Drainage Model in Sandbox

. . . take a large, thick piece of glass and slope it lengthwise in a sand table. The glass may be painted blue on one side or . . . a light blue desk blotter [may be placed] under the glass. The entire glass is then covered with sand. . . . Trace a depression in the sand to represent a valley. The exposed glass will represent the water. Tributary valleys may be traced.

[You] can carry this project still further by placing bridges across the rivers and a house or two on a hill. If greater detail is desired, small twigs may be added for trees and a lake placed at the head of a stream. At one end, the glass may be uncovered to represent part of an ocean. The river may be shown as flowing into the ocean. Other items representative of the local environment may be added.[18]

Sandboxes are very useful in demonstrating drainage. Very slowly pour water and have it run off. Having the whole underlying surface on a slope as described above probably gives a deeper understanding of the total drainage pattern in the local area (slope the total surface as the local neighborhood is sloped) than is possible with only modeling hills and having the water run off. Small models can also be made by individual children in planting flats. They might reproduce some area seen on a trip or in a picture. Fill the box with soil and put in appropriate miniature shrubs, trees, hills, rocks for bare mountains, exposed painted glass for water, etc. Sand from the beach should be used for sandy areas; appropriate soil should be used for natural vegetation, cultivated crops, forest areas, or fields with animals that are to be represented. These models should be authentic as far as possible or they can produce misconceptions.

The children can also build a table model of their neighborhood (Figure 23).

Figure 23

Model of Neighborhood

Tangible mapping experiences in themselves do not guarantee understandings. Discussion and discovering of relationships require planning and guidance on the part of the teacher. The children must also be helped to make the transition from the tangible to the abstract. The teacher should be ever watchful that misconceptions are not developed. Constant check has to be made with reality even when tangible symbols are used. They are still symbols for children although adults often forget this.

Pictorial mapping experiences involve working with crayons, paints, scissors, and paste to portray on individual drawings or murals what was seen on a trip. Children do not worry too much about perspective and scale. What can be shown is relative location and relative distance. Such map pictures not only are a means of rethinking relations and re-organizing data but also provide a good opportunity for the teacher to check errors in perception.

Preston studied a third-grade class and found that children often lack experiences for interpreting a three-dimensional landscape from a map; they need to develop a bird's-eye-view.[19] He suggests that they practice drawing a book that is lying upon the floor or make informal sketches as they look down on something. It would also be worthwhile to study pictures that were taken looking down at a landscape. The children may also draw such pictorial representations of their own (Figure 24).

Whittemore recommends pictorial representation for primary grade children as the step between third-dimensional and more abstract inter-

Figure 24

Children Sketching Nearby Landscape

pretation. In pictorial representation streets and roads, ground plans, buildings, lampposts, and trees are realistically drawn. No abstract symbols are used. Yet pictorial representation provides an opportunity for representing relative size, relative location, and relative distance. "The child must have the concept that is expressed by a map symbol or the symbol will be meaningless."[20]

With the streets or roads of the neighborhood forming the ground plan, symbols can move gradually from realistic pictorial toward the more abstract pictorial; this is the kind of mapping second-graders will often do following experiences in which they have seen the real landscape.

Mapping with semipictorial and abstract symbols comes next. When children have had a background of concrete and pictorial mapping and are able adequately to conceive of the map as a representation of the landscape seen from above, they can move toward more conventional symbols. A street or road can easily be represented by a double line (▬), buildings by squares (□) or rectangles (▭), a school by a square flying a little flag (⌐□), a church by a square with a little cross extending from one side (✝□). Even a river becomes a line (∿) following proper background experiences.

When teacher and children draw a large-scale map of the neighborhood or some part of it (the marketing area, a park, a wooded area, cultivated fields) and then play on it, the ground plan is more abstract than teachers often realize. The younger the children, the larger the ground plan should be. Seven-year-olds can play on the floor with an outline map painted on a large sheet of paper or linoleum (6′ × 8′— larger if practicable).

Much more definite work in orientation is suitable at this age.

> A certain amount of direct drill . . . in orientation is welcomed by the children. I should never recommend it for young children in and for itself; only in so far as it makes for better play. Maps must be kept functioning and for six- and seven-year-olds this usually means they must be played upon. Children like to take imaginary trips on a map, particularly if it is large enough to permit impersonations of pilots or engineers or bell buoys or hills and so extend the "drill" beyond a merely locational exercise into the realm of images, of play.[21]

Though the map itself becomes more and more abstract, the use of it brings back the reality. The symbolic is possible only when children can recall the genuine image in response.*

---

* See "Map and Globe Symbols," Appendix B, for examples of pictorial and conventional abstract symbols.

Scale becomes increasingly important, and the teacher should draw the map to scale. The first maps are drawn large—on playground or floor; later the maps can be drawn smaller on paper. As the same area is reproduced in different sizes and the child recognizes the same features and realizes it is the same landscape, he is learning about scale on a map. However, base maps should usually be drawn to scale by the teacher; only the very advanced child can handle scale properly at this age.

On a base map drawn by the teacher, the children can manipulate small toys as symbols, then little pictures pasted on cardboard, and eventually semipictorial and more abstract representations. At this later point they should begin to use a legend. The purpose of the legend is to explain to anyone else using the map what the symbols stand for. Children can now look at a city or county map and employ some of the same symbols used there. The legend should be placed in the lower left-hand corner; it is best to develop the habit of placing it correctly from the start. Wherever possible, use accepted practice. Also, use the same symbols consistently.

The street plan of the neighborhood can be made a permanent base map for second grade. The children then add just those features they have seen on a particular trip. At a given time they may be concerned with one basic human activity and put on the symbols only for that—for example, agreed-upon symbols for the firehouse, hydrants, and fire alarm boxes. Another day, the children may remove these symbols and use the map for another purpose. With the teacher's guidance, they might discover that gasoline stations are on important street or highway intersections, that schools are usually in residential areas, or that marketing areas are near routes of public transportation. In this way they will be helped to make inferences by comparing different facts about the same area.

Again the point needs to be made that important geographic generalizations and mapping skills can be gained by studying comparable and contrasting neighborhoods that are seen in pictures or described in sounds and spoken words of others. No teacher needs to feel constrained to deal exclusively with the neighborhood in which the children live. A look at other neighborhoods that may solve the same problems in different ways is important to growth of understanding. And mapping these described communities is very productive in seeing similarities or contrasts in spatial distribution of schools, libraries, playgrounds, fire departments, etc. But the objective is not the study of a faraway neighborhood; come back to the central purpose of understanding better the set of interlocking communities of intimate contact and let the contrasts and comparisons enrich this understanding.

READING AND INTERPRETING MAPS MADE BY OTHERS

Aerial Photographs.

Airplane views are the easiest of maps because they are only extensions or variations of the familiar instead of being expressed in difficult symbols. If the water in an airplane rotogravure is painted blue to bring it out more clearly, an airplane view becomes a transition map from a play-scheme map to a symbolic outline map where the representative quality of the symbol is practically lost.[22]

The aerial photograph is useful, then, as a step from the three-dimensional to the more abstract symbolization. It is an aid in visualizing a more abstract symbol on a map. Also, it does something that even a trip might not do. It provides the overall perspective of the area traversed, and it shows it all at one time. There are problems of aerial translation, however, that are treated in a later section.

It cannot be assumed, however, that an aerial photograph of the pupils' neighborhood will always be available or that children will understand it at first view. They should view the neighborhood from a hill or tower in order to recognize the similarity with an aerial photograph

Figure 25

Aerial Photograph of Airport

when one is available. As with all experiences, the teacher must have clearly in mind the purpose for which the photograph is being used. Without guidance the children may well overlook important relationships. A teacher should not say "Study the photograph," but, "Locate the hangars (center, north), and the Terminal Building (center, south). Do you see the parking lot across the road from the hangars? Where else do you see parking lots? When a car comes over the bridge, what must it pass before it gets to the Terminal Building?" Etc. (Figure 25.)

Pictorial and Semipictorial Maps. Pictorial maps use the simplest symbols: drawings or photographs of real objects. They must be placed accurately and *not be too cluttered.* The base map must be accurate and in proper scale.

All of the play-scheme maps (as in Figure 20) that are made and used with three-dimensional objects can eventually become pictorial maps by replacing the objects with pictures. Pictures can be removable, or added gradually, so the pupils are able to handle without confusion the concepts represented. But pictorial maps can become too cluttered. If the teacher remembers that maps at this age level are to be used for a single purpose, clutter can usually be avoided. However, if the relationships to be developed do require many symbols, these relationships might wait until some of the picture symbols can be replaced by conventional symbols, which use less space.

Pictorial maps can be works of art as well as accurate. If any such maps of the neighborhood are available, they certainly should be obtained. It is also possible to provide exercises in looking at a pictorial landscape and remapping it into a semipictorial version.

Teacher-Made Maps. Teacher-made maps can be adjusted to the children's level of development in map skills. The teacher's map will be accurately scaled. It will contain the area that the children have studied on trips, in aerial views, and in photographs. The symbols used will be those the children are familiar with, but they will be accurately placed (within the limit imposed by their size). The teacher should make several enlargements of the neighborhood area by projecting it from the city or county map. (This is done by projecting a city or county map with an opaque projector onto paper hung on the wall or chalkboard and tracing off a simplified version of the neighborhood area.) When several such enlargements have been made for base maps, the particular features needed for a given lesson can then be added to one map. First the map is placed on the floor or table for the children to use as a play-scheme map. Then pictorial and semipictorial symbols are substituted, always with agreement from the class as to what they represent in reality. Eventually, even at second-grade level, conventional symbols can be used, but only for those features seen and discussed by the class (Figure 26).

The teacher will also want to make maps of the same area in different scales so that the children can begin to recognize features and relation-

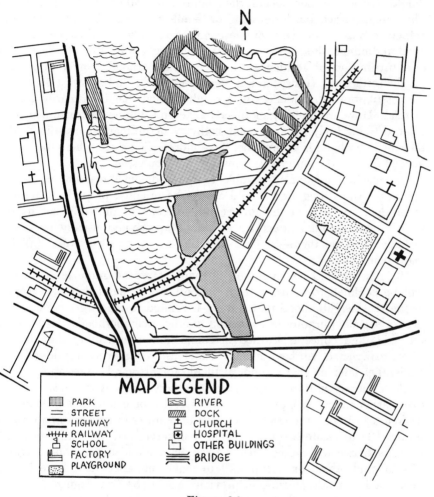

Figure 26

Semi-pictorial Map

ships regardless of size. The smallest map of the neighborhood should use a scale of twelve inches to a mile. This might be the size of the map given to the children for individual use at their seats or to take on trips as a guide or to which they each add new features.

Street or Road Map of the City or County. The teacher can probably get from a service station a road map of the city or county. Maps of different oil companies should be analyzed so that the simplest and the one most suited to the given purpose can be chosen. The children should learn to locate their neighborhood on the city or county map. They should also locate their school, their homes, and other familiar features. They might trace out extensions of familiar streets. They might be helped to make some very simple comparisons between their neighborhood and others. For example, the teacher might want them to discover the distribution of residences in their neighborhood, which may be totally residential (except for a shopping area), and contrast it with the distribution of residences in a neighborhood that is primarily commercial. How are the neighborhoods alike and different with respect to a large water body, an important highway or railroad or coastline? If their neighborhood is a rural one, the children should see where they are in relation to the county seat, transportation routes, etc.

The teacher might also be able to get a precinct map, to be used similarly. Maps thus used should always be oriented properly in terms of outdoor space even though second-graders will probably not have been taught cardinal directions as yet. Maps should usually be read looking down on them—on floor or table—not hung on a wall. (Wall maps come later.)

The reading and interpretation of maps at second-grade level, then, will be confined to maps of the neighborhood or parts thereof, except as the real neighborhood under study is related to the larger communities for specific purposes or compared to other neighborhoods. However, the skills and concepts learned in connection with sensory data from direct experience will have much broader use for interpreting described landscapes later on that are not available for firsthand observation.

The children will use maps made by others much as they used their own earlier maps: (1) to observe relative size or extent of any feature or area, (2) to observe relative location of features of concern in a given lesson, (3) to locate features previously observed, (4) to study relative distance between features, (5) to serve as a guide in planning a trip, (6) to guide them *on* a trip, (7) to make inferences that have been developed or made possible in previous work, (8) to recognize certain physical features and their relation to selected cultural features that are within their understanding.

Maps should be used as often as possible, and the teacher should always check to see that they are properly oriented in space and that the children are not developing misconceptions.

Using the Globe. As previously indicated (pp. 41–42), modern geographers agree that a simple globe, for informal use, should be present in all primary classrooms. It need show nothing more than land, water, the poles, and the equator. The neighborhood under study should be located on the globe. The pupils should have opportunities to study the globe, and their questions should be answered.

SUPPORTIVE CONCEPTS TO BE DEVELOPED

Natural Features. Thralls discusses how natural features may be found in miniature in any locality where bare earth is exposed to action of sun, wind, frost, rain, and running water:

> Pupils may observe, on a limited area of bare earth, actual illustrations of streams, tributaries, flood plains, meanders, divides, deltas, distributaries, lakes, cliffs, shore lines, islands, peninsulas, and other features. A field lesson for the observation and interpretation of such features and their relation to the larger but similar features of the local region helps to prepare for correct and vivid visualization of the real features of the earth on a larger scale.[23]

Not all these natural features will be available to the children in full scale in the neighborhood environment. But even when they are all available in miniature, only those features that are pertinent should be focused on.

Roadside streams can be observed after a rain, when the children can see the stream cutting its channel and gathering its load. The place where the stream deposits its load as it slows down on entering a pool or larger stream, or when it strikes a stone or stick, is also there for the looking. Little deltas are formed where one stream comes into another or where it enters a pool of water. Even the building up of an alluvial fan may appear at the foot of a sharp roadside slope.

Another condition that should be focused upon in the out-of-doors is sun behavior. While all studies do not agree in encouraging the teaching of cardinal directions in second grade, some sun behavior should be noted. Poole, Barton, and Baker suggest concepts that might be developed at first- and second-grade level.

The sun shines on the earth.
The sun rises in the east and sets in the west.* [Whether to teach this or not at this grade level is in dispute. The teacher may try it and see if it is confusing to his particular group.]
The sun is high in the sky at noon.
The sun helps to show the time of day.[24]

Attention should also be called to the changing seasons and how they affect the landscape, man's activities, and the behavior of plants and

---

* It may be more accurate to have children learn: In the early morning, the sun is seen in the east. In the late afternoon the sun is seen in the west.

animals. Pictures of an area might be drawn during each season and then the seasons compared. The daily changes in weather could also be noted and recorded on the calendar. Rain, sun, and wind can be shown using agreed-upon symbols, either pictorial or color.

Plants, Animals, Soil. Experiments with plants, soil, and animals can develop concepts such as the following:

Some plants are cultivated.
Some plants grow naturally in the surroundings.
Many plants grow from seeds.
Plants help to provide food and fibre.
Most plants change through the seasons.
Most plants grow better in some places than in others.
[The class might set up pots with different kinds of soil; some in sun, others not; some getting morning sun, others getting late sun; some being watered more often, others less often, etc.]

Some animals are domesticated.
Some animals live naturally in the environment.
Animals live and move about in different ways.
Animals help provide food and clothing materials.
Animals require food and water.
Some animals require human care.
Animals eat different things and have different feeding habits.

Soil is found on yards, farms, and gardens.
Plants grow from the soil.
Food comes from soil.
There are different kinds of soil.[25]

Population. Attention might be called to variations in population distribution:

In urban areas, sections with apartment houses have a greater concentration of population; single homes with lawns around them have fewer people. In the country, the greater spaciousness is even more apparent and should be compared with city population distribution. Variations in homes and kinds of buildings might also be noted.

Landforms. The concept of landform in map reading and map interpretation is a basic yet difficult one. Sharp contrasts in elevation are quite easily observed in the landscape, but on maps it is especially hard to represent three dimensions adequately for young children. Therefore, as much background in noticing elevation as possible should be provided in the primary years to prepare for interpreting maps of places that are not possible for the pupils to see or experience directly.

Children should be given opportunities to observe how landforms affect activities—how going upstream feels compared to going downstream; how climbing a hill feels compared to going down a hill. Climbing the stairs of a high building helps develop in the sensorimotor system an awareness of what height can mean to human activity. Children can be made to realize that a river or lake can help or hinder transportation or that a high elevation can be an obstacle. Some dramatic play in the room using a covered chair or other physical prop as a mountain can help build or reinforce concepts of an obstacle to movement on land. Making three-dimensional models of various kinds may be helpful. Nothing beyond realistic or pictorial representation of elevation should be attempted at this level. Geographers agree that at this age color layers on maps are too far removed from reality to be of much help.

Distance. At this grade level distance is understood mainly in relation to the time it takes to get from one place to another. Perhaps, with enough opportunity for experience, the number of city blocks takes on meaning for city children just as the number of miles becomes meaningful for rural children. Walking a mile and counting the city blocks walked are suggested as activities for city children.

Children may experience the feeling of distance by walking and traveling to specific places if they are *told* the distance in miles. They might compare the distance from home to school among the various children in terms of blocks or miles. Without such direction or opportunity for informed experience, children do not have the means for expressing distance.

For most of us, distance is time as well as miles. In the "time-to-get-there" sense, distance varies with the means of transportation and the state of technology. Even in first and second grade, children should begin to look at distance in its relative sense.

Let us move now to a discussion of the map skills and geographic understandings to be developed by primary grade pupils within the context of the next larger communities of which any neighborhood is a part: the local communities.

REFERENCES

1. Harold V. Baker, *Children's Contributions in Elementary School General Discussion*, Child Development Monographs, No. 29 (New York: Bureau of Publications, Teachers College, Columbia University, 1942), pp. 117–130.

2. David S. Hill, "Personification of Ideals by Urban Children," *Journal of Sociology*, 1:379–392 (1930).

3. Lucy S. Mitchell, *Our Children and Our Schools* (New York: Simon and Schuster, Inc., 1950), pp. 12–13.

4. Arnold Gesell and Frances Ilg, *The Child from Five to Ten* (New York: Harper &

Row, Publishers, 1946), pp. 381–383.

5. *Ibid.*, pp. 157–158, 186–187, 443.

6. Faculty of the University School, *How Children Develop* (Columbus: Ohio State University, 1946).

7. George F. Howe, "Teaching of Directions in Space," *Journal of Geography*, 31: 207–210 (May, 1932), pp. 209, 210.

8. Gesell and Ilg, *op. cit.*, p. 443.

9. Lucy S. Mitchell, *Young Geographers* (New York: The John Day Company, Inc., 1934), p. 22.

10. N. V. Scarfe, "Geography Education and Teaching Methods," *Journal of Geography*, 55:57–67 (February, 1956), p. 63.

11. Mitchell, *Young Geographers*, pp. 25–26.

12. Thomas F. Barton, "Geographic Instruction in the Primary Grades," *Geographic Approaches to Social Education*, Nineteenth Yearbook, National Council for the Social Studies (Washington: NCSS, 1948), pp. 205–217.

13. *Ibid.*, p. 210.

14. Baker, *op. cit.*, pp. 122–123.

15. Mitchell, *Our Children and Our Schools*, p. 198.

16. Katheryne T. Whittemore, "Maps," *Geographic Approaches to Social Education*, Nineteenth Yearbook, National Council for the Social Studies (Washington: NCSS, 1948), pp. 117–130, 120.

17. Mitchell, *Young Geographers*, p. 32.

18. Barton, *op. cit.*, p. 214.

19. Ralph Preston, "Implications of Children's Concepts of Time and Space," *Social Studies*, 36:218–219 (May, 1945).

20. Whittemore, "Maps," p. 120.

21. Mitchell, *Young Geographers*, pp. 46–47.

22. *Ibid.*, p. 45.

23. Zoe A. Thralls, Isabelle K. Hart, and Erna Grassmuck, "Geography in the Elementary School," *Teaching of Geography*, Thirty-second Yearbook, National Society for the Study of Education (Bloomington: Public School Publishing Co., 1933), pp. 219–245, 221.

24. Poole, Barton, and Baker, "Concept Chart," *Geographic Foundation Series* (New York: The Bobbs-Merrill Company, Inc., n.d.).

25. *Ibid.*

chapter six

THE BEGINNING GRADES

EMPHASES

/ 4. *The Local Communities*

General Introduction to the Local Communities

Previously learned geographic understandings and map skills now need to be reinforced and extended, and new generalizations and skills are to be initiated with the local communities as the focal arenas. First we will consider the development and learning abilities of eight- and nine-year-olds, the general age level of Grade 3. Next the nature of the local communities will be analyzed and their position within the social studies framework described. The four major objectives and the pupil experiences possible to achieve them will be analyzed for each basic human activity, after which the material will be correlated into a suggested sequence of pupil experiences, given in detail for this age level. Studies will be cited from the psychological and geographical literature to lend support.

In planning general geographic and more specific map experiences, we may obtain cues from psychological literature exploring children's interests, concept development, and reasoning ability. In any single grade there is a considerable spread of ability, and the material is presented with this in mind. Also, the experience sequence not only allows for but emphasizes flexibility in meeting individual and group differences.

CHILDREN'S INTERESTS

There is a gradual extension in children's interests from those that are immediate and personal toward those that range beyond direct experience. Baker, in a previously cited study of children's discussions, found that at the third-grade level the greatest concern is still with immediate, personal activity and experience and is dependent on personal presence and direct contact.[1] Hill found that children of this age idealized people mainly of the immediate environment.[2] Interest in human work is emphasized by Mitchell: "It lies around them, in and out of their homes: they share it dramatically, practically, as investigators, as participators. It is a deep and abiding interest—perhaps it has no rival interest as strong."[3]

We are not ignoring the fact that modern mass media of communication have widened the child's horizons to include activity beneath the sea, in outer space, and in other local communities far removed from direct contact possibility for most children. We definitely utilize the new geographic content carried by these channels. But we contend that an understanding of the pupil's own local communities is of greater value at this point in his development of a sense of a set of interdependent but expanding communities of men than could be the alternative program of depending primarily on the vicarious stimuli of the faraway in time and place. Enrichment excursions into the described activities of other local communities are to be used to deepen the understanding of the rationale of the expanding set of family, school, neighborhood, and local communities in which the pupil is a member and an active participant; they are not to become independent and isolated studies with their own ends.

These assumptions encourage a map program centered on the local communities and concerned with the basic activities of people with whom children come into personal contact. Its underlying purpose is not to develop map skills as such, but to develop them as a tool to better understanding differences in the way people carry on their activities in different settings. Thus the interest in people and relationships, in human work, is of tremendous importance.

In addition, Witty points out, these interests are only a starting point in the introduction of many activities; it is the teacher's responsibility to extend them:

> . . . every teacher should aim to modify old patterns and create *new* interests. . . . The interests of boys and girls on coming to school constitute the opportunity and responsibility of teachers; their interests on leaving a class or school reveal the [teacher's] contributions made to their growth.[4]

CHILDREN'S CONCEPTS

In general, children are becoming more objective, able to see a little beyond the immediate self and immediate present. Piaget says that from age seven to age eleven, some appreciation of relativity develops.[5] Children can now conceive of the world as it might be perceived from another perspective. They become aware of the existence of objects and relationships apart from themselves. Mitchell finds that at this age children's curiosities gradually extend beyond the here and now to the faraway and long ago.[6] However, she says that although eight- and nine-year-olds are more capable than younger children of learning through words (a descriptive approach), they still need to translate these words into action in their own ways to make them have real meaning. They still need direct experience to support or test the ideas or concepts they have been formulating.

For our purposes, this would mean that we can and should continue to build concepts primarily by inductive learning based on expanding communities—a program in which the children still have opportunities for direct experiences with reality in the immediate environment. Children are more verbally able to generalize, are more objective, but it is still best to help them first build images through direct experience and then verbalize the experiences.

The ability to understand time relations is a necessary skill in map interpretation. However, the child's knowledge of conventional time is a matter of gradual development, beginning before the age of three or four and reaching the minimum adult level at thirteen and fourteen. The power to think of the past as different from the present does not seem to develop noticeably before age eight. This does not mean that children eight years old can suddenly understand any and all time relations. Chronology still seems to be beyond the grasp of most children below eleven years of age.[7] Nevertheless, from research studies it would appear that children in third grade can explore a given period in the past and contrast some of the ways in which conditions and happenings may have been alike or different.

Third grade has been chosen as the most favorable period in the primary grades to teach space comprehension.[8] Lord says there is a real need for out-of-door exercises, observations, and drills with regard to directions.[9] He found that children often lack the foundational experiences necessary to make directions in space meaningful. It is necessary, he says, to develop in the child a close relationship between the arrangement of cardinal directions and self. Howe devised a procedure to teach primary grade children directions in space and had great success with third-graders. (This procedure is incorporated in the detailed sequence of experiences presented later in this chapter.)

Preston emphasizes the need for children to have a bird's-eye view of space before they are expected to use two-dimensional maps with comprehension.[10] He points out that children can verbalize 93,000,000 miles to the sun but cannot estimate the distance of fifteen feet required for parking distance from a water hydrant. He suggests that trips be taken which give children opportunities to look down at a landscape and get a bird's-eye view, followed by informal sketching, construction of floor plans, diagrams of routes to school, etc.

The eight-year-old, according to Gesell, has a deeper understanding of wider community relationships.[11] There is a beginning interest in primitive people and times past. The child is much more adventurous, more willing to try new things and visit new places. He walks quite a distance in his own neighborhood and tries new routes. He is eager for trips to new places beyond his neighborhood. He can travel by bus outside his neighborhood on a prearranged route if he is put on the bus and met by someone at the journey's end. Gesell infers that this willingness to venture out into the "broader world" is due to the child's greater feeling of familiarity in space.

At nine, Gesell says, the child is interested in the concerns of expanding community life: local community problems of health, life, property; mercantile businesses, manufacturing industries; agricultural industries; inter-neighborhood transportation; weather; animal and plant life beyond the neighborhood; holiday and seasonal activities.

At about eight, the child can distinguish right and left on others as well as on himself and so has added a new objective perspective to space.

CHILDREN'S REASONING AT THIRD-GRADE LEVEL

Many investigations have shown that children are capable at an early age of the same reasoning processes exhibited by adults. However, Jersild cautions, "there are limitations when children are called upon to deal with problems that go beyond their understanding and experience. Some of these characteristics also appear in the reasoning of adults when they are on unfamiliar ground."[12] Croxton's study supports this view regarding early capabilities of reasoning.[13] He found that children are able to reason inductively even in kindergarten.

The conclusions of these studies have direct bearing on our desire to develop geographic reasoning about local communities. Because children are capable of reasoning when the problems are kept within their realm of experience and understanding, it becomes our duty to provide the necessary experiences and help establish understandings to the extent that growth and experience will permit.

Mitchell,[14] who has spent many years working with children in developing geographic understanding and map-making skills, offers specific guidance in relating interests and concepts of eight- and nine-year-olds to curriculum in map making and map thinking:

> Interest drives. What children observe in their environment.—This age children are beginning to leave the "here and now," but the distant and

long-ago still have to be closely connected with the present environment. Interest in skills and techniques begin. Children are interested in work now and in the past.

Relation of people to people.—Organized dramatizations can begin. Children are able to work in committees. Workers in the city or work of farmers in the country are related to children's own lives. Workers in Indian communities long ago or far away can also be related to the children's own lives. In their dramatic play, children seem to live the roles they play. Children are concerned with attitudes among people.

Tools and children's methods of expression.—Symbols of general ideas begin, but they are still closely tied up with direct images. Children can draw rough maps with crayons. They can use books and other written source material, also simple maps and charts. They can use the compass, pilot maps, out-of-door maps. They can conduct simple experiments in erosion; experiment with seeds; experiment with food preservation. They can conduct experiments in handwork technology of earlier people; pump, drill, loom, windmill, etc.

Curriculum implications: trips, map making, map thinking.—Concept of erosion—rivers and sea-drainage—should be investigated. Children can make rough modeled maps showing drainage from mountains to the sea. Children should practice representing relief. Children should make maps of out of doors. They can play out on these maps, work they have seen. Tool maps (base map on which children play and move their toy symbols) can be made on oilcloth and re-used to develop and clarify land-water relations and their effect on activities. Attention should be called to how the growth of living things are conditioned by earth forces. Trips should be taken in connection with the here-and-now. Photographs can be shown of the far away. Stories should be read about the far away in which the dramatic control is geographic; e.g., grass or earthquake.

In summary, research seems to point to third grade as a period of expansion in time and space. Children should be taught cardinal directions, and a time dimension can be added to the study of the local communities. Children are becoming more objective, more realistic, and more concerned with expressing relative size of objects, perspective, and correctness of detail. We might expect a marked improvement in ability to handle the semipictorial and more abstract concepts in their mapping.

Within our social studies framework, based on the expanding communities of men, Grade 1 was concerned with the family community and the school community; Grade 2 emphasized the neighborhood community; Grade 3 will focus on the local communities, which encompass the previous three emphases and look ahead to subsequent study of the state community. Although all the larger communities of men (state, nation, even world) impinge on the activities of the local communities, attention will be focused on the larger-than-neighborhood local arena which is still within the direct sensorimotor contact of the child. All his future map interpretation depends on the fund of accurate images and concepts he can develop in the geographic reality in which he lives.

According to conditions, the local communities constitute a clustering of neighborhoods and can be called by a variety of names: a town, a city, a county, or a metropolitan area. The local communities are composed of all the neighborhoods that touch each other in this larger population complex.

This is a new arena for the children to explore. In it they can discover multiple examples of people working together in various ways to provide for their basic needs. They will find the central organization for many of the protecting and conserving functions (police, fire protection, water) that they have observed in their previous emphases of family, school, and neighborhood. The possibilities of studying producing, distributing, and consuming are multiplied and enriched. There is a greater opportunity to discover the interdependence of farm and city communities and the relationships of smaller communities to the larger metropolitan community within the area designated "local." There are the interurban rail and bus systems tying suburbs to metropolitan center. Exciting trips to investigate the "how" of our communicating media can be made to the local telephone exchange, central post office, city press, radio and TV stations. Recreational opportunities abound. Understanding of the organizational and administrative aspect of education can be gained in the county or city school system offices through investigating the nature of the relationships and the spatial distributions within the new arena. The governmental aspects of many of the functions previously witnessed in the neighborhood now come into sharper focus. Children can experience directly the way people work together at the political level to solve the problems faced by all who live in the local arena—problems that cannot be solved wholly within the lesser communities of family or neighborhood.

In this emphasis we plan to begin systematic study of earlier times in this geographic area. It is not chronology as such that concerns us, but a comparison of how people at different times in the same natural setting use that base differently according to the conditions of their culture and the state of their technology.

Analysis in Terms of the Basic Human Activities

In the section to follow we will analyze the local communities (town, city, county, or metropolitan area) and their ways of carrying on each of the basic human activities. This new arena enlarges the pupil's horizon and opens for investigation new relationships. Not only are additional functions to be observed here, but the differences and relationships among the neighborhoods within the same local communities become a province for study. Also to be analyzed are the relationships of smaller local communities within the larger complex of county or metropolitan arenas.

THE LOCAL COMMUNITIES (EMPHASIS 4)

Basic Human Activity: Protecting and Conserving Life, Health, Property, and Resources

OBJECTIVES	PUPIL EXPERIENCES
1. *Ability to observe thoughtfully.*	1. *Firsthand experiences.*

1. *Ability to observe thoughtfully.*

Observe local communities as places in which protecting and conserving functions occur. Question who is involved. Where? With what? Why? Consider human beings as resources to be protected and conserved as well as natural resources and property.

1. *Firsthand experiences.*

Observe location and distribution of protecting and conserving functions and associated features in local communities, such as police and fire protection, water distribution facilities, safety controls, hospitals and health centers. Visit the county office. Investigate role of the county clerk, county court, sheriff, coroner, justice of the peace, and health agencies in relation to protection of all. Locate city and county parks as examples of conservation of resources. Differentiate between natural and man-made conservation features. Check for whom these functions are most easily available. For whom are they more difficult of access?

2. *Ability to reason about things geographic.*

Fire protection as an example:
(1) relative location of fire-fighting facilities: What are they near? Are they equally distributed in all areas?
(2) relation of location to function: How large an area is served by each fire station? Are congested neighborhoods, commercial and industrial, residential, or farm areas equally

2. *Reorganized experience.*

a. *Discussion.* Analyze one function thoroughly and develop relational thinking as described in column of objectives, item 2. Then contrast fire protection with police protection. Discuss conservation in terms of land care, land use, and use of human resources. Is current conservation practice maintaining or enhancing resources? Are resources being depleted and run

well protected? Who has most protection? Why?

(3) relative direction: How large an area is served by each installation: Do fire stations in the local communities cooperate with each other? What is the pattern of cooperative service?

(4) changes in solutions to protecting and conserving that resulted from introduction of larger population, new tools and technics, etc.

3. *Ability to map in some form what has been observed.*

Design street or road maps, accurate as to blocks or miles, three-dimensional, with pictorial, then semipictorial or abstract symbols, to show, for illustrative protecting and conserving activities, e.g., hospitals, clinics, erosion dams, etc.,

(1) relative location;

(2) relative distance and direction;

(3) same features on maps of different sizes (crude use of scale);

(4) cardinal directions;

(5) legend.

4. *Ability to read through symbols of maps.* Ability to use simplified map of the local communities prepared by teacher, using symbols for familiar features; ability to locate local communities on commercial street or road map of city or county.

down? Could our local communities plan more wisely? How can even children protect plants, animals, land, man-made features, and other people?

b. *Dramatic play or dramatization.* Dramatize a large fire in a department store, in a flat in a poor congested neighborhood, in a small residence, or on a farm. Which firehouses or other facilities will be alerted? How will they converge on the fire? What will they do? Dramatize the same incidents

(1) one hundred years ago in your local communities, and

(2) twenty-five years from now in the future.

c. *Mapping.* Use above acquired information to project a simple street or road map of one of the local communities. With help of teacher trace off *main* features: water bodies, landmarks —only what is pertinent. Discuss any new symbols. Add familiar features representing protecting and conserving. Orient map with out-of-doors. Create a map to represent the action in a story. Draw a map from a picture. Construct a map in a sand table to study drainage, for conservation. Draw picture maps for beauty, but make them accurate as to relative location. Make maps showing changes over the past decades. Make maps in which pupils imagine distribution in the decades ahead.

3. *Using and interpreting maps made by others.*

Teacher can enlarge, by projection, maps of the local communities and trace off the pertinent data. Features can be added as needed. Main streets and roads, water

Ability to relate "our local communities" to other local communities for comparison and contrast. Ability to recognize symbols for smaller local communities within a metropolitan area.

Differentiate commercial, residential, industrial, etc., areas on map of local communities. Note relation of these areas to each other and to protective features. Locate local community on state map. Locate sources of rivers and their basins that are important to the local community.

bodies, important landmarks should be included. Plan each trip using the map. Have children carry maps with them on trips to follow their route. Make sure children are oriented on map. Use cardinal directions as learned. Locate own neighborhood and use to compare and contrast with other less well-known areas of town, city, county, or metropolitan area. Use supplementary sources of information to answer questions raised by map study.

Study maps made by Red Cross, conservation district engineers, etc., to show changes in function and in spatial distributions of the imagined future.

Basic Human Activity: Producing, Exchanging, Distributing, and Consuming Goods and Services

OBJECTIVES

PUPIL EXPERIENCES

1. *Ability to observe thoughtfully.*

Observe local communities as places in which producing, exchanging, distributing, and consuming functions occur. Question who is involved. Where? With what?

1. *Firsthand experiences.*

Take trips to observe how some of the major needs of the local communities are met. Be selective. Observe *key* functions—those necessary to the needs of the local communities: water purification and supply; distribution of light, heat; sewage disposal; complete cycle of milk production from cow to consumption in a city home; distribution of produce from farm to wholesale market, to retail market, to city home. Observe the key functions for which our local communities are of importance to others.

Observe consuming of utilities (water, electricity, heat, etc.), of food, clothing, shelter, of transportation and communicating facilities, etc. Is any group being excluded in these functions?

2. *Ability to reason about things geographic.*

Analyze what features are necessary for producing, exchanging, distributing, consuming:

(1) relative location of these features;

(2) relation of land use to land form and cultural features: influence of elevation, water bodies;

(3) distribution of features: city layout, farm and town complex of county; influence of lines of transportation;

(4) effect of technology: relative time necessary with hand processes compared to various levels of machine processing; difference in education and number of people needed for work with hand processes compared to other levels of machine processing.

2. *Reorganized experience.*

a. *Discussion.* Discuss what the fathers and mothers of members of the class contribute to producing, exchanging, distributing, consuming activities; what community workers do; what farmers do; what children do. Help children see how their roles will change as they grow up. Discuss the functions necessary to meet the needs of the people. Discuss the unique contribution this city or county makes. Is it a port? Is it a center for redistribution of farm products? What main products come in from the surrounding area? What products or raw materials go out? Is it mainly a financial and light industrial center? Is it mainly a manufacturing center? Is it an agricultural area? What are its *key* functions or products? Where are producing or consuming features located? What is the pattern of distribution? How do products or raw materials come in and go out of the community? Where do they come from? Where do they go? How are people engaged in these functions? Do all people have equal opportunities to engage in these activities? If not, what is needed?

b. *Dramatic play or dramatization.* Have children dramatize their roles in producing, exchanging, distributing, consuming. Have them dramatize the roles of fathers, mothers, industrial workers, agricultural workers, and other people on whom the local communities depend and whom the local communities serve. How do people feel who are unemployed? What do they do? Have children dramatize what they have seen on trips. Help children select those items that will build key understandings. Dramatization may take place on a base map and show the route of distribution: milk from cow to city home; tractor from manufacturing plant to farm. Or the floor plan may be a diagram on which an agricultural or manufacturing process is re-enacted.

3. *Ability to map in some form* what has been observed. Ability to sketch maps of walks or short trips, with key landmarks, accurate as to relative location and relative distance. Ability to mark routes on city or county maps; ability to add features to base maps of local communities. Ability to use cardinal directions when learned. Use of legends. Ability to discover symbols to represent new features (full range from three-dimensional to conventional symbol, when ready). Ability to add familiar symbols in new locations and possibly to use color symbols to differentiate residential, commercial, industrial, agricultural, park, and natural areas in local communities. Ability to use historical maps to note changes that have happened during the generations in the distribution of these activities in the local communities.

c. *Mapping.* Take a trip to observe important producing, distributing, or consuming functions and associated activities. Study pictures before and after depicting the same or similar function. Where the trip is not possible, pictures and aerial photographs and directed study may serve. Map in following order of difficulty:

(1) *Tangible:* Re-enact using props to depict relative location. Examples in city: plant layout in bottling plant, newspaper or printing plant and route of process; major routes of transportation bringing people to work and bringing produce into city to wholesale market and reloading and distributing to retail groceries. Examples on farm: farm layout, milking barn layout; daily route of cows; transportation routes to take farm products to market, to take people to work.

(2) *Pictorial:* Draw pictures of what has been seen or dis-

cussed, accurate as to relative location and relative distance.

(3) *Semipictorial:* Draw large sketch on floor, large paper, or oilcloth, under teacher guidance, using agreed-upon symbols to depict features. Put legend in lower left-hand corner. Add cardinal directions when learned.

(4) *Creative mapping:* Draw a map to represent the action in a story. Draw a map from a picture or aerial photograph. Construct a map in a sand table to study land use as it might relate to land form. Draw picture maps for beauty but make them accurate as to relative location and direction.

4. *Ability to read through symbols* of maps and associate with imagery of realities thus represented. Ability to read a map of local communities, first teacher-made, then commercial. Ability to read pictorial, semipictorial or abstract symbols of familiar features. Ability to locate neighborhood on map of local communities. Ability to contrast own neighborhood and other areas in local communities (town, city, county, metropolitan area).

Locate each local community on commercial street or road map of metropolitan region or county. Recognize relation of own most immediate community to others in same county or other local communities within same metropolitan region. Locate local communities on map of state.

3. *Using and interpreting maps made by others.*

Read a simplified map of city or county using an enlarged version of a local map simplified by teacher. Features of familiar places with familiar symbols should appear, but not too many at one time—only those pertinent to or important for a given lesson. Note cardinal directions when learned. Locate neighborhood on local map as basis for broadening understanding to areas less well known. Locate local communities on map of surrounding area. Analyze simple relations between town, city, or metropolitan area and adjacent agricultural, mining, or fishing areas, etc., in terms of producing, exchanging, distributing, and consuming functions. Use supplementary sources of information to improve map work. Use maps both historical and of the planned or imagined future.

Basic Human Activity: Transporting People and Goods

OBJECTIVES	PUPIL EXPERIENCES

1. *Ability to observe thoughtfully.*

    Observe the local communities (town, city, county, metropolitan area) as places dependent on transporting function. Question who is involved. From where? To where? With what? Why?

1. *Firsthand experiences.*

    Observe roads and streets in the neighborhood and in the local communities. Notice trucks, buses, cars, streetcars, taxis, trains, helicopters, and the facilities necessary to make them operative. Look at transporting within the local communities involved in producing, exchanging, distributing, consuming. Look at transporting of people and goods into and out of the local communities. Stand on a congested downtown corner when office workers arrive in the morning. Visit a factory gate when workers are arriving or leaving a shift.

2. *Ability to reason about things geographic.*

    Analyze distance in relation to time to get from school to home, from school to other places in the neighborhood, from school to places on trips. Analyze distance in relation to blocks or miles. Estimate and check distance. Compare distance by different means of transportation and by obstacles that prevent a direct route. Compare transporting in urban and rural areas. Compare transporting of times past with present and project solutions of transporting into the future.

2. *Reorganized experience.*
    a. *Discussion.* Discuss relations of time and distance to means of transportation used. What means are used in the neighborhood, in connecting neighborhood to other areas in local communities, in bringing goods and people into and out of local communities? What helps determine the type of transportation used? Compare means of transportation and their use in local communities of county and metropolitan area. Compare difference in distances involved. How do different kinds of workers get to their jobs?
    b. *Dramatic play and dramatization.* Dramatize the time it takes for things to get places by various means of transportation. Dramatize the difference in route and the difference in handling occasioned by the different means of transportation used.

3. *Ability to map in some form* what

    c. *Mapping.* Take walks, keeping

has been observed. Ability to make sketches of small areas visited or routes to get there, showing key changes of direction on a short trip. Ability to map ground plan of out-of-door places visited, such as roundhouse or airport as seen from a tower, accurate only as to relative location and relative distance, using cardinal directions, when learned, and legend. Ability to use symbols: pictorial, semipictorial, moving toward conventional, of carbarn, train terminal, railroads, roundhouse, bridges, shipping by water, airport, water bodies, streets and roads.

track of time, blocks or miles walked. Time trips. Keep record of route. If driving, note time and mileage and changes in direction if not too complex. Take boat trip. Keep time and try to get information as to distance traveled. Compare to travel time on land. Sketch a trip over a bridge, past a railroad track. Compare routes when different means of transportation are used. If the local communities have a port, map the harbor. Map a railroad roundhouse floor plan. Get an aerial view of airport and sketch, accurate as to relative direction and relative distance. If the local community is agricultural, map transportation connections to city. If local area is a city, map transportation connections to surrounding area bringing in food or raw materials for manufacture or shipping. Map routes and means of transportation used to get people to work: in the past, now, and in future.

4. *Ability to read through symbols* of maps and associate with imagery of realities thus expressed. Ability to read a simplified map of local communities and locate features concerned with transportation.

Read from a county map some of the transportation routes connecting various parts of the local complex. Follow through the main lines of transportation as they extend beyond local boundaries into the state.

3. *Using and interpreting maps made by others.*

Read a simplified street or road map of the local community using symbols that represent familiar features. Locate local community on map of larger area. See what lines of transportation run in and out of local community and where they lead. Get information about the number of vehicles using various main routes each day. What means of transporting are available to move people and goods among the local communities? What helps determine the type of transportation used?

Basic Human Activity: Communicating Facts, Ideas, and Feelings

OBJECTIVES	PUPIL EXPERIENCES

1. *Ability to observe thoughtfully.*
   Observe local communities as places dependent on communicating functions. Question who is involved. From where? To where? With what? Do all people within local communities interact?

2. *Ability to reason about things geographic.*
   (1) Note distribution of post offices, mailboxes. Compare pattern of distribution in different types of neighborhoods. Do the same with telephone, TV, and other forms of communication to try to discover reason for location pattern. Are some neighborhoods less well covered? Why?
   (2) Compare means of communication and time involved.
   (3) Compare differences in function and who uses different means.
   (4) Recognize calendar and clock as means of measuring and communicating time.

1. *Firsthand experiences.*
   Observe distribution of communicating activities and associated features in neighborhood and in local community. Locate post offices (main and branches), telephone exchanges, TV stations and aerials, radio stations, mailboxes, telephone wires, newspaper office, etc. Are there special areas where certain minority groups live? Do they have their own newspapers and broadcasting stations?

2. *Reorganized experience.*
   a. *Discussion.* Discuss relative location of features of communication. Do different patterns emerge in different types of neighborhood? Are people in some neighborhoods isolated from people in other neighborhoods? Why? Compare distances involved in urban and rural communities. Where are radio and TV stations located? What problems do telephone wires create? Study the calendar as a means of recording time of week, month, season, year. Study clock as means of learning time of day.
   b. *Dramatic play and dramatization.* Dramatize various forms of communication, their operation, problems of repair and maintenance. Note the difference that means of communication might make in an emergency. How might people have reached a doctor before the time of phones? How much longer might it take for news to get

3. *Ability to map in some form* what has been observed. Ability to locate familiar features concerned with communication and add others on a simple large base map of the local communities. Ability to do the same on individual base maps at seat (may use colors to differentiate forms of communicating features; cardinal directions, when known; legend). Ability to use symbols of newspaper office, telephone exchange buildings, telephone poles and wires, TV stations, radio stations, post offices, applying simple use of color.

4. *Ability to read through symbols* of maps and associate with imagery the realities thus represented. Ability to read a simplified map of the local communities, noting pattern of distribution of symbols representing familiar means of communication.

Locate local community in complex of county or metropolitan area.

known without radio and TV? Without newspapers? What effect would distance have on news if these media did not exist? What happens in a poor, congested neighborhood when a fire breaks out or police protection is needed? Dramatize the ways that a general alarm might be communicated regarding an approaching tornado or a tidal wave. Why would some means of communication be more appropriate than other means under such emergency conditions?

c. *Mapping.* On large base map of the local communities, locate pertinent features under discussion—one medium at a time. If a minority group is isolated in one area of the community, pupils should be aware of this. Do the same on identical desk-sized base maps, one for each child. Add features gradually; agree on symbols (conventional, when possible). Add legend. Orient map and note cardinal directions. The pupils should not overlook the wide range of local communities' communication activities, e.g., posters during political campaigns prior to election, street and highway marking signs, outdoor electrical signs and billboards, etc. These features can be mapped.

3. *Using and interpreting maps made by others.*

Read a simplified street or road map of local communities. Locate places visited in studying communication. Locate same features elsewhere on map. Note how lines of communication connect neighborhoods within a local community, local communities of small size with

Locate local community complex within the state.

other parts of a larger community complex like a metropolitan region or a county. Note relation between central point of origin of communicating features and distribution into neighborhoods. Locate local community complex on a simple map of the state. Look for familiar communication symbols. Note ties of own local community to surrounding area.

Learn to find and use additional symbols. Learn to use additional source material to supplement and improve map work.

Basic Human Activity: Expressing Aesthetic and Spiritual Impulses

OBJECTIVES

1. *Ability to observe thoughtfully.*

    Observe local communities as places in which aesthetic and spiritual impulses find expression.

2. *Ability to reason about things geographic.*

    Analyze location of churches in relation to types of neighborhoods: residential vs. others. Why this distribution? Relate location of parks, trees, lawns, to types of neighborhoods, local communities. Where is there greenery? Where none? Why are concert halls, museums, and similar cultural facilities located as they are in the local community complex?

PUPIL EXPERIENCES

1. *Firsthand experiences.*

    Locate parks, gardens, landscaping, natural beauties of local communities, and agencies concerned with enhancing the cultural offerings. What has been added by man that enhances? Note distribution of these features. Locate museums and concert halls. Locate churches of various kinds. Note architecture, religious denominations. Look at pictorial maps as aesthetic products.

2. *Reorganized experience.*

    a. *Discussion.* Discuss location and extent of areas of natural beauty in local communities. How are they being preserved or encroached upon? Where are the largest areas? Where none? What might be done to improve the situation? Where are the parks and whom do they serve? Where are the churches and whom do they serve? How are locations of churches related to kind of area and to population?

    b. *Dramatic play and dramatiza-*

3. *Ability to map in some form* what has been observed (three-dimensional, pictorial, semipictorial). Ability to locate on large base map of local community areas of beauty, churches, museums, noting relative and exact location.

Agree on colors to show areas of greenery and on symbols for church, museum, trees, water bodies, etc.

4. *Ability to read through symbols* of maps and associate with imagery of the landscape or the realities thus represented. Ability to read simple maps of local communities and locate symbols concerned with expression of aesthetic and spiritual impulses.

Locate neighborhood and local communities (town, city, county, or

tion. Act out a visit to a place of beauty—how it smells, sounds, feels, as well as how it looks. Roll in the grass or climb a hill. Re-enact route to get there. How long does it take? Dramatize planting and caring for flowers, bushes, trees. Dramatize appropriate behavior in a concert hall, museum, place of worship, a private garden, a city park, the shrine of a hero, etc.

c. *Mapping.* Estimate extent of areas of beauty in terms of blocks or miles. Take trip to check correctness of estimate. Estimate distance to arrive by preplanned route. Check in terms of time, blocks, or miles with mileage meter on car or bus. Draw pictures of places of beauty. Get pictures of nearby places of beauty, e.g., war memorials, a hero's monument, a historical site, a park, a beach, etc., place around map and draw a string from each to exact location on map. Agree on pictorial symbol for each. Place three-dimensional, pictorial, or semipictorial symbols on base map of local communities. Note pattern of distribution of features in relation to types of neighborhood or locale of community. Are some areas neglected? Locate places of worship and places of beauty on desk-sized base map.

3. *Using and interpreting maps made by others.*

Read simplified street or road maps of local communities. Recognize symbols and note distribution of above features in own neighborhood and in other areas of local community complex. If some areas are less well supplied, why? Is some group being deprived? Lo-

metropolitan areas) on map of larger area, noting symbols for aesthetic and spiritual expression.

cate local communities in larger state complex. Compare relative spaciousness, areas of greenery, churches, museums in surrounding area. Locate city or county parks on map of state.

Basic Human Activity: Providing Recreation

OBJECTIVES	PUPIL EXPERIENCES

1. *Ability to observe thoughtfully.*
   Observe local communities as places in which recreational functions occur. Analyze distribution of recreational features.

2. *Ability to reason about things geographic.*
   (1) relative location in terms of residents: Are recreational facilities equally available to all?
   (2) relative distance: How far must one go to get to areas of recreation in each area? What means of transportation is necessary? Is this means available to all?
   (3) exact distance in blocks or miles;
   (4) relation to physical and cultural features.

1. *Firsthand experiences.*
   Observe distribution of features of recreation (natural and cultural). Locate community centers, swimming pools, parks, movie houses, libraries. Where are they located in relation to various residential, commercial, industrial, and farming areas? Where are they spacious? Where are they cramped? Where are natural areas?

2. *Reorganized experience.*
   a. *Discussion.* Where are recreational facilities found? What kinds are available? Whom do they serve? Are they equally accessible to all? Are any areas unduly neglected? What can be done to improve such a situation? How far must one go in terms of time and blocks or miles? Do the physical features of the landscape influence location? Does land use influence location? Is there adequate space for recreation? Note distribution in residential areas of different types (small homes, apartments in "better" neighborhoods and in poorer neighborhoods). Contrast distribution in urban and rural areas. Where inequalities exist, can something be done?
   b. *Dramatic play or dramatization.* Re-enact routes to get to recrea-

3. *Ability to map in some form* what has been observed.

Discover use of symbols (three-dimensional, pictorial, semipictorial). Sketch large base map and locate areas devoted to recreation. Trace routes from various neighborhoods of local communities. Agree on color to differentiate recreational features. Differentiate between areas of natural and commercial recreation. Locate parks and playgrounds in own neighborhood and in other areas of local communities. Show cardinal directions. Make legend.

4. *Ability to read through symbols* of maps and associate with imagery of the landscape or realities thus represented. Ability to recognize familiar features and symbols on teacher-made and commercial map of local communities and compare to recreational features of the neighborhood. Ability to note how the neighborhood depends on the local communities for many of its recreational needs.

tional areas. Are they near or far? What means of transportation is available and most appropriate? (Bring all senses and muscles into play.) Who can't get there? How might they feel? Act out recreational activities of people in different communities. Contrast rural and urban; home, commercial, and public types of recreation.

c. *Mapping.* Create maps based on trips, pictures, discussion. Make crude map for dramatic play mentioned above. Draw pictures of recreational facilities. Set pictures around base map and draw strings to location on on map. Put semipictorial symbols on map. Locate parks and other features. Note if any residential area is neglected. Agree on symbols and color, if used. Discuss conventional symbols, if any used. Draw ground plans of some recreational features. Show cardinal directions; make legend.

3. *Using and interpreting maps made by others.*

Read a simplified street or road map of city or county. Locate or add features of recreation. Discuss any different symbols used for familiar features. Locate own neighborhood on city or county map and compare pattern of distribution of features. Locate local community complex in map of surrounding area. Compare areas of natural recreation and commercial recreation and indicate how far it is to travel to each from different neighborhoods. Locate city and county parks. Get and interpret maps of city and county parks if available. Get additional information about how city and county parks come into being. Compare recreational activities and their sites today with old maps to show changes in location, quantity, and quality.

Basic Human Activity: Providing Education

OBJECTIVES	PUPIL EXPERIENCES
1. *Ability to observe thoughtfully.* Observe local community (whether town, city, county, or metropolitan area) as place in which educational activities occur.	1. *Firsthand experiences.* Take trips to elementary schools in a variety of neighborhoods. Take trips to junior high, high schools, and colleges in the local community. Visit other educational facilities—community centers, libraries, museums. Note their location. Visit central representatives—board of education, main library, etc.—so as to contrast and compare physical plant and function and to discover relation with neighborhood facilities. Attend meetings of various agencies concerned with providing quality education for all.
2. *Ability to reason about things geographic.* (1) number and distribution of various types of schools and informal educational features and relation of functions; (2) relative distance from home to schools at different grade levels; (3) effect of physical features; (4) effect of cultural uses of land.	2. *Reorganized experience.* a. *Discussion.* In what ways are elementary schools in different neighborhoods different? Why? In what ways are schools of different age levels different? Why? What is the relation of the central representative to neighborhood facilities? Are schools and supplies fairly distributed in various types of neighborhoods? Do physical features of land affect location? Do cultural land uses affect location? Which seems to affect location more? Can something be done to improve the situation? How have location of educational facilities changed through time? b. *Dramatic play or dramatization.* Dramatize going to school on base map of neighborhood.

Dramatize something seen at the board of education, main library, museum, or another school. Act out a relation between main representative and own school: a supervisor visiting own classroom; getting help with a room project from the main library. Act out "in the library" using a rough sketch of library floor plan drawn on classroom floor. Dramatize similar educational activities in great-grandfather's time in the local communities.

3. *Ability to map in some form* what has been observed. Ability to use simplified base map of local communities to sketch routes of short trips to nearby educational facilities.

Agree on symbols to represent educational facilities. Use color, cardinal directions, legend.

c. *Mapping.* Sketch routes to school and other educational facilities on simplified base map of local communities. Count blocks, estimate distance in terms of time, city blocks, miles, method of transportation used. Show distribution of main library and branches, museums, board of education, and schools throughout the local community. Develop symbols for schools, libraries, community center, and other educational features of the local communities. Become aware of the quality of a school building as well as its location. Map routes to school in great-grandfather's time and show appropriate symbols for means of getting to school.

4. *Ability to read through symbols* of maps and associate with imagery of the landscape and realities thus represented. Ability to read teacher-made and commercial maps of local communities using familiar and conventional symbols. Ability to read map of county and state and locate familiar symbols. Ability to analyze pattern of distribution and contrast pattern found in different areas. Ability to contrast distribution of educational facilities

3. *Using and interpreting maps made by others.*

Locate educational facilities (especially central, organizing ones) on map of local communities. Note familiar symbols in new places. Read legend for any new symbols for familiar features. Analyze pattern of distribution of educational facilities as to type of neighborhood and relation to central office. Become aware of neighborhoods in which improvements in educational

throughout local communities over historic periods.

facilities are needed. Locate familiar features on map of larger area. Compare on maps distribution of educational facilities today with distribution throughout the history of the local community complex.

Basic Human Activity: Organizing and Governing

<table>
<tr><td align="center">OBJECTIVES</td><td align="center">PUPIL EXPERIENCES</td></tr>
</table>

1. *Ability to observe thoughtfully.*

Observe the local communities to discover their organizing and governing activities. Who is involved? Where does the activity occur? How is it done? For whose benefit? What are the interlocking levels of organizing and governing: neighborhood, precinct, city, county, metropolitan?

1. *Firsthand experiences.*

Take trips to institutions and organizations where organizing and governing at neighborhood and local community levels can be seen and functions related and contrasted. Be sure to visit city hall when local governing board is in session and again when planning commission or other important committees meet. On county level, visit courthouse and observe some of the activities which go on. Visit county clerk, justice of the peace, sheriff, constable, coroner, etc.; become acquainted with their functions. Visit agencies concerned with improving education, cultural offerings, and providing social services (health, job training, aid, etc.).

2. *Ability to reason about things geographic.*

Analyze examples of organizing and governing in the local communities centrally and their relation to various neighborhood branches. Review organizing and governing functions of home, school, neighborhood agencies. Analyze relationship with city or county government. Note relative location of central features to subsidiary. Reason why more organizing and governing is essential as local community complex has grown from primitive neighborhoods into mod-

2. *Reorganized experience.*

a. *Discussion.* Review organizing and governing in home, school, neighborhood. Compare government at central level with familiar forms. Discuss role and functions of city or county government and organizations at level where children can see effect in the neighborhood. How does city or county help finance and provide fire and police protection, see that justice is done, provide educational and job-training facilities, cultural facilities, social services, etc.? What

ern cities and metropolitan districts.

3. *Ability to map in some form* what has been observed.

Discover use of symbols (three-dimensional, pictorial, semipictorial) to represent agencies involved in organizing and governing functions in local communities. Map layout of some of these institutions and agencies so as to clarify functions. Use symbols for police stations, firehouses, roads, traffic lights and road lighting, postal facilities, parks, public-supported educational, social, recreational, and aesthetic features, city hall or county courthouse.

groups are active in the community to guarantee civil rights of all citizens?

b. *Dramatic play and dramatization.* How are problems discussed and decisions made in home, school, neighborhood. How do city and county functions compare? Study relation of city or county government and agencies to neighborhood: How does one get a policeman assigned for school crossings and for training traffic guides at school? How does one get a mailbox where it is needed or the fire department to come to school for fire drill? How does one get a stop sign or traffic light installed where needed? Who paints the white lines on streets and roads for intersection crossings and traffic lanes? How does a citizen get police protection in his neighborhood? How might these organizing and governing activities have been carried on in past time in the local communities?

c. *Mapping.* Locate city hall, county courthouse and other important metropolitan governing agencies. Review all basic human activities and their associated features and locate on large base map. Make sure the central organizing facilities appear. Analyze location of city hall, county courthouse, police headquarters, etc., to their functions. Show relations between centrally organized functions (interrelated controls). Review all symbols for above. Note cardinal directions. Make legend. Map old buildings that once housed these organizing and governing activities.

4. *Ability to read through symbols* of maps and associate with imagery of realities thus represented.

Recognize symbols for all organizing and governing agencies at neighborhood and local community levels: city hall or county courthouse and also the central bodies that organize and direct the way the local communities and neighborhoods that comprise the complex carry on all the basic human activities. Recognize and relate these familiar features on a teacher-made or commercial map of city or county. Compare and contrast distribution of these activities over time through maps drawn during the life of the local communities.

3. *Using and interpreting maps made by others.*

On map of city or county locate central organizing and governing agencies and draw lines to the neighborhood facilities with which they relate. Use a different color line for each of the basic human activities: for example, red lines from central police headquarters to all neighborhood branches. Locate city hall and county courthouse. How do these relate to organizing and governing bodies of other basic human activities? Review all symbols above. Note cardinal directions. Read legend. On map of state, locate state capitol. Find and use other sources of information to supplement concepts of local government and organization. Compare and contrast old maps with contemporary maps to see what changes have taken place. Speculate on the reasons for changing activities and related facilities and their spatial distribution.

Basic Human Activity: Creating Tools and Technics

OBJECTIVES

PUPIL EXPERIENCES

1. *Ability to observe thoughtfully.*

Observe the local communities as places in which tools and technics are used and created.

1. *Firsthand experiences.*

Observe major construction or repair taking place anywhere in the key functions of the local communities and in major transportation lines bringing goods and people into and out of the local communities. What tools and technics are being used in various jobs? Who operates the necessary equipment? How many people are involved? What training is necessary? Where is it provided? Who can get it? Where differences in the use of tools and technics occur, can you account for them?

Visit major industries of the local communities. Ask the same questions about tools and technics being used. If possible, visit industries doing similar work but using less advanced technology for comparison.

Visit a research and development institute or talk to a foreman of a new construction to find out what innovations are being made to solve the problems of the local communities.

2. *Ability to reason about things geographic.*

   Analyze the effect of the tools and technic being used:

   (1) What happens when an operation gets larger?

   (2) What happens when more automatic tools and technics are used?

   (3) What happens when the geographic space of local communities expands rapidly? Are subways, elevators, monorails, helicopter ports related to such problems?

2. *Reorganized experience.*

   a. *Discussion.* Analyze the difference between a small operation and a large one: production, construction, transportation. Why do larger operations tend to have more automated machinery? What brought about their introduction? What happens to the people replaced by machines? What can the local communities do about automation and jobs?

   b. *Dramatic play.* Re-enact what was seen on any of the visits and discussed above.

   c. *Mapping.* Have the children draw maps based on firsthand observation, e.g., floor plans of industries or section of an industry visited. Add or change symbols on a base map of the local communities to show changes in roads, etc., that are planned for the future. Draw contrasting maps based on information about the local communities 100 years ago and today.

3. *Ability to map in some form* what has been observed.

   On a base map, add symbols for any of the new construction visited. What changes in the local landscape appear during a year? What new inventions are most needed to solve problems of modern local communities? Where?

4. *Ability to read through symbols* of maps to the realities thus represented. Ability to read a map prepared by the teacher or a simple commercial map using familiar symbols which depicts the local

3. *Using and interpreting maps made by others.*

   The teacher can prepare maps of the communities long ago and today. It might be best to start with pictorial symbols and focus on one

communities of 100 years ago and compare it to one of today.

Films and pictures will be necessary to build visual images and the teacher will have to direct pupils' attention to certain key features. Examine maps of planning commission, highway engineers, and private corporations to see what and where they are planning for the future.

basic human activity at a time. The change in land use as population increased and tools and technics improved should become obvious. Attention should be directed to the effect of population pressure on land use.

Trace the relations between the urban community and the surrounding land use through study of semipictorial maps which show land use and by studying the roads, railroads, or water bodies used to connect the metropolitan area and its environs.

Sequence of Pupil Experiences

The experiences suggested above disclose many possibilities for geographic thinking and map making for eight- and nine-year-olds within the local communities in relation to each of the basic human activities. Such an analysis becomes an excellent source of material for a unit of work based on any given cluster of activities, for example, "Transportation in the Local Communities," or "How the Local Community Protects Itself," or "Interdependence of City and County in Producing, Exchanging, Distributing, and Consuming." *Within the analysis of any basic human activity, the complete map study sequence is used.* The children start with firsthand experience in space and move gradually and step by step to making maps of their own, and finally to reading maps made by others; they go from three-dimensional mapping in dramatic play to reading conventional symbols on a commercial map of their local communities; finally, they locate their local communities complex on a state map.

Now we will correlate all the material of the preceding section into a more detailed sequence of pupil experiences which is *developmental in its overall framework.* It uses the same methodology but cuts across the basic human activities. The section as a whole starts with observation and trips into the local communities and ends with the most abstract map interpretation of which third-graders are capable. It is also sequential in relation to previous chapters. The arena of concern here is the local community complex, which encompasses the previous emphases of family, school, and neighborhood community and looks briefly ahead into the state community.

This sequence may serve as a guide for the teacher or researcher in the classroom who is working with a group of eight- and nine-year-olds. Skills developed in previous levels will be reinforced and extended in considering the local communities (town, city, county, or metropolitan area)—any or all in combination. More difficult aspects of previous skills and understandings will be initiated. It is hoped that this section will serve as a guide in the classroom, to be adapted as need be in light of local conditions.

Scarfe has characterized the period of growth from six to nine as the "Age of Observation."[15] Children should be encouraged to observe carefully the behavior of sun and weather and of plants and animals. They should take note of the hills and valleys, rocks and minerals, and the kinds of work people do. The close observation of what is laid out for them to see becomes the basis for extending their thinking now or in later grades to exploration in other lands. It lays the foundation for the concept that people the world over have *similar* needs and *similar* as well as *different* ways of satisfying them.

Surveys of child development agree that children of primary school age are interested in almost everything of the present time and of the immediate environment. As their interests begin to move outward in time and space, the present and the immediate must be used to build a firm foundation from which they can take off. How much a child will observe, and how much he may benefit from such observation, however, is to a large extent dependent on the direction and encouragement he gets. This does not suggest a haphazard study of details as facts in themselves. We are concerned with building clear images of landscape features in the immediate environment that will make it possible to interpret landscapes both at hand and far away. Geographers agree that early, accurate observations and interpretations in the local environment are the basis for good geographic understanding and map thinking from this age on. Social studies in the first three grades offer the opportunity to have children observe carefully the important features, both natural and cultural, available in the immediate environment of the local communities.

TRIPS AS A MEANS FOR OBSERVATION

At third-grade level trips will have three interrelated purposes: (1) to discover how a city, county, township, or metropolitan community carries on the basic human functions, (2) to gain ideas of the interdependence of people in carrying on the basic activities within these several enlarged communities of slightly different scale, and (3) to gain new insight into the fundamental relationships of the set of interlocking communities—family through metropolitan.

Experiences designed to help youngsters discover how the local communities carry on their basic functions will be considered for each of the nine basic human activity clusters. We do not suggest that trips and other experiences be undertaken in the order given here, however. Trips should be an outgrowth of the larger social studies units. It is important that a spirit of inquiry, purposeful exploration, and discovery be built in advance. The pupil should know what he is looking for: how some of the basic human activities not capable of full satisfaction in the lesser communities of family, school, and neighborhood are more adequately cared for in the larger local communities of township, county, city, or metropole.

Protecting and Conserving Life, Health, Property and Resources. Previous trips into the neighborhood community may be recalled or repeated. Trips not taken in the second grade may well be scheduled, but the rationale is now focused on how the lesser communities are complemented in their efforts to protect and conserve by the activities of the larger and more inclusive local communities. Children should be able to discover for themselves, with wise guidance from the teacher, the reason neighborhoods join with other neighborhoods of like scale in order to form larger communities with more complete resources to satisfy human needs.

A trip can be taken to the central fire headquarters of which the neighborhood fire station is a branch. Maps can be observed that show the distribution of all the lesser fire station branches throughout the local community complex. A trip to the public health agency will demonstrate how the neighborhood clinics and the several hospitals are related, and maps will show the areal distribution of such facilities. Similar excursions to central headquarters will help pupils discover the networks of services that exist throughout the local communities: sewers, power lines, phone lines, substations for water, police, fire, sanitation, fire hydrants, fire alarm boxes, traffic lights, and a host of "everyday" objects, agencies, people, and events that a child by himself may never sort out and organize into a system of services of protecting and conserving provided by the public and private agencies created by the set of communities.

Producing, Exchanging, Distributing, and Consuming Goods and Services. In this focus the pupils will discover how the goods and services consumed in the home, school, and neighborhood are produced and exchanged in the larger local communities. Key industries and key distribution mechanisms can be visited at this time. Not every producing or exchanging facility could possibly be visited; choices must be made. These choices should be carefully weighed so that pupils experience one or two of the *key* or *major* activities that characterize their particular local communities. An automobile manufacturing center would logically suggest a visit to observe this significant enterprise. A flour milling industry of major proportions likewise would be logical for a different local community complex. Activities that make the local communities important beyond their own boundaries must be looked at. For example, if the pupils were studying their local community of San Francisco, the fact that it is a major port and exchange center, a major financial and trading center, must be adequately covered. If one had to make a choice of a trip in San Francisco, a trip to a leather processing plant, interesting as that might be, could not take precedence, for example, over a trip to the harbor to see the ships come and go. If children live in a major port and do not watch a ship being loaded or unloaded, they are not being introduced to the very personality of their local community. What is more, the trip should be planned when important activity is taking place. If the local community is a port, children should see longshoremen at work. They should examine types of products and find out where they come from and how they differ from those produced within their own locale.

The neighborhood distribution services should be reviewed and relational thinking extended by visiting areas of similar functions in the local community. Where previous trips were made to the neighborhood grocery, the concern could now be shifted to the wholesale market. The routing of food from farm to processor, to wholesale market, and finally to neighborhood retail market should be analyzed. The complete process of milk from cow to city home should be of interest to both farm and city children alike. City children should see trucks bringing in produce or milk, refrigerator cars and milk tanks being loaded or unloaded. Food can be seen coming in and going out by freight trains. What determines the means of transportation? More distant relationships in food distribution could be considered. What is being shipped out? What is coming in? The same questions would apply to rural areas; rural children are just as much in need of seeing where their produce goes and what comes back in exchange. At the local community level, it is time to develop concepts showing the interdependence of city and country. Children need to compare and contrast nearby communities. Small local communities within the same county may be very similar in function. However, many of them are often very closely associated economically with a large city or metropolitan area. Such ties should be identified. They may help make more understandable the contribution of the small local community and, in turn, its dependence on the larger community.

Trips must also be taken to discover how the local community supplies some of its own needs. Every local community needs a water supply, sewage disposal, materials and labor to provide shelter, and a food supply. How are they obtained? A trip can be taken to the water purification plant. The source of the water should be discovered and the plan of distribution to the pupils' neighborhood studied. What other neighborhoods or local communities share the source?

It is still in order to plan a trip to see a house being built in the neighborhood and to observe the carpenters, plumbers, electricians, painters, glazers, roofers, etc., at work. Discuss the type of building. Is its construction in any way related to the climate or the building materials available locally? Now is the time to follow materials to their sources of supply in the larger local communities. Question the wholesalers to discover where *they* get their supplies. It is wise to find out in advance from a builder when a load of materials from the district wholesaler will be arriving at a site of construction. If the trip is planned to coincide with such a delivery, the children can see lumber, glass, plumbing fixtures, or other equipment as it arrives and observe what means of transportation is used and how the materials are handled. A trip might be taken to the wholesaler to see lumber coming in by truck or train and being unloaded and stored, or to follow its delivery to the neighborhood building job. Such trips are possible in rural as well as urban communities. Seeing the processes firsthand helps develop and tie fragments of information together. In discussion periods afterwards children should be helped to understand where they personally fit into this activity cycle of producing, exchanging, distributing, and consuming goods and services in the wide arena of the local communities.

Children should become aware of who does the work of the community: construction, maintenance, major production, service. Where do these people live? How do they get to work? How hard do they work? How well are they paid? How are they trained? Who has no work at all?

Transporting People and Goods. Previous trips have already demonstrated some transportation means. The ride to the harbor, or other major trip in the local community, might well have involved a train, a bus, a streetcar, or an automobile, depending on where the children were coming from. Observations there meant walking and perhaps other transportation. Loading and unloading may have involved vessels, trucks, or trains. If a trip is taken to the train terminal or freight yards, to the roundhouse or airport, deepened understandings should be built by relating previous transportation experiences in the neighborhood to the present experiences, which are focused on more centrally organized aspects of transporting.

In addition, there is a broader view to be taken toward transporting at the level of the local communities. Our focus now includes transporting as the means of moving people to and from work and the problems that arise at peak hours of traffic. We become concerned with moving products in and out of the city, distributing products within the city, and interchanging products between local communities in urban and rural areas. These aspects lend themselves very well to mapping. In turn, mapping routes and relations becomes an important means of developing insights.

The possibilities of looking through files of newspapers and magazines in the library or historical society to discover changes that have taken place over time in transporting within the local communities are great. These time changes are important bench marks in projecting changes in moving people and goods in the decades to come.

Communicating Facts, Ideas, and Feelings. Trips can be taken to the main post office, central telephone exchange, main library. Their functions should be related to those of the neighborhood branches. How do they maintain their lines of communication? Trips to radio and TV stations could be taken now if the group has not already done so previously. Perhaps a trip to a large metropolitan or county newspaper could be arranged to see how the neighborhood news is gathered. A visit to a county sheriff's headquarters could include observation on how communication is maintained with police cars cruising anywhere within a county or metropolitan area. Trips to a variety of neighborhoods will reveal how other people within the larger local community live, information that otherwise might not be communicated to pupils.

Expressing Aesthetic and Spiritual Impulses. Trips can be made to parks, gardens, areas of natural beauty, and areas that have been beautified by men. Eyes should be alerted for the birds and small animals to be seen. Attention can be directed to the different kinds of trees, bushes, and flowers. Many of the plants are imported from places all over the world. Some are local varieties. Discussions of where the plants originated, how they are transplanted, and the special care or conditions needed to maintain them in their new environment can help build geographic concepts. Planners in local communities are becoming more and more aware of the necessity to conserve and protect areas of natural beauty. Many states have undertaken a program of building county parks as centers of recreation and enjoyment: waterfront parks, playfields, golf courses, landscaped areas, tourist camps, picnic facilities. Children should be introduced to these county parks where they exist nearby. And equally or more important, children should be introduced to the kind of thinking that makes the parks possible. In terms of mapping, the routes coming and going can be mapped. The children can then help their parents take the trip with them. The distribution and availability of such areas to various neighborhoods is important. Children's attention should be called to means of transportation available for getting to places of beauty. If public transportation is not available, who suffers? The ground layout would also make an interesting and worthwhile map project.

Churches, museums, art galleries, concert halls, historic monuments, etc., can be visited. They often reflect architectural influences which are well worth discussing. The floor plan can be sketched as well as the setting of the building in its surroundings. Children should also be interested in the distribution of these places and should study their location before taking the trips. These experiences can become the bases of pictorial maps which can be aesthetic expressions in themselves.

Providing Recreation. There are many opportunities for firsthand observation of recreational facilities in the local communities. Trips can be taken to community recreational centers, swimming pools, parks, playgrounds, and commercial recreation areas. Attention should be called to the kinds of neighborhoods in which they are located and the pattern of their distribution in the city, county, or metropolitan communities. Are recreational facilities equally accessible to all? Are there any areas unduly neglected? If so, why? How far are they in time and distance from each neighborhood? Is transportation easily available? Are additional recreational facilities needed in some neighborhoods? The relation of the physical features of the landscape to location of recreational facilities can be noted. How does land use influence the amount of land available for recreation? Where are recreational facilities spacious? Where are they cramped? Who is being neglected? Why? What can we do to improve recreational facilities for all? As children take trips and analyze them from a geographical point of view, we are helping them develop the kind of thinking that can make local communities more beautiful and more equitable areas in which to work and play.

Providing Education. A trip to the board of education of the city or of the county would be in order. Probably both county and city school administrations should be noted. If possible, pupils should attend a meeting at which an important local issue is being discussed. The child is broadening his view from the immediate neighborhood to the local community organization, and this should be the focus in the trips at this level. He should now be noting the quality as well as the quantity of schools provided for a variety of neighborhoods. Are certain neighborhoods more neglected? Why? What can be done to improve the situation?

A visit to the main library, also, will have two purposes: one will be to compare in size and complexity the main library with the neighborhood branch; the other, even more important, will be to analyze the relation of the main library to the smaller neighborhood branches and the quality of the neighborhood branches.

Organizing and Governing. Trips to the city hall, to the county courthouse, to social agencies are musts. Preparation should be made in advance so that the children are able to get maximum benefit from their observation. If possible, each trip should be made when a meeting of a committee or governing body is in session. The size and layout of the building as such are not important unless they are seen in relation to its function. The kind of question to raise with the children is: What kind of problems come up in the neighborhood community that are too big to be taken care of there? Children must be helped to see, for example, that the neighborhood community would find it very difficult to provide schools and pay the teachers and other school personnel. One neighborhood community alone could not very well set up its own traffic lights, support adequate police and fire protection facilities, or provide work for the people living there. Third-graders who have analyzed functions of the home, school, and neighborhood communities as suggested in earlier emphases should be able to understand that many of the problems of the neighborhood must be handled by the larger local communities of which it is a part.

Creating Tools and Technics. The importance of tools and technics in the local community has been obvious in trips taken in relation to most of the other basic human activities: in protecting and conserving of resources—natural, cultural, and human; in producing, exchanging, distributing, and consuming; in transporting and communicating; in providing recreation, education, and the means for expressing aesthetic and spiritual impulses.

Organizing and governing functions of the local community often do and often still need to concern themselves with the effect of changes in tools and technics on the lives of human beings. Education must be improved and must provide training and retraining programs for people who lack the skills to participate in an increasingly automated society. The need for innovation and creative effort in tools and social institutions should be a fruitful subject of challenging discussion for pupils. The study of the local communities on such a broad perspective provides an important firsthand experience for understanding the tremendous progress we have made and some of the problems we face. It also helps supply background for understanding some of the problems faced by many nations in the world today, background that will be valuable in later grades when other areas in the world become the major focus.

We have briefly discussed trips that might be taken to discover how the township, city, county, and metropolitan communities carry on their basic functions. What can children learn from trips that will help them understand the interdependence of people? People do not live unto themselves. To understand the local environment, children must note something of the needs and doings of outsiders. Each neighborhood is part of a larger whole: the city, county, or metropolitan area. City children should get out into the country to see cows being milked, chickens being raised, grains harvested, fruit and vegetables grown. They might observe some of the arrangements for marketing. Trips are meant to furnish the sensory data with which to discover that the city neighborhood could not exist without the country to support it. Farm children must get into the city to see where their farm products go, and in turn to find out where they get what they cannot produce at home in rural areas. Trips to the harbor, to railroad yards, to the wholesale market, mentioned previously, are not just sightseeing tours. They lay the foundation for discovering where materials come from that are used in the neighborhood. If a trip can be taken to a relatively distant lumbering operation, mine, or fishing wharf when appropriate activity is in progress, this should be done.

Through the age of seven, children's interests are mainly in the present time and of the immediate environment. At eight, interests are reaching out in time and space. The extension beyond the phenomena close at hand is thus possible, and necessary, so long as teachers make sure that children have ample opportunity to build an adequate background of immediate experiences. Studies seem to agree that eight-year-olds, as a group, can do some systematic thinking about the past.

The study of the local community can now be extended to include a time dimension. Some trips can focus on remnants or relics of previous times in the community. As Mitchell points out, "Eight- and nine-year-olds are intrigued by what happened long ago on the very spot where they now live. Few places have not some traces of the early environment left which they can explore."[16] However, she warns,

> Eight-year-olds, who are still young children, should not be plunged simultaneously into the past and the distant. Either they should take their first step back in time to people who long ago lived in the same place in which the children live, or their first step should be far away in space to living people with whom their own lives have a real and tangible relation.
>
> The first approach either to the faraway or to the long ago should be closely tied up with immediate world around the children which they can to a certain extent explore at first hand.[17]

Why do we give all this attention to observation and trips when the concern of this study is with map making and map interpretation? Experts in geography agree that study of the immediate environment is a necessity for good map work. Parker says,

Maps . . . can have meaning only through abundant experience in translating landscapes observed *into* maps, and map symbols into landscape realities. Experiences essential in so doing are needed in *connection with every locality studied.* It is only as one learns gradually to translate landscapes into maps that one can, in turn, acquire the ability to use maps in gaining those concrete concepts of the world whole. . . .[18]

It is the responsibility of the teacher to make proper use of the landscape as a laboratory:

It becomes the first task of a teacher who would base her program with younger children on an exploration of the environment to explore the environment herself. She must know how her community keeps house—how it gets its water, its coal, its electric power, its food, and who are the workers that make the community function. . . . she must know the geographic features which characterize her particular environment and strive constantly to see how they have conditioned the work of which she is a part and how they have been changed by that work.[19]

REORGANIZATION OF EXPERIENCE THROUGH DISCUSSION

Discussion is one means of helping children develop the ability to reason about things geographic. Geography today is less and less a study of purely physical features and their relations and more a study of the relations of man to his environment. Thus when children explore local communities and their functions as suggested above, they are preparing themselves to understand the little dot or circle or other symbol that stands for a city or metropolitan area on a map. That little symbol does not stand for the *word* city. It represents all the streets, buildings, activities, institutions, technologies, and people that make a city go. Every city carries on all the basic human activities, and in this respect they already know something about every city they see on a map. A similar relation exists between the area shown on a map representing a county and the basic human activities carried on by all the people who live within its borders. Each city or county is also different, however; each has separate location and each carries on a role peculiar to itself. The teacher must help the children form a distinct understanding of their own local community complex so that they may use this knowledge as a basis of comparison with other communities of similar scale.

In providing opportunities for relational thinking, we are hoping pupils will acquire the following map skills and understandings: (1) ability to recognize and express geographic distribution and relative location, (2) ability to understand time relations, (3) ability to orient self and note directions, and (4) ability to judge or measure distance. In the pages to follow we will analyze how best to help children develop such relational thinking.

Ability to Recognize and Express Geographic Distribution and Relative Location. Since no community lives unto itself, children should see a series of relationships in their local communities. They must try to understand their local communities as entities within which the basic human activities are carried on. Then they must understand their local communities as they relate to all other communities of lesser, the same, and greater size. What counts is the functional significance of the location of a place. Meyer asks six questions which can guide teacher and pupils in analyzing the importance of the relative location of "our particular local community."[20] Reworded for our third-grade emphasis, these questions follow:

1. Where is our local community in terms of a large water body (a river, lake, sea, or large bay) and type of climate? (If the children have studied latitude as distance from the equator, they might also locate the community in terms of latitude.)
2. Is our local community in the valley, the mountains, on level or hilly land?
3. What towns, cities, counties, and metropolitan area is it in or near?
4. What natural vegetation and what mineral resources are found in or near our local community? (If a distinctive kind of soil is present that helps explain the vegetation or mineral deposits, this too should be called to the children's attention.)
5. What is the *main* type of work carried on in our local community: farming, manufacture, mining, fishing, etc.? What specific kind? How does our local community's particular function relate to that of other nearby towns, cities, or metropolitan area within or bordering our county?
6. What means of transportation or commerce connects our local community to nearby towns, cities, or metropolitan area within or bordering our county?

This kind of thinking is not the direct result of trips, but trips and directed observation are necessary to help find answers to these questions. The discussions that follow trips must encourage such thinking.

Mitchell describes the value of discussions with children of things they have spontaneously noticed in the neighborhood, local communities, or elsewhere, and of planned group exploration.[21] Discussions should be held before planned exploration to focus the children's questions and prepare them to observe effectively. A trip is primarily to teach the children the technique of gathering information through observation and provides an opportunity to answer questions previously raised. Then a follow-up discussion is necessary. Emphasis should be on the immediate environment and the *work* that different people are doing. But one cannot confine discussion to the here and now; children will on their own and should be encouraged to bring in the related activities of local communities far away in time or space.

Maps themselves become a tool in learning of relations. Whittemore points out that a child cannot "gain a full knowledge of the world by exploring it bit by bit and piecing together in his mind his own concrete experiences . . . only maps will enable him to understand the relation of one place to another and the significance of the location of places. The *purpose of a map* is to reduce the patterns of the physical and human features on the earth to a size that can be seen at one place."[22] By third grade, then, a map will often be present during discussions.

It is important for children to begin to see the *structure* of the local communities. In a city, they should become aware of the relative location of industrial, commercial, transport, and residential neighborhoods. They should locate the physical features and cultural items that influence location. They should see how streets, roads, rivers, airports, and railroads are related. Analysis of a county's structure would be very similar: residential neighborhoods might coincide with farms or a village; relative location of industrial and commercial areas, physical and cultural features, roads, rivers, and railroads would be equally important in understanding the county (see Figure 27).

Even *within* a city or a county, children cannot visualize the pattern of distribution of various features unless they can see the whole city or county at one time. Only with a map can they analyze where the physical features, like hills and water bodies, appear that in turn influence where cultural features may be located. They cannot get an overall picture of transportation lines from any one or even a dozen walks or rides. To see the structure of a city, a county, or a metropolitan area in terms of residential, commercial, industrial, and agricultural areas, they must see their bits of experience spread out in one place before them.

Thinking, however, should not stop with analyzing how things are or how they came to be. Even a third-grader can wonder, at his own level of experience, whether things could not be otherwise. The effects of previous lack of planning can be called to his attention. Sometimes level land needed for agriculture in an area has been used up for houses which could have been built in the foothills. Even children can grasp ideas of conservation. A continuous destroying of forests and cutting down of orchards in order to replace them with asphalt parking lots and roads will eventually destroy the beauty and food-producing features of that land. More and more children must also be led to think of human resources and potential human resources that are often being destroyed or wasted. Children can be helped to think of alternative courses of action in the choices they make daily and in the larger choices being made by the people of the local communities.

The technological processes available to a community are a vital factor in determining the kind of work and life possible there. Children can observe enough on their trips and in their own immediate environment

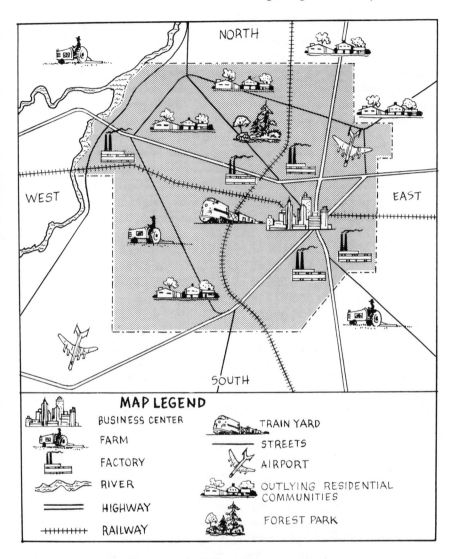

Figure **27**

Pictorial Map of a City and Surroundings

to have a basis for comparing simple hand processes with semiautomatic and more complex automatic productive processes. The following examples are readily available and not difficult to understand: baking at home or school, in a small neighborhood bakery, and in a large commercial bread plant; ironing at home, in a small dry-cleaning establishment in the neighborhood, and in a large central laundry; building something of wood at home or school, in a small upholstery shop, and in a mass-production factory. There are still many processes to see in operation in any city or county that are at different levels of technological development. Children can quite easily grasp the difference in amount of time it takes to produce things by different methods and the comparative size and cost of plant and machinery needed to mass-produce. Also, education becomes a factor in nurturing human resources to keep up with the new technology.

Similar thinking can be fostered about improved means of transportation if it is held to a level of concreteness that children can think about. If they see a stretch of road or a street being built and watch the many processes and machines used to build one or two miles of road or blocks of street, they can begin to comprehend why public thoroughfares are costly. This will be important in their understanding of roads and streets or lack of them when they study maps of larger areas. Even within their school experience they will be able to see a constant shift away from hand-operated small tools to the use of more and more automated large tools. What happens to the people who now do the unskilled labor? Attention to such processes is not something that is imposed on children for future use only; the human aspect of them in their immediate environment can interest them at the moment.

The ability to reason and see relations is not accomplished in one long discussion period. Questions are raised and discussed before, after, and during each trip. The discussions are kept short, but the learning can be cumulative. As Jersild says, "In many areas it appears that in order to grasp certain meanings it is necessary for the child to have an accumulation of impressions and experiences distributed over a period of development as distinguished from lessons or impressions concentrated within a limited period of time."[23]

Children do not learn to reason by words alone. Follow-up discussions should also recall sounds, smells, sights, touch, feelings of people, etc. Questions such as the following, about cultural items seen, encourage reasoning which is supported by other senses: How did the machinery sound in the milk bottling plant? Did the men seem to mind the noise? Did it smell clean and fresh? How would you like to work in the bakery? What kind of education is necessary in order to perform these jobs? Why did the men wear those heavy asbestos gloves when they took the loaves out of the oven? Why was it so warm in the room where the sponge for the bread was rising? Did you like the smell?

Dramatic play brings senses and muscles and feelings into operation and, especially when guided and combined with discussion, often helps clarify ideas. Concepts relating to features in the natural environment can be built by encouraging children physically to act out: climbing a mountain, rolling down a grassy slope, lying on a hot sandy beach and feeling the breeze blown over the water, or bending down to pick beans hour after hour.

Ability to Understand Time Relations. Time relations can enter in a more systematic form in children's thinking at this age. Concepts that have a time dimension can be given support with dramatic play. For example, Indians are often studied in third grade when teachers and pupils go back in time to learn about people who lived on this very land long ago. Eight-year-olds identify with people whose culture is very unlike their own as they try to re-enact *how* those people lived and worked. We can raise questions such as: What was the land around us like before people with modern tools changed it? How did the Indians use this land? Mitchell describes the kind of learning possible when other kinds of thinking are brought into support words:

> The lives of Indians were obviously and dramatically conditioned by the natural conditions they found around them. Here is a basic relationship which makes the Indian culture, or any other culture, understandable. How can children discover, not merely be told, that the work of the Plains Indians sprang from the wide grassy plains and the buffaloes that roamed over them? If children can be made to feel the enormous flatness stretching to the horizon under the great arch of the sky; if they can come to love the infinite variety of grasses bending in the wind; if children can know all about buffaloes, their strange shapes against the sky, their many entertaining habits, the paths they made to water holes, what they did when snow came—then the problems of the Plains Indians will become the children's problems. They will feel like Plains Indians. . . . all the time the children will be thinking and working out the relationships between the land of the Indians and the work of the Indians. . . .[24]

We certainly should make use of this fact in planning a third-grade curriculum.

Studies in child development agree that eight- and nine-year-olds are more capable than younger children of learning through words. But they still need to translate the words into action in their own ways to make them have real meaning.

Ability to Orient Self and Note Directions. A sense of direction is one of the first requisites in learning to map. The following pages will discuss three aspects of orientation: (1) learning E-W and N-S directions in space, (2) understanding "up" as being away from the center of the earth and "down" as being toward the center of the earth, and (3) following directions in space.

Since a sense of direction is not inborn, it is important to provide children with experiences which will make the language of direction meaningful before they are expected to note directions on a map or orient a map.

With respect to *learning cardinal directions,* Howe undertook two important experimental studies: (1) to find out what primary age children know about directions and (2) to see if children can be taught a clear concept of directions in space systematically and accurately. In the first study he found that "Children do not know directions as well as commonly supposed."[25] In the second study he showed that children can be taught directions in space systematically and accurately, and that third grade is the most favorable period of comprehension.[26] His step-by-step procedure follows:

Step   1: *Outdoors* about 8:45 A.M.
   a. Children observe position of sun.
   b. Teacher tells them: this is the *eastern* part of the sky.
   c. Same as (a) and (b) in a new location on the next day, or day after.
   2: Children state in what part of the sky the sun appears.
Step   3: *Outdoors* about 11:30 A.M. Children observe noon sun. Told this is *southern* part of sky.
   4: Children say *where* the noon sun is.
Step   5: *Outdoors* as late in the afternoon as possible. Children observe sun; told this is the *western* part of the sky. Children urged to watch the evening sun at home.
   6: Children say *where* the late sun is.
Step   7: *Shadow stick* to show *northern* direction at noon. (Shadow stick built on a 1-foot square wooden base. A round or square peg 1-inch by 30″ is attached perpendicular to the base.)
   8: All shadows point in the same direction at a given time. The shadow stick is carried on trips to eliminate local association.
   9: *Counter directions*—The sun is in *eastern* sky, where is shadow?
           The sun is in *western* sky, where is shadow?
           The sun is in *southern* sky, where is shadow?
   10: *Semi-cardinal points*—to show in between points—shadow in northeast, northwest, etc.
       (First use shadow stick; then telephone poles, trees, human shadow substituted for shadow stick.) [Figure 28.]

This intensive study is extended over ten weeks with a gradual lengthening of the lapse between instruction periods. It is important that instruction be carried on over a long period of time and in varying situations around the school building.

Howe added a prolonged procedure to be continued throughout the school year which makes use of seasonal change. The necessary information is summarized here:

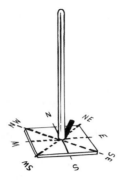

Figure **28**

Shadow Stick

If the drill cycle is introduced in September, the sun will be nearly east at the beginning of the school day and the varying positions of the morning sun may be followed.

About September 22 (the autumnal equinox), the day and night are of equal length (12 hours each); the morning sun can be seen exactly in the east and the evening sun exactly in the west everywhere within the mid-northern latitudes.

About December 22 (the winter solstice), we have the shortest day of the year in the Northern Hemisphere, representing midwinter.

About March 21 (the vernal or spring equinox), the day and night are again of equal length (12 hours each), and the morning sun is again to be seen exactly in the east and the evening sun exactly in the west everywhere within the mid-northern latitudes.

About June 21 (the summer solstice), we have the longest day of the year in the Northern Hemisphere, representing midsummer.

Many geographers have recommended simple plans for teaching children direction by the sun. Kohn suggests using the hands to learn directions: In the morning point with right hand toward sun to be seen in the east; in late afternoon point with left hand toward the sun to be seen in the west. Front of body is facing north; back of body is toward south. Kohn too says that "Exercises like these require frequent repetition. Time should be permitted during third grade to allow the children opportunities to practice orienting themselves in the morning, at noon, and in the afternoon."[27]

Involving the body in the learning of directions may be an important factor in orientation. Lord, in his studies, found,

Those persons who have well-developed abilities with regard to orientation seem to have the cardinal directions related to their bodily position at any given time. The pattern of arrangement of the cardinal directions needs to be as well fixed as the association of right-left and front-back.

He continues,

> There is a real need for out-of-door exercises, observations, and drills with regard to directions. Children lack the foundational experiences necessary to make directions in space meaningful. There is need, if directions are to function as instruments in orientation, to develop in the child a close relationship between the arrangement of cardinal directions and self.[28]

Whittemore suggests that with every change in classroom from third grade on, the teacher should help children orient themselves in the classroom.[29] She suggests that the points of the compass be reviewed with the children outdoors at the time of the high sun and that the children then be brought indoors into the new classroom and be oriented again to the points of the compass. Whatever map is being used should be placed on the floor and also oriented with outdoor space. The children can be helped to place themselves and their new classroom in respect to directions in space and to the way their local communities spread out around them. This relationship should be taught in the primary grades and maintained at higher levels.

Anderzhon lists *understanding "up" as being away from the center of the earth and "down" as being toward the center of the earth* as one of the prerequisite skills in map reading.[30] If maps are kept in a horizontal position on floor or table or desk, there should be no difficulty in teaching up as away from, and down as toward, the center of the earth.

Children carry on many activities to further their understanding of directions by *following directions.* They may plan a short walk and follow their own directions, which include cardinal directions. They might practice giving directions to a stranger who wants to find a place that is familiar to them. They might give each other directions to follow on a map of the county or city to see what the destination is. They or the teacher might dictate a simple walk, which the children would sketch, noting cardinal directions. The teacher might plan a picnic lunch at a new spot and have the children sketch the selected route and then really go. For example: "Go north two blocks and turn right. Travel in this direction for three blocks and you will cross a bridge over a railroad. Continue two blocks further until you come to a river where the road turns sharply north again. Pull off the road to the south, and this is where we will have our picnic. Mark an X where we will have our picnic. Note the cardinal directions on your sketch." (See Figure 29.) Such exercises can be good learning experiences for using symbols as well as directions.

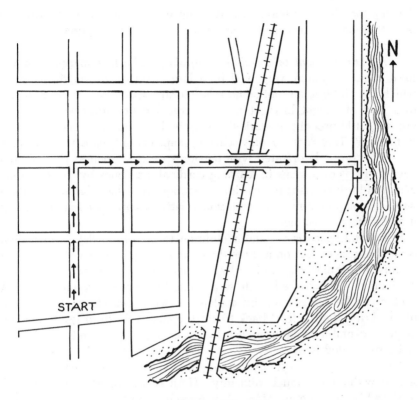

Figure 29

Following Directions: Sketch Map

Ability to Judge or Measure Distance. Children continue to measure distance by time to get somewhere as well as by number of miles or blocks. They may estimate the length of short walks by blocks, time, or number of paces. They should be checked by some more accurate estimate—a pedometer or a car mileage gauge or other source of information. Whenever the group goes on trips, the mileage should be noted. In discussing transportation and communication as a means of overcoming distance, children should be reminded of the influence of mechanical inventions on the time it takes by the various means at our disposal to cover equivalent distances.

REORGANIZATION OF EXPERIENCE THROUGH MAPPING

We have discussed ways of reorganizing experience gained from first-hand observation and trips. We have analyzed the role of discussion (with support from dramatic play) as one means of helping children develop the ability to reason about things geographic. Now we will turn our attention to mapping as a means of reorganizing experience.

Three-Dimensional or Tangible Mapping. The first mapping of the local community may very well be a large map drawn on the floor on which the children act out some relationship. Examples: What happens to a load of freight brought in to a large redistribution center? How are the cattle brought to market? What is the route of lettuce from field to market? This floor, or play-scheme, map, like all maps used to date, should be properly oriented with outside space. As soon as the children have had several lessons in learning cardinal directions by the sun, they may add to their maps the cardinal directions they have learned. Otherwise, the map continues to represent relative location of features being used in the re-enactment.

Horizontal space is easier for children to map on a flat surface than is vertical space. But on a three-dimensional map it is less of a problem because a real obstacle can be placed where an obstacle occurs in nature. A chair can be covered with something to represent a mountain. A bridge can be represented by a plank between two chairs, but only if planks bring the roadbed back to earth again. (By third grade it is no longer acceptable to children, if it ever was, to allow the ends of a bridge to be suspended in space.)

A sand table is a must. On a sand table vertical surface can be represented without too much difficulty. Here is an opportunity to clarify "up" and "down" again. Since all geographers and cartographers recognize the representation of elevation as difficult on a flat map, the sand-table map should be used for its advantages. It is especially helpful in demonstrating relief, drainage, flow of rivers, erosion. Children can read from such a map that *A* is in the mountains, *B* is on a river. "Land" can be built up and the table flooded to show the formation of an island, a peninsula, or a body of water such as a lake. Farm children can also be helped to see why a field may become flooded after a heavy downpour.

Barton describes how a sand table might be constructed and used:

> . . . take a large, thick piece of glass and slope it [gently] lengthwise in a sand table. The glass may be painted blue on one side or . . . a light blue desk blotter [may be placed] under the glass. The entire glass is then covered with sand. . . . Trace a depression in the sand to represent a valley. The exposed glass will represent the water. Tributary valleys may be traced.
>
> [A group] can carry this project still further by placing bridges across the rivers and a house or two on a hill. If greater detail is desired, small twigs may be added for trees and a lake placed at the head of a stream. At one end, the glass may be uncovered to represent part of an ocean. The river may

be shown as flowing into the ocean. Other items representative of the local environment may be added.[31] (See Figure 22, page 176.)

The understanding of slope as well as actual height in elevation is very important for interpreting maps and seeing how man has used the land around him. A sand table as described above serves this purpose admirably for third-graders. The total underlying slope is particularly valuable in eliminating misunderstandings of slope since large land masses have a general slope from mountains to ocean in addition to local variations in elevation.

Children can also make small models of landscapes in planting flats, in cigar boxes, or in baking pans, using sand, clay, putty, or plaster of Paris. In these small individual or group projects they can portray many of the same features possible on a sand table. However, if each child or group chooses a different symbol or concept to represent, the whole class can thus have a variety of three-dimensional models from which to learn. Such projects could serve as a liaison between reality and pictorial representation. Some models might be built from a particular section of the landscape seen on a trip. Other models might be built from aerial photographs, from pictures, or from maps with which the children have already become familiar—maps that they have made themselves or that represent landscapes they know from previous learning.

Since at third-grade level the local communities of today, and perhaps yesterday, are being studied, natural and cultural features and relations in this area should be explored in three-dimensional maps. It might be very interesting to take the same physical plot of land (the local communities) and build three models—one representing the way it looks today, another showing how it might have looked when the Indians lived on it, and a third illustrating how it might look in the future.

If a large sand-table model and a small individual model are made of the same landscape, and recognized as such by the children, here is an opportunity to develop concepts of scale that are needed in map interpretation. The children will see that the same area can be represented by maps of different size. Conversely, if two children bring flats to school in which to build their models, one model to represent a farm and one the school grounds, the children may also be led to realize that the same size model can represent different sized landscapes.

Chace describes a unit in third grade to teach the geographic background of Cape Cod.[32] A sand table would be admirably suited to mapping in a tangible form the understandings being developed:

1. Land surfaces or relief: Children take a trip to a hill. Looking down they recognize many familiar landmarks—hills, dunes, farmland, wooded

regions, marshes, but they see in them a relationship that was not previously possible.

2. Water bodies: The children see lakes, rivers, bays, harbors, Cape Cod Canal, the four seas. Having seen the relationship of these water bodies, all of these areas can be seen in greater detail on pictures but properly placed in space, not only as individual bodies of water.

3. Political divisions: Children locate villages and towns.

4. Climate: Children keep records of daily temperature, prevailing winds, rainfall, seasons, weather records. This is supporting data to help children understand the land use of the area.

5. Natural resources: Children's attention is called to the soil around them, forests, plants, animals dependent on that soil, fish and shell available from the waters nearby. The sand table was used to show natural resources and products of the region in proper location.

6. Location of Cape Cod: The children locate Cape Cod by:
   a. Directions on compass.
   b. Directions by routes on gas station road map.
   c. Relation of Cape Cod as a county of Massachusetts, as a part of New England and the United States, on the continent of North America, and on world maps and globes.

Some questions might have been raised, such as: What are Cape Cod's major products? Why? What are the recreational uses of Cape Cod? How did Cape Cod get its name?

Any area can be analyzed using Chace's six points. Children can climb a hill on a farm. How better to discover relative location of house, barn, stream, well, irrigation channels, distribution of planting areas and areas set aside for animals? Likewise they can observe the several farms and towns which make up a part of the county. If the children reproduce this layout on a sand table, they may discover, with guidance, why these particular locations were chosen and perhaps how some particular function might have been more advantageously located. It should be remembered that a sand-table map is developed gradually and is meant to be an aid in learning relations; it is not just a display project.

Maps have two functions: as source material (when one uses maps made by others) and as tools. Three-dimensional maps, maps on which children play and to which they add things, are tools. When children set important buildings, means of transportation, etc., in three dimensions on a large-scale base map of the local community, this is a three-dimensional mapping experience, using the base map as a tool. Another example would be setting up the tower, hangers, runways, planes, on the ground plan of an airport.

Pictorial Mapping. The next step in our sequence, after three-dimensional mapping, is pictorial mapping. Pictorial mapping can refer to (1) drawing pictures, (2) using pictures, or (3) adding pictures to base maps. We will discuss pictorial mapping in that order.

When children *draw a picture* or mural of something they have seen, they are in a real sense making a map. Relative location and relative distance are expressed. By third grade we hope the pictures can become increasingly accurate in depicting location and distance. If the children can first draw a mural in chalk and then check it before putting it into more permanent color, they can improve their accuracy and, it is hoped, their relational thinking.

Children can *use pictures* in several ways. They can study an aerial photograph of a familiar area and then draw what they see, checking with the photograph for accuracy. It would be well for them to compare an aerial photograph taken quite close to the ground and one taken further away to see what happens to size, third dimension, and the amount of detail that can be seen. This is a good exercise for developing concepts of scale.

If children are trying to draw an area they have not seen, pictures of that area would be of help in getting better ideas of relief—how smooth or rugged the landscape is; what kind of trees, vegetation, and water bodies are to be found. Pictures are useful as sources of detail, but looking at pictures alone does not produce the overall perspective that only a map can give. Pictures are a supplementary aid. As with first-hand experience, children cannot piece the world together bit by bit, but they can use fragments from experience or pictures in the maps they draw.

Drawing from air photographs helps children develop more abstract symbols: "If children are asked to make from a simple air picture . . . a rough sketch showing the arrangement of the chief things they see as they look down from the air, they naturally represent streets as straight lines, buildings by squares or rectangles, and so on."[33]

Just as children put three-dimensional buildings, toy trains, and toy tractors on base maps, they can also make and *add pictured symbols* instead. Any of the basic human activities can be studied separately or contrasted. Features can be added and removed to emphasize certain patterns of distribution. Transportation or recreational facilities throughout the city, county, or metropolitan area can be studied, for example; or it is possible to make a study of the overlap of county and city school boards' jurisdiction.

Pictures put on maps are sometimes too unwieldly, so pictures are often put *around* the map and a string is drawn from the picture to its exact location on the map (Figure 30). This is especially suitable in studying basic human activities in a city, county, or metropole.

Pictorial maps are often used to show the products of a region. Care should be taken not to display too many products. Always be selective. Choose the key products and discuss why they are the basic ones of this locale. Remember, the maps we make are primarily to develop relational thinking. A clutter of unrelated products adds very little to

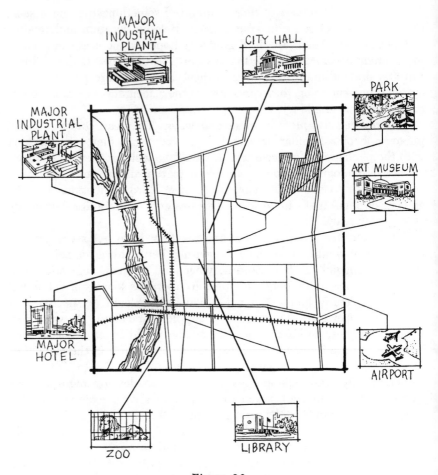

Figure **30**

Map of City with Pictures of Landmarks

lasting knowledge or understanding.

A flannel map can be used to make a pictorial representation. Symbols of rivers, mountains, transportation routes can easily be added with yarn or cord. Pictures pasted to sandpaper will also adhere to the flannel.

Semipictorial Mapping. As ability to use more abstract symbols increases, so can accuracy in depicting relative location and relative distance. Children can estimate a location, check with other sources of information, and be more accurate in their final location of the feature on a map. Semipictorial maps can be used to compare various routes as to distance and time between places within the local communities. Ground plans of a harbor or a farming landscape could be semipictorial with symbols and colors for features agreed upon. Floor plans of the inside of a building, the wholesale market, the cooperative farm produce exchange, the roundhouse, the airport, etc., fall in this category. Still better would be a plan of the larger local communities. Colors could be used to differentiate the commercial, residential, and industrial areas of a city; or the marshes, water bodies, forests, and cultivated and uncultivated areas of a farm county. Children's attention should be called constantly to land use and re-use, to areas of deterioration and the need of the local community to correct it. Cardinal directions should

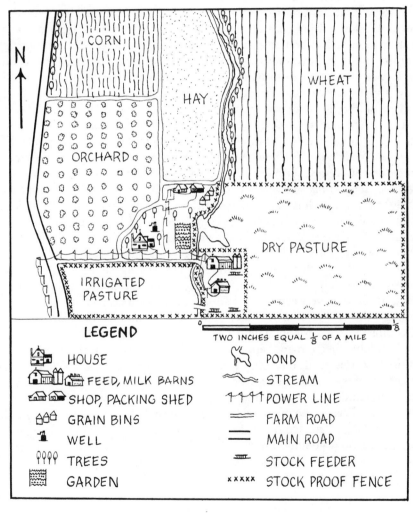

Figure 31

The Bailey Farm

be shown. A legend should appear in the lower left-hand corner explaining the symbols used (Figure 31).

A teacher can draw simple large maps of the city, county, or metropolitan area, on which the children as a group add features or trace travel routes. The teacher can also duplicate small individual base maps for the children to use at their own desks, to which they can add symbols concerning a particular basic human activity or analysis of a certain problem area. Such maps can be used to plan trips and can be carried on trips. It is important that the teacher know exactly what he expects the pupils to gain from any map activity.

However, it is also to be remembered that map making has the attribute of requiring careful observation in order to be able to place a feature accurately, and this in itself can be a purpose. The caution is against trying to have one map exercise do too many things at the same time. Map making can provide an opportunity for using facts in a new way and hence can encourage relational thinking.

Any of the features the children have seen on trips, focused their attention on, and discussed should be capable of translation into some kind of symbol that they can agree upon and understand. They should have no difficulty "looking through" their own drawing to the real landscape it represents because they themselves expressed in their own symbols *what they saw*. They should be able to represent streets as straight lines, buildings by squares and rectangles, and so on. Together they might agree how best to represent a rounded hill, a group of hills, rugged hills, a quick-flowing river on a sharp incline, a slowly flowing river where it enters a larger body of water, a sharp drop to the ocean, a gradual slope, etc. They should be able to agree how to portray marshes, wooded areas, dunes, farmland, cultivated and uncultivated land, if they have seen it, talked about it, dramatized it, and gone through the earlier steps of developing understandings of relationships. A peninsula or an island should be capable of semipictorial portrayal if models have been made and flooded, landscapes looked at, pictures studied, stories read, etc. The teacher should be on hand to help with selection of symbols. Wherever there is a choice, the teacher should help the children to choose the symbol most like the conventional one.*
However, there is no gain in having children's own maps go beyond their thinking. The symbol must stand for a reality in the child's mind; there must be a genuine image behind it. Once the symbols are agreed on they should be used consistently and a legend should be placed in the lower left-hand corner.

---

* Refer to "Map and Globe Symbols," Appendix B, for examples of symbols that may be helpful to teachers and pupils.

Though there is no symbol as such for distance, understanding of any map is based on distance concepts. Children can learn to gain insight into the relationship between time and space by estimating and comparing the time to get from place to place with different means of transportation. They can estimate distances by city blocks and miles. Time and distance should always be noted and discussed when making or using maps and locating features or routes. There is disagreement as to whether children at this level should learn to use scale of miles or only relative distance.

After having had many experiences in walking a mile, checking it against the time it took and the number of blocks walked, riding a mile and comparing it to a mile walked, a child should be able to use simple statements of scale on his maps. He should be able to say about his own map that one inch represents one block or that one inch represents one mile. Or he should be able to show graphically: ⌞_____⌟ 1 inch to 1 block ▬▬▬▬▭ 1 inch to 1 mile. The child's finished map should always contain (1) a legend showing the symbols used, (2) a statement of the scale, (3) a direction arrow. When using a map made by others, he should check these three major items before looking into the map.

The teacher must make sure the children have some understanding of scale before work with maps made by others is begun. In Figure 32 the children can use the scale to measure a mile from Highway 31 to the church, three-quarters of a mile from Highway 2 to the farm, less than one and three-quarters miles from the filling station to the farm, three-quarters of a mile from the bridge over the Marion River to the school. This kind of exercise on their own maps is essential.

If large wall maps for checking scale are not available, maps like those pictured on page 243 can be projected and exercises conducted showing how bar scales, all of the same length, can stand for different sizes. (Figure 33).

USING AND INTERPRETING MAPS MADE BY OTHERS

The first maps to which a child is introduced should be as simple as his own sketch of a ground plan and should consist wholly of some pictorial symbols for features which he already can see in his mind's eye. Children should not be allowed to get their first ideas of the appearance of a given kind of feature from the map. They should meet the symbol only after, from observation of that feature in a real landscape or a photograph, they have a clear idea of the appearance of features of that kind. Introducing symbols of features children have not seen in real or pictured landscapes is one of the chief causes of failure to learn to read maps—that is, to see *through* them to the *realities* the map symbols represent.[34]

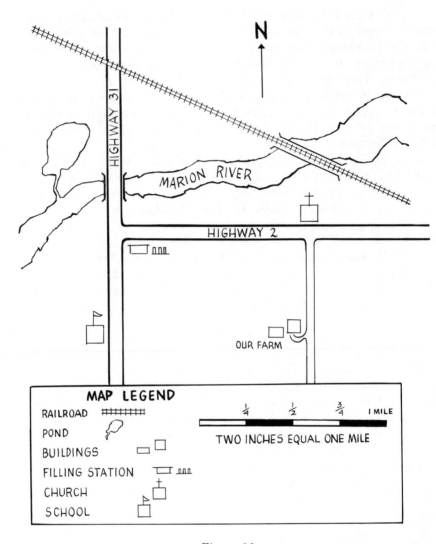

Figure 32

Exercise in Scale

A teacher cannot assume that children have had the previous experiences they should have had and must always check to see where they are. It is better to err in starting with the simple and moving rapidly ahead than to teach misconceptions. So in using maps that the children have not made themselves from their own experience, it might be wise to start through the same process of three-dimensional to pictorial to

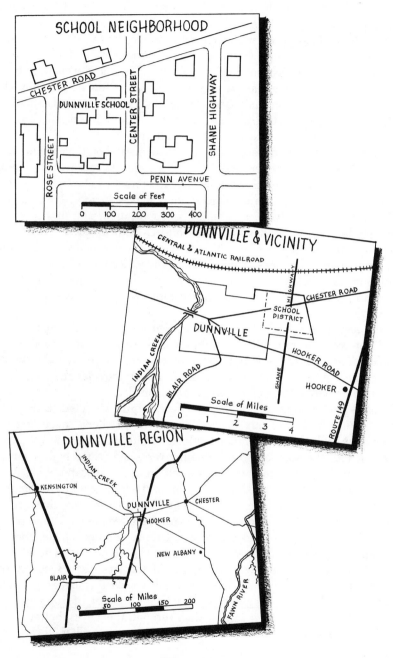

Figure 33

Maps Drawn to Scale

semipictorial.* Also, dramatization is extremely useful at this age for developing concepts. The children may act on a base map.

The three-dimensional map will be a simple, large one (six by eight feet, if possible). Land, water bodies, important relief features should be shown in some pictorial representation. If it is a city map or one of the county, it will have main streets or roads and a few outstanding landmarks. From there on, under teacher guidance, the symbols should be added and manipulated by the children. The base maps, however, should be accurate as to scale and orientation.

For pictorial map experiences, the base map should continue to be simple and large—teacher-made or commercial (Figure 34). Pictures can be used instead of three-dimensional symbols. They may be movable or tacked on. A large flannel map makes a good base map for adding symbols of rivers, mountains, transportation, and any natural or man-made features with which the children are familiar. This type of map has the advantage of making it easy to remove features and to add only the particular ones wanted for a given lesson. Commercial pictorial maps with features already on may be very useful if artistic, accurate, and not cluttered. Such a combination is not easily available, however.

Aerial photographs belong in the category of pictorial maps. If clear and not covering too large or complex an area, they are probably very useful. The aerial photograph, when it covers a large area clearly, does something neither trips nor pictures can do—it provides the overall perspective as only a map of the same area can do.

Aerial photographs, like maps, however, require directed study. There is too much to see in one place without the teacher's specifying what should be looked for. Familiar landmarks and main transportation lines coming into the city, coastlines, main rivers, and water bodies must be located to help the child orient himself in the landscape.

As mentioned previously, elevation and drainage are difficult for children to see on a map, though sharp changes in elevation are easy to see in the natural landscape. Geographers recommend that primary children do not go beyond the pictorial representation of elevation and slope; some kind of shadow or perspective must be added to elevation so that it can call forth correct images of the landscape seen. A relief map in third dimension would seem to fall within this category. In fact, Mitchell finds children get more adequate images of roughness and smoothness "through their fingers than through their eyes, better through actual relief than through symbols which stand for relief."[35] So, as far

---

* The sequence from three-dimensional to semipictorial mapping described here is clearly demonstrated in an eleven-minute film, *Maps, an Introduction.* (See "Aids for Teaching," Appendix A.)

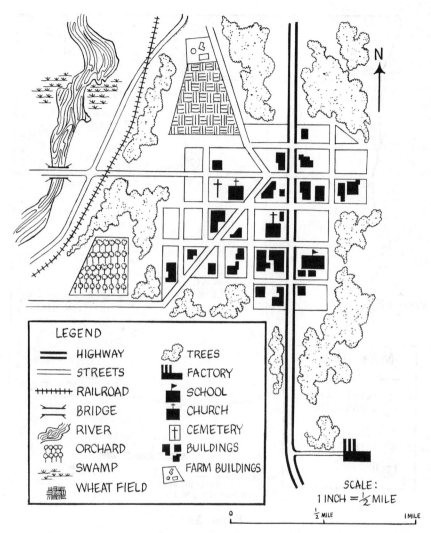

Figure 34

Semi-abstract Map

as slope of land is concerned, portrayal should be in actual relief or pictorial. Color layering is too abstract at this level.

A base street map of the city, county, or metropolitan area should now be understandable to children if it is not too detailed. When third-graders can orient themselves in terms of cardinal directions, they should use them and diagram a route of a trip before leaving the class-room. If a duplicated copy of the diagram is then given to each child, he should be able to refer to it from time to time during the trip and

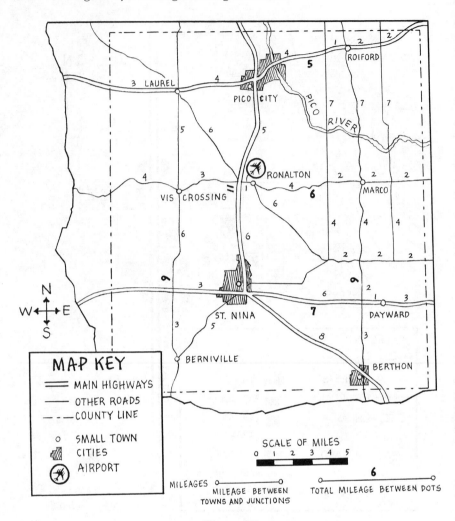

Figure 35

Map of Rose County

note the direction in which he is traveling. At third and fourth grade, a pupil should also be able to sketch the route of the trip *as* he travels, keeping it in proper orientation.

City children should be using simple street maps of the city regularly in the classroom for planning trips and laying out routes (it is nice when each child can have such a map to use at his seat) and as a source of information and location. They should be able to find a familiar park and note its exact extent, to locate familiar features and features represented by familiar symbols. With guidance, they should be able to analyze the pattern of distribution of certain features throughout the city or to compare the same features or lack of features in different areas of the local communities. They should be able to play games of location —telling a stranger how to get somewhere, giving each other directions and finding where they take them, etc. They should be able to trace out a major transportation route with guidance. They should be able to locate a specific feature on a river, near a railroad crossing, etc. However, a teacher cannot take for granted that each child can do this but must investigate, helping each child until he *is* able. A similar use of maps can be readily conceived for the rural local community, so that the children are able to use a road map to plan a trip to a nearby city and estimate distances. Figure 35 can be projected and alternate routes and distances compared, symbols located, etc.

The grid now becomes a factor of concern in exact location. Can third-graders learn to use the grid for exact location? Logically, it would seem that they should be able in terms of their developmental level and their previous experiences. For example, even first-graders can find supplies in an open shelf arranged with vertical dividers. A teacher can direct them to get the crayons from the middle cubicle of the top shelf, etc. Cannot a lettered and numbered grid on a simple map be used in the same way and understood if the teacher plans a few simple exercises with the children? (See Figure 36.)

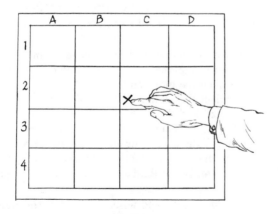

Figure **36**

Using a Grid for Exact Location

Commercially produced maps of the local communities should also continue to be used as tool maps in the same way that children previously used their own cruder maps—to add features and analyze relative location and distance, where the content is limited to a direct relation not involving analysis of too many factors simultaneously. Now, in addition, children can learn to use the grid for exact location.

Maps should be kept oriented to outdoor space even when used in the classroom. It is the teacher's responsibility to make sure the children are oriented in space whenever they change rooms—even during the same day. Cardinal directions should be added to maps and used in speech.

The geographic generalizations and skills learned at this level are very much like those summarized for the second grade, only the arena in which pupils operate has become greater and more complex. In third grade the local communities have been encompassed and some of their vital extensions into the surrounding hinterlands with which they interact explored. Expansion has been in terms of time also, as consideration was given to this same locale in earlier times when perhaps the Indians made it their home or when pioneers first settled the land and the relation to the natural geography was more direct and obvious. Cardinal directions and exact location have been introduced. Psychologists, geographers, and educators—through their studies—give us reason to believe that such activities and understandings are possible. It is the responsibility of the classroom teacher to verify such a program.

Using the Globe

As previously indicated, even in the primary grades globes should be available for informal study by the pupils. Kohn said,

> When the children have learned to locate places on maps, they are then ready to learn to locate them on the globe. They should be made aware of the similarity in form between the globe and the earth. This can be done in the primary grades . . . when the children first handle and examine a globe to discover the location, size, and shape of areas of land and water. After locating, comparing and counting land areas and bodies of water, the children should learn the names of the continents and of the ocean basins. They may also place a symbol on the globe to indicate the location of their home community. This will help emphasize the fact that the earth is their home.[36]

Since we cannot provide direct experiences, learning the names of continents and oceans beyond our own cannot be justified as a *major* aim for all pupils at this level. However, many areas of the world are constantly being mentioned in the mass media, and when the children discuss current events in class which involve knowing the names of the continents and oceans, the teacher should supply that information freely as the need arises. The teacher should stress the fact that at a later stage in the sequential program herein proposed the expanding communities will systematically develop the geographic understanding and mapping skills for the entire globe. Just how far the third-grader can go in developing concepts about the globe is at the moment an unsettled point. When children enter the intermediate grades, teachers often use latitude, longitude, parallels, and meridians in map and globe work as though the children have had some previous experiences with them so it might be advisable to build some simple concepts of their use with globes at third-grade level.

The Grid. It should be possible for the grid to be understood as a means of location, with no more complicated concepts attached. If children are given a large ball with no markings on it but an X and asked to describe the location of the cross, they can be brought to see the usefulness of a numbered grid to help describe the location. The same exercise can be repeated on a large blank piece of paper, asking the children to locate an X when there is no grid and then to locate it when a grid is present (see Figure 36). The value of the grid is instantly apparent. If then the poles and equator could be explained as providing a starting place, children can understand the placing of other parallels as a measuring scale on a globe's surface. It would seem that they could also understand that the first meridian had to be placed somewhere to provide a starting place and that the particular starting place chosen was arbitrarily agreed upon. How well third-grade children could accept this reasoning has yet to be determined. From the evidence on child development and map work with children reported, they probably could use a grid for location purposes as described above without difficulty.

Latitude. Latitude on a globe must be taught first and must be well established as referring to distance from the equator before any work is begun with longitude. Since confusion can easily result from presenting latitude and longitude too closely together, only latitude should be considered in the third grade. There are four relationships involving latitude that can be considered at primary school level: (1) latitude and seasons (summer and winter), (2) latitude and length of day, (3) latitude and length of growing season, (4) latitude and position of noonday sun.

Lord studied the ability of seventh-graders to explain the activity of people in relation to the latitude in which it is performed.[37] He found that they understood the relation of latitude and activities appropriate to summer season and winter season in middle northern latitudes and winter season in high northern latitudes, as well as the long growing seasons in regions of low latitude and the short growing season in regions of high latitude. This supports what we have learned from child development studies: that children understand best things with which they come into direct contact and have simple direct relationships.

What then might be done with third-graders? They can be told the latitude at which their local communities are located in reference to the starting point of zero, which is at the equator. Their attention has been called to sun behavior and seasons throughout the three beginning school years. For third grade we have suggested a systematic study of cardinal directions in terms of sun behavior. It should not be too difficult, then, to develop the following three relationships: (1) length of day at various seasons, (2) heat of the sun in its various positions in the sky by simple experiments with a thermometer, and (3) length of growing season. These are concepts the children can check through direct sensory data. They may then be guided to compare their local communities with other cities they have visited or read about at the same latitude, at higher latitudes, and at lower latitudes. In what direction does change occur as we go farther from the equator toward higher latitudes? In what direction does change occur as we go closer to the equator into lower latitudes? The equator is the starting point, and the position of the noonday sun is the key factor. If children can be helped to relate position of the noonday sun to their other observations, some of the misconceptions of latitude reported in many studies might be avoided. It may be that some third-graders can grasp only the concept of latitude as distance from the equator. Even this is a worthwhile beginning.

The Beginning Grades: A Summary

The overall purpose of map making and map interpretation in the primary grades is to help children develop the beginnings of a geographic point of view. We wish to imbue children with a spirit of inquiry and thoughtful exploration into similarities and differences which exist from place to place, similarities and differences in the ways men carry on their basic activities in varied natural settings. There is a great need in our world today to know enough about other peoples to enable us to live and work constructively with them. However, many of the actions of human beings appear reasonable or even understandable to a young person only when viewed in the light of direct experiences with his own unique environment and of the problems emerging out of his relations to it. Once the geographic understandings and skills are carefully evolved out of these intimate experiences with family, school, neighborhood, and local communities, the child is prepared to move beyond the more immediate into the larger communities whose borders extend beyond the horizon.

Early in this volume, an analysis of studies and surveys was made to check the state of our geographic knowledge as a justification for building a systematic program of geographic concepts and skills in the primary social studies. There is only one conclusion possible from these reports: we are a people sadly uninformed geographically. Furthermore, the skills in using maps whereby one might progressively gain geographic information are also lacking. Just as a trained musician can look at a score and hear the music, so a person skilled in the use of maps can look at a map and bring forth imagery of the landscape—the hills and rivers, the arid and growing regions, the crops; he can feel the heat and the cold, the dryness and the dampness. The cultural symbols—highways, railroads, cities, etc.—tell him something of what the people have done with the land, their climate, and their resources.

The importance of a geographical point of view in today's world, the widespread lack of map skills and geographic understandings, and the many suggestions for remedying the latter situation point to the need for a primary school program that will lay the foundation for developing such skills and understandings within the social studies framework.

Our concern is much broader than map *reading*. We want our young children to begin to approach geographical *thinking*, which is too often neglected in present social studies programs. Within a more widely conceived curriculum, map making and map interpretation become an integral part of developing relational thinking in all social studies.

In the early chapters of this book, we set ourselves the task of analyzing (1) what studies in child development and the learning process contribute to understanding of children's abilities, (2) what map skills and understandings geographers and educators think children ought to have, and (3) what classroom teachers, teachers of geography, and geography specialists have tried successfully with groups of children.

On the basis of this detailed analysis, an integrated overall sequence with specific pupil experiences for each of the three primary grades has been presented to develop map skills and understandings within a scope and sequence framework of the social studies. Our plan has been based on a methodology that will help children think more clearly and more accurately about commonplace everyday conditions in their immediate environment, help them observe more searchingly, help them find answers to the "how" and "why." This in turn will help them develop clear-cut concepts, a rich background of firsthand experiences from which to derive imagery of the landscape, a vocabulary, and the map skills with which to express their experiences. This background will be of value to them in understanding the more distant and more complex communities that are the larger bands in our set of expanding communities of men to be presented in the middle grades.

REFERENCES

1. Harold V. Baker, *Children's Contributions in Elementary School General Discussion*, Child Development Monographs, No. 29 (New York: Bureau of Publications, Teachers College, Columbia University, 1942), p. 2.

2. David S. Hill, "Personification of Ideals by Urban Children," *Journal of Social Psychology*, 1:379–392 (1930).

3. Lucy S. Mitchell, *Our Children and Our Schools* (New York: Simon and Schuster, Inc., 1950).

4. Paul Witty, "Some Recent Research in Child Development," *Childhood Education*, 19:398–404 (May, 1943), p. 399.

5. Jean Piaget, "Principal Factors Determining Intellectual Evolution from Childhood to Adult Life" (1937), *Outside Readings in Psychology*, Eugene L. Hartley and Ruth E. Hartley, eds. (New York: Thomas Y. Crowell Company, 2nd ed., 1957).

6. Mitchell, *op. cit.*

7. Ralph C. Preston, "Implications of Children's Concepts of Time and Space," *Social Studies*, 36:218–219 (May, 1945).

8. George F. Howe, "Teaching of Directions in Space," *Journal of Geography*, 31: 207–210 (May, 1932).

9. Francis Everette Lord, "A Study of Spacial Orientation of Children," *Journal of Educational Research*, 34:481–505 (March, 1941).

10. Preston, *op. cit.*

11. Arnold Gesell and Frances Ilg, *The Child from Five to Ten* (New York: Harper & Row, Publishers, 1946).

12. Arthur T. Jersild, *Child Psychology* (New York: Prentice-Hall, Inc., 4th ed., 1954), p. 450.

13. W. C. Croxton, "Pupils' Ability to Generalize," *School Science and Mathematics*, 36:627–634 (1936).

14. Lucy S. Mitchell, *Young Geographers* (New York: The John Day Company, Inc., 1934).

15. N. V. Scarfe, "Designing the Curriculum to Develop Geographic Concepts," *Journal of Geography*, 52:98–108 (March, 1953).

16. Mitchell, *Our Children and Our Schools*, p. 7.

17. *Ibid.*

18. Edith P. Parker, "Gaining Insight into Human Problems," *Geographic Approaches to Social Education*, Nineteenth Yearbook, National Council for the Social Studies (Washington: NCSS, 1948), pp. 12–13.

19. Mitchell, *Young Geographers*, p. 25.

20. Alfred H. Meyer, "Geography in the Teacher Education Program," *Geographic Approaches to Social Education*, Nineteenth Yearbook, National Council for the Social Studies (Washington: NCSS, 1948), pp. 283–299.

21. Lucy S. Mitchell, *Research on the Child's Level* (New York: 69 Bank Street Publications, n.d.).

22. Katheryne T. Whittemore, "Maps," *Geographic Approaches to Social Education*, Nineteenth Yearbook, National Council for the Social Studies (Washington: NCSS, 1948), p. 118.

23. Arthur T. Jersild, *et al.*, *Child Development and the Curriculum* (New York: Bureau of Publications, Teachers College, Columbia University, 1946), p. 459.

24. Mitchell, *Research on the Child's Level*.

25. George F. Howe, "A Study of Children's Knowledge of Directions," *Journal of Geography*, 30:298–304 (October, 1931), p. 303.

26. Howe, "Teaching of Directions in Space."

27. Clyde Kohn, "Interpreting Maps and Globes," *Skills in Social Studies*, Twenty-fourth Yearbook, National Council for the Social Studies (Washington: NCSS, 1953), p. 148.

28. Lord, *op. cit.*, p. 504.

29. Whittemore, *op. cit.*, p. 121.

30. Mamie L. Anderzhon, *Steps in Map Reading: A Map-Reading Workbook* (New York: Rand McNally & Co., 1955).

31. Thomas F. Barton, "Geographic Instruction in the Primary Grades," *Geographic Approaches to Social Education*, Nineteenth Yearbook, National Council for the Social Studies (Washington: NCSS, 1948), p. 214.

32. Harriet Chace, "Map Skills in the Third Grade," *Social Education*, 20:13–14 (January, 1956).

33. Edith P. Parker, *Seeing Our World through Maps* (Chicago Heights, Ill.: Weber, Costello Co., 1942), p. 6.

34. *Ibid.*

35. Mitchell, *Young Geographers*, p. 50.

36. Kohn, *op. cit.*, pp. 157–158.

37. Francis Everette Lord, "The Ability to Make Geographic Uses of Ideas of Longitude and Latitude," *Teaching of Geography*, Thirty-second Yearbook, National Society for the Study of Education (Bloomington: Public School Publishing Co., 1933), pp. 466–468.

chapter seven

THE MIDDLE GRADES EMPHASES

5. *The State Community*

6. *The Region-of-States Community*

General Introduction to State and

Region-of-States Communities

In the middle school grades social studies program we plan to initiate and develop new geographic concepts and skills as well as to reinforce and extend to larger and more meaningful patterns those developed in the primary school grades.

The primary grades program in social studies emphasizes the more intimate communities of men: the family, the school, the neighborhood, and the local communities. In the middle grades we will emphasize the next larger in the set of interdependent and interlocking communities: our state, our region-of-states, and our national communities. We repeat: the particular allocation of one of these expanding communities to a specific grade is of much less importance than is the principle of moving through the set in an orderly manner, from the lesser to the larger communities. With a strong belief in systematic programming of the sequence, the typical grade allocation over the nation appears to be following a pattern that emphasizes the state community and the region-of-states community in Grade 4 and the United States national community in Grade 5.

It must be clearly understood that the particular design of the social studies program presented in this volume does not stop at the boundaries of the national community. We do stress the importance of helping children first understand their own national complex or set of interlocking communities in order that they may live more rationally and behave more acceptably in pursuit of our values from family through nation. But the age of Shangri-La isolation and extreme nationalism is passing. Repeatedly, through the aeons of societal development, technology and science have broken up the older patterns of self-sufficient communities and forced communities to join with other communities in pursuing some common goal that was of greater value than that of their previous isolation and independence. Once again in our era we see the outer barriers of national communities breached as nations join other nations to create new values, institutions, laws, customs, and mechanisms. By this process of greater association a region of nations is slowly formed to fulfill far more of the human aspirations than can the individual nations working separately. In the lifetime of youngsters now in school, much of their thought and energy will be spent on creating the new and larger-than-national communities—the emerging region-of-nations communities and ultimately (and hopefully) a worldwide community of associated nations.

In the junior high school emphases, as presented later in this volume, we will treat the geographic concepts and skills for the remainder of our set of expanding communities of men: the emerging United States and inter-American community (Emphasis 8), the emerging United States and Atlantic community (Emphasis 9), the emerging United States and Pacific community (Emphasis 10), and the emerging World community of nations (Emphasis 11). These four communities, more embryonic than mature, are to be developed after the completion of the national set, Emphases 1 through 7.

Returning to the purpose of this "middle grades emphases" section of Part Three: We will (1) briefly review the geographic content and skills considered by the scholars in geography and cartography to be of importance in this developmental sequence; (2) consider the characteristics of pupils, aged nine to twelve, in the middle grades; and (3) illustrate how experiences can be provided to help pupils both inductively and deductively gain greater mastery over the structure of geography as it is analyzed out of the total web of the social studies in the pupils' own state, region of states, and nation.

Our objectives are those described in earlier chapters: (1) the ability to reorganize geographic data gathered from firsthand and vicarious experiences and to represent the distribution of these data on maps with appropriate symbols, (2) the ability to read geographic data recorded on maps and globes, and (3) the ability to interpret the distributions represented on maps and globes and to reason about things geographic. Too, each expanding community emphasis will deal with the same list of nine basic human activities described earlier but will treat each according to the interests and problems pertinent to that particular community. Thus within the social studies sequence design each basic human activity is examined in each expanded geographic arena as a new aspect of a familiar problem. Likewise, each of the three objectives is examined in each of the communities in a similar manner. A particular geographic generalization or map skill, consequently, *cannot* be studied once and for all at a particular grade level.

The teacher must continue to be aware that not all pupils have reached identical stages of concept development or skill performance. Each of the geographic skills and understandings must be checked, and, whenever necessary, appropriate teaching-learning experiences pertinent to the new community emphasis should be arranged to develop a simpler but key skill or understanding that may be lacking.

Child Development and the Learning Process

The teacher is faced with a wide spread of maturation and experience levels at every grade in the school. While the chronological age range may be narrow for a single grade, usually encompassing nine- and ten-year-olds in the fourth grade, for example, the maturation and experience range can be extremely broad. Furthermore, not all fourth-grade children are at the same stage of readiness for the various geographic activities. Careful consideration must be given to what each child is like within any grade grouping. Some children have not had the opportunity for developmental experiences in geography or lack maturity generally and are younger than their chronological age might lead the teacher to expect; others are more advanced than their chronological years would suggest because of maturation factors and experiences. Some of the children have accumulated knowledge from having lived in other locations in the national community and the lesser communities of states and regions of states. Others, who have had opportunities to take trips and use air, water, or road maps with adults, have learned through firsthand experience some of the functions of maps. These are only a few of the many ways in which children differ. Children in the middle school grades respond differently to the teaching-learning experiences offered by the school because of these variations in maturation and experience. The need for attention to individual differences is present in any classroom.

Attention is now directed toward studies of children in the middle grades age groups for clues to organizing a program of teaching-learning experiences aimed at developing geographic concepts and map skill performances. Children viewed as a group exhibit many common characteristics. The nine-year-old has an eye and ear for significant details that come from a variety of sources including motion pictures, television, pictorial magazines, and other mass media. Often he is so interested in perfecting skills that he likes to do the same thing over and over. A favorite pastime of this age group is poring over maps, and frequently drawing them as well. A typical nine-year-old is a great reader of books. Animal stories, biographies, mysteries, and the encyclopedia for reference—all are of interest to him. He especially likes to read for facts and information.

Millard points out that one of the important characteristics of the nine-year-old period is the rapid rate of growth and learning. At this stage the child has expanding capacities for work and a growing ability to work independently of the teacher and other children. He likes to make out lists and plan activities along with schedules and procedures.

It is at the fourth-grade level that the pronounced separation of the sexes begins; interests and activities of boys and girls begin to diverge. Millard points out too that the nine-year-old is susceptible to slight outside motivations; he is sensitive and alert to stimuli and responds accordingly. His attention span increases to the point where he is able to stay interested in a project for a considerable length of time. For example, he will practice on mechanical skills for an extended period of time. He will repeat drills and exercises which can be timed or scored. Furthermore, his enthusiasm makes him susceptible to unimaginative as well as creative teaching. Thus this caution offered by Millard should not be ignored when planning activities for fourth-graders:

> Constructively, what this child needs is intelligent and understanding manipulation of potential environmental stimuli. He responds to everything so well that he can be led into blind alleys or inconsequential learnings. The job of guidance . . . is to see that the child is provided with stimuli that will bring out his most important individual characteristics related to his temperament, emotion, personal-social needs, and cultural surroundings.[1]

Hence it is essential that the teacher, the most important member of the class, provide the necessary guidance at all times so that all of the child's geographic activities are within the broad and flexible framework of the total coordinated social studies program.

The wide spread of maturation and abilities continues in fifth and sixth grades. The teacher must keep this in mind when arranging teaching-learning experiences and selecting instructional materials. Any sequential framework of classroom activities must allow for much flexibility to meet these expected individual and group differences.

The Ohio State University study of *How Children Develop*[2] offers a useful summary of what can be expected from middle grade school children in the observation, investigation, discussion, dramatic play, and mapping activities planned for them. This study, which is an analysis of the scientific literature in child development, reports,

At age 9: Children can read for information. A range of four or five years in reading may be expected.

They are interested in measuring and counting larger quantities and also smaller quantities.

Reasoning is still largely based upon direct observation. Abstract principles are still rudimentary. They learn better by doing and need to be confronted by immediate situations.

At age 10: Their desire for facts as well as their imagination finds outlet in books of travel, stories of other lands, mechanics, and biography. The story and drama begin to take on added significance to the child in helping him to understand relationships between factors such as place, time, ideas, and happenings.

Most children have become interested in teamwork. They are becoming more aware of, and concerned about, the other person's ideas and beliefs.

From ages 9–10: They are eager to extend their horizons intellectually. They have a great interest in facts, in what things are made of, and how they work.

Imaginative play decreases and interest in facts and realism increases.

They are able to work with more effectiveness with concrete materials such as clay, paints, wood. They are passing from the symbolic stage into the realistic stage and want their pictures to look "real."

They have increased ability to fit past events into their proper sequence.

From ages 11–13: This is the period of rapid growth.

Children at this age have an increasing ability to deal with the quantitative aspects of the environment. Words are their most common medium of expression, but they still profit from expressing ideas through tangible materials.

They have the ability to analyze situations verbally and have an increased understanding of cause and effect.

There is an increased ability to make accurate associations, comparisons, and estimates. However, children of this age level still tend to draw conclusions from scanty and improperly observed data.

Their understanding of abstract concepts continues to grow. They enjoy concrete manipulation of things.

They are increasingly better able to use books, lists, books on how to do or how to make things, charts, maps, and so forth.

Children at this age level who have similar interests quite frequently group themselves.

Children within any organized classroom group represent a wide growth and experience range. For instance, when a random group of eleven- and twelve-year-olds enters the sixth grade, the range in general intelligence, disregarding the extreme 2 per cent at either end, has in the past been found to be about eight years. Likewise, the educational achievement of this same sixth-grade group shows a range of approximately eight years in reading comprehension, vocabulary, reasoning, arithmetic computation, and other fields.[3] It cannot be assumed, furthermore, that children with the same mental ages are at the same stages of readiness for all map-making and map-interpretation activities. Consequently the teaching-learning experiences presented for the emphases on state, region, and nation are arranged so as to allow for flexibility in meeting individual and group differences.

If children in the middle school grades are to acquire concepts and understandings that contribute to the development of a geographical point of view and competency, the school program must offer relevant experiences, both direct and vicarious, appropriate thereto. Field trips, motion pictures, photographs, charts, books, models, and so on are suggested for each of the basic human activities on the assumption that each activity invoking the use of these materials will contribute to the growth of particular geographic concepts and skills. There is little evidence, however, to show what kinds of experiences facilitate the formation of particular concepts and understandings; thus the teacher must hypothesize. The effects of the various suggested mapping experiences must be evaluated in terms of the ease with which the children grasp the concepts and acquire the skills and of their ability to recognize new instances of a concept in other contexts.

The middle school teaching-learning experiences make systematic use of the learnings acquired in the primary school emphases and offer opportunities to facilitate and enhance new learnings which are introduced within the context of the larger communities of the state, the region of states, and the United States national community. Teachers need to keep in mind that the overall framework of both the map skills and interpretation program and the geographically related concepts and understandings is formulated in advance. On the other hand, teaching-learning experiences in the classroom situation are cooperatively planned with the pupils so that the actual program of activities meets their particular needs and interests. Furthermore and significantly important, the proposed teaching-learning experiences described for each of the nine basic human activities within each of the community emphases are merely suggestive and not to be followed slavishly by the teacher as they are listed in this chapter.

Amplification of Emphases Assigned
to the Social Studies Program

The sequence of emphases for the social studies program is based on the expanding communities of men. It is important to have the meaning of the generic term *community* clearly in mind. Both structural and functional elements of a community must be recognized. Several things are true of all communities: Each community is made up of people who have similar customs and who think of themselves as belonging to that community; they live in a reasonably concise and definable space; each community has laws and institutions to serve its people; each community has certain problems that unite its people in a common cause; and each community can communicate over the geographic space occupied. For instance, men have found it easier to meet the basic human needs of protecting and conserving, providing recreation, transporting, and organizing when they group themselves together into larger communities such as the state or nation. However, a community need not be a politically organized entity, nor is self-sufficiency one of the chief characteristics in today's highly interdependent society. We live within a number of communities simultaneously whether we recognize it or not. Every fifth-grade pupil, for example, is a citizen of a national community, a state community, a neighborhood community, and so on. Citizenship in any one of these communities need not be in conflict with citizenship in other communities in the set, for each community has its own structure and functions, complementary to but not duplicated by those in the other communities of lesser or greater size in the system.

Likewise, it is extremely important that teachers understand the particular emphasis or emphases assigned to their respective grades. To illustrate: A focus of study on transporting people and goods in the state community is not concerned with aviation transportation in all its global dimensions and does not stress the national network of railroads, waterways, and highways. Transportation within a state is centered on moving goods and people via a state system of highways, using truck and bus routes on a state basis, the state automobile associations, the state Department of Motor Vehicles and Highways, and so on. There will be peripheral and related areas of attention and interest in the study of each basic human activity in each community that should receive some consideration, but it should be clear that they are not the focus of attention for the particular community being emphasized at a given moment in the sequence.

Analysis in Terms of the Basic Human Activities

The state, the first community to be emphasized in the middle grades, exhibits both structural and functional characteristics. The state community has a definable physical space clearly prescribed by its political boundaries. Its geographic space is a specific area of land with variations in landforms, water bodies, vegetation, climate, natural resources, and cultural features built by men. Within the state arena both public and private sectors pick up each of the basic human activities and expand it in ways that are impossible for the smaller populations of the lesser communities within the state. For instance, it would be next to impossible for each of the many local communities to provide adequate higher educational facilities. One thinks of statewide systems of higher education or of private institutions that draw their strength from many local communities. One also thinks of providing recreation in terms of a state system of parks and beaches or a state high school athletic association; of protecting and conserving in terms of a state highway patrol force or a state association of insurance underwriters. Countless facilities and ways of carrying on the basic human activities are provided by these larger than local or neighborhood governmental and private associations and agencies. Their programs are directed at promoting better ways of meeting the needs of the smaller communities that comprise the state community. And in turn the state community is not self-sufficient but depends upon the region-of-states, the national, and the larger-than-national communities for many of its basic requirements.

The region-of-states community represents an emerging community rather than a well-established polity such as a state or a nation. People living in a region-of-states community have numerous common interests and problems. Aware of the need for cooperative action beyond the state level, they join together to achieve common goals. They often share common memories and values and customs in their historical antecedents; they may face the same climate pattern and live in a geographic area characterized by similar landforms and vegetation. Within this arena many of the children in the fourth grade have done most of their vacation traveling. They have a fund of firsthand experiences and images of ways people in the several states carry on the various human activities. To communicate facts and ideas, there are regional radio and television networks that carry news and weather reports and other information of importance to travelers who in a day's trip by car may cross several state lines. There are well-known magazines that carry accounts of activities, holiday events and celebrations, and travel information of interest to the region-of-states community. There are regional playoffs in sports, with a single team representing the region in a national championship event. Manufacturing concerns have regional offices to serve the several larger-than-state communities.

The program of map skills and understandings and geographically related concepts of relative location, distribution, and areal association for these two emphases (the state and the region of states) is developed within the context of a social studies program that has two sets of coordinates as its framework: the expanding communities of men and the basic human activities. In this chapter the nine basic human activities are analyzed as they function within the state and region-of-states communities in terms of the three basic geographic objectives described earlier. The left-hand column on succeeding pages lists the three major objectives for the geographic program; the right-hand column contains examples of mapping experiences that apply to the basic human activity being analyzed and that may be used to develop specific map skills and understandings. These teaching-learning activities are organized as (1) map-making activities, (2) map-reading activities, and (3) map-interpreting activities. The suggested sequence is based on the principle that children first learn the skills and understandings through direct experience in making maps and then are able to profit more by reading and interpreting maps made by others. The teaching-learning experiences described for each of the three stages are suggestive, not prescriptive. The distinctive geographical character of the pupil's state community and his region of states and the maturation and range of experiences of particular fourth-grade classes will have much to do with what specific mapping experiences are undertaken.

THE STATE COMMUNITY (EMPHASIS 5) AND THE REGION-OF-STATES COMMUNITY (EMPHASIS 6)

Basic Human Activity: Protecting and Conserving Life, Health, Property, and Resources

OBJECTIVES	TEACHING-LEARNING EXPERIENCES
1. *Ability to reorganize systematically data gathered from firsthand and vicarious experiences and represent them on maps with appropriate symbols.*	1. *Mapping activities.*

1. *Ability to reorganize systematically data gathered from firsthand and vicarious experiences and represent them on maps with appropriate symbols.*

The state community is concerned about the protection and conservation of all its resources. Some of these functions are performed by the governmental agencies of the state; others are performed by private agencies and groups organized on a statewide basis. Likewise there are regional organizations interested in protecting and conserving. For example, the need to protect a common source of water supply in a border region finds the several states

1. *Mapping activities.*

Many of the state functions of protecting and conserving life, health, property, and resources reach into the local communities. Begin with the observation of one of these agencies such as the local unit of a state highway patrol. Gather information about the location and distribution of these offices in your state. On a highway map of your state locate the division offices. Have a large-scale base outline map of your state for this mapping activity. Locate the central state headquarters. Using the class-made map, discuss the location of various units in relation to function: How large an area is

working cooperatively together. Children develop an understanding of how people in the state and region-of-states communities work together to carry on this important basic human activity through participation in such teaching-learning experiences as observation, investigation, discussion, reading, and mapping activities.

2. *Ability to read data recorded on maps and globes.*

Develop reading skills in identifying symbols portraying protecting and conserving activities within the arena of the state community and the region-of-states community. Develop the ability to translate these symbols into meaningful imagery and verbal descriptions. Maps pertaining to organizing and governing activities and features include
   (1) development and conservation of natural resources;
   (2) use and conservation of native plant life;
   (3) use and conservation of wild animal life;
   (4) use and conservation of state public lands;
   (5) use and conservation of water resources by governmental agencies;
   (6) soil maps;
   (7) water pollution control;
   (8) control and protection of public forests;

served by each unit? Are there greater concentrations of units in certain sections of the state? Help the class interpret the areal distribution of the units. Contrast protection on the highways with other kinds of protection such as fire, health, and so on.

Discuss the work of a volunteer agency in protecting and conserving life and resources. An excellent example is the American Red Cross. Gather information from your local chapter on the regional organization, its headquarters, how this office serves the several states, etc. On a small-scale outline map of your region-of-states community locate the regional office. Make a map key and explain symbols.

2. *Map-reading activities.*

Considerable class time should be spent to help children develop meanings for the concepts symbolized on the maps they are going to read. Pictures of the features portrayed on maps should be introduced and discussed to bring out the salient points that might suggest the pictorial symbols used. Build a three-dimensional model of a state game refuge to scale. Invite a state game warden or a member of the state game commission to visit the class and discuss the features of this game refuge. What are its functions? Why is it located where it is? Is there any relationship to climate? Obtain maps from the state game commission. Compare the symbols used to portray certain features with the class model and the pictures of the actual refuge. Have children trace the boundaries of the refuge on the map. Find its location on a large-scale wall map of the state. Read its location by using a simple grid.

(9) control and protection of forests owned by private citizens and companies;

(10) conservation and development of grassland to prevent erosion;

(11) state hunting and fishing grounds;

(12) private hunting and fishing grounds;

(13) private agencies and their activities designed to protect and conserve resources both natural and human.

Develop the ability to locate places on maps with the use of a grid system and the ability to locate the sources of rivers and read the direction of water flow.

3. *Ability to interpret distribution and location on maps and to reason geographically.*

Analyze the geographic location and distribution of protecting and conserving activities within the state and region-of-states arenas as to

(1) relative location;

(2) relative distance;

(3) relative direction;

(4) spatial distribution.

Plan for studying other protecting and conserving activities carried on within the arena of the region-of-states community. Help children to develop meanings for the map symbols that show protecting and conserving activities within these two communities. Plan appropriate map-reading activities designed to develop skills in reading the following groups of symbols: point symbols for ranger stations, dams, fish hatcheries, state hospitals, clinics, state penal institutions, and the like; line symbols for streams, rivers, aqueducts, boundaries; area symbols for forests, conservation districts, range of movement of certain animals.

3. *Interpretation activities.*

Develop the ability to perceive possible relationships in terms of relative location: What is the relationship of the various conservation activities to the landforms and water bodies of the state community? The region-of-states community? For example, where are reforestation programs being carried on? Where are these activities in relation to metropolitan centers of the state? The region of states?

Conceive relationships in terms of relative direction: What is the relationship between water conservation programs and the slope of the land? The direction in which the rivers flow?

Conceive relationships in terms of relative distance: Where are fire ranger stations located? How far apart are they? How difficult is it to get fire-fighting equipment to various areas? Where are the access roads? Where are the main highways? Where are the airports? What is the spatial distribution of protecting and conserving features in the state community and the region-of-states community?

Basic Human Activity: Producing, Exchanging, Distributing, and Consuming Goods and Services

OBJECTIVES

TEACHING-LEARNING EXPERIENCES

1. *Ability to reorganize data gathered from firsthand and vicarious sources and represent them on maps with appropriate symbols.*

At the state and region-of-states levels people produce, exchange, and consume goods and services. Various areas within each of these communities specialize in the production of certain goods or services and in turn depend on other areas for other goods and services. Thus the state and region-of-states communities are characterized by specialization and interdependence. The geographical patterns of agricultural production vary from local community to local community and from state to state within the regional arena. The products are distributed to all sections of the state or the region. Many industrial concerns establish a single plant to serve a state or region of states. The manufactured goods are sold to wholesale companies, which also have a statewide organization to sell to the many retailers in all sections of the state or region of states. Electrical power produced in one section of the state may be distributed statewide. The services may be consumed on a state community basis.

1. *Mapping activities.*

Begin by having the class investigate the local communities to find out if any industries produce goods and services for consumption by the state community or the region-of-states community. Find out the sources of raw material. How are raw materials brought to the plant? To what wholesale centers in the state are the finished products shipped? To what distribution centers in the region-of-states community? Discuss the plant's location in terms of transportation facilities: highway, rail, water, air. Do transportation facilities figure in the plant's economical operation? These data may be conveniently summarized on a map of the state and the region of states. Make two large bulletin-board-size maps, one of the state and one of the region of states. Decide on the data needed for the base map, such as main transportation networks, etc. Show the source of raw materials, the manufacturing centers, and the market outlets within these two emphases. Explain all of the symbols used in the map's key, lower left-hand corner. Choose a suitable title for the map. Indicate the scale used and include it in the key. Show the cardinal directions. Discuss the use of appropriate semipictorial symbols for the raw materials and finished products. Use these maps

2. *Ability to read data recorded on maps and globes.*

Develop map-reading skills in identifying symbols portraying producing, exchanging, and consuming features and activities within the arena of the state and region-of-states communities. Develop the ability to visualize and understand the realities represented by the symbols. Maps showing features and activities pertaining to this basic human activity include

(1) agricultural production and distribution: cultivated farm-lands and agricultural products—plants, livestock;

(2) development of industrial resources: power resources—coal, oil and gas, electrical; mineral resources; building resources — lumber, cement, stone; textile resources—wool, cotton, synthetic; rubber production — natural and synthetic; industrial goods—manufacturing with iron, steel, aluminum; chemical plants;

(3) financial centers;

(4) wholesale centers;

(5) market areas.

Develop the ability to locate on maps using a grid system and the ability to read the areal distributions on maps.

2. *Map-reading activities.*

Many symbols (pictorial, semi-pictorial, and abstract such as points, circles, squares, etc.) are used to represent producing, exchanging, and consuming features and activities. Pupils learning to read maps should understand the meaning of what they are to read before they learn the symbols. Various symbols representing products, raw materials, and so on often indicate the object, such as a milk bottle for dairying. However, the pupils should always go to the key for reading all symbols. Extensive use of pictures, motion pictures, and filmstrips should parallel all of these map-reading activities. Using appropriate pictures, discuss the characteristic features of a commercial area. Find out how such an area is symbolized both on a large-scale map and on a small scale map. Plan reading activities to develop functional use of needed symbols. (See "Map and Globe Symbols," Appendix B, for suggestions.) Symbols include point symbols for manufacturing centers: plants, mines, oil wells, gas wells, sawmills, power plants, and so on; line symbols for power transmission lines, flow of raw materials, flow of finished products, pipelines, boundaries for districts, etc.; area symbols for distribution of raw materials, markets for finished products, agricultural regions, manufacturing regions, extending market service regions, and so on.

Help pupils to read large-scale maps of metropolitan areas to note

in class discussions to point out relative locations of outlets in relation to the size of the market, and so on.

3. *Ability to interpret distribution and location on maps and globes and to reason geographically.*

Reason geographically about the location and areal distribution of producing, exchanging, distributing, and consuming goods and services within the state community. Analyze the geographical locations and areal distributions of these basic human activities as to relative location, relative distance, and relative direction. Correlate the spatial dimensions of these activities with other cultural features as well as with the physical features in each of the two communities under study. Develop the ability to make inferences about data read on maps.

the relationship between plant locations and transportation facilities.

3. *Interpretation activities.*

Provide many map interpretation activities to help pupils use maps as basic tools in the study of geographical aspects of producing, exchanging, and consuming goods and services in their state community and the region-of-states community. For example, note the location and distribution of farming activities, manufacturing activities, lumbering activities, and so on. Help the pupils to make inferences about the interrelatedness of locations and distributions of two or more features. Several maps are needed for purposes of gathering and interpreting such data. What areas of the state community have a concentration of lumbering activities? Manufacturing activities? Note the location of lumbering activities in the forested regions of the state or region of states. Many of the lumber products are manufactured in centers located some distance from the place of logging operations. Have the pupils make inferences from maps showing population centers, distribution centers, and transportation facilities.

Basic Human Activity: Transporting People and Goods

OBJECTIVES

TEACHING-LEARNING EXPERIENCES

1. *Ability to reorganize data gathered from firsthand and vicarious experiences and represent them on maps with appropriate symbols.*

Maps are an important tool to the people who are engaged in the basic human activity of transporting people and goods. In the state

1. *Mapping activities.*

Observe kinds of transportation systems connecting the local community with other communities in the state. Discuss ways in which communities in various parts of the state are dependent upon the transporting activity. Note the

community many different kinds of transportation equipment are used. New developments are being made to improve and expand the transportation of goods and services, thus bringing the many local communities of the state and region of states closer together. Some transporting activities are provided by private venture, some by government, and some by joint efforts of private and public. The ability to sort out these authorities is important.

different kinds of transportation equipment—land, water, and air. Are there state centers of transportation? Where are they located? Are they connected to similar centers in the region of states? If so, how? With what? Visit a major airport or trucking center. Find out how it uses maps. Does it handle bulk commodities? Where are they being transported? Decide on the use of symbols to show the various transportation facilities. Note the connecting and/or terminal facilities of the state and the locations of regional transportation systems in the state. Include harbors, airports, railroad yards, and the like. Use these class-developed maps to trace the route of goods and people some time ago and now. Relate this to population maps. Classify various transportation features into public, private, or joint public and private. So identify them on maps.

2. *Ability to read data recorded on maps and globes.*

Develop skills in reading features involving transporting people and goods as they are portrayed on maps. These include
(1) paths, trails, and other routes of foot travel;
(2) city streets, traffic arteries, truck and car routes;
(3) underground pipelines;
(4) highway maps;
(5) railroad maps, routes, terminals, division points;
(6) water routes, harbor facilities, docks, piers, anchorages, floating docks, buoys, beacons, lighthouses, and the like;
(7) air routes, airports, landing fields;
(8) ferries and bridges, ports, har-

2. *Map-reading activities.*

Transportation maps are exceedingly common today. Provide opportunities to read road maps of the state and region of states. Select maps that have a minimum of detail on them. Plan a make-believe trip by auto to some interesting place in the state. Read the road map to plan a possible route; note distances involved, kinds of highways, and so on. Have another group in the class plan a trip to the same place using other means of transportation—bus, train, and airplane. Obtain bus and railroad maps, air maps. Check them with the classroom wall maps because some railroad maps, for instance, are diagrammatic. If possible, visit a large metropolitan center, obtain

bors, docks, locks, canals, etc.; (9) transportation construction. Develop the ability to visualize the realities representing these transporting features as symbolized on maps. Develop the ability to read the relative locations and distances between the local community and the other centers in the state and the region of states in terms of the various modes of transportation.

a large-scale map, and read it to find the location of different terminal facilities. Note the location of the airport, the bus station, the harbor. Where are the major state highways? Is there a concentration of terminal facilities in certain areas? What symbols are used to show these facilities? If possible, get an oblique aerial photograph of the area. Read transportation maps of the state and the region of states to find areas that have few roads and no railroads or airports. Note the areal distribution of features involving transportation—trails, paths, highways, winter roads, summer roads, ferries, bridges, air routes, railways, and water routes. (See "Map and Globe Symbols," Appendix B, for suggestions.)

3. *Ability to interpret the distribution and location that are portrayed on maps and to reason about things geographic.*

Analyze examples of transporting people and goods in the state and region of states to note relative location of terminal transportation centers; the concentration of facilities and transporting features in certain areas; the absence of transporting features in other areas; geographic features such as landforms and their effect on the kind of transportation and their routes between centers in the state and region. Reason about the kind of transportation most appropriate to the earth's surface or landscape. Reason about the route most appropriate to that particular geographical region: boats follow inland waterways; railroads take the least grade route; large airplanes fly straight routes between centers. Why are airways the responsibility

3. *Interpretation activities.*

Where would you expect to find the greatest flow of goods within the state and the region of states? Where would you expect to find the greatest movement of people? Relate these movements to the location of the large metropolitan centers in the state. Describe the geographical locations of these centers. Are they at the junction of several major waterways? Is there a large bay suitable for an excellent harbor? Interpret the shift of certain important transportation centers with the advent of new ways of transporting goods and services. Why have certain population centers grown faster than others? Did transportation have anything to do with this growth? Reason about the kinds of landforms most favorable to the development of transportation facilities. Contrast a plains region with a mountain region. Reason about the location of trails

of the public, while most air transport is private enterprise? Is rail transport the same or different? Why?

used by pioneers in the state. Relate their location to modern highway routes.

Basic Human Activity: Communicating Facts, Ideas, and Feelings

OBJECTIVES

1. *Ability to reorganize data gathered from firsthand and vicarious experiences and to represent them on maps with appropriate symbols.*

Within the state and region-of-states communities the communicating of information, ideas, and feelings is carried on in many different ways. There is a need for a network of communication organized on these larger community levels to provide all kinds of information such as weather reports, market quotations, the ordering of special supplies to meet emergencies, and so on. Only when communication networks are so organized can this vital information be provided to each of the smaller local communities. A statewide or regional system enables messages to be transmitted to many people at the same time. Improvements and new means of communicating are being developed continuously, thus bringing communities closer together.

TEACHING-LEARNING EXPERIENCES

1. *Mapping activities.*

Pupils are well aware of and have some understanding of several media of communicating information, ideas, and feelings from their study of the several lesser communities in the primary grades. The class may observe the operations of the local telephone company to find out that it is a part of a larger network. What facilities are needed to relay messages to other parts of the state or the region of states? What route would a message take if direct long-distance telephone dialing were used? Record this information in a notebook for use in the classroom. Where are coaxial cables used? What centers in the state or region are connected by a microwave relay system? On returning to the class arrange these data on an outline map of the state and the region of states. Locate the "nerve" centers, the main cable lines of communication between major centers of population and between regional centers of population. Using the class-constructed maps, discuss the significance of these networks and the part they play in communicating information rapidly and efficiently to all the people of the community. Discuss the many uses telephone people have for

2. *Ability to read data recorded on maps and globes.*

Develop map-reading skills in identifying symbols portraying communicating features and activities with focus on the state and region-of-states communities. Develop the ability to visualize and understand the realities represented by these symbols. Maps pertaining to this human activity include

(1) state system of libraries;
(2) telephone maps of the state;
(3) telegraph maps;
(4) radio networks and stations;
(5) television stations and networks and areas served;
(6) news service systems;
(7) radio beams for shipping and aviation;
(8) mail routes—land, sea, and air;
(9) newspaper production and distribution;
(10) printing and distribution of periodicals, books, records, etc.

Develop the ability to read the areal distribution of the communication features within the state and the region of states.

maps in their work: location of underground cables, location of relay stations, etc. Discuss which types of communicating are run by the private sector and which by government. Why are newspapers private while the highways which carry the newspaper to the reader are a public responsibility?

2. *Map-reading activities.*

Initial activities should be designed to help pupils develop meanings for the various communication concepts symbolized. Concepts introduced at a prior grade level are extended and examined in light of the expanding communities of the state and the region of states. New concepts and understandings are introduced. Through the use of photographs, charts, illustrated material, and textbook matter, plan activities to help pupils identify and read the following group of symbols: point symbols for radio stations, television stations, transmitting stations, post offices, newspaper plants, radio beam stations, telegraph offices, microwave relay towers, repeater stations, and the like; line symbols for telephone lines, coaxial cable, telegraph lines, mail routes, distribution routes for newspapers and other printed material, etc.; area symbols to indicate the listening range for radio stations, television stations, coverage range for newspapers, aviation radio beams, and so on.

Use the map key to read the symbols used on communication maps. Develop skills in reading the distance between relay stations, distribution centers, etc. What is the terrain of the area like? Help children to become aware of the danger of reading ground distances

3. *Ability to interpret distribution and location on maps and to reason geographically.*

Analyze the geographic location and distribution of communication features and activities in the state and region-of-states communities as to
(1) relative location;
(2) relative distance;
(3) relative direction;
(4) spatial distribution.
Help pupils to understand the association of several conditions in the state or region, to understand the areal association of several communication features, and to understand the areal association of communication features with natural features.

over mountainous regions on maps. They will have to make allowance in their answers. Have a pupil check their map measurements with mileage data from a local telephone or TV engineer.

3. *Interpretation activities.*

Analyze examples of communication means and facilities to note relationships in terms of
(1) relative location and concentration of telegraph and telephone facilities with population centers: Why is there a concentration of these facilities in large cities? What kinds of communication facilities do you find in the rural areas? Why? Discuss the problems of communicating in mountainous regions, for example.
(2) relative distance and terrain: Are physical barriers such as mountains or open water a factor in communicating ideas by telephone? By mail? By telegram? By radio? By television? Were mountains ever a barrier to communication? For example, local communities in a state 100 years ago were often a week apart. Today these same two communities are only seconds apart. Is Telstar or Comsat an appropriate communications solution within a state? Why?
(3) relative direction and the use of communicating features and activities: Where are the microwave stations located? Does the distance or the direction of a radio or television receiver from the transmitter affect reception? Can mountains interfere? Why?

Basic Human Activity: Expressing Spiritual and Aesthetic Impulses

OBJECTIVES	TEACHING-LEARNING EXPERIENCES
1. *Ability to reorganize data gathered from firsthand and vicarious experiences and translate them into map language.*	1. *Mapping activities.*

1. *Ability to reorganize data gathered from firsthand and vicarious experiences and translate them into map language.*

Members of the state community meet the human need of expressing spiritual and aesthetic impulses in various ways. The people may express spiritual impulses through membership in a religious group. Aesthetic needs find expression in such activities as music, art, ballet, and drama. Places of historical, scenic, and cultural interest and beauty are enjoyed by all citizens of the state and by people who live in the region of states—and even the national community and the world. Children are helped to gain an understanding of how people make provisions for carrying on the basic human activity of expressing spiritual and aesthetic impulses through participation in teaching-learning experiences such as observation, investigation, discussion, reading, and mapping activities.

1. *Mapping activities.*

Spiritual and aesthetic phenomena assume state and regional characteristics because people from various parts of the state and region-of-states communities visit and use them. Observe and map these places, both natural and cultural, that facilitate spiritual and aesthetic expression. Discuss the location and extent of each area. What festivals or celebrations are held and who participates? When are they held? In what ways are they related to the climate of the state? The region of states? List and discuss the events that are held. Plan to make a map showing the location and size of the area. What symbols might appropriately symbolize the various locations and activities? Give every child in the class an opportunity to make a map. Encourage the children to make an artistically balanced composition with appropriate pictures to fill in the blank spaces. Pleasing borders may be placed on the map sheet. Include a key to explain the symbols used, along with the date and name of the map maker. Other maps may be made showing the locations of museums, libraries, theaters, etc., that have assumed state and regional characteristics. Include various buildings that are used by different groups for worship. Discuss the use of appropriate symbols for large-scale maps of a section of the state and for small-scale maps of the state or the region of states.

2. *Ability to read data recorded on*

2. *Map-reading activities.*

maps.

Develop reading skills in identifying symbols portraying ways people express spiritual and aesthetic impulses in the state and region-of-states communities. Develop reading skills for identifying features, both cultural and natural. Develop the ability to translate these symbols into meaningful imagery. Maps pertaining to spiritual and aesthetic phenomena include churches, synagogues, temples, mosques, etc., shrines, monuments, museums of painting and sculpture, structures of architectural interest, location of musical organizations, locale of works of literature, and locale of artists, musicians, writers.

Help children develop meanings for the symbols used on maps that portray cultural and natural features of spiritual and aesthetic phenomena. Use a variety of instructional materials, both visual and written, to help them develop meanings for the concepts. If most of the members of the class live in a rural setting, plan activities to help them build meanings for a theater district in a large metropolitan center that is symbolized on a large-scale city map, for example. Show pictures of theaters that have architectural interest. Read accounts of historical aspects of the district. Now see how the map maker symbolizes these cultural features on the large-scale map of the city. Are they shown on a small-scale map of the state? Why? Plan other appropriate map-reading activities for understanding the following groups of symbols: pictorial and point symbols on large-scale maps for places of worship, shrines, theaters, museums, etc.; point symbols on small-scale maps for parks, gardens, historical buildings, etc.; line symbols for boundaries of gardens, scenic routes of travel, etc.; and area symbols for areal distribution of religious groups, musical organizations.

3. *Ability to interpret distribution and location on maps and to reason geographically.*

Reason geographically about the distribution and location of phenomena that facilitate the expression of spiritual and aesthetic impulses.

3. *Interpretation activities.*

In reading the location of certain cultural phenomena on maps, what might account for the location of museums, art galleries, etc., in certain sections of the state? Are they located in rural areas? Where are the historical museums and places of interest? Are they near present highways? Interpret their location in terms of the location of the trails and roads of 100 years ago. Are cultural features such as art galleries, etc., related in any way to centers of learning? Investigate the geographic locations of historic churches, missions, etc. What is the pattern of their distribution? Note that some of the historic churches are located in various sections of the state and are being used today. Interpret the locations of new art galleries, theaters, and the like in relation to present population centers. Where are there plans for the construction of new cultural centers? What is the geographical location?

Basic Human Activity: Providing Recreation

OBJECTIVES	TEACHING-LEARNING EXPERIENCES

1. *Ability to reorganize data gathered from firsthand and vicarious experiences and represent them on maps with appropriate symbols.*

In the state community and the region-of-states community people engage in various kinds of recreational activities. Facilities for these activities are provided by government and private agencies. Recreational areas and facilities have form, function, and a pattern of areal distribution. People engage in recreation as participants, spectators, and sponsors. They have more free time to spend than did their forefathers; they have more income to spend on recreational pursuits. Modern transportation facilities make areas in all parts of the state and the region accessible to most people. Looking forward, we can expect an ever increasing demand for more recreational facilities. Both government and private agencies will be asked to provide the needed facilities which are be-

1. *Mapping activities.*

Many pupils have been to recreational places located in various parts of the state community and the region-of-states community. Perhaps several have been on fishing expeditions to remote areas of the state; others may have been to a remote mountainous area in the region of states. Many of them have been spectators at sporting events, the state fair, and other special festivals and events that have assumed state and regional characteristics because people from all parts of the state and and the region-of-states communities attend. Discuss these events and their recreational features. In what part of the state are they located? What time of the year do they occur? What are the physical characteristics of the area like? Make a collection of pictures and brochures describing these areas. Plan to make a large bulletin-board-size map of the state or the region of

yond the ability of the smaller communities to provide by themselves.

2. *Ability to read data recorded on maps and globes.*

Develop map-reading skills in identifying symbols portraying recreational phenomena in the state community and the region-of-states community. Develop the ability to translate these symbols into meaningful imagery. Maps pertaining to recreational features and activities include

(1) public recreational areas and institutions;

(2) commercial recreational areas and institutions;

(3) public lands for recreation such as state parks and beaches, state forests, and the several county and local public recreational areas and parks within the state;

(4) cultural features such as cities, state fairgrounds, and amusement parks.

Include both small-scale and large-scale maps in the reading program. Develop the ability to read the areal distributions and relative locations of recreational phenomena in the state community and the region-of-states community.

states. On this outline map locate the phenomena, both cultural and natural, that facilitate recreational activities. These may include a mountainous region, a seacoast, a lake region, a forested region, and so on. Decide on areal symbols to show these regions. Select appropriate point and line symbols to represent picnic tables, riding trails, boating docks, etc. Include special festivals and the state fair. Use pictorial symbols to show the kinds of activities connected with each facility. Give the map a title. The class may want to arrange the exchange of the map of their state with that of a class in another state.

2. *Map-reading activities.*

Help pupils develop meanings for the symbols that portray recreational features on the state and the region-of-states community maps. Gather information from both first-hand and vicarious sources to develop and extend concepts. For instance, plan a make-believe trip to a well-known recreational area in the state. Read road maps, both small scale and large scale, to determine a route. What kinds of road surfaces will be traveled on? What are the mileages between towns and cities? If it is a camping trip to a remote region, are there any nearby stores for supplies? Small-scale maps may not show this kind of information. These reading activities should be arranged so that pupils find out that there are dangers in trying to read too much into a small-scale map. To help them visualize various features discussed, collect pictures of the campsite, the kinds of roads traveled, etc. Make a bulletin board display of the trip, including the map and the pictures. Plan other appropriate map-reading activities for the following groups of symbols: point symbols for small boat harbors, rest camps on mountain trails, ski lifts, skating rinks, bowling lanes, public swimming pools, etc.; line symbols of boundaries of state parks, ski runs, riding paths, hiking trails, winter roads, summer roads, etc.; area symbols for state parks and beaches, forest regions; dots for the quantitative distributions of motels, theaters, etc.

Bring into the classroom various recreational maps published by travel companies, etc., and read them for recreational information. Help children to recognize certain exaggerations that may appear on these maps. Compare these maps with those prepared by the state Beaches and Parks Commission.

3. *Ability to interpret distribution and location on maps and to reason geographically.*

Analyze the recreational phenomena in the state community and the region-of-states community as to

(1) relative location;
(2) relative distance;
(3) relative direction.

Analyze geographical location and distribution of recreational features to help children conceive relationships in terms of areal associations of the man-made features in recreation, areal associations of natural features with the man-made features, and areal associations of several man-made features.

3. *Interpretation activities.*

In reading the locations of certain recreational features and activities on maps, what reasons account for the particular distribution in the state community? What recreational phenomena characterize mountainous regions in the summer? In the winter? Where are the state parks? Relate their locations to water forms, flora and fauna, and the climate of the state. Reason from the distributions on a map about the greatest tourist attractions in the state community and in the region-of-states community. What will be the future demands in providing facilities for growing population areas and an increasing amount of free time for recreation? Have recreational features in either of these two communities assumed national characteristics in that they attract people from all parts of the nation? Interpret patterns of areal distribution of outdoor recreational facilities in terms of the climate, the land forms, major bodies of water, flora and fauna, transportation features, man-made features such as reservoirs, dams, motels, and other tourist facilities. What is the state doing to lay out future parks and beaches? What are private agencies and individuals doing to provide additional recreational facilities?

Basic Human Activity: Providing Education

OBJECTIVES

1. *Ability to reorganize data gathered from firsthand and vicarious experiences and to represent them on maps with appropriate symbols.*

At the state and region-of-states community levels people work out ways for carrying on the basic human activity of providing education for both children and adults. Each state community provides its own system of public and private education. All states have a state-wide system of public schools and most states have a system of higher education to provide educational facilities beyond the secondary school. Many organizations sponsor state conferences to provide opportunities for adults to engage in additional educational activities. Many colleges and universities assume regional characteristics because they attract students from various parts of the region-of-states community. Many regional conferences are arranged by various private as well as governmental agencies to provide adults with opportunities for further education. Children are helped to gain an under-

TEACHING-LEARNING EXPERIENCES

1. *Mapping activities.*

The class may begin with a discussion of the various occupations followed by the adult members of the families represented in the classroom. Where are the institutions located to train the skilled workers, tradesmen, servicemen, professional men and women needed in the state or in the region of states? Locate on a state map the secondary schools of agriculture, trade and industry, etc. Locate the state Department of Education. Is it in the same city with the state legislature and the other departments of state government? Where are the institutions of higher education located to train doctors, nurses, engineers, farmers, merchants, teachers, lawyers, dentists, etc.? There may be one state professional school that serves a region of states. Where is it located? How large is it? Discuss the role of private colleges and universities. Where are they located? Do any members of the class have older brothers and sisters attending any of these colleges or universities? How far

standing of how people make provisions for carrying on the basic human activity of providing education through such teaching-learning experiences as observation, investigation, discussion, reading, and mapping activities.

2. *Ability to read data recorded on maps and globes.*

Develop map-reading skills in identifying symbols portraying educational facilities in the state community and the region-of-states community. Develop the ability to translate these symbols into meaningful visual or spatial terms. Maps pertaining to providing educational functions include

(1) public elementary and secondary systems and buildings;
(2) private elementary and secondary systems and buildings;
(3) institutions of higher learning, private and public;
(4) libraries;
(5) museums;
(6) historical museums;

away is their school? Perhaps the class can take a field trip to a nearby vocational or comprehensive high school or a junior college or a college or university campus. Plan the trip in advance. Prepare a map of the route the class will take. Indicate the cardinal directions and the scale used. Calculate the traveling time. After making the trip, the class may want to contrast the educational facilities of higher education with those of the secondary schools: size of the library, science laboratories, etc. The class may want to make a bulletin-board-size map of the state showing the location of all the colleges and universities in their state. On a map of the region-of-states community they may locate all the facilities that serve the region. Give these maps appropriate titles and keys. Explain the symbols used in the key. Indicate the nature of the facilities, i.e., technical school, medical school, graduate school, etc.

2. *Map-reading activities.*

Plan activities designed to develop meanings for the symbols used to portray educational features and activities with focus on the state community and the region-of-states community. Have class discussions and dramatizations and gather information both firsthand and vicarious to develop and extend basic concepts involved in providing education. For example, collect pictures of buildings and grounds of a regional university. Identify the various buildings and special facilities. Send to the university for a map of the campus (Figure 37). Project it on a screen with an opaque projector. Read the symbols representing the main build-

(7) training facilities provided by many business firms.

Develop the ability to read the location of these sites relative to the ings on the campus: library, gymnasium, football stadium, bookstore, and so on. Read the directions and describe the location of various

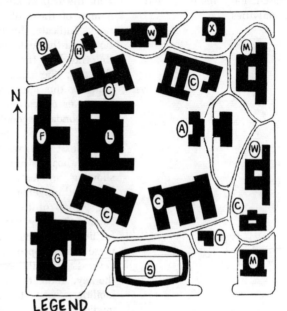

LEGEND

A. ADMINISTRATION BUILDINGS
B. BOOK STORE
C. CLASS BUILDINGS
F. FINE ARTS BUILDING
G. GYMNASIUM
H. CHAPEL
L. LIBRARY
M. MEN'S RESIDENCE HALLS
S. STADIUM
T. FACULTY BUILDING
W. WOMEN'S RESIDENCE HALLS
X. MAINTENANCE & POWER BUILDING

Figure **37**

Map of a University

local community and the ability to read the patterns of distributions in the state community and the region-of-states community.

buildings in relation to the library, for example. Is the library centrally located? Why? Read the scale and determine how large the campus is. Compare it with the size of the pupils' elementary school plant. On a small-scale map of the region of states, how is the campus portrayed? Is there a conventional symbol for universities and like facilities? A bulletin board display of a small-scale map showing educational facilities with pictures of the campuses around it should be helpful in these exercises. Connect the pictures of the campuses to the map symbols by strings.

3. *Ability to interpret distribution and location on maps and to reason geographically.*

Reason geographically about the location and areal distribution of educational features serving the state community and the region-of-states community. Analyze these geographic locations and distributions of educational structures and activities as to

(1) relative location;
(2) relative distance;
(3) relative direction.

Correlate the locations of educational features with other cultural features and physical features of these two communities. Develop the ability to compare maps and to make inferences concerning the distribution of educational features and activities shown on them.

3. *Interpretation activities.*

After children have read maps showing the locations of educational institutions serving the state or a region-of-states community, have them analyze the pattern of distribution as to population centers in the state, geographical regions or sections, and type of economic endeavor being carried on. Compare a map of the location of higher educational institutions in the state with a map showing the population distribution for the state. Are there large centers of population without a university or college? Why is a large university often located in a small population center some distance from a large metropolitan center? Is this always true? Help children to make inferences about these locations 100 years ago. Where do they think a new college or university might be located? Help them explain the location of vocational and technical schools. Use a map showing the location of major industrial centers. Note the location, for example, of experimental agricultural stations in the state community and in the region-of-states community. Explain the fact that a forestry school may be located in one state and not in a nearby one.

Basic Human Activity: Organizing and Governing

OBJECTIVES	TEACHING-LEARNING EXPERIENCES

1. *Ability to reorganize data gathered from firsthand and vicarious experiences and to represent them on maps with appropriate symbols.*

    The people of the state work out ways for organizing and governing the state community. Many of the governing activities are centralized in one location. The city where the state government is located is called the state capital. The people elect representatives who go to the capital of the state to carry on the activities of government. Many of the state governmental agencies have branch offices in various local communities of the state. The private sector also organizes and manages. Pupils should develop the ability to analyze the location and areal distribution of the centers within which these private ventures carry on this cluster of activities.

1. *Mapping activities.*

    Readiness activities should include a review discussion of how the county government in the local community is centralized in one place with some branch offices located in other parts of the county. The center of the state government is called the state capital. The class may be able to take a field trip to visit the site of government for the state. Use maps of these state grounds and plan the visit so as to include several centers such as the governor's mansion, the legislative building, the department of education, and so on. Make a large-scale map of the area. Decide on symbols to represent the various buildings. Include the streets and gardens. Indicate the cardinal directions. Explain the symbols used in the map key. Discuss ways the capital may be symbolized on a small-scale map of the state. What is the conventional symbol used by map makers? (See "Map and Globe Symbols," Appendix B.) Members of the class may do some research on the various locations in the state that have at one time been the state capital. Locate these on a small-scale map of the state. Have the class make inferences about the various historic sites and possible reasons for the changes. Locate on state and regional maps the headquarters of private agencies in which pupils have a special interest.

2. *Ability to read data recorded on maps and globes.*

    Develop reading skills in identifying symbols portraying organizing

2. *Map-reading activities.*

    Maps showing political organizations contain much information about the basic human activity of

and governing activities and the ability to translate these symbols into meaningful imagery. Maps pertaining to organizing and governing activities include features such as

(1) political divisions — states, counties, districts, precincts, and so on;

(2) metropolitan areas, cities, towns, villages, unincorporated areas;

(3) centers of government — state capitals, county seats;

(4) historical aspects of political divisions, centers of government, territories.

Develop the ability to visualize the realities representing the above organizing and governing activities as symbolized on maps. Develop the ability to read the relative location and distances between the local community and the state center of government.

3. *Ability to interpret distribution and location on maps and to reason geographically.*

Use maps to reason geographically about the location and areal distribution of organizing and governing features.

organizing and governing. Plan activities to help children understand the meanings for the symbols representing organizing and governing features in the state and region-of-states communities. Discuss the concept of political boundaries: Are they visible? How do you know where they are? Are there actual markers? Where? Plan activities to help children identify and read the following groups of symbols: point symbols for centers of county governments, state governments, cities, towns, and the like; line symbols for boundaries of county units, states, precincts, senatorial districts, etc.; area symbols for state units, metropolitan regions, counties, etc.; areal symbols for management districts of private enterprise.

Read maps to describe the locations of centers of government: near the center of the state, in a metropolitan center, in a rural area, and so on. Note the direction of the state capital from the pupils' local community. How far is it from the local community? Use the map scale to read the distance.

3. *Interpretation activities.*

Relate the location of the center of the state government to present distributions of

(1) population;

(2) landscape features;

(3) transportation facilities;

(4) communication facilities.

Help children to make inferences about the data they gather. Reason about the location of the early state capital cities. Relate the old cities to present population centers. What areas in the state community are growing rapidly? Will they have more representatives in the state government? Help pupils make inferences about the distribution of management and sales offices of private corporations and associations throughout the state and region.

Basic Human Activity: Creating Tools and Technics

OBJECTIVES

TEACHING-LEARNING EXPERIENCES

1. *Ability to reorganize data gathered from firsthand and vicarious experiences and represent them on maps with appropriate symbols.*

In the state and region-of-states communities, people are working out new and better tools and technics to carry on the basic human activities. In the state community, for instance, new tools and technics in communication and transportation have brought the many local communities together; in the region of states widely separated geographical areas are only a matter of hours away by aircraft. The introduction of new tools and technics in agriculture has brought about many changes in production methods. Universities and other research centers of industry are continually developing new tools and technics. Conferences and demonstrations at these centers assume regional characteristics in that they attract people from various parts of the region to attend them. Children develop an understanding of how people create new tools and technics through participation in such teaching-learning experiences as observation, investigation, discussion, reading, and mapping activities.

1. *Mapping activities.*

Begin with a discussion of the various tools and technics pupils have observed in use as they have traveled about the state community or the region-of-states community —perhaps special road-building equipment at work on a state highway project such as large earth-moving vehicles, giant bulldozers, or huge shovels. Contrast these tools with those used by the early pioneers. Compare the technics of road construction. Project into the future and contemplate the kinds of tools and technics that might be in use then. Discuss the use of new tools and technics to provide water for agricultural regions and large metropolitan regions. As an example, read accounts of the cooperative efforts of the several states in the Colorado River region of the Southwest. Gather information about the dams, aqueducts, and canals that were built to distribute water in the states of Colorado, Nevada, Arizona, and California. Collect pictures of the dams, reservoirs, sections of the canals, etc., and make a bulletin board display. On a base outline map of this region, show the key dams and their locations, the main aqueducts, canals, and so on. Find out the conventional cartographic symbols for some of these features

2. *Ability to read symbols recorded on maps and globes.*

Develop map-reading skills for identifying symbols portraying tools and technics people are working out to carry on the basic human activities within the state and the region-of-states communities. Develop the ability to translate these symbols and their distribution into meaningful imagery. Maps showing these features and activities include

(1) research and development centers;

(2) areas producing machine tools;

(3) experimental farms and stations.

3. *Ability to interpret distribution and location on maps and to reason geographically.*

Analyze the geographic location and distribution of places using different kinds of tools and technics in the state and region-of-states communities as to

(1) relative location;

(2) relative distance;

and use them on the map. (See "Map and Globe Symbols," Appendix B.)

2. *Map-reading activities.*

Plan activities to help children develop meanings for the symbols used on maps to portray the creating and use of tools and technics in the state and region-of-states communities. In the state community, for example, discuss the part universities and colleges take in the promotion and development of new tools and technics in agricultural and forest production. Where are the experimental farms and stations located? What kinds of work do they carry on? Collect pictures of some of the activities and discuss them in class. Obtain maps from the university and plan activities to read the symbols used. The map may be a large-scale one of an experimental station. Read the scale to find out the amount of geographical space the station occupies. Plan appropriate map-reading activities for the point, line, and area symbols used on this large-scale map. How are these facilities symbolized on a small-scale map of the state? Read these maps to describe the locations of the various experimental facilities in relation to the land forms, water bodies, and agricultural regions of the state and the region of states. Note the areal distribution.

3. *Interpretation activities.*

Analyze the examples of tools and technics in the several basic human activities to note relationships in terms of

(1) relative location and use of large power tools in agricultural production in terms of such landforms as plains, plateaus, valleys in mountain-

(3) relative direction;

(4) spatial distribution.

Help children to perceive relationships in terms of areal association of man-made features and areal association of natural features and man-made things.

ous regions; small farms in valleys cannot make use of large farming implements; plains areas facilitate their use;

(2) relative location to function: for example, the use of such tools and technics as conveyor belts to transport ore from mines over difficult terrain to mobile transportation facilities;

(3) relative direction of land slope: What is the relationship between the direction and pattern of canals and the slope of the land?

(4) relative distances between specific places; gorges, for example, make transportation of ores mined impossible by the usual wheel transportation technics; the relative distance between a farming region and a source of water may be great because of an intervening range of hills or mountains;

(5) possibilities for states and regions with seacoast to create tools and technics to mine and harvest the riches of the oceans; discuss the importance of resources disclosed on new maps of the oceans.

An Illustrative Sequence of Pupil Experiences

Thus far we have analyzed many possibilities for map making, map reading, and map interpretation in relation to the geographical dimensions and characteristics of each of the nine basic human activities within the state community and the region-of-states community. The organization of these learning experiences into a detailed sequence of activities is crucial, for no matter how effective an individual learning experience may be, it must be followed up in subsequent phases if there are to be significant and permanent impacts on the understanding and behavior of the learner. Thus the previously learned map skills and geographic understandings which have been introduced and developed to varying levels of competency in the primary school social studies program need to be reinforced and expanded into larger and more meaningful patterns in each of the community emphases assigned to the middle school grades. In addition, new skills and understandings need to be systematically introduced and developed within the context of the ongoing social studies program and used and applied subsequently as they are needed. Complete mastery of a map skill or a geographic understanding is *not* expected in any particular community emphasis; rather, provision is made for systematic maintenance and reinforcement over the span of the elementary school grades. Consequently, there is a need for providing articulation of the teaching-learning of these skills and understandings as the pupil moves from one community emphasis to the next in the set. A teacher at any middle school grade level must see how and where the specific learning experience he is developing with his children will fit into the overall developmental geographic concept and map program.

This section sets forth in detail an illustrative sequence of suggested teaching-learning experiences designed to contribute to the development of selected map skills and understandings in conjunction with one basic human activity within the context of the state and the region-of-states communities. It will lead naturally into the program of teaching-learning experiences for the third emphasis for the middle school: the national community.

These teaching-learning experiences are only suggestive and must be adapted to the capacities and backgrounds of particular pupils by the teacher in each classroom situation. Descriptive statements of the learning activities for each of the expanding community emphases are intended only as general guides; substitutions to fit the needs of particular groups of children are to be expected and encouraged. While it is important that the essential features of the sequence be maintained, the content may have to be extended for some classes and reduced for others. The level of understanding and conclusions pupils are able to attain with respect to the three major objectives for the program will vary widely from one class to another and, of course, will vary within any one class. It is well to understand that the sequence begins with firsthand experiences provided in the more immediate locale of the pupil's home, school, neighborhood, local, metropolitan, and county communities and proceeds to build upon these experiential backgrounds as the larger and more remote communities of the state, region of states, and nation are studied in turn.

One basic human activity, providing recreation, with focus on the outdoor activities, has been selected from the social studies program for detailed sequential development for illustrative purposes. Any of the other eight clusters of basic human activities would have served our purposes of illustrating sequences of experience equally well.

EXPLORING THE BASIC ACTIVITY OF PROVIDING RECREATION

In every community people engage in outdoor recreational activities. The specific understandings children bring into the classroom will depend to some extent on where they live and the experiences they have had outside of the school. Children continue to have many kinds of experiences with the environment throughout their years in school. However, this largely incidental and haphazard interaction with the environment in one or several of the expanding communities may be educationally unproductive and may result in isolated and often weak or false concepts and generalizations. It is the responsibility of the elementary school's social studies program to help these children to observe, sort out, expand, revise, clarify, organize, and develop the many geographical concepts related to outdoor recreational phenomena. Understandings typical of a social studies program for the elementary school grades related to this topic of study are as follows:

> People engage in various kinds of outdoor recreational activities. These activities may vary from one season to the next.
> The kinds of outdoor recreational activities in which people engage vary with the kinds of land and water features and climate found in the geographical arena in which they live.
> Outdoor recreational areas and facilities have form, function, and a pattern of areal distribution.

Learning activities are then arranged to help children develop these generalizations about man's many ways of providing recreation by making use of the earth's features—water, plains, hills, mountains—for a variety of outdoor recreational activities. For example, hills and mountains, when covered with snow, provide slopes for skiing and tobogganing. In summer, these same slopes provide opportunities for sightseeing, hiking, fishing and hunting, and camping. Thus the concept of elevation may be taught as a closely related part of the ongoing social studies program rather than as an isolated concept illustrated with examples randomly selected by the teacher and then used incidentally thereafter. Maps, too, can contribute to helping children become more aware of the various geographic dimensions that influence outdoor recreational phenomena in any given community emphasis.

Instruction in how to represent and to read elevation on a map is an important element of map language that must be planned carefully in a developmental sequence. Classroom instruction should be given at the time children are called upon to make or read maps for a specific purpose connected with a specific concept or generalization from the social studies and when they have the necessary readiness and capacity to understand the geographic concepts involved. Likewise, children should understand the ideas represented by various combinations of symbols used to stand for recreational features. The initial phases of concept learning should begin with examples that represent differentiating characteristics of the concept rather than the rote memorization of a number of arbitrary associations. The sequence of learning experiences, for instance, should be such that children do not *first* encounter the abstract symbols of contour lines or colors on a map for elevated land features of the earth's surface. Such learning properly follows direct and/or described experiences.

DEVELOPING MAPPING EXPERIENCES

The remainder of this chapter will be devoted to coordinating a suggested series of learning experiences in map making, map reading, and map interpretation related to man's ways of meeting recreation needs through a variety of outdoor activities. Children will have opportunities to broaden and deepen their understandings about how recreational activities are related not only to where people live but also to the values and customs by which they live. Mapping experiences will be designed to help pupils acquire the ability to use and understand symbols and visualize the realities for which these symbols stand.

Usually several geographic skills and understandings will be represented simultaneously in each of the mapping experiences, and ideas and understandings from all ten skill categories will be interwoven throughout the sequence. The detailed descriptive statements of teaching procedures and mapping activities which follow are planned to further (1) the ability to organize systematically data gathered from firsthand and vicarious experiences and to represent them on maps with appropriate symbols, (2) the ability to read geographic data recorded on maps and visualize the realities represented, and (3) the ability to interpret the locations and distributions represented on maps and to reason about things geographic.

Before outlining an illustrative map program for the middle school grades emphases, it might be helpful to review the social studies experiences and the related geographic understanding and mapping activities the children working with this design may have had previously. A brief summary of these probable antecedent teaching-learning experiences concerned with the ways people engage in recreational activities follows. The communities emphasized included the home and school in the first grade; the neighborhood community in the second grade; and the city, metropolitan, and county communities in the third grade. The most important source of content for the program has been the school's deliberate use of the everyday experiences of children in these several expanding communities of which they are simultaneously members.

One of the initial steps in teaching children to make and to read the symbols on maps has been firsthand contact with recreational features in the school community. The first-grade teacher, for instance, has taken the pupils outdoors to observe and discuss the various recreational structures and areas on the school playground. There was probably a flat or level area for ball games; another area had elevated structures such as slides, jungle gyms, swings, and teeter-totters. Teacher and pupils probably discussed the steepness of the slide's slope that enabled children to slide from the higher level to the lower level. In the classroom the teacher helped pupils make large floor maps using blocks and other objects to represent the playground and its recreational structures. They mapped the observed playground arrangements and noted the spatial dimensions as they described their floor map to their classmates and the teacher. The children may have made crude representations of recreational structures from clay or papier-mâché and in this way begun to develop the ability to observe carefully and to note characteristics and locations of various features and facilities. Through these activities they were learning how to make maps from data gathered through firsthand observations of real objects in their immediate environment.

The teacher then helped the children learn to use pictorial symbols to represent these features on large sheets of paper. If they decided to make a map of the school playground, the class discussed and agreed on the use of appropriate pictorial symbols to represent the recreational structures. The symbols may have been either drawn directly on a base map prepared ahead of time by the teacher or drawn on sheets of paper, cut out, and then placed on the map. These pictorial symbols helped the children to picture in their minds the realities being represented. In addition the teacher could quickly check both the children's understandings of the concepts being developed and their mapping skills. They were forming the habit of associating various objects represented on the map with the actual objects being mapped. The maps made by the children were read and interpreted in connection with the understandings being developed in the ongoing social studies program.

The neighborhood community, studied next in sequence, offers many opportunities for outdoor recreational activities—in parks, community centers, commercial sports parks, playgrounds, water bodies, and wooded areas. For example, a neighborhood center may have a public swimming pool adjacent to a wooded area supplied with barbecue pits, tables, benches, and so on, for family picnics. The neighborhood playground may be equipped with swings, slides, and fields for playing a variety of ball games. Field trips during which second-grade children observed and noted the natural and man-made features in neighborhood parks and playgrounds provided opportunities to observe and discuss outdoor recreational facilities and the activities associated with them. The children may have observed geographical phenomena as they were related to specific activities. Sloping areas covered with grass and shaded with large trees may be set aside for group activities such as picnics and evening musicals. Large open areas that are level may provide space for group games. The children observed with the intention of building a three-dimensional model or making a sketch upon return to the classroom. They noted the particular arrangements and the relative locations of the facilities. These activities allowed them to learn spatial relationships from observations they had made through actual field work.

Map-making activities helped the children reorganize their field observations in their neighborhood. They probably made large-scale maps of the recreational areas using pictorial symbols for the natural and man-made features. They could have made a large small-scale map of the neighborhood community using appropriate pictorial and conventional symbols to show streets, buildings, and other prominent features. The outdoor recreational areas such as parks were represented on this latter map with appropriate area symbols that were explained in the map's key. All of these maps may have been mounted on bulletin boards and referred to throughout the class's study of how people provide for recreation in the neighborhood community.

As the emphasis in the social studies program progressed to the larger city, metropolitan, or county communities, other recreational features were studied. For example, there may be larger natural features such as streams, lakes, seashore, and wilderness areas which are not found in the lesser neighborhood; many recreational activities are associated with each of these natural features. The class may have planned a field trip to view firsthand a nature park that offers people living in this larger local community complex an opportunity to enjoy a wide range of activities such as hiking, boating, observing plants and animals, hunting and fishing, camping, and so on. The field trip made it possible to observe and note recreational phenomena that were closely related to the various land features of the local communities. The children were probably asked to observe the direction in which the stream or river flows, to note places where it flows rapidly and places where it doesn't appear to be moving at all. The class may have planned a hike along a nature trail that took them over small hills or knolls and eventually to a hilltop overlooking the entire park. From this promontory they noted that the land surface in this arena is not flat. There probably is an almost level area at the entrance of the park; the hiking trail follows the section of the valley that is not as steep and rugged as other parts of the valley;

and so on. They should have made notes of the various recreational structures associated with each of the particular land forms. For instance, the campsites and playgrounds are probably located in the more level entrance areas of the park.

Back in the classroom, the various physical features of the park and the locations and distributions of recreational structures were listed and discussed. Where was the trail in relation to the range of hills? Why did the trail wind around the highest hill in the park? How could a map help them locate and relate the various natural and man-made features of the park? By using a map, spatial relationships and directions could be noted and described with a measure of accuracy. A large oblique aerial photograph of the park might have been used to help the class identify and locate the various structures and land features before they began their mapping activities.

There were many possibilities for map making at this third-grade level. One group of children may have made a three-dimensional relief map of the park using the aerial photograph to help them locate the base data such as the stream, the range of hills, and the park's boundary. Molding sand and putty are excellent materials for making relief maps. A relief map helps children to visualize and understand the unevenness of the earth's surface.

Another group of children may have made a large-scale map of the park on a large sheet of paper, using pictorial symbols to represent the natural and man-made features. They may have discussed ways of representing the elevated features such as the hills on their maps. They may have recalled the hills where walking was easy and those with steeper slopes where walking was more tiring and breathing difficult. Was this the highest hill in the park? The information gathered from the discussion could have been checked with the aerial photograph and the relief map. Pictorial mounds or hills may have been used to represent the range of hills. The children probably found it hard to portray the exact nature of the surface features through the use of these symbols and thus they may have wanted to have the photograph of the park near at hand along with the three-dimensional relief model. The children recalled the various recreational structures located in the park and then agreed on the use of suitable pictorial symbols to represent them on their map. The map's key in the lower left-hand corner explained each of the symbols used. (See "Map and Globe Symbols," Appendix B.) Ways in which the map differs from the photograph were noted.

During the course of the third school year the children should have had opportunities to read and interpret maps of the city, metropolitan, or county communities made by others showing recreational features like swimming pools, resort areas for water activities—boating, water skiing—and so on. Some of these maps will have used pictorial symbols and others will have used abstract symbols having no visual relationships to the objects being represented. Children should not have been asked to read abstract symbols without first having had an opportunity to see either the object or a picture of it. After reading the pictures, for example, they may then have read the symbols on the map.

Children following the social studies design herein described in the primary grades should have developed the habit of making and using maps as a regular part of their social studies work. Ideally a systematic plan has been followed for building concepts through geographic work that was closely associated with the study of the basic human activity of outdoor recreation within the several smaller communities previously studied. Specifically, they have been introduced to the concept of elevation through learning experiences ranging from firsthand observations made on field trips to making three-dimensional maps and simple pictorial representations on a plane surface. They have observed that the kind of geographic area in which people live probably makes a difference in the kinds of outdoor recreational activities in which they engage. Likewise, outdoor recreational activities vary with the seasons of the year. Children who have had a variety of learning activities such as those described above have had an opportunity to experience how land forms affect one of the clusters of human activities. They have been building visual images of contrasts in elevation and land forms from numerous direct observations. All of these experiences will help them, in the study of state and region, to interpret maps of places which cannot be seen directly. If the pupils entering the intermediate grades have not had such experience, the teacher would be well advised to undertake such teaching-learning activities before going on to those suggested here for the middle grades.

Children in the middle school grades have developed wide and active interests in outdoor recreational activities. Many of them are skilled in skiing, ice skating, swimming, boating, hiking, or camping. From these firsthand out-of-school experiences with the physical environment of the several larger-than-local communities, they are forming geographic and recreational concepts and generalizations. These experiences are often directly related to the middle school program in social studies. They should be used wherever and whenever they are relevant to the ongoing social studies program.

To turn specifically to the state community and the region-of-states community, we find that the members of these communities engage in various kinds of outdoor recreational activities in areas related to the land forms, water bodies, and climatic conditions of the state and region of states as well as to the availability of transportation.

The teacher should foster a spirit of inquiry in the class discussions, directing the attention of the children to the kinds of outdoor activities each one engaged in and how these activities were related to the land forms, water bodies, and climatic conditions characteristic of the area. For example, these questions might be asked with respect to a hiking or camping expedition: How rugged was the terrain of the region? Was it possible to climb the highest hill or mountain? Why? Was there a great difference in elevation between the high and low ground in the region? Did the hiking trails follow the lower or higher elevations? Why is it harder to walk a steeper slope than a gradual one? Where did the streams or rivers flow the swiftest?

The teacher may be able to arrange a field trip to a nearby state park and a short hiking expedition to make these firsthand observations. The sequence of map-making activities should begin with teaching-learning experiences to expand and extend the ability to make accurate observations such as noting locations and distributions of natural and man-made recreational features. Such firsthand experiences help children to form sensorimotor images through what they do with their big muscles, what they see, hear, smell, and touch. Photographs and motion pictures of recreational phenomena are useful sources of visual images when firsthand observations are not possible. The teacher should, if possible,

1. Plan a field trip to a state park in a nearby section of the state to provide experiences to extend observational skills such as selecting and classifying data; recording what is seen; noting the shape of natural features like hills, mountains, valleys, bodies of water, and so on; noting the slope of these features; making estimates of distances; making some actual measurements to check the estimates.
2. Provide experiences to maintain the ability to orient self and note the cardinal directions out-of-doors. Review the cardinal directions. Continue to relate the cardinal directions to the position of the sun. Introduce the intermediate points of the compass. Have the children identify features in the park and describe their locations and directions.
3. Have pictures of the park for the class to study and discuss the essential characteristics of both the natural and man-made features. Organize the information gathered from reading these pictures into meaningful patterns. Note where such man-made features as roads are located. Record significant details for later reference.

Map-making activities to develop the ability to represent data on maps with appropriate symbols should follow the observational experiences. Natural and man-made features observed and studied during field trips can be translated into symbols and placed on maps. Previous map making in the primary grades will determine the children's readiness to use pictorial and abstract symbols to represent selected features. The process of symbolizing things provides opportunities to enhance concept learning. However, this does not mean that children should have a completely developed concept of the object before they are asked to symbolize it on a map. The teacher should keep in mind when planning mapping activities that the natural features and the recreational structures and activities lend themselves to many possibilities and varieties of symbolic treatment on maps. It is important that children be helped to develop skills in the use of conventional symbols to represent these features, both natural and man-made, whenever and wherever possible. Map making activities might include

1. Making a large-scale map of a state park visited by the class or a well-known national park in the region-of-states community. Decide on a scale of miles and include this information in the map's key. Use a line symbol of dashes for the park's boundary. Have members of the class decide on appropriate pictorial symbols to represent the man-made structures and special areas set aside for various recreational activities. Where appropriate use the conventional colors of black and red for these features. Identify road surfaces to and in the park by using various ribbon patterns and colors. Be sure that all of the symbols are explained in the map's key. Give the map a title and include the date the map was made. Use manuscript writing for all lettering. *Key* in lower left and *title,* date, and cartographer in lower right of map.

2. Making a map of the state or the region-of-states community to show the locations of recreational facilities, both private and governmental. Introduce the use of conventional symbols: line symbols for highways, railroads, boundaries (a long dash and two short dashes, repeating the pattern for the state boundaries), trails, rivers, streams, etc.; point symbols such as dots, circles, squares, rectangles, triangles for buildings, small towns, large cities, historical landmarks and monuments, docks, lookout stations, airports, lighthouses, etc.; area symbols for parks, resorts, beaches, forested regions, water bodies such as lakes, etc. Here again use blue to represent water bodies, green for vegetation, and black and red for man-made things. (See "Map and Globe Symbols," Appendix B.)

Recommended beginning maps for reading the relief features of the state and the region-of-states communities are raised plastic relief maps. (See "Aids for Teaching," Appendix A.) Commercially prepared and available from several sources, these maps enable children to feel as well as to see the shape of such terrain features as hills, mountains, valleys, and plains. The differences in elevation between high and low ground stand out plainly and are visually and haptically apparent. However, the teacher should recognize that it is necessary to exaggerate the vertical elements on these maps if all mountain ranges and other elevated features are to be perceptible. Some of these relief maps may be marked with colored crayons, thus providing opportunities for further map-making activities. For example, the state parks, state forests, and other well-known privately provided recreational areas in the region of states may be located on the map with appropriate area symbols. Pictures of the land forms, water bodies, and recreational structures should be mounted at the side of the map to help children associate the symbols used on the map with the actual locations and distributions of things being represented. As Whittemore points out, "Pictures should be correlated with map symbols throughout the grades, not only to help in the introduction of map symbols, but also to check and test what meaning such symbols have for the child."[4]

A raised plastic relief map helps children to visualize the slope of the land and to reason about the direction in which the rivers and streams flow. Have the children trace the courses of rivers from their sources to their mouths, noting the land forms through which they flow. Ask questions like: Where do you think the rivers are swift? Where do you think the rivers are slow and meandering? Where would you expect to find wide and shallow river valleys? Relate this information to possible recreational uses of rivers for fishing and water sports.*

These map-making and map-reading activities should be followed by carefully organized classroom activities to help the children develop the ability to interpret and understand the locations and distributions of outdoor recreational phenomena represented on maps. The map interpretation activities should be directed toward the discovery and understanding of relationships between natural features of the state and the region-of-states communities and the many ways in which people use them for recreational purposes. Evidences of areal relationships may be gained by comparing the distribution of man-made structures and facilities shown on a recreational map with the land-form features portrayed on a raised plastic relief map. "In almost every social studies unit," Kohn points out, "children should discuss and explain the distribution of physical and cultural features by comparing maps which give different facts about the same area."[5] Maps reduce the patterns of areal distribution and locations to a size that can be seen at once and at one time and thus are invaluable tools in helping children develop relational thinking skills. The teacher may lead the pupils to

1. Analyze and interpret the significance of the location and distribution patterns of recreational phenomena within the state and region-of-states communities. Reason about the presence or absence of summer resorts and winter resorts in various geographical regions in both of the communities. Look for associations of summer resort areas with bodies of water and mountainous regions. Develop the ability to make inferences about the location and distribution of winter resort areas and the geographical char-

---

* An eleven-minute film, *Rivers*, produced by the Audio-Visual Center, Indiana University, Bloomington, Indiana, would be useful for developing the concepts needed to answer the questions raised here. (See Appendix A.)

acter of a region. Help the children gather their data from two or more maps.

2. Use two or more special kinds of maps—relief, population, transportation, vegetation—when discussing questions such as these: What will the future demand in providing facilities for growing population areas in each of the communities and an increasing amount of free time for recreation? What is your own state doing to lay out future parks and beaches? What are private agencies and individuals doing to provide additional recreational facilities? What kinds of activities will they provide? Have members of the class propose possible recreational areas for the state community and the region-of-states community and explain and defend their choices using a relief map, a population map, a transportation map, and a climate map.

In summary, this illustrative sequence of teaching-learning experiences and suggested teaching procedures described for the two community emphases of the state and the region of states focuses on each of these three geographic skills and understandings: making maps to record information gathered from firsthand observations, reading maps, and interpreting maps to form associations and to make inferences. If children can develop a beginning competency in these fundamental map skills and in geographic understanding, they will be able someday to use maps as tools to help provide more adequate recreation in the state and region-of-states communities.

REFERENCES

1. Cecil V. Millard, *School and Child* (East Lansing: Michigan State University Press, 1954), p. 44.
2. Faculty of the University School, *How Children Develop* (Columbus: Ohio State University, 1946), pp. 29–48.
3. Walter W. Cook, "Individual Differences and Curriculum Practice" (1948), in Arthur P. Coladarci (ed.), *Educational Psychology* (New York: Dryden Press, 1955), p. 331.
4. Katheryne T. Whittemore, "Learning to Read Maps," *Childhood Education*, 14: 175 (December, 1937).
5. Clyde Kohn, "Interpreting Maps and Globes," *Skills in Social Studies*, Twenty-fourth Yearbook, National Council for the Social Studies (Washington: NCSS, 1953), p. 175.

chapter eight

THE MIDDLE GRADES EMPHASES

/ 7. *The United States National Community*

In this chapter we will analyze each of the basic human activities carried on within the arena of the United States national community for geographic experiences which can further the development of map skills and areal understandings in this middle grade emphasis. A fundamental principle of organization must be kept in mind by the teacher: Each expanding community in the social studies sequence deals with the same list of basic human activities and the same basic list of geographic objectives and map skills but treats each according to the interests and problems pertinent to that particular community.

Analysis in Terms of the Basic Human Activities

The program of teaching-learning experiences for this emphasis is organized as follows: In the left-hand column of the succeeding pages, for each of the nine clusters of human activities, are listed the three major objectives for the geographic concepts and mapping program: (1) the ability to reorganize data concerning the physical and cultural landscape gathered from firsthand and vicarious experiences and to represent these data on maps and globes with appropriate symbols, (2) the ability to read data recorded on maps and globes, and (3) the ability to interpret and reason about the distributions, locations, and interrelationships of the phenomena of geography represented on maps and globes.

The right-hand column contains examples of teaching-learning experiences, organized in three stages: map-making activities, map-reading activities, and map-interpreting activities. The sequence of mapping activities described for each stage is suggestive, not prescriptive. An illustrative series of geographic and mapping experiences suggesting a developmental sequence of map work is spelled out in detail following this outline.

THE UNITED STATES NATIONAL COMMUNITY (EMPHASIS 7)

*Basic Human Activity: Protecting and Conserving
Life, Health, Property, and Resources*

OBJECTIVES	TEACHING-LEARNING EXPERIENCES

1. *Ability to reorganize data gathered from firsthand and vicarious experiences and represent them on maps with appropriate symbols.*

The national community, by virtue of its vast resources, provides many mechanisms for protecting, conserving, and improving the life, health, property, and resources of all members of the nation. Our national defense guards us from military aggression from potential enemies. Internally, national organization of law enforcement protects the rights of all citizens against encroachments. Functioning within the national community are many private and volunteer agencies providing services in protecting and conserving resources, both human and natural. The joint action of the smaller state and region-of-states communities within the arena of this larger community of the nation makes it possible to provide a greater range of services in protecting and conserving than is possible for the lesser communities working alone. New and better ways are being developed continuously.

1. *Mapping activities.*

Many problems of protecting and conserving are of such scope that the state or region-of-states communities by themselves. do not have the resources or the facilities to solve them. Agencies which function on the national level are both governmental and private. As an example in the private sector, discuss the work of a national volunteer organization such as the National Tuberculosis Association. What is the concern of this agency? What activities does it engage in? Where? How? Why should concern about this disease merit national action? Write to the local county unit for information. Find out where the national headquarters are located. Where is the state headquarters office? On a base map of the United States locate these organizational features of this national organization. Discuss the work of such federal governmental agencies as the Defense Department, the Federal Bureau of Investigation, the United States Coast Guard, or the Bureau of Narcotics. Each is organized on a national basis. Obtain data about the spatial distribution

2. *Ability to read data recorded on maps and globes.*

Develop skills in reading symbols portraying protecting and conserving activities within the national community. Develop the ability to translate these features into meaningful imagery. Maps pertaining to protecting and conserving both human and natural resources include:

(1) development and conservation of natural resources;

(2) use and conservation of native plant life;

(3) use and conservation of native animal life;

(4) use and conservation of national public lands;

(5) use and conservation of water resources by federal and national private agencies;

(6) soil maps;

(7) water pollution control maps;

(8) conservation and protection of areas of natural beauty;

(9) national flood control;

(10) military installations: air bases, army bases, naval bases, training facilities, and missile bases;

(11) distribution of national volunteer agencies concerned with health and welfare.

Develop the ability to locate places on maps using a grid system and the ability to read the relative locations of places and features. Develop the ability to read the cardinal directions and areal distributions.

of these agencies. Where are units located in your state? Appropriate maps made in the class can be helpful in discussions. If you can get historical data on any of these national efforts, map former spatial distribution and compare with current distribution.

2. *Map reading activities.*

Help children develop meanings for the symbols used on maps and globes portraying features of protecting and conserving activities in the national arena. As an example, discuss the work of the United States Weather Bureau. What is the importance of weather information to people within the national arena? Could this information be gathered by a less-than-national organization? What is the organization of this bureau? What is the work of a single weather station? Collect information from various sources. Get photographs of weather stations. What are the physical features? How are they portrayed on a map? Are all weather stations alike? Do they all perform the same duties? How are the differences shown on maps? Obtain copies of weather maps from the United States Weather Bureau. (See "Aids for Teaching," Appendix A.)

Map-reading activities should be planned to help children develop skills in reading the following groups of symbols used to portray protecting and conserving features and activities: point symbols for weather stations, coast guard stations, federal prisons, reservoirs, military academies, military airports, naval docks and stations, and so on; line symbols for boundaries of military installations, classified areas for security purposes, etc., lines of communication, boundaries

3. *Ability to interpret distribution and location on maps and to reason geographically.*

Analyze the geographic location and distribution of protecting and conserving features and activities in the arena of the national community as to:
(1) relative location;
(2) relative direction;
(3) relative distance.
Reason about the distribution of these features in relation to major land forms and water bodies and climate features.

of conservation districts, etc.; area symbols for wildlife refuges, federal forests, and various other federal districts; watershed lands, and so on. (See "Map and Globe Symbols," Appendix B.)

3. *Interpretation activities.*

Reason about the protection and conservation of wildlife, for example, referring to the locations of some 300 refuges of the United States Fish and Wildlife Service. What geographical considerations must be taken into account in locating refuges? Is there any relation to landforms? Water bodies? What about the kinds of vegetation that exist? Has vegetation any relation to the climate of the region? Why is it necessary for the national community to take these steps to conserve national resources such as wildlife, forests, soil, minerals, and the like? Discuss the work of the Audubon Society or the American Forestry Association in protecting and conserving wildlife. Through these activities help children to develop the ability to perceive relationships in terms of relative location, relative distance, and relative direction. Help them to establish areal associations between natural features such as annual precipitation, the relative slope of the land, and the construction of dams and reservoirs to conserve water and prevent destruction of soil resources through the control of floods (Figure 38).

Basic Human Activity: Producing, Exchanging, Distributing, and Consuming Goods and Services

OBJECTIVES

TEACHING-LEARNING EXPERIENCES

1. *Ability to reorganize data gathered*

1. *Map-making activities.*

Figure **38**

Dam Site

from firsthand and vicarious experiences and represent them on maps with appropriate symbols.

Within the United States national community people produce, exchange, distribute, and consume goods and services. The major characteristic of our national society is its high degree of industrialization and specialization. For instance, regions with rich soil and adequate water resources plus a favorable climate specialize in agricultural production while manufacturing activities may predominate in other regions. Thus no single lesser community produces

Manufacturing steel is an example of a major private-sector industry producing and distributing a basic material to serve the needs of many other industries. Large capital investments are required to provide the facilities to produce steel in large quantities. Show a motion picture describing the making of steel to the class. Have the class investigate the location factors of this industry. In what states are the main producing facilities located? What raw materials are used in the production of steel? Locate the chief sources of these materials on a large outline map of the United

all the goods and services needed by its members. Each one relies upon many other communities for its basic needs of food, clothing, manufactured goods, and services. Likewise, the major industries exhibit national patterns of organization. These include steel, auto, aircraft, major household appliances, furniture, radio and television, foods and drugs, etc. Many industrial concerns have major production centers to serve the entire national community; finished products are distributed through regional centers to serve widely separated geographical areas. The national community has a vast complex of networks for producing and exchanging goods and services. Children are helped to gain an understanding of this complex interrelationship through participation in teaching-learning activities such as observation, investigation, discussion, reading, and map-making activities.

2. *Ability to read data recorded on maps and globes.*

Develop skills in identifying symbols portraying producing, exchanging, distributing, and consuming features and activities within the national community. Develop the ability to translate these symbols and their areal distribution into meaningful imagery and conceptual patterns of landscape. Maps portraying symbols pertaining to this basic human activity include:

(1) forest products;
(2) agricultural production and distribution: land use, culti-

States. Locate these three major steel manufacturing centers: Chicago, Illinois; Cleveland, Ohio; and Detroit, Michigan. All are situated on the Great Lakes. Locate other major centers, in Pennsylvania and Ohio. Note how this industry exhibits sharp localizations and close areal associations with raw materials, transportation facilities, and users of its products. Place these major production centers on an outline map of the United States. Have a committee investigate the large users of steel products, such as the auto industry, and the location of their major production centers. Place these production centers on the same map. How are finished steel products shipped to the auto industry? Contrast the shipment of bulk material such as coal, limestone, and ore with the shipment of sheet steel, for example. Gather information about the recent shifts in the location of new steel-producing facilities—St. Louis, Utah, and Southern California. Locate these on the same map. Discuss the impact of new technologies on future geographic locations of this industry.

2. *Map-reading activities.*

Many symbols—pictorial, semi-pictorial, and abstract—such as the geometric shapes of the point, circle, square, triangle, are used to symbolize producing, exchanging, and consuming goods and services within the emphasis of the national community. In planning the map-reading exercises for identifying these features the teacher should be sure the pupils understand the realities symbolized on the maps before they learn the symbols. There are many excellent motion pictures, filmstrips, photographs, and textual

vated farm lands, and pasture and grazing lands;

(3) agricultural products (plants): food and fiber products, industrial products, and consumption areas;

(4) livestock products: food products, industrial products, consumption areas, and irrigated areas;

(5) development of industrial resources: coal mining areas, distribution of coal for domestic and industrial use, oil and natural gas fields, pipelines for the distribution of oil and gas, oil refineries and storage areas, production and distribution of electricity, and areas with potential power sites;

(6) development of mineral resources: mining of industrial metal ores, mining of precious metal ores, mining of radioactive ores, mining of mineral salts, and manufacturing with iron, steel, aluminum, etc.

3. *Ability to interpret distribution and location on maps and globes and to reason geographically.*

Reason geographically about the location and areal distribution of producing, exchanging, distributing, and consuming goods and services within the arena of the national community. Analyze the geographic location and areal distribution of these phenomena as to relative location, density, relative distance, and relative direction. Correlate the spatial dimensions of these phenomena with cultural features such as the locations of metropolitan centers as well as the physical features of the national community. Continue to develop the ability to make inferences about data read on maps.

materials that can be used to help pupils develop the mental images of the essential characteristics of many of these production and distribution features. For instance, show pictures of the iron ore docks at Duluth, Minnesota, and the typical docks of an ocean port such as New York, Seattle, New Orleans Help the pupils develop the conceptual landscape patterns for these iron ore docks. Help them identify new instances of these docks in other parts of the Great Lakes. Use both large-scale maps of small areas and small-scale maps of large areas in the reading exercises. Plan activities to help them translate symbols showing steel-producing centers, oil-producing fields, financial centers, industrial research and development parks, and so on, into imagery of the realities thus represented.

3. *Interpretation activities.*

Help pupils develop the ability to use maps as basic tools in the study and interpretation of geographic dimensions of producing, exchanging, distributing, and consuming goods and services in the national community. Industrial manufacturing can be used as an example: Note whether the industry's factories are located in or near cities. What geographical factors were probably taken into account in locating these factories? Is there any relation to the climate of the region? Landforms? Water bodies? Help pupils to make inferences about the interrelatedness of locations and distributions of two or more factors, for example, raw materials, markets, adequate transportation facilities. Several kinds of maps are needed for gathering data and interpreting them. Help the children to reason about associations of two or more of the factors mentioned above. Many manufacturing plants are located some distance from the source of raw materials. What factors make this economically feasible? Help students to look for possible relationships by using several kinds of maps—transportation maps, population maps, natural resource maps, and special maps showing the locations of institutions of higher learning and advanced research. Help students recognize areal associations between a natural resource such as oil and the concentration of chemical plants, for example.

Basic Human Activity: Transporting People and Goods

OBJECTIVES

1. *Ability to reorganize data gathered from firsthand and vicarious experiences and represent them on maps with appropriate symbols.*

The activity of transporting people and goods efficiently and rapidly is of vital importance to the national community of the United States. Spatial connections and interactions between the many state and region-of-states communities are provided by water, land, and air transportation facilities. The development of each of these modes of transportation on a continental basis helped our nation expand from a number of widely separated local and state communities into a national community. New tools and technics are resulting in improvements and changes in transporting

TEACHING-LEARNING EXPERIENCES

1. *Mapping activities.*

Observe the nation as a large community that makes use of the transporting function to move people and goods. Describe the kinds of transportation facilities available in the local community to all points of the nation. Find out if any members of the class have used any transcontinental travel facilities. Have them trace their trips on a map of the United States. Reorganize these firsthand experiences of the children and translate them into map symbols. On a large bulletin-board-size map of the United States locate the local community and the state. Decide on symbols (conventional wherever possible) to show the routes, the kinds of facilities used, and the people and goods that bring the local and state communities closer together and make living better in each lesser community within the national community.

2. *Ability to read data recorded on maps and globes.*

Develop reading skills in identifying symbols portraying transportation features and develop the ability to translate them into meaningful imagery. These include:

(1) continental paths, trails, and other routes of foot travel;

(2) continental wagon trails, turnpikes, and other early routes;

(3) national highway maps;

(4) interstate and transcontinental railroad maps, routes, terminals, division points;

(5) national water routes, harbors, docks, piers, warehouses, beacons, lighthouses, etc.;

(6) national air routes, national and international airports, landing fields;

(7) military airports;

(8) charts for navigation on water;

(9) charts for navigation in the air;

(10) ferries and bridges.

Develop the ability to read the relative location and relative distances between national points. Relate these to the various kinds of transportation. Develop the ability

places visited. In the key explain the symbols used. Use the scale to locate the distances between the places visited. Give the map a title. Contrast the transporting of people today with that of colonial times. Gather information on the early continental trails and their location. Locate these on the class map. Compare the travel time of old and new transport between places on the map. Note how present interstate highways have shortened the distances between many places. Speculate about future developments in the transporting of people and goods throughout the nation.

2. *Map-reading activities.*

Maps showing national systems of transportation are important to many segments of our population. Discuss what would happen if the operations of major land, water, and air transportation facilities were to come to a sudden halt. Bring out the understanding that we live in a highly specialized society which is dependent on the transportation of many kinds of goods from one region of states to another. Our system of production and distribution of goods and services relies on an efficient and carefully planned network of primary inland waterways, highway, railway, and airline routes. Help children to read maps to identify these major continental routes. Be sure to include Alaska and Hawaii and the territories. For instance, read highway maps of the United States and trace the major interstate systems of roads. Learn to read the numbering system used for these roads: even numbers refer to roads that run in an east-west direction, while the odd numbers run in a north-south direction. Read the key to find out the symbols used

to read the areal distribution of various kinds of transportation.

for freeways of more than two lanes, the kinds of surfaces, the seasons the road is open, and so on. Read weather maps of the region to find the kinds of weather conditions to be expected on major interstate highways. Discuss the importance of this information to truckers and others who travel over these highways. Have children read maps to find the arterial routes between large distribution centers such as New York City, Detroit, Chicago, Seattle, San Francisco, and Los Angeles. Read maps for the areal distribution of railways, water routes and canals, and airports. For example, read physical maps of the nation for landforms of areas having many railways fanning out in many directions.

3. *Ability to interpret distribution and location on maps and globes and to reason geographically.*

Reason geographically about the location and areal distribution of transportation features in the United States national community. For example, interpret the location and distribution of national highway systems, transcontinental railways, the major continental air routes, and the major water routes and harbors. What factors determine the volume of interchange between rural areas and metropolitan centers? Between manufacturing centers and sources of raw materials? Reason about the route most appropriate to physical features: boats follow inland waterways; railways follow river valleys and routes of least grade; transcontinental airplanes such as jet passenger and cargo planes follow great-circle routes. Reason geographically about areas and centers that draw general traffic from the larger areas

3. *Interpretation activities.*

Children should be helped to make inferences from the data they gather from maps about the significance of the location and areal distribution of various kinds of transportation in certain areas of the national community. Why are cities such as Chicago and St. Louis the hub of major transportation facilities and routes? What kinds of products would you expect to flow through St. Louis and other cities in the national community? Reason about the number of spatial connections and interactions a city like Milwaukee would have. What inferences can be drawn from reading a topographical map of the state of Montana with regard to the routes of railways and highways? In what ways does a mountainous landscape limit the development of extensive water and land transportation facilities? What kinds of landforms favor the development and ease of transportation of goods?

of the nation. Interpret the number systems for routes found on maps.

Relate the cost and ease of building highways and railways over various kinds of terrain. Discuss the interest of our national government in the development of national transportation systems. Reason about the significance of the first national highway from the Atlantic coast to the interior of the Midwest in the early 1800's. Reason about the location of present-day highways and the early continental trails such as the Santa Fe. What advantage can you see in starting the most easternly national highway with the number 1? Where would you expect to find U.S. Highway 101? Where would you find the low even-numbered highways?

Basic Human Activity: Communicating Facts, Ideas, and Feelings

OBJECTIVES

1. *Ability to reorganize data gathered from firsthand and vicarious experiences and represent them on maps with appropriate symbols.*

   Our highly industrialized society is dependent upon fast and efficient systems of communication. Many business concerns are dependent upon these systems of communication for vital information such as the latest weather reports or market quotations; they must know when to order extra supplies to meet sudden emergencies or market demands, and so on. These vast communication networks span the nation and are in constant states of change and expansion. Some of the media of communication such as radio reach into the most remote regions of the nation; others such as closed-circuit television and the telegraph reach only larger centers of population. Recent develop-

TEACHING-LEARNING EXPERIENCES

1. *Mapping activities.*

   A beginning point for discussion may be a recent address of the President of the United States to the nation. Discuss the vastness of a communication network that enables people in all regions of the national community to hear the message as it is being delivered by the President from the White House in Washington, D.C., and to see the President. When was the news of the talk carried in the local newspaper? Find out how the local newspaper receives the news it prints. Plan a field trip to the newspaper's newsroom to see how the news is collected from all parts of the nation. Gather information about such agencies as the United Press, the Associated Press, etc. What is their organization and what kinds of facilities are needed to provide a network of national cover-

ments such as the electronic transmission of blueprints, pictures, and other data are available in only the major centers of the national community. The need for a national system of communication was recognized from the time of the beginnings of our nation. Projecting into the future, more efficient and more rapid means of carrying on this basic human activity will be worked out.

age? Reorganize these data and represent them on an outline map of the United States with appropriate symbols. Contrast this communication system with the carrying of the news in the early days of our nation. How were ideas, facts, and other information communicated from one section of the nation to another? Read accounts of the pony express and map its routes on an outline map of the United States. Read this map to estimate the approximate time needed to carry a message from the President, in Washington, to a local community in California. Find out how man today uses the air to send messages from one place to another. Read accounts of the national microwave network and the part it plays in relaying television programs direct from New York to San Francisco, for example. Find out how satellite communication systems may again modify national communication networks.

2. *Ability to read data recorded on maps and globes.*

Develop skills in identifying symbols portraying communicating features and activities within the national community. Develop the ability to translate these symbols and their patterns of distribution into meaningful imagery and conceptual patterns of landscape features. Maps portraying symbols pertaining to communication features and activities include communication systems and routes:

(1) telephone and microwave networks;
(2) telegraph stations and networks;
(3) radio networks and stations;
(4) television networks and stations;
(5) news service systems;

2. *Map-reading activities.*

Plan map-reading activities to develop the ability to identify new instances of communicating features and activities within the national arena. Discuss the essential characteristics of the various features. Many of the symbols used to represent communicating features are semipictorial, as, for example, telephone lines, telegraph lines, radio and television broadcasting towers. In developing meanings for the many concepts discussed, it may be helpful to correlate the work with that of the science classes. Plan activities to help read the following kinds of symbols: point symbols for radio stations, television stations, broadcasting towers, microwave relay stations, newspaper publishing

(6) radio beams for shipping and aviation;
(7) mail routes: land, air, water;
(8) newspaper and periodical production and distribution;
(9) printing and distribution of books, records, etc.;
(10) communication satellites, laser beam communication.

plants, book publishing plants, post offices, terminal facilities; line symbols for telephone, telegraph, and coaxial lines, radio beams, newspaper routes, mail routes (airmail, railroad, and highway), microwave beams, distribution routes, other communication routes; area symbols to show the distribution of communicating features, range of coverage of radio broadcasts, news services. (See "Map and Globe Symbols," Appendix B.)

Plan activities to help children to read the relative location of these features. For example, television broadcasting stations and their transmitters are located in large centers of population. Impose a grid system on maps and describe the relative locations of various communicating features in reference to each other.

Plan a map-reading exercise using a U.S. postal rates map. Compute the rates for sending parcels to various sections of the national community.

3. *Ability to interpret distribution and location on maps and globes and to reason geographically.*

Reason geographically about the location and areal distribution of communicating features and activities within the United States national community. Analyze the geographical location and areal distribution of communication phenomena as to relative location, relative distance, and relative direction. Correlate the spatial dimensions of these phenomena with other cultural features and the physical features. Continue to develop the ability to make inferences from maps.

3. *Interpretation activities.*

Help pupils use maps as basic tools in the study of geographic aspects of communicating structures and activities within the national community. Note the location and distribution of microwave networks and the television stations. Explain this distribution by comparing maps which give different facts about the national community such as the major population centers, the physical features of the land, and so on. Help the pupils to make inferences about the interrelatedness of locations and distributions of two or more cultural features. Several maps are needed for gathering and interpreting the data. What regions of the national community have a concentration of communicating facilities? Why should such cities as New York, Chicago, St. Louis, Seattle, San Francisco, and Los Angeles become key nerve centers of communicating features? Compare communication routes of the pony express with the modern microwave networks of today. Use both maps and a globe to make inferences about the future use of satellites in communicating facts, ideas, and feelings.

Basic Human Activity: Providing Education

OBJECTIVES

TEACHING-LEARNING EXPERIENCES

1. *Ability to reorganize data gathered from firsthand and vicarious experiences and to represent them on maps with appropriate symbols.*

People at the national community level work out ways for carrying on the basic human activity of providing education. While our nation has not had a federal system of education at the elementary, secondary, or higher education levels, nevertheless, at the national community level the people through their federal government are interested in and very much concerned about educational opportunities for all citizens of the nation. Universities and colleges have assumed national characteristics because students from many states of the nation attend them. National conferences sponsored by private and governmental agencies provide adults with opportunities for further education. In addition, museums, libraries, conservatories, art galleries, and so on, provide programs so that people from all parts of the nation can learn about, as

1. *Mapping activities.*

A member of the class may have visited an older brother or sister who is attending a college or a university in another region of the nation. Have him describe the campus, using any pictures, bulletins, and maps to illustrate and give detail to the presentation. Compare the size and facilities of this university with those of a state university or college nearby. Are there many students from a wide geographical area also attending this university? Why does it attract students from so many parts of the nation? Find out whether there is special equipment such as an outstanding collection of library books, special laboratories, outstanding research facilities for the training of scientists, research technicians, etc. Are there other universities that have special facilities and staffs in such professions as medicine, engineering, and education that attract students from many sections of the nation? Have a committee investigate various sources and references

well as enjoy, many different things. Children are helped to gain an understanding of how people make provisions for carrying on the basic human activity of education through such teaching-learning experiences as observation, investigation, discussion, reading, and mapping activities.

2. *Ability to read data recorded on maps and globes.*

Develop skills in identifying symbols portraying educational phenomena in the national arena. Develop the ability to translate these symbols and their distribution into meaningful imagery. Maps pertaining to educational features and activities include:

(1) U.S. Office of Education;
(2) institutions of higher learning, private and public;
(3) libraries;
(4) museums: art, science, etc.;
(5) historical museums;
(6) industrial training centers provided by various private concerns;
(7) language centers, art schools, music conservatories, etc.;
(8) educational status of the population;
(9) conference centers and facilities for national groups.

Develop the ability to read the relative location of these features and the patterns of distribution. Develop the ability to read distances on maps and the globe.

3. *Ability to interpret distribution and location on maps and to reason geographically.*

to prepare a list of universities and colleges prominent in such fields as agriculture, medicine, forestry, education, science, art, and music. Translate these data into map symbols on a large bulletin-board-size outline map of the United States. Decide on appropriate symbols to show the fields of specialty. Give the map a title. Impose a grid on the map to describe the locations. Use this map for class reading and interpreting activities; for example, interpret the relative location of the School of Forestry at Oregon State University, Corvallis, Oregon.

2. *Map-reading activities.*

Many symbols, pictorial, semi-pictorial, and abstract, such as points, circles, squares, etc., are used to symbolize educational features and activities on maps. Plan activities to extend the meanings and associations for the education features portrayed on maps of the national community. Discuss: In what ways are universities of the nation different? Why? What are some of the physical features of these institutions? Make a bulletin board display of some of the campuses that draw students from the entire nation. Discuss the essential features of great "national" universities that are different from local colleges. What conventional map symbols are used to show these features? Read maps showing the distribution of colleges and universities 100 years ago. Read their locations in terms of the population centers of the time. Read large-scale maps of several colleges and universities that have assumed national characteristics.

3. *Interpretation activities.*

Have the students compare two sections of the United States on a

Analyze the geographic location and distribution of educational structures and activities in the national community as to:

(1) relative location;
(2) relative distance;
(3) relative direction;
(4) spatial distribution.

Correlate the location of these educational phenomena with other cultural and physical features. Develop the ability to compare two or more maps and to make inferences concerning the spatial distribution of educational phenomena shown on these maps. Develop the ability to make inferences from maps.

map showing the distribution and extent of state universities and colleges. For example, how might you account for the large number of institutions of higher education in the states of New York and California as compared with the states of Montana or Arizona? They might also be asked to note that large private institutions of higher education are concentrated in particular sections of the national community. What inferences might be made from this information? Locate the centers of such cultural and educational activities as the music conservatories, libraries, and so on. Reason about their particular locations. Why would one not find large libraries in sparsely populated areas? Reason about the locations of conference centers and facilities for national groups who make regular provisions for in-service education of employees. Note areal relationships of cultural features. For example, nationally known medical schools are located in certain sections of the nation, usually in centers that have well-regarded hospitals nearby. Why?

Basic Human Activity: Providing Recreation

OBJECTIVES	TEACHING-LEARNING EXPERIENCES
1. *Ability to reorganize data gathered from firsthand and vicarious experiences and represent them on maps with appropriate symbols.* The United States national community provides facilities for people to engage in various kinds of recreation as participants and spectators. Recreational facilities and services are supplied by both government and private agencies. Phenomena both natural and cultural facilitate	1. *Mapping activities.* Many children in the middle grades have had firsthand experiences in using recreational facilities provided by the national parks of our nation. Have these children share their experiences with the class. Carefully selected pictures, brochures, maps, etc., should be shown in class. Have each child describe the location of the national park he visited. What is the relative

recreation. Certain areas of our nation such as Hawaii or Florida, the New England coast, the lake country of Minnesota, the Rocky Mountains, and the like, have assumed national characteristics because people from all parts of the nation visit and use them for recreational purposes. Metropolitan centers such as New York City, New Orleans, and San Francisco likewise have assumed national characteristics as recreational centers. Modern transportation facilities have made most recreational facilities available to most of the people of the nation, and further make possible nationwide athletic leagues, musical organizations, etc.

distance, direction, and location of the park from the local community? Describe the recreational features of the park and the kinds of activities available. Trace the route taken to get to the park on both the globe and a map of the United States. Discuss the advantages and disadvantages of using a globe and a map. As a mapping activity have each child map the route to the park or parks he has visited. Decide on symbols to show the locations of these parks. Discuss the element of "whereness." How would a grid system help in describing locations? Place a grid on the map. Provide a title and key for the map. Be sure to include the cardinal directions. The class may want to make a map showing the parks members of the class would like to visit. Decide on appropriate semipictorial symbols for the activities of the area. Give this map an appropriate title. Place a grid on this map and have the children describe locations. Decide on what land forms are needed to make the location of certain activities meaningful. Note the kind of recreational activities that characterize a mountainous region. Compare the children's maps with commercial maps. A large sheet of acetate with a system of coordinates drawn in ink can be placed over the more permanent map. Then with a china marking pencil the pupils can add recreational features. Discuss some of the cartographic features of commercial maps. Many commercial maps are not strictly maps but only pictograms with the shape of the land serving as a framework to show the approximate shape and location of recreational features. Make national maps showing locations of baseball, football, hockey, basketball, etc., teams that belong to one or another national league.

2. *Ability to read data recorded on maps and globes.*

Develop skills in identifying symbols portraying recreational phenomena in the United States national community. Develop the ability to translate these symbols into meaningful imagery. Maps pertaining to recreational functions include:

(1) public recreational areas and institutions serving the national community;

(2) commercial recreational areas and institutions serving the national community;

(3) public lands for recreation: national parks, national monuments, national forests;

(4) hunting areas, fishing areas;

(5) national game reservations.

Develop the ability to read the areal distributions and relative locations of recreational phenomena in the national community. Develop the ability to read scale and grid networks.

2. *Map-reading activities.*

Plan activities to gather information about a national park. Use a small-scale map of the United States and a large-scale map of a park such as Crater Lake National Park in Oregon. What information can you get from a small-scale map? Relative location, distance from the major centers in the United States, highway connections, etc., may be obtained from such a map. Read a large-scale map such as the map of the park in the U.S. Department of the Interior publication. Read the key for the symbols used. Find the relative location of the park headquarters, the lodge, highways, hiking trails, etc. Make a collection of pictures of the various features of the park portrayed on the map. Display these on a bulletin board. What time of the year do you think the pictures were taken? Help the children to visualize the recreational features in various seasons. How are the mountain peaks symbolized? How are these peaks in Crater Lake National Park different from peaks in Glacier National Park, for example? What symbol is used for the fire lookout station? Study maps and brochures put out by motel or hotel chains, by resort chains, by airlines and railways and bus companies, all advertising the variety of recreational opportunities that exist in our nation.

3. *Ability to interpret distribution and location on maps and to reason geographically.*

Develop the ability to reason geographically about the spatial distribution of selected recreational features and activities portrayed on

3. *Interpretation activities.*

For example, where are the national parks located in the United States in terms of certain landforms? Interpret the significance of the location of several national parks in the Sierra Nevada. Inter-

national maps. Develop the ability to perceive relationships in terms of:

(1) relative location;
(2) relative direction;
(3) relative distance.

pret the significance of the location of national monument parks. What is the relative location of these parks in terms of population centers? Landforms? Water bodies? Weather? Vegetation? Transportation? What is the relative direction of these features in terms of the pupils' local community? The large population centers of the national community? What is the relative distance of recreational features from the pupils' local community? Can people from all parts of the nation get to the facility conveniently? Why is it that people in some sections of the nation must travel considerable distances to national parks? Relate the national monument parks to the historical development of our country. What is the areal association of man-made recreation features to natural features? In what ways are summer resorts related to terrain? Winter resorts? All-year resorts? What might account for the increased interest in areas for natural recreation? What are possible national trends in providing recreation in the future? How well does the airway network make parks easily accessible to national population distributions? What are possible trends in national networks of private enterprise entertainment? How are hotels, motels, shops displaying local crafts, etc., aiding tourism in the nation?

Basic Human Activity: Organizing and Governing

OBJECTIVES	TEACHING-LEARNING EXPERIENCES
1. *Ability to reorganize data gathered from firsthand and vicarious experiences and represent them on maps*	1. *Mapping activities.* Begin with a review of the concept of the centralization of the gov-

with appropriate symbols.

Just as the people in the state community work out ways of organizing and governing, so do all of the people in the many state communities of the nation carry on central governing activities for the national community. These governing activities for the most part are centralized in one location. The city where the national government is located is called the national capital. The capital of the United States of America is located in Washington, in the District of Columbia. The people in each of the state communities elect officials to carry on the important function of organizing and governing on the national level. Hundreds of private (nongovernmental) agencies have national organizational headquarters: CIO-AFL, NAM, U.S. Chamber of Commerce, American Red Cross, etc. Many but not all of these are located also in the nation's capital city. Industrial, commercial, financial, and professional organizations have their national headquarters usually scattered throughout the nation.

ernmental function for the county or local community and for the state community. Our federal government is concerned with matters that affect the welfare of the total national community. Discuss some of the activities of our national government such as the distribution of the mail, protecting and conserving life and health, and so on. Plan to make a large-scale map of the District of Columbia. Collect pictures of the main buildings in the capital city. Make a bulletin board display. If possible, obtain an oblique aerial photograph of the Capitol Mall area. Locate the Capitol Building, the White House, the National Art Gallery, and so on. Place these main buildings on the class map. Include the cardinal directions. If any members of the class have visited Washington, have them describe their visit. Discuss the use of a symbol to show the national capital on a small-scale map of the United States. What symbols are used to show our national boundaries? On the small-scale map of the United States draw the national boundaries using the line symbol of a long dash followed by two short dashes. Be sure to include the border for the state of Alaska. Explain this symbol in the map key. (See "Map and Globe Symbols," Appendix B.)

Select a few nationwide corporations and find out where their headquarters offices are. Map the distribution of some of them—say, insurance companies, or automobile manufacturers, or furniture factories, etc.

2. *Ability to read data recorded on maps and globes.*

Develop skills in identifying symbols portraying both public and

2. *Map-reading activities.*

Help children develop meanings for the symbols portraying organizing and governing features in the

private organizing and governing activities and facilities within the arena of the national community. Develop the ability to translate these symbols into meaningful imagery. Maps pertaining to organizing and governing activities and facilities include:

(1) national, colonial, and territorial government and centers;

(2) historical aspects of the national community;

(3) quasi-public and private associations that are national in scope.

Develop the ability to visualize the realities representing the above organizing and governing features and activities as symbolized on maps. Develop the ability to read directions, areal distributions, map scale, and location.

arena of the national community. Have class discussions and activities to extend and broaden the concept of national boundaries. Are the national boundaries of the nation visible features of the landscape? If so, where? How? Collect pictures of border-crossing points and discuss the features. There may be fences and lines drawn across roads, for example. What about the other sections of the border? In what ways are international boundaries different from state boundaries? How do map makers show international boundaries? How are these boundaries different on maps and globes from the state or county boundaries? Have children trace with a pointer our national boundaries on a wall map and the globe. Include the boundary for the state of Alaska. See if the map makers show any boundaries for the state of Hawaii. Plan appropriate map-reading activities for the following groups of symbols: point symbols for the national capital, ports of entry, state capitals, etc.; line symbols for international boundaries, federal judicial districts, the boundary for the District of Columbia; area symbols for the extent of such political divisions as federal districts of various kinds, federal lands and forests, territorial regions, etc.

Describe the relative location of the national capital, the local state capitals, along with the relative directions. Do the same for national private associations.

Look in an encyclopedia or a *World Almanac* for names of national associations and the location of their organization headquarters. Map these locations. What do you see in the patterns of distribution? Is there any relation between the great financial centers of the nation

3. *Ability to interpret location and distribution on maps and globes and to reason geographically.*

Use two or more maps to reason geographically about the location and areal distribution of organizing and governing features in the United States national community. Analyze the location and distribution of national organizational headquarters of private (non-governmental) agencies within the United States. Compare the locations and distribution of these agencies with the locations and distribution of governmental agencies. Correlate the spatial dimensions of these locations and distributions with other cultural and natural items within the national community.

and headquarters of, say, insurance companies?

3. *Interpretation activities.*

Relate the present location of our national government center to present population centers, transportation centers and facilities, areal extent of the fifty states in the Union, and the major communication centers. Reason about the relative location of the national capital to the pupils' own state community and to the newest states of Alaska and Hawaii. Relate the present location of the center of our national government to population centers, transportation facilities, communication networks, and the areal extent of states in the union in 1800, for instance. What was the relative distance of Vermont or Illinois to Washington, D.C.? Help the pupils to make inferences about the relative locations of the states and the national center by using several maps showing different man-made and natural features. Compare this information with the relative distance and location of such states as California, Hawaii, and Alaska. Compare a map showing the locations and distribution of headquarters and regional centers of several well-known national corporations with a map showing the major metropolitan centers of the nation or the major transportation and communication centers. Note kinds of areal relationships which exist among the items mapped.

Basic Human Activity: Expressing Aesthetic and Spiritual Impulses

OBJECTIVES

TEACHING-LEARNING EXPERIENCES

1. *Ability to reorganize data gathered from firsthand and vicarious experi-*

1. *Mapping activities.*

Begin with a review of the basic

ences and represent them on maps with appropriate symbols.

The human need of expressing spiritual and aesthetic impulses is met in many ways by the national community. People who may live in widely separated geographical areas of our nation but who possess a common cultural background form national associations to perpetuate these ways of life and enjoy engaging in their unique expressions of artistic and spiritual feelings. These many and varied spiritual and aesthetic expressions make a significant contribution to the richness and beauty of life in the United States. Pupils are helped to gain an understanding of this basic human activity through participation in teaching-learning experiences such as observation, investigation, discussion, reading, and mapping activities.

concepts of expressing spiritual and aesthetic impulses in the local, state, and regional communities. Discuss the relevant characteristics of the various forms of expression and how people react to the forms of expressions of others. Within the national community the various features and functions have taken on more formalized expression. Various groups attract talented students and adults from all parts of the nation. Have the class read accounts of art schools, music conservatories, drama workshops, and so on, that have a national reputation. Members of the class may have attended musical performances, plays, folk music or folk dancing festivals that are nationwide in appeal. Have them describe their experiences. Locate these places on a large wall map of the United States. As a class mapping project have each pupil select an artistic or a spiritual event or activity that is nationwide in character that he would like to visit or attend. Gather information from reference sources as to its location, when it is held, where, and other pertinent details. Bring all these data together on a large bulletin-board-size map of the United States. Help each pupil to decide on an appropriate symbol to represent his selected activity or event on the map. Sample events: summer festivals of American Indians, the religious expressions of people in summer camp meetings, national youth summer camps for orchestral music, summer plays in New England, jazz concerts in California, etc. Give the map an appropriate title. If pictorial symbols are used, view this map as an aesthetic product.

2. *Map-reading activities.*

2. *Ability to read data recorded on maps and globes.*

Develop skills in identifying symbols portraying spiritual and aesthetic phenomena in the national community. Develop the ability to translate these symbols into meaningful imagery and conceptual patterns of landscape. Maps pertaining to these features and activities include:

(1) national headquarters of religious groups, churches, temples, cathedrals, synagogues, shrines, etc., that have national fame;

(2) national museums of art, sculpture, or history;

(3) architectural structures of national interest;

(4) location of musical organizations, ballet, theater groups with national fame;

(5) locale of important concentrations of artists, musicians, writers, composers, etc.;

(6) historical aspects of the arts;

(7) national headquarters of garden clubs, park and beach conservation organizations, and organizations supporting other types of natural beauty.

Develop the ability to read the patterns of distribution of any of the above features and human activities, the relative locations, and relative distances.

Help children develop meanings for the symbols used on maps to portray cultural and natural features and activities of spiritual and aesthetic phenomena. Use a variety of materials both visual and printed to help the pupils develop mental images of the relevant characteristics of the concepts. The concepts introduced at a prior grade level are extended and expanded within this next larger community of the nation. For example, help the pupils read symbols representing gardens and parks. Gardens located in Florida are much different in appearance and vegetation from gardens located in the more northern sections of our nation. Yet on a map these features may be symbolized by a point symbol such as a dot or circle. Also, the appearance of these gardens may vary greatly from one season to the next: in the southern latitudes of the nation they may be green the year round, whereas in more northern latitudes there is little green vegetation to be seen during certain seasons. When reading these symbols pupils should be on guard against associating a single image for some of the features portrayed on maps. Plan reading activities for these features represented on large-scale maps. Help the pupils to use the key to explain the symbols used. Find out whether there are conventional symbols to represent certain of the spiritual and aesthetic features and activities. Make a list of the conventional symbols and help the pupils to gain a ready recognition of them without referring to the key. Give the class practice in reading various kinds of maps to gain information about spiritual and aesthetic phenomena. Give special at-

3. *Ability to interpret distribution and location on maps and to reason geographically.*

Reason geographically about the location and areal distribution of aesthetic and spiritual structures and activities within the national community of the United States. Analyze and interpret the location and areal distribution of these phenomena in relation to geographical regions, ethnic groups, rural areas and metropolitan areas, and so on. Correlate the spatial dimensions of aesthetic and spiritual phenomena with other cultural features and physical features. Continue to develop the ability to make inferences about data from two or more maps.

tention to mapping the distributions of national headquarters or concentrations of various organizations and performers of the arts, and membership of religious groups.

3. *Interpretation activities.*

Help the pupils interpret the presence or absence of spiritual and aesthetic structures and activities in various regions of the national community. Note and explain the existence of many variations in the patterns of areal distribution of musical organizations, ballet groups, theater groups, and so on. Interpret the interrelatedness of the locations and pattern of distribution of these activities with other cultural features. For example, note any correlations of population density with the presence or absence of these groups and activities. Help the pupils to make inferences by comparing the content of one map showing the location of nationally recognized musical groups and organizations with that of another map showing the population centers. Children will find that small communities often have nationally known groups whereas metropolitan centers may be without any such organizations. Note similar variations in the distribution patterns of nationally known art centers, and other cultural activities expressing aesthetic and spiritual impulses. Compare maps showing the locations and distributions of such features.

Basic Human Activity: Creating Tools and Technics

OBJECTIVES   TEACHING-LEARNING EXPERIENCES

1. *Ability to reorganize data gathered*   1. *Mapping activities.*

from firsthand and vicarious experiences and represent them on maps with appropriate symbols.

In the national community people are creating new and better tools and technics to carry on the basic human activities. All segments of the national community —government, education, private agencies, foundations, business, labor, and industry—are expending large sums of both human and financial resources in research and development. Many new products and processes are introduced each year. Research in the fields of science and technology has enabled us to produce new and better ways of doing things. The introduction of new tools and technics in manufacturing and agriculture has brought about changes in production methods. Conferences and demonstrations at key centers in the nation have assumed national characteristics in that they attract people from all sections of the national community. Children continue to develop an understanding of how people create new tools and technics through participation in such classroom teaching-learning experiences as observation, discussion, and mapping activities.

Begin with a discussion of the tools and technics people have used from the beginnings of settlement in the New England colonies. Analyze: What kinds of tools did people use to produce clothing? What was the principal source of power? How many hours per week did people work? What were the characteristics of this rural handicraft culture? Contrast the methods of producing goods by these pioneers with the methods used during the nineteenth century in the factory system. What were the sources of power? How would you account for the current reduction in the work week? Discuss some of the new tools and technics currently used in agricultural production. Machines such as the reaper made it possible to harvest larger acreages of grain but still depended on men to perform certain tasks. Today new inventions have resulted in the production of complex automatic machines which need only one man to operate and are capable of performing many operations at one time. These machines make it possible to harvest thousands of acres of grain in a relatively short time. Today large manufacturing complexes located in key centers specialize in the manufacture of farm machinery. Collect pictures of farm equipment and discuss how these machines serve farmers. On a base outline map of the United States locate the beginnings of these agricultural tools and technics. Indicate the areal extent of the use of machines that work cotton fields, wheat fields, citrus groves, etc.

2. *Map-reading activities.*

2. *Ability to read data recorded on maps and globes.*

Develop skills in reading symbols portraying tools and technics people are using to carry on the basic human activities within the arena of the national community. Develop the ability to translate these symbols into meaningful imagery and conceptual patterns of landscape. Maps portraying symbols pertaining to tools and technics include:

(1) public and private research and development centers of national importance;

(2) nationally important areas producing machine tools;

(3) experimental farms and agricultural stations run by public and private national agencies;

(4) agricultural areas using highly specialized tools and technics;

(5) manufacturing centers using and creating specific and highly specialized tools and technics;

(6) specific tools and technics used and being researched and developed in national transportation;

(7) specific tools and technics used and being researched and developed in national communication.

Develop the ability to read national maps showing the areal extent of phenomena using such symbols as dots, circles, and shadings. Develop the ability to gain information from maps showing the amount or quantitative dimension of objects or things being symbolized.

All map-reading activities should be preceded or accompanied by teaching-learning experiences that help pupils to develop an understanding of the items being symbolized on maps. Have class discussions, dramatizations, and other activities to extend and clarify meanings of various kinds of tools and technics characterizing such activities as agriculture, industrial production, transportation, communication, and protecting. Continue to use visual aids such as pictures, filmstrips, and motion pictures to help the pupils develop mental images of the relevant characteristics of the things or processes being represented on maps. Begin with maps using pictorial symbols which show the character and distribution of tools and technics within a region of the national community, such as cotton-picking machines, mechanized coal mine equipment, airplane frames, and the like. Plan appropriate map reading activities for the following groups of symbols: point symbols for national research and development centers, pilot plants and facilities, experimental farms and stations, etc.; line symbols for newly developed or experimental tools and technics such as nationwide systems of pipelines for moving crude oil and natural gas, national communication networks using closed-circuit television, proposed air, rail, and ground systems for transportation, etc.; area symbols for proposed irrigation districts, interlocking grids of electric power, distribution of features that cover extensive areas such as new soil conservation districts, river valley developments, metropolitan or "strip city" governments, etc.

Read distributions shown on United States maps and compare one map with another as to variations in patterns.

3. *Ability to interpret location and distribution represented on maps and to reason geographically.*

Reason geographically about the location and areal distribution of tools and technics within the national community. Analyze the distribution of these features as to relative location, relative distance, and relative direction. Compare the distribution of tools or technics with distribution of other man-made features. Also compare the distribution and location of natural features with the distribution of specific and highly specialized tools and technics. Continue to develop the ability to make inferences about the location and distribution of tools and technics, and the character of areas in which these phenomena are present or not present. Correlate the spatial dimensions of tools and technics with other man-made features and natural features of the United States national community.

3. *Interpretation activities.*

Analyze examples of the creation of new tools and technics in several basic human activities to compare distributions and locations with the natural features of the region or regions. Note location and use of large tractors and other power equipment in agriculture relative to the kind of natural features such as plains with wide expanses of level land, and narrow valleys in mountainous or hilly regions. Compare the locations and distributions nationally of research and development centers with the locations and distributions of universities having outstanding faculties and research facilities. Notice the locations of tools and technics relative to specialized functions. Mechanical devices such as pipelines or conveyor belts are used to transport ore and other materials over rough terrain to nearby transportation facilities such as railroads, waterways, and highways. Discuss how these technics save time and energy. Discuss what happens to people displaced by increasing automation in several fields of endeavor. Note efforts to minimize effects through job reeducation and unemployment insurance. Have the children make inferences about other tools and technics which might be used in the future to move materials. Arrange activities to help pupils look for relationships by using several maps showing different features.

An Illustrative Sequence of Pupil Experiences

Now we suggest a developmental sequence of mapping procedures and activities specifically designed to analyze the geographic distribution within the United States national community, Emphasis 7, of one basic human activity: providing recreation through outdoor activities. We have noted that the national community has a definable space on the earth. There are wide variations in the terrain, water bodies, climate, flora and fauna, etc., which provide opportunities for people to engage in recreational activities during all seasons of the year. Many regions have become nationally known for their recreational attractions—some for summer sports such as camping, fishing, boating, and swimming; some for winter sports of skiing, tobogganing, and ice skating; and others for all-year recreation features.

EXPLORING THE BASIC ACTIVITY OF PROVIDING RECREATION

Prior to this emphasis of the national community, the social studies program does not expect pupils to have acquired a complete understanding of the many ways in which people use the major land and water forms and features—mountains, hills, lakes, rivers, islands, bays, gulfs, deserts, and forests—to satisfy their needs for outdoor recreation. On the other hand, the geographic concepts of elevation, mountain, desert, bay, cove, slope, climate, and others need not be fully developed before national maps representing them can be used. However, new meanings and additional associations are developed for these concepts as they are studied systematically within the expanded community emphasis. This distributed study and analysis approach to building concepts and generalizations over the span of several community emphases is supported by statements such as this one by Jersild: "In many areas it appears that in order to grasp meanings it is necessary for the child to have an accumulation of impressions and experiences distributed over a period of development as distinguished from lessons or impressions concentrated within a limited period of time."[1]

DEVELOPING MAPPING EXPERIENCES

Mapping activities should be organized to capitalize on children's interest in adventure and travel. There probably will be some in the class who have lived in other regions of the national community, and they will have contributions to make to the unit on national recreation being studied. Others will have taken trips and enjoyed recreational activities afforded by the cool breezes and sunny weather of the seacoast in the summer months. Through firsthand experiences they may have observed coastal regions that are rocky and steep or that are flat and sandy. Gently sloping sandy beaches lend themselves to swimming and other play activities whereas the steep rocky coastline may provide an ideal spot from which to cast for fish. Thus children begin to understand that one of the limiting factors of land use for recreational activities is its slope, an important generalization to be developed in understanding the distribution of outdoor recreational structures in the national community.

Children need help in visualizing places and things through the use of selected photographs, preferably in color, motion pictures, filmstrips, and other visual aids such as charts and sketches. They should not be permitted to form their first visual impressions of a resort area from reading a map of the region. When color is used on a physical map to represent elevations or altitudes of large areas of land, for instance, children may falsely visualize identical terrain features for lowland regions over the entire Atlantic coastline of the United States. Maps of this scale hide many of the important small features of the landscape. It is equally important for the children to have some understanding of the concepts being represented on maps by abstract geometric symbols such as triangles, squares, and circles; otherwise the symbols are without meaning even though they can read them by referring to the map's key. New meanings and associations should be developed for both natural and cultural items through carefully planned teaching-learning experiences—the more firsthand experience and observation, the better the understanding of the symbols. As Parker succinctly points out,

> Maps . . . can have meaning only through abundant experiences in translating landscapes observed into *maps,* and map symbols into landscape realities. Experiences essential in so doing are needed in connection *with every locality studied.* It is only as one learns gradually to translate landscapes into maps that one can, in turn, acquire the ability to use maps in gaining those concrete concepts of the whole world.[2]

Let us suppose, for example, that the pupils in a classroom are gathering information about outdoor recreational facilities in well-known national parks located in several regions of the United States. (See "Aids for Teaching," Appendix A.) Divide the class into several mountain-hiking parties and plan imaginary expeditions. One group could plan a trip in White Mountain National Forest in New Hampshire, another group a trip in Glacier National Park in Montana, and still another group a trip in Mount McKinley National Park in the state of Alaska. Have the groups gather pictures of the landforms, water bodies, and flora and fauna found in each of these parks. Have them obtain weather data and decide on clothing needs. Locate the parks on a large raised plastic relief map of the United States and have class discussions comparing and contrasting their terrain features. The map and the pictures tell the children that the mountains in the western United States are much higher in elevation and more rugged than the mountains in the eastern United States. The most rugged mountains, however, are in Mount McKinley National Park in Alaska, where they have many sharp-edged pinnacles and glaciated surfaces.

Much of the high land in the western United States is rough and rugged. The canyons and river valleys are deep, and most of the rivers flow swiftly over steep rocky slopes with countless falls and rapids. In contrast, most of the Appalachian region in the eastern United States is smooth and rounded and much lower in elevation. The river valleys are not so deep, and the rivers flow slowly. Hence the scenery which the hiking groups see along the trails in each of the parks will be different in many ways. Walking along trails in the higher elevations will be more tiring and make breathing more difficult. The distance covered along a given trail in one day's journey will also vary in each of the parks. The general climate, the local weather, and elevation will all have an influence on shelter, clothing, and equipment, for the hiking parties. Discussions in the classroom should help children to become aware of relationships between the kinds of land features and their impact upon outdoor recreational activities; the same for climate, weather, and elevation. Each of the questions and explanations given should be carefully planned. Detailed information should be made readily available so that children can grow in the ability to think more clearly about the arrangement of natural and man-made recreational facilities and structures and the relationships that exist within any given geographic area devoted to meeting the basic human activity of providing recreation.

The teacher should continue to provide experiences to expand and extend the ability to make careful and accurate observations such as noting locations and distributions of natural and man-made recreational features pictured in a variety of visual media. Firsthand experiences such as field trips to resort areas located in distant parts of the nation are not possible for a class though individual children may have had them. Large colored photographs and motion pictures of recreational phenomena of different parts of the national community are useful sources of visual images and details, the next best source after personal direct experience. High oblique aerial photographs which include the horizon should be used extensively. These picture-reading activities should be designed to help pupils visualize (1) outdoor recreational phenomena in the national community setting that are considerably more extensive than those located in the local or state communities; (2) the wide variations in the physical features such as hills, mountains, canyons, water bodies; and (3) the wide variations in man-made structures and activities. The teacher should:

1. Continue to take children on field trips to study specific landform features in the local or state community. Help the children draw field sketches of the landscape features from an elevated observational point. Have them note the spatial relationships and relative directions of features. Attach titles to these sketches.
2. Have pictures for the class to study. Excellent sources of pictures are the travel maps, calendars, and brochures which are available from local travel agents and the major transportation companies. These pictures should show ways people are engaging in recreational activities typical of the region for a particular season of the year. Interpret recreational structures in various kinds of resort areas—mountain, forest, lake, river, and seaside. Note such details as the roof pitch of cabins, piers, break-waters, and so on. Make inferences about these items. Check the in-ferences by having the children do further research in reference books such as atlases, encyclopedias, dictionaries, and earth-science reference books.
3. Show filmstrips and motion pictures of recreational phenomena. These should include such well-known resort areas as New England, Florida, Arizona, the Pacific Northwest, the Lake of the Woods, California, Hawaii, etc. Organize information gathered from these sources into meaningful patterns and types of recreational activities. Compare and check this information with that obtained from reference books and maps.

Map-making activities of various kinds are important in helping children reorganize information gathered from many sources. They will need to make large- and small-scale maps of both the national community and regions within it. Desk maps for individual map-making activities as well as large wall or bulletin-board-size maps and transparencies for wall or screen projection will be needed to record data with appropriate symbols, both pictorial and conventional. Making map outlines can be fascinating for children and highly rewarding if the teacher will help them learn a few simple technics. The teacher should:

1. Help the children to make their own maps by basing them on other maps. Use the method of squares to enlarge an original map in a text-book for display on a bulletin board featuring Florida, for example. Florida is a resort area with national visibility; people from all parts of the United States visit and use it for recreational purposes during all seasons of the year. The suggested procedure is as follows: Draw a grid of horizontal and vertical lines *one inch apart* on a sheet of paper and trace the base map in the textbook or atlas over this grid. The tracing sheet should be plastic or celluloid to protect the base map in the text-book. To enlarge this map draw a grid of horizontal and vertical lines *three inches apart* on another sheet of paper. (The new map will have squares three times as large as those on the base sheet. The map scale has been tripled, too.) Number the squares on both sheets of paper. The

final step is transferring, one square at a time, the outline boundaries in the smaller squares to the larger squares by redrawing the map free-hand but three times as large (Figure 39).

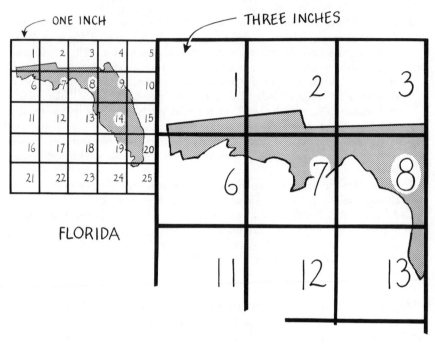

Figure 39

Enlarging a Map by Use of a Grid

2. Develop the idea that this method of squares may be used to reduce the scale of the base map as well. This is done by reducing the size of the squares of the transfer grid on the new map. A small-scale map may be used to advantage for insert purposes to show the comparison of area of recreational regions.

In the United States national community emphasis, it is suggested that skills be developed for reading and using the landform map. The landform or pictorial terrain map employs an effective mapping tech-nic that visually suggests the nature of the surface features of the earth. (See "Aids for Teaching.") Maps of this nature are seen in newspapers and magazines regularly because they give a realistic appearance to the surface features of the land being represented. They show the rugged-ness and shape of the mountains, hills, and vegetation from an oblique or side view which makes it easy for the reader to visualize. Interest-ingly, the conventional symbol for swamps is derived from side views of water plants. Raisz, the cartographer, has this to say about the pictorial terrain or landform map:

> The advantage of the landform map is that it appeals to the average man. It suggests actual country and enables him to see the land instead of reading an abstract diagram. It works on his imagination even if he is not able to recognize the exact geomorphologic types. It is a method that makes mountains look like mountains.[3]

The visual effectiveness of such a method of presenting the major landform features should be of primary concern to teachers at this early stage of map reading in the elementary school grades. Unfortunately this type of map has not been commonly used in social studies textbooks at these grade levels. It is designed primarily for small-scale maps and thus lends itself to representing large areas of land surface such as the New England resort area, the Pacific Northwest, or the Rocky Mountain region. Pictorial or landform maps help children to understand the slope of the land and to reason about the direction in which rivers and streams drain. Here again, it is important for the teacher to remember that when actual observations of such natural phenomena are not possible, photographs should accompany the maps to allow the children to build accurate visual images of smaller detail than can be shown on the maps. The teacher should:

> Have the children make a collection of high oblique aerial photographs of the area being represented on the map. Note the major characteristics of the features in the picture such as the shape of the mountains, hills, plateaus, volcanic forms, mesas, plains, and the vegetation. Now go to the landform map and identify the symbols used for each of these features. Note how each symbol suggests actual country. Be sure to use the map's key as a check in reading the symbols used. Have the children note the conventional symbols used for the rivers, streams, coastline, cities, etc. Use the scale of miles to measure distances between selected features. Encourage the children to make landform maps of their own. Have practice sessions for drawing symbols representing mountains, hills, water bodies, forests, etc.

As pupils develop skills in making and reading maps, they should have many opportunities to learn how to recognize and understand relationships between recreational phenomena and natural and cultural features in the national community. The ability to recognize and express relative locations and distribution patterns of cultural and natural features is important in relational thinking. Being able to use two or more maps is a must for interpretation activities. For example, the class might compare a recreational map showing summer and winter resort areas that have assumed national importance with a map showing such cultural features as the major population centers of the nation or the network of transportation facilities or with a map showing the variations in temperature during the winter months and the summer months. "By comparing maps which give different facts about the same area," as Kohn points out, "students can see the different kinds and degrees of area relationships which exist among items being mapped."[4] To develop the ability to compare maps and make inferences, the teacher may have pupils:

1. Compare maps showing the areal relationship of recreation phenomena with other cultural phenomena such as, for example, transportation facilities and resort areas. An example: Locate on a United States map the major resort areas for skiing and other winter sports. Note where these centers are located in relation to transportation facilities, population centers, and so on. The children might compare a map showing the distribution of skiing centers in the Sierra Nevada of California with one showing the highways and centers of population in this state. Winter resorts in Florida, California, or Hawaii are only hours away by air from major population centers in the nation. Make inferences about the presence or absence of facilities in various areas of the national community. Discuss the adequacy of present facilities for rapidly growing population areas.
2. Compare maps to bring out the areal relationships of natural features and man-made recreational structures and activities. Note the areal relationships between the location of recreational phenomena and the snowfall and temperature; between summer resorts and water bodies. Have the children think about the cause-and-effect relations through the use of appropriate maps and other data.

In summary, the suggested teaching procedures and learning experiences outlined for the national community emphasis focus on the three major objectives: systematic observations resulting in making maps, reading maps, and interpreting maps to form associations among the many things represented on maps. In mastering these skills and understandings children will be able to use maps as geographic tools to further their knowledge of one of the major ways people in the national community engage in the basic human activity of providing recreation.

The Middle Grades: A Summary

In concluding our discussion on geographic generalizations and map skills for the middle grade emphases on the states, the region-of-states, and the national communities, we make the point once more that our schema has been illustrated with only one of the nine clusters of basic human activities as they are carried on in these three expanding arenas. Only space limitations force us to omit comparable and even much more comprehensive suggestions for sequential experiences in the other eight basic activities as they have been in the past, are now, or might in the future be carried out in these three communities of men.

Our design is built on the theory that each lesser community in the set carries on each of the basic human activities within the conditions and according to the resources available to it. We believe there is merit in guiding children to observe, sort out, organize, and express geographic insights and relationships through making and using maps and globes that record these activities for each of the expanding communities of which he is a member. In the process of analyzing each community in some detail he becomes aware that there are conditions within that community that prevent the full realization of human aspirations. Some of these shortages can be overcome by better laws, institutions, customs, mechanisms, and individual behavior.

But other aspects, of protecting, transporting, educating, etc., cannot be fully implemented within the limits of the lesser community. Only by joining with other communities of similar size and characteristics can it hope to achieve the full benefits possible in these fields. So the intensive study of each community in the set demonstrates (1) what things can be done within that community to improve life and (2) what things can be done by forming new and larger communities out of the numerous lesser communities facing common problems, thus increasing the capabilities and resources for the solution of the problems within the new and expanded association of lesser communities.

This rationale is central to the multidisciplinary program of social studies around which the geographic generalizations and map skills of this volume are designed.

REFERENCES

1. Arthur T. Jersild, *et al., Child Development and the Curriculum* (New York: Bureau of Publications, Teachers College, Columbia University, 1946), p. 459.
2. Edith P. Parker, "Gaining Insight into Human Problems," *Geographic Approaches to Social Education,* Nineteenth Yearbook, National Council for the Social Studies (Washington: NCSS, 1948), pp. 11–12.
3. Erwin Raisz, *General Cartography* (New York: McGraw-Hill Book Co., Inc., 2nd ed., 1948), p. 122.
4. Clyde Kohn, "Interpreting Maps and Globes," *Skills in Social Studies,* Twenty-fourth Yearbook, National Council for the Social Studies (Washington: NCSS, 1953), p. 170.

chapter nine

THE JUNIOR HIGH SCHOOL EMPHASES

/ A Modified Approach and a Preview of Emphases 8–11

The substance of the social studies program comes to life for the pupil when he can discover and employ new skills and understandings and thus deal more meaningfully with new interrelationships, causalities, and developmental histories of the physical and cultural world around him.

History and geography make their most vital contributions to the multidisciplinary social studies experience by presenting the story of man's existence on planet earth and by describing and analyzing the stage setting for human society. The effective citizen needs to know the developmental background of the nations and cultures of the world, to be able to visualize and conceptualize physical and cultural realities, and to understand and appreciate the geographic significance of physical and cultural commonalities and differences.

In his earlier studies of the less-than-national and national communities in the primary and middle grades the child took field trips to observe directly people and their cultural behavior and the land and its promises and problems. Now, as he directs his attention to broader-than-national communities—the emerging inter-American community, the Atlantic community, the Pacific community, and the world community—he must learn to take vicarious trips, making greater and greater use of the described and recorded experiences of others as found in the disciplines of history, geography (astronomy, geology, meteorology, climatology, and cartography), economics, sociology, political science, anthropology, along with other social sciences.

A crucial role of the geographic teaching-learning activities in the multidisciplinary social studies is that of making these vicarious experiences meaningful. The task is closely akin to bringing youth to view a play that has already progressed through many acts by the time that they arrive in the theater. It is not enough to allow them to be entertained and educated by the current events occurring upon the stage, for such events are not self-explanatory; further, the teacher is aware that eventually these pupils—tomorrow's adult citizens—will be responsible for later "acts."

In this "world theater" hundreds of plays are continually being produced. It is impossible to review all that has occurred before and even more impossible to conceptualize all that is currently happening on stage. Obviously the teaching-learning problem is both perceptual and conceptual. The social studies teacher must aid youth with some conceptual frames of reference with which to look for clues that will help them generalize about some of the problems and possibilities inherent in each act of every production. Concurrently, the teacher hopes to present brief highlights of each play's antecedent activities (historical and geological analyses and research) which are responsible for the accumulated cultural and behavioral patterns displayed by human communities in the present physical setting.

With such a viewing procedure it becomes plain that the educational emphasis must be upon interrelationships and problem solving rather than upon mere facts and memorized answers. Soon these pupils will be actors upon the many "stages" of the world and they will need to know and understand yesterday's and today's problems and solutions so that they may make wise decisions for a better tomorrow.

Organization of Chapters Nine to Eleven

The organization of the coordinated and multidisciplinary social studies experiences for the junior high school emphases has been modified from that for the earlier emphases in the following ways:

In this chapter each of the four final expanding communities of men (the sequence) and the basic human activities (the scope) will be generally discussed. In Chapter Ten special consideration will be given to objectives and teaching methodologies for the junior high school social studies program, and the four expanding communities of men (inter-American, Atlantic, Pacific, and world) will be generally, rather than specifically, coordinated with each of the nine basic human activities. Each of the basic human activities (the scope) will include a *prologue* followed by selected geographic concepts and map experiences in the same format employed for earlier chapters. In Chapter Eleven the coordinated program proposals are supported by a section of illustrative developmental classroom lessons and teaching strategies.

This modified and more general approach has been selected because it is recognized that across the nation school districts are employing differing sequences of curricular content for their junior high school social studies programs. Consequently, in order to maximize adaptability of these proposals, the focus is upon sequentially appropriate conceptual and skill-building experiences, without insistance upon any one expanding community as *the* content for a given maturity level in the junior high school social studies. However, because the following program proposals make constant reference to the expanding set of communities, readers wishing to employ this design sequence to structure the curriculum should experience little difficulty in identifying appropriate sequential activities.

Our intent is to help the reader further appreciate how geographic concepts and map skills are highly relevant aspects of the modern coordinated social studies program. While the suggested pupil experiences, topics, and problems may constitute valid curricular experiences, they are not meant to represent a total social studies program. In short, the illustrative materials which follow are proposed as worthy adjuncts to the overall multidisciplinary social studies program; the curricular rationales described constitute maturationally appropriate opportunities for teaching-learning experiences.

It is beyond the scope of these latter chapters to attempt a comprehensive list of specific knowledge and methods of inquiry for the overall program of the junior high school social studies to be drawn from geography, history, and the several social sciences. Thus, broad social studies concepts and generalizations have been employed for illustrative purposes. It is hoped that the reader will recognize the rich possibilities for improved teaching-learning activities which exist in a purposeful and systematically developed social studies program.

Emphasis 8: The Emerging United States and Inter-American Community

The emerging inter-American community, comprising over twenty nations of the Western Hemisphere, on a great land mass known as the North and South American continents and stretching almost from pole to pole, is the home of roughly one-half billion humans. In the far north, Canada and the U.S. state of Alaska border on the Arctic waters. South of Canada, and, like it, spreading from the Atlantic to the Pacific, is the United States of America. South of the United States is the nation of

Mexico. Between Mexico and the northern shore of South America lie the several small nations that are known as Central America. To the east in the Caribbean Sea are small island nations and territories.

The southern continent, South America, is divided into ten independent nations and three small European possessions. These nations can be further grouped into the northern nations of South America, the Andean nations, the southern nations, and, because of its enormous size, the nation of Brazil.

What do the half-billion humans spread over this vast terrain have in common that might lead us to speak of this complex as an emerging inter-American community? Is it only that the lands are continuous and completely surrounded by oceans? No, the reasons for viewing this arena as a larger-than-national community are several:

1. This enormous space was the site of Indian cultures for ten to twenty thousands years before the explorers from Europe claimed it for their kings and queens. During these centuries Indians had gradually spread out from the possible Asia-America land bridge in the Bering Sea vicinity; they spread south and east to establish tribes in what is now Canada, the United States, and Mexico. They worked their way along the narrow bridge of Central America until they came to the northern lands of South America. Here the migrating Indians separated. Some went east and south into the Amazon River basin where over the long reaches of time they gave up many of the civilized ways they had known in more favorable circumstances to the north; others went west and south along the Pacific rim of the continent, establishing permanent sites both along the coastal plain and high in the Andes. These great movements of Indian cultures had distributed civilization fairly evenly over the Americas before the Europeans came.

2. Following the age of discovery the Europeans established their culture throughout the Indian lands. For 300 years the Europeans colonized and multiplied. The Indian cultures, still persistent, were overshadowed by European customs, institutions, and technology. Thus the emerging inter-American community has in common an Indian cultural heritage and a European cultural overlay.

3. With the successful struggle of the original thirteen colonies on the Atlantic coast of North America to win independence from England and from Europe, there followed a succession of wars of independence, encouraged by the growing young nation of the United States, until in the nineteenth century all the lands and peoples of the Americas, with the exception of small land pockets and islands, were free from European rule. This third historic fact is a powerful force, often unrecognized, that binds the more than twenty American republics together.

The idea of a union of the Americas has existed for over a century. Dreamers have talked and even acted to bring such an association into existence. Probably the first important instruments to survive the difficulties of birth were the Monroe Doctrine and later the Pan American Union. World War II sharpened the sense of community, and the Organization of American States was created, with most of the nations joining. Later events have nurtured the community still further, and the great multinational effort known as the Alliance for Progress has been formed.

No one can deny that much tension exists within this vast arena of the Americas. People for the most part are desperately poor; they lack educational opportunity; they lack capital for investment in transportation, communication, industry, agricultural development, and health facilities. They lack experience in representative self-government, and political activity often is dominated by a series of disjointed crash programs. There is fear both of the thrust of communism and of the might of the Yankee nation to the north on whom the Latin American nations have to depend for defense, for capital, and for technical assistance.

But underneath the suspicion and often antagonism, there is slowly developing better understanding. The United States of America is seriously trying to avoid unilateral action in matters that are of concern to all our American neighbors. Mistakes are made on all sides, but with each setback all the Americas realize more clearly the inevitable—the invention of better multinational social technology that will make possible solutions to problems in all of the basic human activities that are not available at present to any one of the member nations working in isolation.

Certainly, we do not claim that a true community of Americans exists at the moment, or that it will come into being within any specified time limit. But we do believe that modern science and technology will in the end break through the walls of national communities and force the nations of North and South America to form more viable institutions and mechanisms for their survival and for their progress. We are, therefore, presenting to pupils in the junior high school the opportunity to view the Americas as a potential community of men and to that end have devised teaching-learning experiences, particularly those basic to developing geographic concepts and map skills, that may be crucially useful in the decades ahead. These pupil experiences are grouped within Emphasis 8, the United States and inter-American community.

Emphasis 9: The Emerging United States and Atlantic Community

Physically, the Atlantic community consists of the land masses adjacent to the Atlantic Ocean and surrounding the Mediterranean Sea, as well as these two bodies of water that now constitute the inland sea of this community. Thus, our geographically arbitrary distinction (Atlantic Ocean-related land masses) brings all of the Americas, Africa, Europe, and the Middle East together for common study. As the land masses stretch across high, middle, and low latitudes and include marine and continental climates, proximity to this inland sea, rather than similarity of physical environment, must lie behind any community of interests.

Culturally, the Atlantic community identifies the homelands and major spheres of influence of the "Western tradition." The Western world has generated significant bonds of common interests through cultural borrowing during centuries of interaction. Modern communication and transportation have proved to be the technological catalysts whereby men of these nations in recent decades have gained new perspective on the common danger and costs inherent in clinging to separatist and irrational nationalistic behavior patterns. Today, leaders of these nations are attempting to rise above legacies of fear and hostility toward their neighbors by focusing attention upon common values, aspirations, and human needs and through economic and educational attacks upon the real enemies—ignorance and inefficiency.

With World War II the United States at last came to realize fully the demanding nature of membership in the broader sub-world communities of nations and the frightful price of failure to work together. However, it is not necessary to marshal only recent events in helping pupils recognize that a "community of the West" exists. So that any illusions concerning United States isolationism may be put to rest, Lippmann reminds us that the United States has been, willingly or not, a part of the Atlantic community throughout its history.

> The Atlantic Community has existed as an historic fact since the Spanish and the Portuguese, the French, the British, the Dutch and the Swedes colonized North and South America some three centuries ago. That there has always been an Atlantic Community since then is attested by our own history. Beginning with colonial times there has been no great war in Europe in which Americans have not become engaged.[1]

Through their studies of the emerging Atlantic community pupils should come to recognize that the same basic human problems found in their immediate communities plague the peoples in all the expanded multinational communities. Along with the other basic human activities they will note the problems of providing, for both children and adults, education that may supply the unifying values and generalizations to make the emerging region-of-nations community viable. They will be able to trace the historic efforts of the Atlantic community to defend itself, increase its productive capability, or develop greater exchange of ideas and values. And pupils will always be encountering new uses for and new needs for additional map skills and understandings as essential tools for interpreting the physical and cultural landscapes of the Atlantic community.

It is interesting to note what the educational leaders of the Atlantic community hope pupils in the United States will learn as they study about the Western world:

> . . .we should like to see all young Americans taught to realize not only the importance of European culture, as the basis of Western civilization, but also the diversity and prospects of the nations of Europe. . . . While the steps taken toward the unification of Europe should certainly be given the importance which they deserve, young Americans should be shown that the division of Europe among many states is due to physical conditions and historical developments very different from those of the North American continent. It is important on both sides of the Atlantic Ocean to emphasize those ideals which all our nations, devoted as they are to freedom, have in common, to study the great historical texts upon which our liberties are founded and to appreciate the main difference in the political and administrative institutions of our several countries.[2]

In recent years all of these nations and emerging national states have become equally aware of the value of available natural and intellectual resources. The recent story of the emerging Atlantic community and its sub-communities, then, tends to focus upon competition for limited supplies of economically productive mineral resources and land, skilled labor, and investment capital as well as upon the efforts to employ wisely the fruits of modern science.

As an outgrowth of beginnings at the Bretton Woods Conference of 1944 and with support via the Marshall Plan, the United States has worked with the nations of western Europe to the point that they have achieved the status of full partners who are beginning to give us useful advice and support for meeting our mutual economic problems. To illustrate what is happening: Recently two groups concurrently were meeting at the supranational level. One group was working toward a monetary union among the six-nation European Economic Community, which included joint development of a "community" budget. In the other meeting twenty nations were represented on the Economic Policy Committee of the Organization for Economic Cooperation and Development. This group, a key instrument of the Atlantic community, was planning guidelines for combating future recessions. As evidenced by the two meetings, these particular nations have come to recognize that the misfortunes of any member nation of a multinational community generally spread to all members; the two organizations were working together to solve a problem confronting *all* peoples of the emerging

Atlantic community—whether or not all of the nations within this vast arena were aware of or interested in the problem and its solution.

These are but two of many examples of growing maturity in the Western world—a maturity which is being achieved painfully over the years. Pupils need to become familiar with the concepts and truths underlying the dynamic changes occurring in the emerging Atlantic community.

Pupils need to understand, too, that, beneath all the surface noise and confusion, the ties between Europe and Africa are stronger and sounder today than they were a decade ago under European colonialism. The French Community, consisting of France and fifteen of its former African colonies, now independent nations, is developing favorably and rapidly. The United Kingdom and the African nations that were once her colonies are working to strengthen their economic and cultural networks. The European interest in Latin America, while it has perhaps waned for some time, has revived, and Europeans and Latin Americans are weaving a fabric of economic and cultural threads that will undoubtedly ultimately add to the strengthening of an Atlantic community. The United States, likewise a member of this community, while outwardly resisted by such leaders as De Gaulle, is deeply involved through history, through the geographic fact of bordering on the Atlantic inland sea, and through its sharing with this huge arena of a "Western tradition." There will be many powerful forces of resistance to the maturing of the emerging Atlantic community, but the forces bringing such a new region-of-nations community into full bloom will be in the ascendancy over the long run.

Of course, there is not likely to be any sudden magical metamorphosis from a state of hatreds, fears, and prejudices to a state of good will and enlightenment within the emerging Atlantic community. Nor should there be a rush to submerge national identities and cultural traditions, even though the momentum is building for uniting Europe. Pupils may study the gradual demise of colonialism and recognize the concurrent reduction in sources of conflict between members of the Atlantic community. They should be fully cognizant of the "cold war" pressures which have encouraged the nations of western Europe to unite. No one knows what easing of tensions among the Russian bloc and the rest of the Western world might do to the timetable of the Atlantic community.

Junior high school pupils certainly should study the advantages and disadvantages to nations opening their borders to freer trade among the other members of the Atlantic community. They also can observe and speculate on the political, social, and economic possibilities when such a broad multinational community establishes a common monetary system, or a supranational federation. These are events which lend themselves to the structured analysis provided by the scope of our design—the basic human activities.

Other ties and associations are developing among the nations of the

Atlantic community in addition to those to be illustrated. As curriculum builders identify the most useful ones for building desirable concepts, they will certainly recognize the fundamental necessity for pupils to have achieved considerable skill and understanding in the use of maps.

Emphasis 10: The Emerging United States and Pacific Community

Is there a sense of community emerging in the Pacific region? Yes, suggest those who have studied the peoples who populate the islands and huge land masses touched by the waters of the Pacific and Indian oceans. Since a third of the earth's surface is covered by the Pacific and Indian oceans, the peoples of the lands bordering them are representative of the full range of biological and cultural differences found in man. Yet, following scholarly study of the past and present history of the Pacific world, Hardy and Dumke could conclude, ". . . more and more East and West merged, with the result that today around her basin a new and greater Pacific community is arising."[3] If these writers have generalized correctly, the great common drive of men in the Pacific may be characterized as the desire for economic advantage, which certainly suggests a basic similarity to the pattern of development of the Atlantic community.

In our search for evidence of emerging region-of-nations communities in the world, we look forward to the time when men are less alienated and insulated by political and cultural barriers. Brown, a student of the Pacific Ocean world, suggests that not only must the problems of human unification be worked out in the Pacific arena but the Pacific may well be the scene for the first success of this evolutionary process.[4] Michener strengthens the case:

> . . . from now on the Pacific traffic will be a two-way affair. I can foresee the day when the passage of goods and people and ideas across the Pacific will be of far greater importance to America than the similar exchange across the Atlantic. Asia must inevitably become more important to the United States than Europe.[5]

In defining the emerging Pacific community, as with the emerging Atlantic one, a geographic arena is employed without any implication that it has uniform physical geographic conditions. Locating this vast "non-Western world" community on a geopolitical map or globe is accomplished by the gross act of including all nations washed by or adjacent to the Pacific and Indian oceans.

In this loosely defined community are the many emerging nations in central, southern, and eastern Asia. Dispersed across the immense reaches of the Pacific and Indian oceans are the scattered island cultures of Melanesia, Micronesia, and Polynesia, which seem to emulate the political achievements of the "Europeanized" nations of Australia and New Zealand. Then to complete the roll call are the nations in the Americas which face their Asian neighbors across the "shrinking" Pacific.

Among these diverse nations exist great cultural divergence and a significant sense of lack of cultural commonality which has led to the descriptive phrase *non-Western world*. Generally, the nations situated to the west of us are facing in common the multiple problems inherent in strivings for national independence and concurrently attempting to "leap forward" into the technological age of the twentieth century. Japan, Australia, and New Zealand are exceptions. The majority struggle with the needs of numerically "exploding" uneducated and underfed masses of population.

Pupils in the junior high school who have explored evolving political and economic structures in the "Western world" will not find such advanced structures in the less modernized nations of the Pacific community. Among several possible approaches, an introductory study of current economic and cultural changes offers rich learning opportunities as well as a means for conceptualizing some of the major common challenges facing Pacific nations.

The economic realities and resultant implications facing the nations of the Pacific community[6] may be traced through study of maps and the employment of geographic thinking. In seeking to aid pupils to understand better the multitude of facts to which they may be exposed while studying the nations of the Pacific community, broadly generalized answers to the following questions might be sought: What is meant by "backward nations" in a technological age? What are the fundamental economic and political problems and issues which most of these nations face in common?

Of the many issues, common and unique, related to cultural change, two of the problems to be faced and resolved by emerging nations are (1) achieving "know-how" and the related attitudes of willingness to employ new knowledge and (2) building investment capital and developing human resources.

To look at the problem of "achieving know-how and being willing to employ new knowledge," pupils should review the fund of technological skills and understandings requisite for a nation to maintain a viable political-economic system. Hence curricular activities might focus upon comparative studies of such modern nations as the United States, Japan, or Australia, and selected Pacific nations lacking modernization, with particular emphasis upon what the "typical" citizen is called upon to do. What vocational attitudes, generalizations, and skills exist? What sense of shared responsibility for political-economic decision making and internalized social values have been attained? Is factual and reliable information available to all citizens and do they have the requisite skills and understandings to utilize it effectively?

Once the pupils have been oriented to the educational needs of the peoples in a few selected Pacific nations sharply contrasted on a modernization scale, they may then begin to ascertain the possible roles and activities which the United States, Japan, and Australia as "more advanced" members of the Pacific community might and/or should play. The sense of community will have been built just to the degree that pupils recognize that the best interests of the United States and all the other members of the Pacific community are mutual. The question for consideration by the social studies class might be "How can the more advanced nations (including the United States) help the less advanced nations of the Pacific community meet their political-economic-social needs?"

Building investment capital and developing the human resources of the less advanced nations may seem at first glance too difficult for junior high school classroom consideration. On the other hand, it should be obvious to youth and adults alike that technologically advanced nations are built with accumulated surplus profits continually reinvested in further intensive capital-producing technology and in more investment in education to create human capital. If pupils are to enjoy a meaningful study of the basic human activity of creating tools and technics, they must come to appreciate the signal value of investment capital and human capabilities as fundamental technics in an industrial age.

Once pupils begin to conceptualize the roles of investment capital and human resource development, they may more readily come to appreciate the underlying economic reality which poses a dilemma for backward nations struggling to catch up with the twentieth century in emulation of the Western world: Investing and reinvesting in intensive capital-producing machines and investment in education must deny to the masses immediate relief from their less than subsistence level existence. For better or for worse, the masses are aware of the discrepancy between their own barren existence and that which is possible in "more advanced" nations. Revolt is rampant among the world's awakening peoples. Impatient of the time lag necessary to build capital and educate the masses, the awakening nations of the emerging Pacific community are often in a weakened position to employ rational economic and educational means to bring about the desired modernization.

Should these developing nations seek foreign investments, seek to raise the levels of living of their peoples entirely through their own efforts, or attempt through dictatorship long-range planning for the eventual good of the masses? When pupils begin to recognize the difficulties in finding "answers," given the conditions found in selected Pacific nations today, they will have made major strides toward readiness for participation in this emerging and expanding Pacific community of men.

Of course, proposing the study of selected emerging nations and the awakening sense of community in the Pacific arena does nothing to resolve the host of curricular questions which existent social studies programs have largely failed to meet. To avoid oversimplification of these curricular issues it seems useful to review briefly the problems of studying Asia.

In undertaking the study of the United States and selected nations from the Pacific arena, there are two approaches which might be employed: (1) Major attention could be devoted to the interests of and problems related to the United States as a member of the Pacific community aiding the development of new nations and of the emerging Pacific community as a whole. (2) Major focus might be directed to one or more selected Asian nations with only incidental reference to the United States and even less to the Pacific community. Designing curricular experiences to introduce the pupil to the Pacific community would seem to call for judicious balancing of depth study in several Asiatic nations with meaningful study of the part to be played by the United States as a member of the emerging Pacific community.

Another consideration is the selection of balanced experiences with current events and "depth" study in the social history of the selected nations and the cultural regions. Analysis of the current scene in light of historical background seems desirable if pupils are to achieve meaningful concepts and useful attitudes which lead to effective membership in the modern world. Content chosen for study must lead to fruitful awareness of potential commonalities throughout the arena of the Pacific and the avoidance of premature judgments.

As we have suggested, the sense of community is just beginning to emerge in the Pacific. Whether it will be possible for the nations of this arena to achieve a multinational community depends upon many factors over which we have little control.

The basic question is, of course, what happens as a result of the declared determination of the leaders of Communist China to bring the general population of Asia into its camp. But as long as the possibility exists to build a Pacific community of cooperating nations, the schools have an obligation to prepare our youth with the values, knowledge, and competencies out of which one day they may participate with their counterparts in other Pacific nations in creating the institutions and mechanisms essential to the maturing of this potential region-of-nations community.

Emphasis 11: The Emerging World Community

The world community is treated here as the entire earth, the home of all of mankind. Such a complex and immense community is almost impossible to conceptualize meaningfully. That is, world community may be "felt" emotionally far more easily than "known" rationally. The pupil's generic definition of *community* may be unduly strained by such a "catchall" category into which the world's widely divergent life styles and philosophies must somehow be made to fit.

The areal space which the world community comprises is easy to define. But what about the unity of the human family in such a global complex? The social studies program would be called upon concurrently to deal with the concept of the United Nations, the Western world, the non-Western world, the inter-American community, the Atlantic community, and the Pacific community. In addition, it must deal with the unaligned nations, the emerging nations and trusteeships, and possibly soon the moon and other planets! And we must not overlook the wide gaps between subgroups in these larger clusters, i.e., Israel and the U.A.R. or Malaysia and Indonesia or India and Pakistan.

Delimitation seems essential. Random illustrations of the basic human activities might be drawn forth, but, taken out of community context, their power to build concepts would be weakened. Such worldwide diversities of cultural traditions, social and political institutions and aspirations, and religious beliefs could be approached only through the crudest of generalizations, which might border upon the miseducative.

One obvious strategy for delimitation is to focus upon the free world community into which the United States has entered with a sense of mission as well as reluctance and anxiety. The free world community is a dream which may become reality. However, the activities and aspirations of the United Nations provide partial evidence of the growing maturity of mankind. The successes of NATO and the various economic associations in Europe as well as the growing bonds between nations in the wider Atlantic community or in the inter-American community suggest what common cultural heritages can make possible.

The Commonwealth community established through Great Britain's overseas activities is misunderstood by many citizens of the United States, for we are products of a history of "Anglophobia" and a predisposition to find all justice in our rebel cause of 1776. We in the United States have not been able always to understand why Britain's former colonies have not rushed to disassociate themselves at the earliest opportunity, especially following the granting of increased autonomy with the Statute of Westminster of 1931.

Many schools are devoting considerable attention to acquainting pupils with the structure, purposes, and procedures of the United Nations. Certainly any social studies program dealing with the emerging world community must draw upon and expand the pupil's knowledge of this experiment in formalized coexistence. The multitude of problems faced by the U.N. provides extensive factual evidence of worldwide recognition of man's common needs and aspirations and offers additional examples of how traditional prejudices and cultural patterns are not appropriate human responses in an age of nuclear weapons.

What are the powerful forces which are shaping the emerging world community? What cultural phenomena have resulted in the emergence of hemispheric, or "inland seas," or other sub-world communities of nations? What has changed the meanings to men of physical phenomena recorded on maps? What has brought about the rapid transformation in the demarcations of political boundaries? It is easy to overlook these forces. Behind them all, however, are the two great contemporary social upheavals of the industrial revolution and the democratic revolution.

The *industrial revolution* has altered the nature of the solutions in the basic human activities in the following ways:

1. Man is becoming the creator and master rather than a source of muscle power requisite for performing essential tasks. Further, man is better able to control his environment and no longer needs to live a hand-to-mouth existence.

2. New processes in production and transportation and related technologies have drawn men to locales of previously unappreciated natural resources and thus altered traditional concepts of "natural value" in the physical environment.

3. New approaches to production and transportation result in urban patterns of living, with highly specialized division of labor. Possession of investment capital brings power and status while possession of land is no longer the prime key to better life for the masses in rapidly industrializing nations. World areas of dense population are facing greater concentrations while areas of thin population are losing inhabitants.

4. Science and medicine are producing major changes in the world's demographic structure. Populations are exploding, the individual's productive years are being greatly extended, and the relative numbers of the young and of the elderly are increasing rapidly.

5. Recent advances in communication further reduce the possibility of any human group's remaining isolated from involvement in the dynamics of the industrial and democratic revolutions.

6. Science has provided men the means to gain more control over natural conditions and thus to challenge traditional value structures dedicated to the rationalized "good" of fatalistic acceptance of "the way things are."

The industrial revolution, then, while seemingly only having to do with man-to-thing relationships, is ultimately forcing mankind to reevaluate accepted man-to-man and man-to-spirit relationships. The industrial revolution first generated drives for national independence. Today many of the world's emerging nations are seeking to industrialize and to achieve national independence concurrently. Sooner or later, however, each nation becomes cognizant of the fact that the demands of an industrial society for markets and materials make all men interdependent; national isolationism and accelerating industrialization do not go together.

The *democratic revolution* must also be recognized as a powerful force in the world today. It demands that each person have protection from those in authority in the form of equal recourse to law, and representation when government formulates laws and taxes. Representative democracy insists that the controlling laws and form of government be decided via secret ballot and majority rule, with a minimum of pressure applied by private interests or by government. Finally, representative democracy is viable only when there exists free access to knowledge, the opportunity to discuss issues and related governmental policies openly, and the right of minorities to plead their causes.

The democratic revolution came, in part, as a response to the recognized need for responsible and wise group decision making. The close relationship between economics and political science becomes evident. As the industrial revolution changes the old social order, the democratic revolution makes its bid for control of the "new order" against the bids of various forms of absolutist government. The evolution of representative and democratic forms, which occurred gradually over the centuries in Europe and in the United States, must be accomplished in fewer years by the peoples in emerging nations today.

The United States and all members of the free world community are vitally concerned with the course of events in the developing nations and in the emerging communities. In particular, we are anxious that the seeds of the democratic revolution shall reach fruition. What topic could be more significant to pupils as they are introduced to their responsibilities as participants in building a better world?

The changes initiated by the industrial and democratic revolutions have resulted in ever increasing interdependence among the world's nations. Neither the United States nor any of the other advanced nations have enjoyed the fruits of science-created technological progress without of necessity developing contacts and ties with other nations throughout the free world.

The free world, product and producer of pluralism and the open society, must hold in check the forces of coerced conformity with their universal single answer as pursued today by the totalitarian blocs. Pupils in our classrooms must be led to realize that as members of the free world community, we cannot rationally or honestly claim to respect pluralism and self-determination while insisting that other nations follow only our lead and accept only our answers. Diversity in the free world needs our support in cooperative programs for improvement. Our pupils must achieve a concept of world community as the opportunity for all nations to practice freely the democratic principles of free association, group planning, a representative voice in decision making, and respect for minorities while accepting and living by majority rule. That such a supranational community does not now exist discloses the challenging task ahead, for only a cooperative free world community can resist world totalitarianism and eventually establish an all-inclusive community of mankind which may make possible universal individual dignity, freedom, justice, and worldwide peace. Pupils, then, should study the problems of an emerging sense of world community. Understanding should be followed by greater efforts of the United States and other more fortunate members of the free world community to help establish ties between developing sub-world communities.

Let us push the argument a bit further. Because coalitions of independent and free nations are not proving effective enough, the free world seems faced with a limited list of alternatives: either follow the lead of the democratic revolution and employ the federalist government concept (with which many Americans are uncomfortable), or accept the monolithic and authoritarian approach to world order. It is not enough that the free world community agrees to be *against* totalitarianism; rather, as with any viable community, it must work actively together *for* something. The United Nations constitutes a useful device for coexistence, but as a meeting place for sharply conflicting interests and life styles it cannot serve also the necessary functions of a world government or even serve as true government for any of the world's sub-communities. Of course, pupils need to study the United Nations, but they also need to study the concept of "world federation of free nations." Events in the inter-American and in the Atlantic communities suggest increasing readiness for such a federation of free world nations.

Pupils in the schools of the United States have an excellent opportunity to compare the story of this nation's long struggle toward federal government with what is happening in the 150 nations of the world. The obvious parallels between our continuing problems of "states' rights" within our nation and our anticipated problems of attaining United States "rights" in any future world federation certainly illustrate the fact that this state of affairs promises to be no Utopia if and when it is ever achieved. Yet if we have faith in representative forms of government, we should seek to study critically in our schools the problems of federal world government. If mankind is to survive its own skills at weaponry it will probably be through the existence of some form of world federal government. The question to be decided in the lifetime of today's pupils may well be whether the democratic revolution will prove viable enough to shape and maintain a successful federation in the face of the industrial revolution.

Pupils may begin to conceptualize the possibilities of world community after careful study of the problems and successes of the emerging inter-American, Atlantic, and Pacific communities. They will begin to appreciate the tremendous problems facing any free world community of the future after they have studied the faltering progress toward community illustrated by the several sub-world region-of-nations attempts to form trade and defensive alliances.

Pupils then might be guided into awareness that the peoples of emerging nations, drawing upon the same information as is available in the classroom, are attempting to assess and evaluate the strength and future of a free world community in order to choose wisely the path for their nation's future. The following are questions that both our pupils and peoples of the recently modernizing nations may be asking: Does the common drive for progress and freedom provide a secure basis for mutual confidence and action? Is the flow of ideas, resources, capital, and people among the nations of the free world such as to suggest viable bonds for the establishment of a secure world community? Will the anticipated rewards of modern technological living be great enough to bring highly divergent cultures into mutual understanding? Is representative democracy as a philosophy and a political rationale strong enough to organize and manage world affairs while retaining cultural pluralism and national identities in the world of tomorrow? These are questions each pupil probably needs to ask and test and seek to resolve for himself if responsible citizenship in all of tomorrow's expanding communities is to become reality.

The implications of the sense of an emerging world community for the social studies program certainly are not easily deduced; attitudes and values acquired by pupils are not direct products only of knowledge or teacher purpose. While any attempt to spell out a comprehensive social studies program is beyond the scope of this volume, it is reasonable to identify geographic concepts, map skills, and social science understandings which seem requisite to logical and systematic intellectualizing of the problems and issues concerning an emerging world community.

Conceptualizing and Mapping the Basic Human Activities

The basic human activities are those commonly found in all of mankind's total environmental adaptations and carried on in some form in all cultures. In each human group these activities are evidenced by some level of formalized social arrangements which are shaped by the mores and values perpetuated and modified from generation to generation. As societies become more complex, these activities tend to become more specialized and at the same time more closely interwoven and patterned. In technologically advanced societies formalized social institutions are established to achieve the desired stability, continuity, and efficiency which the social group (or its leaders) deem essential. Generally, each formal institutional entity adopts a control structure, assigns roles and responsibilities, and develops routines and procedures by which to conduct its internal and external activities.

Hence, each cluster of the basic human activities in each of the world's social settings can be mapped in terms of areal extent, areal association, and areal interaction. However, this is no simple task in complex societies such as the United States national community. It is a long step from the pupil's awareness of the basic human activities as they affect his local communities to the building of sound concepts of international understanding through recognizing the universality of the basic human activities. It is proposed that repeated consideration at ever higher levels of sophistication be offered to keep pace with the pupil's maturational development.

The basic human activities, then, are not social studies "facts" to be memorized but ways of conceptualizing through categorizing. Pupils in the junior high school are just learning to handle this construct. Much planning and careful selection of experiences are essential if the pupils' introduction to the basic human activities found in remote and alien cultures is not to be miseducative. The institutional responses of human groups to basic human needs reflect amazing varieties of life styles, habits, customs, mores, beliefs, and philosophies. Variation seems to be the rule; man and land combine to produce a host of viable, useful responses. However, in the social studies program, map skills and understandings must share in the task of educating youth to appreciate the basic *similarites* of needs and responses of all men; the worthiness of cultural behavior patterns in carrying on the basic human activities must not be arbitrarily judged. In brief, recognizing and mapping the basic human activities require thoughtful observation and broadened cultural perspective.

The basic human activities comprise a "crude form" category for our social observations; they are generalizations, rough categorical discriminations based upon human purposes rather than upon specific means. A trade route is not less a trade route because camels are used instead of cargo planes. A communistic regime and a democratic republic are both illustrations of human organizing and governing activities. Certainly, pupils in the social studies (value sciences) should make discriminations between these forms of government, but such evaluations must be undertaken upon a different basis.

Objective analyses cannot be derived from data which are "contaminated" with other issues, prejudices, or "mental sets." Maps and other social studies materials may be employed for propaganda purposes, but also, "honest" data may be misread by people who have developed un-analyzed subjective responses or habits. Map conventions must be interpreted and responded to by pupils with the same degree of ob-jectivity as is expected of them when dealing with the symbols of the natural sciences.

The social studies teacher will want to increase pupils' understanding of the basic principles of economics if meaningful use of the basic human activities construct is to continue to be fruitful in more advanced work. Surely an effective program of geographic studies will deal extensively with concepts from economics, as the following definition suggests:

> Economics is the social science that analyzes the data, issues, and public policies connected with the production, distribution and consumption of wealth and income. It is a seamless web of reasoning that begins with the facts of scarcity and unlimited wants and proceeds through specialized pro-duction, interdependence, exchange, markets, price, costs, and public policy. Emphasized are economic stability and growth, the allocation of resources to their most important uses, and equitable distribution of income. . . .[7]

In summary: Helping pupils become more familiar with the under-lying economic aspects of men's basic human activities in their set of expanding communities is, then, essential to meaningful social studies teaching-learning experiences. In addition, the teacher should guide pupils to search out *where* cultural and physical phenomena are lo-cated, *how* they came to be so distributed, *what* part the physical en-vironment plays in setting the community "stage," and, to the extent possible, *why* changes have taken place and will continue to do so through time. The historical interest in *when* obviously must be given extensive attention if the changing meanings of the physical and cul-tural environments are to be conceptualized by pupils.

In their social studies experiences pupils must recognize the basic human activities as a *way of thinking about what they observe. Gen-eralizations and principles are not answers to be memorized but products of meaningful learning experiences and ways for sorting out, organizing, and getting at the meaning of the facts.*

As each of the nine basic human activities is studied, pupils should be encouraged to consider all observed interrelationships between man, his institutions, and his physical-cultural environment. Constant reference to what people *do* in terms of *where* and *how* they live is necessary if youth are to become educated and effective participants in society.

The illustrations of coordinated scope and sequence in Chapter Ten were selected as teaching-learning opportunities by which to further ex-tend and refine the map skills and understandings developed earlier in this volume. Repeated, systematically presented experiences are necessary to build concepts, and the quality of generalizations is dependent upon the adequacy of prior knowledge. Thoughtful generation and/or assimilation of broad generalizations occur when learners know how to think and have had many experiences which provided them with something to think about. Unanalyzed generalizations presented as "what to think" have little place in the social studies program in a democracy.

The reader is again reminded that the entire program for developing map skills and understandings adheres to the maturational rather than the mastery rationale. The teacher ultimately must take responsibility for determining each pupil's achievement level. Therefore, before pupils attempt practice activities with any geographic concept or map skill during the study of a selected region-of-nations or a possible world community, previous knowledge should be specifically reviewed, extended, refined, or retaught if necessary. Basic skills and understandings are too critical to effective and meaningful social studies experiences to chance reliance upon incidental learnings and/or untested assumptions concerning pupil readiness. The possibilities for depth study by academically advanced pupils seem limitless in the proposals which follow.

REFERENCES

1. Walter Lippmann, "Walter Lippmann," *New York Herald Tribune,* November 8, 1961.
2. Atlantic Treaty Association, *Transatlantic Understanding in the Schools* (London: R. H. Johns Ltd., 1960), p. 21.
3. Osgood Hardy and Glenn S. Dumke, *A History of the Pacific Area in Modern Times* (Boston: Houghton Mifflin Company, 1949), p. 1.
4. John M. Brown, "Pacific Ocean Questions," *Encyclopaedia Britannica,* Vol. XVII (Chicago: University of Chicago, 1949), p. 20.
5. James A. Michener, *Return to Paradise* (New York: Random House, Inc., 1956), p. 437.
6. Research Center for Economic Development and Cultural Change, *Economic Development and Cultural Change,* Vol. X, No. 3 (Chicago: University of Chicago Press, April, 1962).
7. California State Department of Education, *Report of the State Central Committee on Social Studies,* 1959, p. 46.

chapter ten

THE JUNIOR HIGH SCHOOL
EMPHASES

*Teaching-Learning Objectives and Activities for
Larger-Than-National Communities (Emphases 8–11)*

We have reviewed the emerging world region-of-nations communities and further enlarged our description of the basic human activities. The nine sections that follow emphasize these nine clusters of activities. Each section has a prologue consisting of illustrative material emphasizing an aspect of social studies and geographic education content which could be introduced and/or extended in the junior high school curriculum. The same three broad map skills utilized in earlier grades are retained. These are amplified by statements of more specific objectives that are shaped primarily with reference to map-related *knowledge, translation,* and *interpretation* abilities and skills.[1] Within the frame of teaching strategy, the social studies, and the general intellectual abilities and skills of pupils, we complete a coordinated program by focusing attention upon Emphases 8, 9, 10, and 11: the emerging United States and inter-American community, the emerging United States and Atlantic community, the emerging United States and Pacific community, and the emerging world community.

Basic Human Activity: Protecting and Conserving Life, Health,
Property, and Resources

PROLOGUE

"Good health," "the good life," "property," and "valuable resources" are all relative to the culture developed by the people of a local community, nation, or region-of-nations community. In the social studies

354

program of the junior high school the pupil's knowledge of cultural and areal differentiation may be greatly enlarged through comparative studies of how peoples and nations meet this basic human activity.

While many alternative social studies objectives may be accomplished by means of study of the protecting and conserving activity, the following highlights from cultural geography suggest one underlying content area to give focus to proposed teaching-learning activities. Of course, these ideas may be taught deductively or developed inductively depending upon the abilities of the pupil and the social studies content selected by the school.

At one time it was believed that environment determined biological and cultural responses. Today, however, determinism no longer retains its hold over the social sciences. The physical environment is seen as inert and non-compelling, limiting, but neither encouraging nor discouraging in man any "natural" cultural response. Men will tend to follow easier pathways and will be influenced by physical barriers; but physical phenomena per se do not dictate the behavior of men or nations. Behavior is largely the manifestation of accumulated culture and "culturally tinted" perceptions of reality.

Similar physical environments do not cause similar cultural environments among the nations of men. On the other hand, when human cultures spread, even dissimilar physical environments begin to be overlaid with the cultural attributes of the former homeland. Invention and diffusion are the key cultural processes. Because different ways of life are transmitted to men they react quite differently from one another even when placed in essentially identical physical environments. It is just these great differences in cultural responses which make repeated study of the basic human activities in each of the expanding communities of men new and interesting rather than dull and repetitious. Of course, the teacher is responsible for helping the pupil to gain knowledge of each new culture and its frame of reference before he undertakes a study of such activities as protecting and conserving as practiced among the peoples of the world regions of nations.

What differences exist from area to area in the world today and from period to period through human history become evident and understandable through application of the culture concept. Cultural traditions concerning health, life, property, and resources make for interesting studies. The incidences and diffusions of human belief patterns and ways of life are readily traced by pupils who have been trained to read maps.

Basic Human Activity: Protecting and Conserving Life, Health, Property, and Resources

OBJECTIVES	TEACHING-LEARNING EXPERIENCES
1. *Ability to reorganize data gathered*	1. *Mapping activities.*

from firsthand and vicarious experiences and represent them on maps with appropriate symbols.

Develop knowledge of the many procedures nations employ to accomplish this basic activity. Concern about protecting, conserving, and improving life, health, property, and resources is not unique to any nation or community of nations, but the efforts and achievements vary widely.

Develop knowledge of the importance of international cooperation. Many aspects of carrying on this basic human activity cross national boundaries and thus become matters of concern for communities of nations. For example, diseases do not respect international boundaries, and frequently single nations do not have the resources to protect their people or prevent the spread of disease to other peoples.

Develop knowledge of the existent forms of national and international cooperation. Joint international agencies such as Red Cross and the United Nations have been devised. Of course, local and national communities need not depend wholly or even primarily upon international arrangements to work out ways to improve and conserve life and resources.

Learn to translate and interpret maps, and geographic and social science data related to protecting and conserving life, health, property, and resources. The pupil develops a growing understanding of how nations, communities of nations, and all of mankind may work together through teaching-learning experiences which further develop their powers of observation, investigation, discussion,

Inter-American Community. There are many aspects of this basic human activity within this region-of-nations community. The protection and conservation of wildlife is a matter of international concern. Correlate the discussion of this problem with your science class. Read accounts of and discuss the migratory habits of several well-known birds. What is the flying range of these birds? Where do they make their homes in summer? In winter? Note that the birds cross a number of international boundaries (Figure 40). The definable geographic space of some of these birds is the Western Hemisphere. Trace the routes of these birds on the globe. What distance do they fly? Use the scale of the globe to calculate the approximate mileage.

For a class mapping activity select an outline map of the Western Hemisphere. Use area symbols to show both the summer and winter ranges of selected birds. Use line symbols to show the probable flying routes. Give the maps appropriate titles.

Atlantic Community. Refer to experiences in the above community and discuss the implications for international cooperation in protecting and conserving wildlife in Africa. Read about the problems of saving the famous "zoo animals" which are being overhunted by thrill seekers from abroad and by uneducated natives. What countries are involved? Gather information on the treaties and laws that have been established in an effort to save a number of species. Locate the preserves now established and being

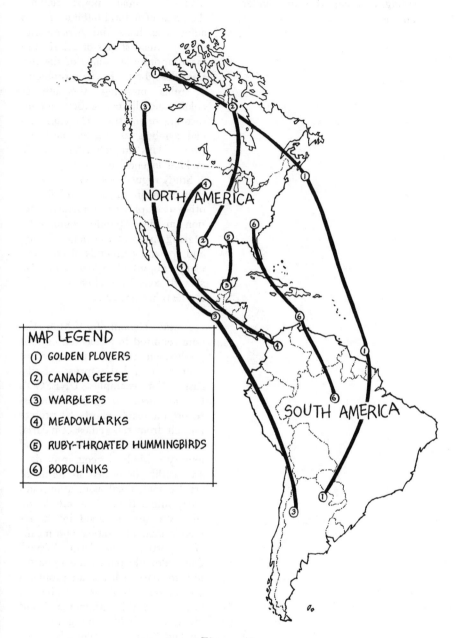

Figure 40

Bird Routes

reading, and map skills and understandings.

planned. Prepare maps showing
the areas of natural habitat of such
animals as lions and African ele-
phants. Read stories of safaris and
make appropriate maps of the terrain described. Review problems
of relief mapping, the use of
colors, and the conventions for indicating orientation. Develop special symbols as needed and improve skills in lettering and in
making legends and scale.

Study regulations concerning the
protection of fur seals and fish as
other examples of cooperative action in the Atlantic community.
Making maps of the major fishing
and spawning grounds of commercially important species of fish
should constitute effective teaching-learning activities.

Pacific Community. Map the
data reported in a selected current
publication concerning efforts of
man to control the spread of disease. For example: UNESCO's
Courier made a global progress
report on man's efforts to protect
himself from tuberculosis, malaria,
yaws, poliomyelitis, influenza, and
leprosy.[2] Medical geography data
are readily described in terms of
areal extent, areal association, and
areal interaction. The article on
"flu" was accompanied by an effective map illustrating one means
of reporting time lapse "wave"
data. Provide pupils the opportunity to map such spread problems
(or fallout problems) by having
available world outline maps and
giving them help in designing useful and "standard" symbols. (See
"Map and Globe Symbols," Appendix B.) The following excerpt
provides data for exact location reporting of a "spread" problem

which may also help children conceptualize how health hazards respect no national boundaries and call forth cooperative efforts by all mankind:

"On May 4, 1957, reports of a "flu" epidemic came to the World Health Organization from Singapore. Within a few months "Asian Flu" had girdled the world. A WHO network of 57 influenza centers in 46 countries went into action. The micro-organism was found to be a "new" virus and was given the name Virus A/Singapore/1/57. All possible measures were taken to isolate the virus and produce a vaccine against it. Headquarters of the battle was the World Influenza Centre in London where a constant search is made for "flu" viruses and a universal vaccine against all types of influenza. . . ."[3]

World Community. Discuss the function of government of the public health profession and other agencies at each community level in dealing with problems such as this. Correlate disease-incidence maps with world maps showing climate, physical relief, diet, income level, educational level, population density, etc. Make a master sketch map of regions of nations or the world to show these correlations.

Discuss the relative effects of physical environment and cultural phenomena on the control of the spread of disease. From these conclusions, reason out possible future activities of world health services and locate on the globe new centers for world health agencies.

2. *Ability to read data recorded on*   2. *Map reading activities.*

maps and globes.

Develop skills in identifying symbols portraying protecting and conserving phenomena within the focus of the inter-American community.

Develop the ability to translate these features into meaningful imagery. Maps pertaining to protecting and conserving functions include:

(1) development and conservation of natural resources;

(2) use and conservation of native plant life;

(3) use and conservation of native animal life;

(4) use and conservation of water resources;

(5) soil conservation and protection;

(6) water and air pollution control;

(7) flood control;

(8) military installations designed to protect the Western Hemisphere;

(9) international volunteer agencies concerned with health and welfare.

Develop the ability to read the locations of places using a grid system, the ability to read the cardinal directions and the intermediate points on the compass, the ability to read areal symbols, the ability to read scale on globes, the ability to recognize the problems of reading scale on maps.

Learn the symbols portraying protecting and conserving activities and features identifying line, point, and area symbols and associating meaningful images with them. Give pupils help in reading maps showing distributions by means of shadings or color patches. Review and extend these reading skills: point symbols for weather

Inter-American Community. Help the class develop meanings for the symbols used on maps portraying features and activities of people within the inter-American community. Continue to use photographs and other visual material to help the pupils associate imagery with the realities symbolized on maps. As an example, read accounts of the work of the various health teams in many countries in Central and South America. Discuss the activities of people connected with these health units. Read pictures of the units' headquarters and various kinds of facilities in the field. How are they symbolized on maps? Include maps showing topographical features, water bodies, and climate of the regions. Read these maps to find out the kinds of clothing the medical people would probably wear, the kind of transportation they would use in getting from one area to another, and so on. What season of the year would it be? What symbols are used to tell the kinds of activities being carried on?

Atlantic Community. Present the generalization: Disease in man is related to climate, altitude, soil, density of population, diet, and income. Provide maps and other information sources for several of the above-named phenomena for a selected nation under study. Obtain similar maps and information for a section of the United States having some common physical characteristics. If possible, select maps projected on similar scale and utilizing common cartographic symbols to expedite comparative study. Ask pupils why

stations, military installations, health facilities, and so on; line symbols for boundaries, districts, rivers, streams, etc.; and area symbols for population distributions of people, animals, insect-infected areas, and so on.

they think you have selected these particular maps rather than others. If common bases and symbols systems are not available, discuss the translation difficulties with the class and be sure that they understand the kinds of error which can occur if mental or actual corrections are not made.

Pacific Community. Now obtain similar maps of a nation in the Pacific region and proceed to compare the above elements with each other and note the incidence of selected diseases. Do the same for two nations to be compared. Correlate the findings and ask pupils to interpret their meanings. While interpretation is a natural outgrowth of map reading, focus upon the accuracy of the class's map symbol translation.

World Community. Now study the cultural maps of selected world nations carefully to discover any phenomena which would explain the superiority of one over another in protecting its population from disease. Are there ways in which these nations are helping or might help each other in fighting disease? Involve the entire class in this activity as probably few pupils will have enough information and imagination to be successful by themselves. Stress application of skills and abilities in order to identify signs of science and technology, communication, medical facilities, education, governmental agencies, sanitation, and high standard of living as depicted by map symbols. Discuss the importance of cooperative action and informed citizenship. What ways are there for comparing historical maps

3. *Ability to interpret distribution and location on maps and globes and to reason geographically.*

Reason geographically about the location and areal distribution of protecting and conserving structures and activities.

Analyze the geographical location and distribution of protecting and conserving phenomena as to:
(1) relative location;
(2) relative distance;
(3) relative direction.
Correlate the spatial dimensions of protecting and conserving phenomena with other cultural features. Develop the ability to make inferences from maps.

Interpret and reason about the following manifestations of the basic human activity of protecting and conserving:
(1) water: flood control, drought, contamination, etc.;
(2) mineral resources and their conservation and distribution among nations;
(3) weather and transportation, agriculture, industry, clothing, shelter, energy, and health;
(4) national rights and international cooperation and conflict: police work, tariffs, customs inspection, military needs, and economic interdependence;
(5) malnutrition problems: backward technology, depleted soils, cultural traditions, overpopulation, etc.;
(6) world life-expectancy patterns and their causes;
(7) safety problems;
(8) human survival and nuclear

in order to "read" with maps the progress made by nations, and mankind in general?

3. *Map interpretation activities.*

Inter-American Community. Provide learning activities to help students use maps as basic tools in the study of the geographical aspects of protecting and conserving phenomena. Note and explain the existence of many variations in the pattern and distribution of flood control structures, hospitals, and so on. Interpret the interrelatedness of locations and distributions of two or more cultural features. Note any correlations of population density with the presence or absence of hospitals, number of medical schools, climate, and vegetation. Several maps are needed to gather information about the area and for areal relationships of physical and cultural items.

Use a globe to note the locations of protecting and conserving phenomena in relation to the equator. Reason about the locations of weather-gathering stations and their distribution in the inter-American community. Note any areal relationship of these locations with the physical elements or the cultural elements, such as transportation features.

Atlantic Community. Make a study of water resources, their utilization and related problems among nations in this region of nations. Locate information on domestic and municipal supplies, industrial uses, agricultural uses, and water power in one or more of the northern European nations. Do not overlook transportation aspects of water in the low countries. In what ways does water aid or hin-

explosions;

(9) world medical needs;

(10) patterns of technological unemployment and utilization of human resources;

(11) the work of the International Red Cross;

(12) the work of international professional groups in this cluster;

(13) the work of the United Nations: UNESCO, World Health Organization, etc.

der the spread of high population density areas? What other physical and cultural resources are dependent upon plentiful water supplies in order to be utilized? Why is Egypt willing to flood some of its historical treasures behind its great new dam on the Nile? Will more water in Egypt make it possible for that nation to industrialize? What other resources must the Egyptians develop? Sketch maps showing anticipated changes in Egypt when the dam is completed. Will the dam solve overpopulation problems for Egypt?

Pacific Community. The layer of topsoil over the earth averages only eight inches deep. Food is all-important to man today as we realize that two out of three people suffer from malnutrition. Soil erosion and leaching are serious problems everywhere; poor-quality soil produces poor-quality foods. Silting tends to increase flooding potentials and to reduce fish population upon which many people are dependent for essential dietary components. Use maps to study these problems in one or more of the Asiatic nations. What are the needs of nations in the Pacific for protecting and conserving the soil? Employ a variety of maps to appreciate the range of cause-and-effect correlations between the soil and other physical and cultural phenomena.

World Community. Good health and long life for all people on earth today could result in a shattering population explosion, yet we want all people to enjoy a healthy and long existence. A population explosion is under way today; we must have a 50 per cent increase in food to nourish those now living; the most backward nations are increasing the fastest. Here is a major social studies problem demanding thoughtful interpretation and application abilities and skills. Plan a study of the U.N.'s efforts in dealing with the results of a worldwide "health revolution" and generally negative attitudes toward reducing birth rates.

Basic Human Activity: Producing, Exchanging, Distributing, and Consuming Goods and Services

Prologue

Map translation and interpretation skills rest upon a growing body of knowledge. Pupils will have difficulty going beyond superficial map reading of exact location if their concepts of basic economics are limited. Hence, renewed consideration of producing, exchanging, distributing, and consuming goods and services in the junior high school may be utilized as an opportunity to initiate "semiformal" studies in economics.

While it may be useful to employ the "standard language" of economics, it is not necessary to introduce a new vocabulary in order to begin building basic concepts. The question "Why economize?" may be answered with simple illustrations of man's unlimited desires and the unfortunate fact that there are limits to the availability of things desired. Once the idea of scarcity is clarified, the major questions of economics may be introduced. Lewis states them in simple form:

(1) *What* shall we produce with our productive resources?
(2) *How much* can we produce in total and how fast shall the economy grow?
(3) *Who* shall get the goods and services produced?

These are the big questions faced by every economic system, be it capitalist, communist, or any other. What? How much? For whom?[4]

Undertake brief studies in the history of selected nations in order to ascertain how their people answered the above questions. Distributional maps of production and consumption of food, shelter, and clothing or medical services could be employed to help pupils visualize these problems. Review how the industrial and democratic revolutions swept the

Western world and people became increasingly dissatisfied with existing *what, how much,* and *who* "answers." Thus, as pupils are introduced to the history of European or Asiatic nations, they can be extending and refining their ability to conceptualize underlying economic principles. Colonialism in Africa, Asia, and the New World, questions of the power to tax and the right to control expenditures, the rise of the guild system and modern activities of labor unions, wars, trade relations, cartels, and recently created supranational bodies such as NATO and the Common Market—all begin to take on more meaning when considered in light of the *what, how much,* and *who* questions concerning the basic human activity of producing, exchanging, distributing, and consuming goods and services.

Study of economic principles may be conducted in the context of this basic human activity. Industrial centers appear as locations of cultural density upon physical-cultural maps. Use physical-political maps for more than merely pointing out the location of "centers" of trade and production. Stress relative location—and draw upon social studies materials to help pupils decide what to look for in the center's hinterland and in its national and region-of-nations setting. Economic needs of the peoples and nations of the world must be considered in order to understand the significance of where economic activities are located.

In each of the regions of nations help the class to locate a "center" for a type of barter system or banking, a source of raw materials or manufacture, a handcraft center or tool and dye producing center, and a dairy products or grain producing and processing center. Locate these centers in terms of their relative location; infer whether *where* the economic activity takes place makes *any difference* to other basic activities of men. Use Meyer's list of "where's" and ask pupils to add to this list following their research activities.

1. Where is the place in terms of latitude, coast line, and type of climate?
2. Where is it in terms of elevation, relief, landform, and water bodies?
3. Where is it in terms of neighboring peoples, cities, and countries?
4. Where is it in terms of types of soil, vegetation and mineral resources?
5. Where is it in terms of dominant types of agriculture, of manufacture, of other land use forms?
6. Where is it in terms of transportation and commerce?[5]

To Meyer's list add "Where is it in terms of other 'centers' of producing, exchanging, distributing, and consuming goods and services and in terms of selected aspects of the other eight basic human activities?"

Industrialization and highly complex economic activities lead to consideration of the geographic aspects of cities and the story of urbanization, which is a worldwide trend today. Generalizations such as the following should let the teacher provide pupils with useful guidelines for better reading of large-scale maps of urban areas. These generalizations relate to mappable phenomena for inclusion in the pupils' own sketch maps. Related studies might include the history of many cities, great and small, coastal and inland, and in densely or thinly populated areas of the world. Geographic generalizations to be considered include the following:

(a) Most cities locate and develop as a result of more than one causative factor, and the functions they perform are likewise seldom singular.

(b) Gateways located between contrasting natural regions are often advantageous sites for the establishment of transport and trade centers.

(c) The demands of commerce usually cause the greatest cities to be located by the sea at the focus of great ocean routes.

(d) The largest cities are in locations having the best communications with the interior.

(e) Cities develop where there is a transfer from one form of transportation to another.

(f) Rivers have always served as desirable locations for the sites of settlements, especially: where transportation routes cross rivers; at the confluence of rivers; on the outer bends of rivers; near the mouths of of navigable rivers which drain productive hinterlands.

(g) Cities tend to rise and grow at the head of a large lake or at the "fall line" on navigable rivers.

(h) The great need for certain minerals has caused the establishment of settlements in extremely remote locales and under the most adverse climatic conditions.[6]

Encourage classes to discover on maps examples of these generalizations and in addition, through their studies, find other interrelationships of place location, economic activities, and development of modern cities. The following map-making experience may prove useful for concept building in both cartography and this basic human activity. Since most Americans today live in or near large urban population centers, the following field activities (either direct or vicarious, through tracing routes on large-scale city maps) for sketching areal extent, areal association, and areal interaction are possible.

Study the city's area of freight yards, warehouses, wholesale outlets, service shops, marshaling yard, and so forth. Make sketch maps of the rail "hubs" and their connecting networks, the truck terminals and highway truck route networks, the locational distribution of major industrial concerns, the locational distribution of population density, exact and relative location of major shopping centers, terrain maps of the city and hinterland, interactional traffic flow patterns between the city and its hinterland, climate maps, and so forth.

Discuss these findings to be sure that pupils do not have fragmented information but can visualize how the whole fits together. Have the class prepare a "total picture" map of areal extent, areal distribution, and areal association. Focus on one phenomenon and check to be sure the map shows the *what, where,* and *how* of the interaction. For example, a flow pattern for bananas may be traced from boat to train to wholesale warehouse to truck to store to handcart to counter to shopping cart to car and home via the freeway. Assign different products to pupils and when the data are collected, discuss with the class the best way to make a broad cartographic description of producing, exchanging, distributing, and consuming goods and services.

Be sure that pupils do obtain an understanding of *why* things are arranged as they are so that they will be able to select significant *whats* and *wheres* to include in their maps of the cultural features of this basic human activity. Learners are making good progress when they cease to ask *what* should go into their maps and start asking for help in finding the most effective way to report significant facts with maps.

Basic Human Activity: Producing, Exchanging, Distributing and Consuming Goods and Services

OBJECTIVES	TEACHING-LEARNING EXPERIENCES
1. *Ability to reorganize data gathered from firsthand and vicarious experiences and represent them on maps with appropriate symbols.*	1. *Mapping activities.*

1. *Ability to reorganize data gathered from firsthand and vicarious experiences and represent them on maps with appropriate symbols.*

Develop knowledge of the needs underlying and the significance of the interdependence of nations. Within all of the emerging world communities people produce, exchange, and consume goods and services. No one national community produces all the goods and services it needs nor can it consume all that it produces.

Develop knowledge of international trading patterns and the organization of trading centers and communities. National economic specializations result from developed physical and human resources and advantageous locations. Trade is both a cause and an effect of a

1. *Mapping activities.*

Inter-American Community. Help the class gather information on the mineral resources of the inter-American community upon which our auto industry is dependent. Discuss how "American" our cars really are. The iron ore may come from Labrador or Brazil; the nickel for the so-called chrome parts may come from Canada; the sulfuric acid used in the battery may be manufactured from sulfur mines in Mexico, and so on.

Make a list of these materials used by various industries and the locations of the principal mines and sources. On a large outline map of the Western Hemisphere, bulletin board size, plan to show their locations or distributions. Decide on appropriate symbols to rep-

sense of community.

Develop knowledge of how individuals participate in world trade. Together with people from many nations, American business concerns and individuals have invested large sums of money and "know-how" in other nations; the theory of money is introduced.

Develop knowledge of map symbols in mapping the *where* of economic activities; reinforce the pupil's appreciation of natural and cultural resources in terms of their distribution, scarcity, and human demand for them. Stress a "problems approach" to determining how to gather, reorganize, and report data on charts, graphs, and maps. Help the class make a collection of the various cartographic devices employed to describe natural and cultural resources and their distribution.

Learn to translate and interpret map data related to basic principles in economics and apply to solving simple problems presented in social studies materials.

resent these data on the map. Discuss ways in which this map can be simple and direct to avoid being overcrowded with detail. The meanings of the map symbols should be made clear in the key or legend.

What happens when the present known resources of nickel mines in Sudbury become exhausted? Read accounts of new discoveries of these mineral resources and the work of developing new mines for production. How is it planned to transport the ores to the markets of the world?

Atlantic Community. Have pupils make original maps to describe the distributions of key minerals; report untapped reserves and current annual production by nations of asbestos, bauxite, copper, cobalt, manganese, nickel, tin, tungsten, etc. Have another group of pupils make maps to describe patterns of power resources, consumption of animal and vegetable resources, utilization of skilled and unskilled labor, accumulation of investment capital, monetary exchange units, etc.

Pacific Community. Ask pupils to prepare maps of the same data as outlined above for the Atlantic region of nations. Compare the patterns of similarities and differences in the clustering of symbols and overlapping of distribution patterns. Discuss both the geographic significance of these patterns and the ways of reporting such data so as to prevent the maps from becoming jumbled and ineffective.

World Community. Study resources and conservation with maps, charts, and pictures. Consider the conservation problems posed when nations compete in producing similar crops and products. Make maps showing the economic specializations practiced by various nations. Discuss the competitive advantages of specialization under free trade. Have pupils map and discuss information about world tariff patterns and resulting problems of exchanging and distributing goods.

2. *Ability to read data recorded on maps and globes.*

Develop skills in identifying symbols portraying producing, exchanging, and consuming goods and services on maps. Develop the ability to translate these symbols and their patterns of distribution into meaningful imagery and conceptual patterns of landscape.

Develop the ability to read map symbols, pictorial, semipictorial, and geometric such as the circle, dot, square, etc., used by cartographers to portray producing, exchanging, and consuming goods and services on maps. Patterns of areal distribution of these features are shown by color shadings, patterns of lines, dots, and such variations as vertically parallel lines, horizontally parallel lines, and varying widths between the lines. Reading exercises to identify the above symbols should provide opportunities for the pupils to develop meanings first.

Map to learn how to portray symbols pertaining to this basic human activity. Include the following:
(1) forests;
(2) agricultural production and distribution: land use, cultivated land, pasture land, grazing land, soil types;

2. *Map-reading activities.*

Inter-American Community. The image of reality must be built from symbolic clues and vicarious experiences. For example, the image of the pampas region and the raising of livestock and grain should be gained through the use of pictures, reading accounts of activities and descriptions of the symbols (pictorial, semipictorial, and areal) which represent these phenomena. Imagery thus developed must be called upon if the pupil is to appreciate the realities represented. The teacher must remember that a map is not a picture. From images of the many producing, distributing, and exchanging features and activities, pupils are helped to develop conceptual patterns of the landscape as represented by the map.

Atlantic Community. American classes will find both similarities and contrasts between what they have experienced in their own culture and what they will discover, vicariously, to exist in the nations making up this region of nations. Becoming informed about this basic human activity as it is conducted in other lands requires that the pupil's learning be carefully guided and richly augmented. A collec-

(3) agricultural products (plants): food products, industrial products, consumption areas;
(4) irrigated areas;
(5) fisheries;
(6) development of industrial resources: coal mining areas, distribution of coal for domestic and industrial use, oil and natural gas fields, pipelines and other distribution facilities, oil refineries, and storage areas, production and distribution of electricity, and areas with potential power sites.

Develop through map study understanding of the development of mineral resources: mining of industrial metal ores, mining of precious metal ores, mining of radioactive ores, etc.

tion of materials should be presented through teaching-learning activities such as investigating, discussing, reading, and viewing motion pictures, filmstrips, and oblique and vertical aerial photographs. Mental images of the essential characteristics of many producing and distributing features which the pupils have not had an opportunity to observe firsthand are developed through these vicarious experiences.

Pacific Community. Once the pupils begin to conceptualize something of the way other peoples produce and consume goods and services, comparative studies are useful. For example, wheat is produced mechanically in major production centers and by ancient methods in isolated marginal producing areas. Ask pupils to make reports for the class which tell about the differing ways wheat (or other grains, particularly rice) is produced and distributed in selected Pacific nations as compared to methods used in the United States. Comparing historical maps reporting grain production would provide an excellent medium for illustrating the effect of the industrial revolution and the shift from animal power to machine power in the agricultural sector of modern industrial nations.

World Community. The activities commenced above may be extended to the total world setting. Agricultural products and their distribution and consumption comprise major social studies topics. Present the pupils with a number of commodity maps and ask them to prepare charts and graphs of the information they have read. Use such a product as wheat and ask pupils to describe how wheat is distributed throughout the world. Use other materials to discover the problems of storing and processing wheat into foodstuff. Obtain large-scale maps of major world wheat exchange centers and chart what contrasts and similarities are discovered. Locate on the globe the world's twelve major wheat-producing areas and help pupils describe their unique and common physical, cultural, and economic conditions.

3. *Ability to interpret distribution and location on maps and globes and to reason geographically.*

Reason geographically about strategic location and areal distribution of producing, exchanging, and consuming goods and services phenomena. Analyze the distribution of these features as to relative location, relative distance, and relative direction.

Correlate the spatial dimensions of these cultural features with physical elements and other cultural features such as transportation and communication facilities. Continue to develop the ability to make inferences about data gathered from specialized kinds of maps.

Translate and interpret map, geographic, and social science data related to producing, exchanging, and consuming goods and services.

Help the class to visualize the physical and cultural realities of world manufacture, trading, and financial phenomena. Patterns of economic areal interaction and trade-flow patterns will become conceptually significant as the class strives to reason about the relationships between man and land phe-

3. *Map interpretation activities.*

Inter-American Community. Provide many map interpretation activities to help students develop the ability to compare maps and make inferences about the geographical dimensions of producing, exchanging, and consuming goods and services. Have students look for correlations of producing phenomena shown on maps.

Read two or more maps to gather information from which inferences can be made about area relationships of cultural and physical elements. Note the locations of major distribution centers in North and South America (Vancouver and Montreal in Canada and Buenos Aires in Argentina are located at or on the mouths of navigable rivers).

Atlantic Community. Interdependence of men and nations may be better understood through asking the economic questions which underlie competition. Through map-based inferences pupils may begin to appreciate the efforts to form trading communities as an enlightened approach to achieving

nomena.

Discover application of the following generalizations:

(1) The location and development of manufacturing is influenced by the occurrence of the potential market for goods and services.

(2) Any nation must depend upon the natural resources lying within its borders, or accessible to it through trade, to supply the physical bases of its industry and its industrial production.

(3) The availability of transportation facilities tends to beget trade, manufacturing, and other industries.

(4) In any industry where mechanical energy required is excessive, the point of fabrication lies as near the source power as possible.

(5) Where the raw materials used in the manufacturing process are bulky, the point of fabrication tends to locate as close to the source of raw materials as possible.

(6) Where processing plants depend upon distant markets, a location near or on the seacoast is an advantage because of the low cost of ocean transport.[7]

more satisfactory answers to: What? How much? For whom?

Study maps of the areal extent of the European Free Trade Association or the European Economic Community. Discuss the implications for arrangements for conducting this basic human activity for the future.

Pacific Community. Symbols showing the areal distributions of "consuming goods and services" such as electricity and natural gas or hotels and hospitals make it possible to make inferences about the character of the country or continent. Correlate maps giving the above information with population maps of the same area. Help students to understand that area relations do not necessarily denote causal relations.

World Community. Draw inferences from information provided by globes and maps about physical factors such as relief and climate and agricultural producing areas in the world. The following "game" provides pupils an opportunity to translate, interpret, extrapolate, and apply economic and geographic facts and principles. A hypothetical situation is set up in which the six generalizations listed in the adjacent objectives column are to be "clues" to resolving the "problem." The problem: A rich uncle has three iron mines and he is giving you whichever one you choose. One is near a seaport, one near a coal field, and one near a great manufacturing center. You may ask ten questions before you must choose. (Pupils could take turns answering questions for each mine and its hinterland by sketching

their responses on maps.) Several
pupils may be the "nephew" and
then the class could discuss the
"problem" and determine what
questions were most useful for making the decision. For able pupils the
scene might be shifted to different
periods in history as well as different nations among the three regions
of nations.

Basic Human Activity: Transporting People and Goods

PROLOGUE

The basic human activity of transportation is a major "consumer" of
maps. Classes will need to make and use many maps in order to appreciate the complexities of transportation today. Insight into cause-and-
effect ramifications and implications having to do with various aspects
of transportation is requisite to generating effective interpretations of
areal extent, areal association, and, in particular, areal interaction. Classes
will need help in computing and reading statistical data in order to identify
and map the qualitative and quantitative ramifications of selected phenomena related to transportation.

An economics-based interpretation of transportation would call for the
use of many sketch maps of spatial interaction focusing upon flow patterns and production cycles of goods within a single unit and between
units. A historical study of transportation might also include sketch
maps of the fantastic feats of the Polynesian peoples in transporting
themselves among the scattered islands of the Pacific. How better to
emphasize the tremendous strides of modern technology?

Take up the concepts of dependent and independent variables having
to do with choice of means of transportation. Meaningful interpretation of areal associations requires extensive geographic factual and
conceptual knowledge, intellectual skills in scientific methods, and inventiveness in perceiving, conceptualizing, and expressing discovered
correlations. Encourage frequent use of freehand sketches of base data
as well as use of prepared outline maps. When evaluating teaching-
learning outcomes remember that interpretative sketch maps provide
a ready means of assessing the learner's grasp and use of the scientific
method, geographic concepts, map skills and understandings, and general orientation to our physical and cultural worlds.

For example, review previous experiences and learnings having to do with the importance of rivers to man. Help the class arrive at a list of criteria for judging the importance of rivers. Prepare a bulletin-board-size sketch map of the world or obtain a large globe which can be written upon with chalk. Ask pupils to locate those rivers of the world which meet various of the "importance" criteria. Help the class devise ways for denoting which rivers (or parts of rivers) are used for different purposes (i.e., the Colorado marked to indicate irrigation but not navigation, etc.). Discover how to classify the age or maturity of a river and devise means for denoting this fact (i.e., is the Colorado young, mature, old, etc.?).

Study the political aspects of transportation. Review the importance to England of control of major world transportation routes. Read map descriptions of the "British lifeline." Use of maps will aid the discussion of the 100-year history of Suez; include consideration of the struggles between England, Germany, Russia, and the rising Arab states related to mercantilism, colonialism, nationalism, and the industrial nation's need for economical transportation for access to the world's resources and markets. Trace the shipments of key raw materials and finished goods through the Suez and other man-made canals.

The mapping of transportation and trade routes provides excellent opportunities for combining geographic concepts, social studies knowledge, and cartographic skills. While in its simplest form the selection of one route over another is based upon distances and ease of movement, political and economic activities bring about many interesting exceptions to the rule.

The teacher might inform the class that an economist has claimed that transportation by water costs about one-tenth as much as transportation over land. From this fact pupils may wish to develop a special water transportation map with the water distances appropriately reduced. This map should focus upon the world's important sea-trading cities and nations.

Another mapping experience might focus upon political considerations of transportation in time of war. Trade maps are concerned with costs, but during a war, *time* is the all-important factor. Likewise political control finds rapid movement important, as illustrated by the roads of the Roman Empire and of Hitler's Germany.

Should the teacher have the necessary background and some pupils disclose interest and appropriate abilities, introductory work in topology may provide a means to enhance appreciation of the significance of physical and cultural geographic phenomena. Topological analysis can provide special insight into the nature of strategic routes, sites, and situations through its concepts of "inside" and "outside" parts. However, for junior high purposes meaningful studies can be achieved without recourse to mathematical analysis, and the significance attached to Suez and Panama can be highlighted as more than "purely" economic.

Basic Human Activity: Transporting People and Goods

OBJECTIVES	TEACHING-LEARNING EXPERIENCES

1. *Ability to reorganize data gathered from firsthand and vicarious experiences and represent them on maps with appropriate symbols.*

Develop knowledge of the importance of transportation to the development of peoples and nations. Central to the history of man is the story of constructing better means for moving people and goods from place to place.

Develop knowledge of the relative importance of various modes of transportation. The principal means of transporting raw materials such as copper ore and crude oil or bulk foodstuffs such as wheat between nations and continents have been ships. Ships were also the main means of immigration and exploration. Today air transportation has become an important means of moving people and goods where time is important. Also, the airplane joins widely separated and isolated centers of population to foster new expanding communities.

Develop knowledge of the problems resulting from changing modes of transportation. New advances in the efficient and rapid transportation of people and goods bring about new kinds of political and economic problems. Pipelines for carrying water, gas, and oil are becoming increasingly important. Political boundaries can cause difficulties when a pipeline runs through several nations.

Learn to translate and interpret map, geographic, and social science data related to transporting people and goods. New modes of transportation have resulted in changes in the relative importance of physi-

1. *Mapping activities.*

Inter-American Community. Most pupils have had vicarious experiences observing the various modes of transportation used by people who live in the inter-American community. Beasts of burden such as dogs pull sleds across the frozen wastes of Canada, and llamas carry loads over rough trails in mountainous terrain in the Andes. Classes have observed motion pictures showing the airplane being used in these same areas to connect them with population centers in all parts of the Western Hemisphere.

Discuss pictures showing the use of land, air, and water transportation in relation to the landform features of the region, the climate, and the population density. How do rugged terrain and vegetation features such as mountains, jungles, swamps, and frozen tundra present particular kinds of barriers to highway and railroad construction? Where would you expect to find rail transportation? Air transportation?

Atlantic Community. A map- and chart-making subject in the study of transportation could take up the identification and location of the world's transshipment activities. Consider the process of "break-of-bulk" which occurs where one form of transportation meets another. For example, following up on previous water transportation studies, the pupils will understand why it is economically possible to move cargo up rivers even when land detours around rapids are necessary.

cal and cultural phenomena. The pupil will develop his knowledge of the changing importance of nations, locations, and resources throughout the world by developing the ability to conduct comparative studies utilizing many kinds of maps.

While studying Africa the class might be required to map the break-of-bulk locales on the Congo between Stanley Pool and the Atlantic port. Effective study of this topic calls for raised relief maps, political maps, cultural phenomena distribution maps, and general consideration of available alternatives. The complexity of this topic allows for the involvement of pupils to the extent of their developed skills and understandings.

Pacific Community. Large cities are usually the centers of transportation. Make a large-scale map of a selected ocean port. Locate the harbor facilities: piers and warehouses for the ships, the connecting network of railroads, highways, airlines, and terminal facilities. Show how goods and people are carried between the port and the surrounding country. Gather data about the kinds of heavy goods of commerce that are carried between continents. Make a large bulletin-board-size map and locate the main ocean trade routes. Indicate key materials being carried. Give the map a title and explain all symbols used in the key. Make maps to show the trade routes of the sailing vessels of the western Pacific. Contrast these routes with those of mechanically powered boats. Help pupils conceptualize the geographic and computational aspects of transportation problems. Map problems of logistics.

World Community. A study of transshipment points may lead to a consideration of continental fall lines. Ask the pupils to prepare sketch maps showing the location of cities on the fall line in a selected country. Such a mapping activity might be the outcome of a map interpretation discussion in which pupils were first asked to study the location of cities and then hypothesize the general lay of the fall line. The class could start with the fall line cities near the eastern coast of the United States and then discover similar situations elsewhere in the world. Such a topic should center upon major cities as viewed on small-scale political maps, both historical and current. Study of industrial nations today may suggest that modern means of transportation is reducing the significance of the fall lines. Hypothetical countries may be invented so that pupils can test their understanding of the relationship between the location of cities and the available means of transportation.

2. *Ability to read data recorded on maps and globes.*

Continue to develop reading skills in identifying symbols portraying transportation features and the ability to translate them into meaningful imagery. These include, among others, the following:

(1) paths, trails, and other routes of foot travel;

(2) international highways;

(3) international railroad maps, routes, terminals, division points;

(4) national and international water routes, both on inland water bodies and on seas and oceans;

(5) international air routes;

(6) international airports;

(7) ports of entry for automobiles, airplanes;

(8) international charts for air navigation;

2. *Map-reading activities.*

Inter-American Community. Identifying symbols for bridges, highways, railroads, and the like, on maps of the Western Hemisphere will be a review for many of the classes. The conventional symbols for these transportation features are the same. All types of bridges, whether they be the modern concrete bridges on a freeway in the United States or a narrow wooden bridge in a South American country, have a common symbol.

Map-reading activities at this level should be designed to help classes develop meaningful imagery. Pictures should be regularly used. Discuss the pictures and note the particular features of various airports in jungle regions, for instance. Locate these airports on a map and draw strings to the actual pictures of them mounted on a

(9) ferries, bridges, pontoon bridges.

Develop the ability to read the relative location and relative distances between international points. Continue to develop the ability to read the areal distributions of various modes of transportation as shown on maps.

Develop the appreciation that transportation depends upon accurate weather maps and charts, relief maps, and pilots who "know" the safe air or water channels leading to port. Make pupils aware of the importance to man of knowledge of latitude, relative location, and exact location, particularly in terms of transportation. Develop the awareness that many transportation and communication problems are dictated by terrain and climatic resultants of wind and water movements across the surface of the earth.

Review the geography of wind and water movements, of precipitation (fog and ice), and of air turbulence and learn the map symbols for these phenomena. Review national and international means of policing the seas and safeguarding shipping lanes from navigational hazards. Learn to read the international symbols for navigational use.

bulletin board.

Atlantic Community. Military campaigns are planned to take advantage of the fastest routes and periods of favorable weather. Read maps of military campaigns to highlight these aspects of transporting people and goods. Place before the class appropriate maps to aid the discussion of the spread of the Roman Empire, the Islamic Empire, or the plans of Alexander, Napoleon, and Hitler. Have pupils use the maps to illustrate how carefully chosen lines of communication and transportation and fortunate weather (or the converse for the Spanish Armada and the invaders of Russia) have tended to make history a story of "might-have-beens," "turning points," and "inevitable outcomes."

Pacific Community. Current events carry constant reminders of the transportation difficulties in the struggle in Indo-China. New interest in the borders of the Himalayan countries is related to new transportation potentials. Compare historical and current maps and read current events to aid the translation of map symbols related to transporting people and goods.

Collect pictures of various parts of the Burma Road of World War II. Mount the map showing this highway on a bulletin board along with the pictures. Connect the pictures to the map symbols with strings. Read the maps to find out what kinds of road surfaces most of the highways have. Have pupils consult maps to find the arterial routes between major distribution centers. Find out what products are being transported over each of these arterial routes.

World Community. Assign the following generalizations about man's movement through river valleys as research themes, discuss findings, and hypothesize concerning the manner in which new technology may necessitate their modification:

(1) The movements of peoples and commerce across the face of the earth in the past have run in "the ruts of the world."

(2) A study of the terrain of the globe discloses areas where rivers and their valleys have provided passes and trails.

(3) Physical-political maps reveal many famous name places from history such as the lower Rhone's "Way of Light" (which in World War II became the "Mohawk Corridor").

(4) Certain rivers have become world famous because they have enhanced the development of the cultures that grew up along them.

(5) Certain large rivers have run their "ruts" into the icy north or into inland seas and as a result have tended to cut off from other men those people who have settled along their banks. (Of this latter group, the rivers of Russia provide an excellent example. Russia's search for a "door to the sea" and a "window to the west" should illustrate the unfortunate consequences, reaching far beyond the immediate area, of physical terrain which impedes transportation and communication.)

3. *Ability to interpret distribution and location on maps and to reason geographically.*

Reason geographically about the

3. *Map interpretation activities.*

Inter-American Community. Help pupils to make inferences from data they gather from maps. For

location and areal distribution of transportation features. Interpret the location of harbors, airports, railroads, and other transportation facilities in relation to transporting people and goods.

Apply the following generalizations as principles to explain cultural phenomena recorded on maps:

(1) Rivers have always served as desirable locations for the sites of settlements, especially: where transportation routes cross rivers; at the confluence of rivers; on the outer bends of rivers; near the mouths of navigable rivers which drain productive hinterlands.

(2) Railroads and factories may be located near rivers both because the land is level and because the river affords a means of transportation and an easy way to get rid of wastes.

(3) River valleys usually provide the easiest lines of human movement, even on plains.

(4) Mature rivers have fewer obstacles to navigation than young or old ones.

(5) The availability of transportation facilities (such as rivers) tends to beget trade, manufacturing, and other industries.[8]

Interpret available data on the past and present of the "non-Western world" and hypothesize about its future in terms of changing modes and methods of transportation.

example, you would expect to find railroads where there are bulk commodities to be moved. Is it feasible to move the bulk agricultural commodities of South American countries to international markets by air transport? If there are no bulk goods to be moved, would you expect to find a vast railway system? Does lack of railroads indicate no need for railroads? What inferences could you make about the activities of people who live in areas where there are few or no railroads? Relate the areal distributions of railways and highways to the land forms of the region. Interpret the significance of the areal distributions in terms of these landforms. Why are there no railroads between North and South America? If an area has no harbors for freighters or large ships, what inferences can you make? If there is a network of air routes to a large airport in the area, what inferences can be made? Read a rainfall map and a highway map and make inferences about road conditions during various seasons of the year.

Atlantic Community. In an age of air travel pupils may tend to overlook the major contributions rivers have made and continue to make to the movement of peoples and goods.

Duplicate the generalizations in the adjacent objectives column having to do with rivers and transportation and provide each pupil with a copy. Have them study a variety of maps of selected rivers and make inferences concerning man's cultural adaptations related to transportation. Prepare sketch maps to illustrate contrasting applications of these principles discovered in European and African nations.

Pacific Community. Mention has been made of England's "lifeline." Help pupils consider the changes in the lives of people in the Pacific region of nations that resulted from their colonial status at the end of the European ocean transportation routes. As these emerging nations develop their own transport system, what new changes will take place in the Pacific? Make reports on Japan, which offers a challenging example of how people through cultural borrowing have successfully struggled to overcome extremely adverse transportation conditions.

World Community. Make inferences concerning the need for cooperation between nations that share the same rivers. Make appropriate maps following discussion and study of selected "river wars" which resulted in interstate or international water rights agreements. What was the result of these agreements in terms of transportation and irrigation uses of water? Study the vital function and role of the United Nations in finding peaceful means for mutually satisfying the interrelated and conflicting movement needs of the world's peoples and goods.

Prepare a world map locating major areas of unresolved controversy over rivers as barriers to commerce and movement of peoples. Suggest how new technological advances (other than flight) may help resolve earth surface movement difficulties experienced today. Compare maps of the industrialized Western world and of the nonindustrialized nations and make inferences concerning the extent of

> man-made physical changes these
> people will soon be making.

Basic Human Activity: Communicating Facts, Ideas, and Feelings

PROLOGUE

In geographic education a central theme (even the "philosophy" of some geographers) is regionalism. In describing a region we seek to point out the core of activities and traits which set it off from other regions. A region of activities is reflected in the common ideas, aspirations, information, and values of the people. Coal mining, grape producing, or wool growing, per se, marked by dots or symbols on a map, cannot characterize the people or their mores and beliefs. Each region has its own life style or provincialism and its own psychological responses or mental attitudes. Pupils need to learn to "read" maps and charts or look at pictures of things and develop the skills and understandings to appreciate the meaning of these man-to-thing relationships in terms of their man-to-man and man-to-spirit concomitants.

The typical slow maturation of pupils warns us that in undertaking such topics we are building readiness for these sophistications and that we certainly should not expect any set degree of "mastery." When producing sketch map series to report on any of the interactional aspects of the basic human activities classes are unavoidably also mapping the communication of information, ideas, and feelings. The educational emphasis for these social studies activities should ever be upon improving the quality of research, planning, structuring of ideas, and cartographic creativity and execution, for it would be paradoxical to present teaching-learning experiences related to this basic human activity and not stress the pupil's active involvement with meaningful information, creative ideas, and positive feelings. A potentially rich educational experience should never be stifled by a teacher's well-meaning distribution of prepared map outlines, charts, or graphs, and assigning classes a task which amounts to little more than "coloring inside the lines." A guideline for selecting the most propitious depth and breadth for any activity might be that of reasonable assurance that currently or in the near future the pupil may make meaningful use of the newly acquired skill and understanding. Just because the pupil "seems to be able" or "ought to be able" to do something is no adequate basis for assigning any curricular experience. Again, it is the teacher rather than the curriculum designer who must make the curriculum implementation decisions.

"Change is the nature of life; critical thinking and the ability to gather information and assess its meanings are essential attributes of social living in all man's communities and in all of his activities." Use this generalization to review map skills related to the basic human activity of sharing information. List symbols and other cues which describe a people's opportunity to seek and share knowledge and feelings. Make inferences concerning the best kinds of maps and reference material to consult. Discuss propaganda maps and how they distort facts and emphasize selected information. Develop a list of pitfalls faced by the map user who compares maps carelessly; give particular attention to map base data, projections, and the use of color. Collect maps produced by chambers of commerce, real-estate agents, and tourist agencies and interpret them. Compare the publicity prepared by competing public and private power and interpret. Compare publicity prepared on both sides of the "iron curtain." Review all the foregoing with the class and then help them formulate some generalizations to apply to any such problem.

The Western world has pulsed with new ideas and feelings which followed new information from the time of the Crusades until the present. Many maps are readily employed in recording the spread and impact of ideas and their related social movements.

All of the following topics might be developed through the case study approach; through current events clippings, historical references, biographies, etc., the activities could be presented or organized in story form. Map "picture statements" of the outcomes of teaching-learning experiences related to these topics might make excellent culminating devices. Topics which might be considered are:

1. The spread of religions: Judaism, Christianity, Mohammedanism, etc.
2. The spread of the ideas of modern science: Locke, Newton, etc.
3. The development of the printing press and its outcomes.
4. The development of English law and its spread.
5. The French economists and social reform movements.
6. The development of political reforms: representative government, democracy, etc.
7. The age of empire building: concept of the "white man's burden," racial superiority, etc.
8. The formation of national states and national ambitions.
9. The search for international languages (note the advent of Telstar and renewed interest in Esperanto).
10. The rise of international professional groups with interests related to science, medicine, law, banking, music, the arts, etc.

Basic Human Activity: Communicating Facts, Ideas, and Feelings

OBJECTIVES	TEACHING-LEARNING EXPERIENCES

1. *Ability to reorganize data gathered from firsthand and vicarious experiences and represent them on maps with appropriate symbols.*

   Develop knowledge of the importance to man of effective communication. Contrasts between the means of communication of yesterday and today are dramatic. The rapid development of more and better means of communication makes possible broader communities of shared facts, ideas, and feelings. Science has provided man with the ability to know his neighbor; now men must learn to use this tool for positive ends.

   Develop knowledge of how men are using new communication media. Vast networks of communication systems spanning the world flash news of disasters; help may arrive at the stricken area in a matter of hours.

   Develop knowledge of how communication makes global communities possible. Troposphere and electronic equipment now permit telephone, telegraph, and data transmission without the use of cables, thus in effect reducing the distance between men who are widely separated geographically.

   Learn to translate and interpret map, geographic, and social science data related to communicating information, ideas, and feelings. Both new and old forms of communication systems may be compared and contrasted to help the pupil appreciate the importance of communication. Mapping communication systems will help him visualize

1. *Mapping activities.*

   Inter-American Community. Discuss the role of fast and efficient systems of communication in the daily lives of people in the inter-American community. For example: information about earthquake-stricken regions are relayed to all parts of this community. Help is mobilized and dispatched within hours from major cities in the United States. Information relayed to all parts of the Pacific coast region often saves people from the tidal waves that are set up by the quake. Using a globe, measure the distance between Chile and Hawaii. Calculate the time it takes a tidal wave to travel this distance. (A tidal wave travels at a speed of approximately 460 miles per hour.) Make a large outline base map of the inter-American community.

   Locate the major communication networks such as telephone and telegraph. Note the coverage of communication systems in the United States. Include the location of television and radio stations. Use a project globe and locate these same features on it. Note the kind of map projection being used and compare the shapes of the land masses as well as the distances between places.

   Work on the project globe and suppose you are interested in seeing local television on a tour of South America. Locate the television and radio stations. Reason about these locations. Compare their number with the number found in the United States.

man's achievements in overcoming time and distance.

Atlantic Community. Employ sketch maps to capture a "picture" of the interrelationships of areal extent, areal association, and areal interaction of selected aspects of the information, ideas, and feelings men share. Help pupils prepare sketch maps, reports, and picture collections to tell the story of cultural diffusion. For example: How do people contribute their ideas of foods and their preparation to others? Prepare charts of these data. Show areal distribution of basic dishes and customary ways of preparing foods.

How have nations and peoples influenced our political ideas and practices? Trace on maps the locales which produced key ideas to our "way of life."

How is communication established between nations in the Atlantic community necessary to maintaining our system of money, credit, exchange, and banking? Study maps reporting such data and select the best means for preparing a classroom map of these data.

Pacific Community. Social studies textual materials are not always too effective at drawing attention to great commonalities and extensive sharing among peoples and nations. Continue the kinds of activities listed above. For example: Do geographical features influence diets, clothing, and shelter? Prepare comparative maps of selected Pacific regions and illustrate cultural diffusion of several elements. Is there a correlation between physical and cultural environments? Is this correlation as high in the emerging age of technology as it was previously?

How have various Pacific cultures

and nations influenced ideas about building design used by other peoples? Study pictures of buildings. Read about their distribution. Select appropriate symbols for indicating design features. Represent their distribution in this region of nations using both small- and large-scale maps.

Map the historical channels of communication throughout this region of nations. What is "saving face"? Make maps showing different national viewpoints concerning this cultural idea.

World Community. Introduce the topic by reading to the class Ralph Linton's illustration of cultural diffusion.[9] In *The Study of Man* he notes that "There is probably no culture extant today which owes more than ten per cent of its total elements to inventions made by members of its own society." Have each pupil research one or more major cultural element to trace it back to its origin. For example: What has influenced us to dress as we do; where did pants originate? Are people all over the world dressing more alike today than formerly? Prepare a bulletin-board-size world map on which each pupil may report his findings concerning sources and/or distribution of his selected element. Discuss and select the most effective means to illustrate on the map these accumulated reports.

2. *Ability to read data recorded on maps and globes.*

Develop skills in reading symbols portraying communicating features and activities. Develop the ability to translate these symbols into meaningful imagery and concep-

2. *Map-reading activities.*

Inter-American Community. Plan activities to help pupils conceptualize the pattern of communication landscape for the telephone network through northwestern Canada to Alaska. Show pictures of this

tual patterns of landscape. Maps portraying symbols pertaining to communication features and functions include the following communication systems and routes:

(1) telephone and microwave networks; trunk lines and international communication centers;
(2) telegraph stations and networks;
(3) radio networks and stations;
(4) international hookups for television systems;
(5) inter-American news service systems;
(6) radio beams for inter-American shipping and aviation;
(7) mail routes: air, land, water;
(8) newspaper, magazine, and book distribution.

Review basic concepts to extend meanings and form new associations. Develop the ability to identify new instances of communicating features and functions within the inter-American arena. Review the point and line symbols for radio stations, telephone, telegraph, and microwave lines, etc. Plan activities to help the pupils to read symbols showing the areal distributions.

Continue improving the ability to read the locations of places using a grid system, the ability to read areal symbols showing spatial distributions of communicating facilities, the ability to read scale on the globe and translate this into communication time—by airmail, for example.

network—the single telephone network with repeater stations located some seventy to a hundred miles apart. Contrast this landscape pattern with the concentration of lines in a metropolitan center. Note the relationship between central points of origin of communicating features and distribution to several nations.

Atlantic Community. Read a map showing the distribution of telephone facilities in the Atlantic community. What conceptual patterns of landscape do pupils have of regions without telephone facilities? How do you communicate with people who are separated from you by geographical space? Read maps to find the areas that are served by telephone facilities. Look for familiar communication features. Note how lines of communication connect major population centers. Do these lines extend into rural areas? What is the pattern of distribution in a rural area in contrast to that in an urban area? Help pupils to associate large centers of population with the landscape patterns of communication features.

Pacific Community. The Functional Commissions of the Economic and Social Committee (ECOSOC) provide avenues for special-interest reports by pupils. Read maps to aid understanding of U.N. activities in the Pacific region of nations. These commissions include the Human Rights Commission; International Commodity Trade; Narcotic Drugs; Population Commission; Social Commission; Statistical Commission; and Status of Women. The activities of the

Regional Economic Commissions and especially the Economic Commission for Asia and the Far East should certainly not be overlooked. The problems being faced by the commissions should be clarified by study of physical and cultural maps. Discuss how governmental structures respond to ideas and feelings. Compare communication networks in the Atlantic and Pacific communities.

World Community. As pupils study the structure of the U.N., they may be encouraged to review the site and situation of nations previously studied in "lesser" communities taking part in the U.N. General Assembly meetings. What ideas and feelings do they express? For example, the membership of the Security Council may be canvassed for representation from Pacific nations. The cases before the International Court of Justice which involve Pacific nations and/or community problems might be discussed in class. The work of the Economic and Social Council with and for peoples of the non-Western world should be considered when the activities of the Trusteeship Council are reviewed. Read maps to clarify the distance and language barriers which must be overcome. As these U.N. activities are studied, extensive use of maps of all kinds is essential. Likewise map-making and map inference skills will be called upon in order to appreciate the "message" conveyed by what does not appear on a map!

3. *Ability to interpret distribution and location on maps and globes and to reason geographically.*

Reason geographically about the location and areal distribution of

3. *Map interpretation activities.*

Inter-American Community. Note the location and distribution of many variations in the pattern and number of telephone networks, communicating features and activities. Reason geographically about the physical and cultural elements of the following: Commonwealth Relations Office; Commonwealth Agricultural Bureaus; British Commonwealth Scientific Offices; Commonwealth Shipping Committee; Commonwealth Telecommunications Board; Commonwealth Economic Consultative Board; Commonwealth Economic Committee; Commonwealth Conferences; and the work of the High Commissioners who represent member nations to one another. As part of the study of trade among members of this community pupils might consider the communication aspects of the British Commonwealth preference system and the world's sterling area.

Analyze the geographical location and areal distribution of communication phenomena as to relative location, relative distance, and relative direction. Correlate the spatial dimensions of these phenomena with other cultural features and the physical features.

Continue to develop the ability to make inferences from maps. Correlate maps showing communication patterns within selected nations with maps showing locations of headquarters of key U.N. agencies. What are the reasons for scattering the headquarters' locations?

radio stations, television stations, telegraph stations and networks, and so on. Have the students make inferences about the location patterns. Several maps are needed to gather information such as the location and areal extent of mountains, tundra, dense jungles, and so on. Note that major centers of population and industry have a concentration of communicating facilities whereas small population centers with few or no industries have limited communication facilities. Compare means of communication such as radio, telephone, telegraph of today with the carrying of messages by men of an earlier period as to the time involved. Explain the location of the major airline routes of today. Reason about the centers these airlines connect. Use the globe to explain the relative locations of these centers of communication within the inter-American community.

Atlantic Community. Put generalizations and other skills to work. For example, the British Commonwealth represents a sub-community of the Western world centered in the emerging Atlantic community which has been generally successful at maintaining communication bonds and close relationships through long periods of dramatic world changes. Why? Collect information and maps of the Commonwealth both as it appears in its world setting and for its many member nations. Review the concept of community and then study the relative and exact location of the member nations in terms of both physical and cultural phenomena. What are the bonds that can be described cartographically? What common problems and actions have the member nations taken? How were these common feelings communicated? Subtopics may include study of various Commonwealth organizations listed in the adjacent objectives column.

Pacific Community. Challenge pupils to locate with maps areas of the Pacific community where people have found that reliance (for human food) solely upon plant life will allow the earth to support more people than when the plants are fed to livestock, which in turn are used for food. What kinds of maps would best convey this information? Continue to build concepts related to ideas and feelings with the following guide questions: Is there a geographic-biotic reason why many people in certain parts of the world do not eat meat? Do social customs sometimes follow geographic-demographic dictates? What implications for diet (and for new tools and technics) do you see from studying maps of areas most hard hit by the "population explosion"?

Have the class prepare a chart listing the world's meat-producing countries, their density of population, their access to modern transportation, their standard of living, their religious beliefs concerning diet, their use of mechanical harvesting devices, and other similar correlations. Check to be sure pupils recognize map symbols for cultural distributions. Read maps of physical characteristics of these same lands.

World Community. Learn about and interpret the communication implications for maintaining these

U.N. agencies: International Bank for Reconstruction and Development (BANK), Food and Agriculture Organization (FAO), International Monetary Fund (FUND), International Civil Aviation Organization (ICAO), International Labor Organization (ILO), Inter-Governmental Maritime Consultative Organization (IMCO), International Trade Organization (ITO), United Nations Educational, Scientific and Cultural Organization (UNESCO), Universal Postal Union (UPU), World Health Organization (WHO), and World Meteorological Organization (WMO). How are people's ideas and feelings made known to these governmental bodies?

Basic Human Activity: Providing Education

PROLOGUE

Education is a process whereby we learn by sharing common ideas. History is filled with examples of individuals or small groups who have used education to further selfish objectives by restricting the flow of common ideas. Often real but solvable problems have arisen, but through use of propaganda and indoctrination selected solutions have been promoted. Seldom have these "solutions" brought lasting satisfaction to the masses of the world's peoples. The social studies program should introduce classes to the processes for solving problems rather than demanding merely the memorization of someone's selected answers. It is hoped, then, that pupils may gain insight into their own educational experiences as teachers guide the study of educational problems in the world region-of-nations communities.

Education is the means for transmitting to future generations all of the accumulated skills and understandings (culture) which man has found useful in adapting to his physical and cultural environments. One focus of the social studies is upon the phenomena which shape each nation's concept of normative and psychological needs. If an education is "good," it must be good for something. Classes must come to realize that that "something" is both different and similar for every person.

Pupils want to find out about what people do to earn their living. Young adolescents tend to develop considerable interest in vocations as for the first time they take serious stock of their future aspirations and educational plans. Charts and graphs showing ratios of various types of economic activity, extent of education, extent of unemployment, occupations threatened by technological change, population mobility, and the trend toward urbanism may be included in the social studies. Help pupils become aware of the relationship between the basic human activity of education and jobs for themselves and their peers. Once having assessed their own society's occupational patterns, they are more likely to be ready to give thoughtful consideration to the opportunities for livelihood, economic security, and a reasonable standard of living available to young people in the world's various "have" and "have-not" cultures and nations.

Pupils might strive to interpret cultural maps in order to respond to the following question: Do cultural maps give us clues as to "life styles" i.e., do cultural phenomena suggest whether an area's inhabitants "fight to overcome nature" or "accept the limitations of the physical environment"? What do various nations want from education?

With such a question as this, high-level sophistication is not to be expected, for we are concerned with readiness-building activities rather than "mastery" content areas. Thus, the teacher could help classes to search (through the various vicarious experiences available—movies, pictures, stories, maps, etc.) for the following types of clues: (1) major alterations of physical surface; (2) diversified activities, classes, beliefs; (3) evidence of resistance to change; (4) signs of population and social mobility; (5) evidence of the institutionalization of the basic human activities; (6) evidence of relative importance given to communication, transportation, trade, education, etc.; (7) evidence of interest in things, in man-to-man relationships, and in spiritual values.

Finding such clues calls for the ability to "read between the lines." But first, pupils must become aware of the nature of the "things" that might be there so as to gather meaning from the observations.

Basic Human Activity: Providing Education

OBJECTIVES	TEACHING-LEARNING EXPERIENCES
1. *Ability to reorganize data gathered from firsthand and vicarious experiences and represent them on maps with appropriate symbols.*	1. *Mapping activities.*
Develop knowledge of how man meets the universal need for education. The pupil will discover that the peoples of different national states meet the basic human activity	*Inter-American Community.* Read accounts of the school systems and facilities of various countries in the inter-American community. For instance, in Canada there are special school classrooms that travel to remote geographical areas so that the pupils there have an opportunity

of providing education in many ways. He will learn that wide variations in educational expectations and outcomes exist within nations, between nations, and among communities of nations.

Develop knowledge of how man has institutionalized educational roles and functions. In some nations there is a federal system of education; in others it is organized on a state, provincial, or even tribal basis. Opportunities for formal education vary from nation to nation. Institutions of higher learning are limited to a select sector of the population in many nations.

Develop knowledge of international aspects of education. There are colleges and universities that have assumed international characteristics because students from many nations attend them. International conferences and institutes are arranged by private, national, and international agencies to provide opportunities for the exchange of information and to develop scientific and leadership skills needed by all nations.

Learn to translate and interpret map, geographic, and social science data related to providing education. The pupil is helped to enlarge his understanding of the problems facing people striving to maintain and improve upon existent provisions for education through observation, investigation, comparative studies, discussion, reading, and mapping activities.

Develop further understanding concerning how to select base data, symbols, and means of achieving visual significance on maps so that the pupils can make effective maps to describe locations, areal extent, areal distribution, and areal

to go to school. Find out why various communities have no regular school buildings. Use a map of Canada to locate these sparsely populated regions.

International conferences in many of the basic human activities by private and governmental agencies allow people to learn from one another. Have the entire class keep a log of such conferences and meeting places during the year. Note the topics of discussion. On a map of the Western Hemisphere represent these data with appropriate symbols. Select a suitable title for the map and explain the symbols used in the key. Indicate the cardinal directions. Discuss possible reasons for the particular meeting places. Relate to communication and transportation facilities. Impose a grid system on this map. Locate the equator and the North and South Poles. Orient the map with the globe. Describe the relative location of the meeting places with regard to the equator, elevation, and the North and South Poles.

Atlantic Community. Histories of social movements abound which were nourished by new ideas and maintained by changes in education. Such events include the change in philosophy in Europe from fatalistic acceptance of "this vale of tears" to optimistic seeking for "the kingdom of heaven on earth"; the rise of the middle class to challenge the landed gentry; the rise of nationalism; the rise of democracy and representative government; the rise of mercantilism; and the development of the university. As the class takes up any one of these topics, provide historical,

interaction related to the spread of new ideas. The history of cartography provides a natural device for reviewing basic map facts and building appreciation for maps as sources of information and as educational devices.

political, and cultural maps so that the pupils may trace the changes these powerful ideas brought about. Discuss what kinds of new knowledge and skills had to be learned by workers, leaders, and professional men. Make sketch maps to locate the new universities that came into being. Help the classes make time lines, charts, and graphs to record the march of events.

Pacific Community. Discuss the "population explosion." Study the findings of demographers and convert the data into map statements. What is the challenge to education if "life styles" must be modified? Present the generalization "Population pressure begins when any considerable proportion of the inhabitants find themselves unable to achieve a minimum standard of living—what that minimum standard is depends upon the attitudes, objectives and technical abilities of the people."[10] (Introduce the concepts of function and role of the institutionalized school and the generalization that schools reflect the community. Explore the possibilities of placing selected facts from the history of education into graphic form.)

World Community. Provide map correlation experiences by asking different pupils to map (provide a common outline map) arable land, water resources, climate, relief, urbanization patterns, transportation patterns, political patterns, language patterns, educational facilities, and population distribution and density patterns for a given period of history. Have other pupils collect and present in the same map outline the same information

2. *Ability to read data recorded on maps and globes.*

Develop map reading skills in identifying symbols portraying educational phenomena. Develop the ability to translate these symbols into meaningful imagery and conceptual patterns of landscape. The essential characteristics of a university that has become internationally known cannot be adequately represented by the conventional dot or circle symbol on a small-scale map. Plan other map-reading and research exercises for the features symbolized within this arena so that pupils develop appropriate imagery. Maps portraying symbols pertaining to providing education include:

(1) institutions of higher learning, private and public;

(2) libraries, museums, art galleries, and the like;

(3) international training centers, language centers, music conservatories, art schools, etc.;

(4) education status of population distributions;

(5) areas served by school facilities;

(6) areas served by higher educational facilities.

Reinforce the ability to read the relative locations of these features and activities and the ability to read the above patterns of distribution and translate them into a conceptual system.

Discover the educational implications of the following generalization: "Differences in economic activities and kind of production from place to place result from differences in, and unequal distribution

for a later or earlier date. Discuss the meaning of the correlation and discontinuities discovered.

2. *Map-reading activities.*

Inter-American Community. A study of the effect of colonial status may be undertaken through analysis of exports and imports and restricted patterns of trade of colonial and non-colonial countries in the Western Hemisphere since European settlement. What effect did colonial status have upon educational patterns? In what ways did educational patterns in the New World differ from those in other world regions of nations? In what ways can the map describe cultural and educational facility, differences between such nations as, for example, Cuba and Mexico? Assist the children in their attempts to read maps in this way, but avoid freely supplying answers. Give information necessary to prevent them from such errors as reading "into" maps data that are not accurate. No doubt problems of prejudices and defensive rationalizing will arise because of the former colonial control once held by the United States over Cuba and because of the conflicts between ourselves and the present Cuban government. However, an important outcome of the social studies curriculum should be the ability to recognize the bias in observation and adjust accordingly.

Atlantic Community. The prior experiences of pupils have helped them to build a systematic understanding and imagery of the essential characteristics of a university—buildings containing classrooms, library facilities, and other physical structures as well as certain speci-

of natural resources, technological differences, ability and opportunity to trade, cultural differences."[11]

fic functions. A large-scale map shows the configuration of a typical campus. However, on a small-scale map of the Western Hemisphere, the abstract symbols such as points or squares give no clues as to the physical structures of universities symbolized. Nor should the pupil apply a visual image of a university campus in his local community or state. Pictures should be provided to help build accurate imagery.

What are the characteristics of an institution that has become, in a sense, international because it attracts students from all parts of the world? Read reference books to make a list of these institutions of higher learning. What are their physical structures like? What functions occur on the campuses? If possible, obtain oblique aerial photographs of several campuses. Discuss their physical structures. Read accounts of the educational activities in which the staff and students engage. Some institutions may have a single building with no campus as such; others may have many buildings.

Pacific Community. As the class proceeds into the following activities, make constant reference to the generalization included in the adjacent objectives column. Call attention to the fact that on the map the island nations of Japan and the Philippines look somewhat alike. Urge pupils to study maps, photographs, and textual materials to discover why there have been great differences in their economic activities. As soon as some ideas are collected, focus attention upon the question: Did these changes through history result from changes in each nation's educational programs? Look for evidence of borrowed ideas about education. Is the willingness to borrow ideas from other cultures good or bad? Asia "South and East" is today a land of rapid change. Pupils may be aided to conceptualize what is happening by comparative study of "Westernized" Japan and other nations now undergoing rapid industrialization such as China. Obtain or prepare large- and small-scale distributional and political-cultural maps of Japan and the Philippines for the years 1900, 1920, 1940, and 1960. Encourage pupils to record on sketch maps any significant cultural changes they might observe for each period. Does knowledge about educational activities during these periods make changes in the cultural maps more meaningful?

World Community. The following two generalizations may open up activities; support them with more general information. "People in different stages of civilization react differently to similar environments." "Men react to physical and social phenomena according to their inherent nature and according to how they have learned to react."[12]

Ask pupils the following questions: How can we explain the great differences we observe between the world's nations and regions of nations in the things people have and in the forms by which they carry on the basic human activities, even when nations may have physical environments that are much alike? Is a "good" education comprised of the same "content" and experiences regardless of the cultural level of a given social group? Have the class summarize findings and conclusions on charts and maps showing areal differentiations. Consider the functions of UNESCO in relation to these questions.

3. *Ability to interpret distribution and location represented on maps and to reason geographically.*

Reason geographically about the location and areal distribution of educational features serving nations and regions of nations. Continue to provide teaching-learning experiences designed to help pupils to compare the distributions shown on a map with the patterns on another.

Analyze these geographical locations and distributions of educational phenomena as to relative location, relative distance, and relative direction. Correlate the spatial dimensions of educational phenomena with other cultural features and with physical features.

Develop the ability to make inferences from maps to answer questions such as the following: Is there a relationship between economic-technological development of a nation and the level of education achieved by its population? What is the relationship between the degree of developed natural resources and the population's average level of educational achievement? Is there a relationship between size of cities and the educational level of their population? Is this relationship direct or inverse? In what kinds of societies do you find the direct relationship exists? Is there an apparent relationship between "races" and educational aptitude and achievement? What are the causes of any correlations that are discovered? Biological? Geographical? Cultural? Is there a relationship between lati-

3. *Map interpretation activities.*

Inter-American Community. Note that the large internationally known universities are located in or near large metropolitan centers in the inter-American community. Why? Two maps are needed; one showing the location of institutions of higher learning and one showing the major centers of population. Reason about the location of major educational conferences in the inter-American community, for example. What are their relative locations in terms of air travel from major centers of population in each of the nations involved? What inference might one make with respect to the educational levels of people living in a country where there are few public and private elementary and secondary schools? Few public and private colleges and universities? How large an area is served by these institutions of higher learning? Have the class select a nation and gather data for a map showing the extent and distribution of literate people who have completed schooling at the elementary, secondary, and college levels. Correlate these findings with other cultural and physical data about the nation and make inferences about the kinds of curriculum in these schools and what the future may bring to these nations.

Atlantic Community. Study maps and other materials to discover what degree of correlation exists between average level of education and such things as gross national

tude and education level? What inferences or hypotheses might explain the correlation you find? In the future, should this latitude-educational level correlation increase or decrease? Why? What correlation is there between the average length of working day and the achieved educational level of the general population? What inferences might you make concerning the importance of leisure time to improving man's adaptation to his physical environment? Is leisure time a cause or an effect of improved cultural tools and technics (in education especially) for adapting to environment? Is progress possible without some escape from subsistence level of life? What is the relationship between a people's religious and philosophical beliefs and the kinds of educational institutions they establish? Is there any correlation between such beliefs and the speed of social and cultural change experienced by a nation? Is the level of technology achieved related in some way to all of the questions raised above?

product, technological development, standard of living, leadership in world affairs, average life expectancy, and average per family income. Refer to the questions in the adjacent objectives column. Discuss the findings with the class. What generalizations can the class make after analyzing their findings? Follow up with consideration of these questions: What additional knowledge and skills are needed to attack such problems? What level of sophistication in map-reading skills and abilities has been attained? What kinds of important problems in the future will pupils be attacking with their ability to read "between the lines" of maps?

Pacific Community. Guide pupils in their use of a wide variety of mapped information and other graphic and verbal materials. Topics, problems, and projects for analyzing and interpreting geographic and education implications might include:

(1) checking various maps of the Pacific region of nations to become informed about distributions of climate, soil, vegetation, elevations, weather, etc., to see if culturally different areas are ever physically alike;

(2) checking maps of cultural phenomena so as to classify areas of similarity and dissimilarity so that correlations may be run on physical and cultural environments;

(3) checking the history of selected Pacific region nations (using historical maps) to find out what changes have occurred over time;

(4) discussing and thinking about

the differences between dynamic and static societies;

(5) reviewing the basic human activities in terms of the necessary "accumulation of culture" which is requisite to the way of life, for example, of farmers in Thailand, the Australian bush aborigines, the factory workers in Tokyo, or the copra gatherers of Polynesia;

(6) guiding study of the transition of the Philippines to illustrate how primitive peoples through education and opportunity have "leaped into the twentieth century;"

(7) drawing together these and other facts to guide pupils into expressing the relationship between level of education and form of adaptation to environment, being sure that they recognize that the multiplicity of viable and useful ways of living are all relative and that ideas of what is "acceptable" are changing rapidly in developing nations today.

Interpret maps and social studies data to discover any correlations suggesting the educational implications of the following:

(1) crop patterns: ratios and distribution;

(2) population: density and distribution;

(3) average number of inhabitants per household;

(4) energy sources—ratio of man to animal, machine;

(5) life expectancy at birth and at age ten;

(6) average per capita caloric and protein intake;

(7) ratio of export and import to

World Community. The geographic and social studies topics in the adjacent column suggest problems and inter-relationships which might be considered as classes use maps, pictures, and textual materials to generate inferences concerning the nature of Western and non-Western cultures in terms of their problems (and hopes) in obtaining education to meet changing needs (the project for the class as a whole will be to bring these factors together meaningfully).

local consumption;
(8) average years of schooling, rural and urban;
(9) average per capita income, rural and urban;
(10) interactional patterns of organizing and governing and education.

Basic Human Activity: Providing Recreation

PROLOGUE

This basic human activity might better be described as obtaining recreation, for recreation means re-creating, a refreshment of strength and spirits after toil, a diversion, or play. In American society recreation is all too often coming to mean play for the sake of play and play as trifling rather than as active engagement. Providing recreation has begun to be confused with providing entertainment, supplying "things to look at" rather than "things to do." Recreation has tended to become "fun" rather than enrichment and fulfillment.

Sociologists have called attention to the shift from the Puritan "work ethic" to the modern-day "fun ethic," a shift which leaves Americans with conflicting criterion measures as well as emotions. Henry suggests,

> Mr. Average American enters the occupational structure doing what he has to do rather than what he has dreamed of doing, and he buries his lifetime disappointment under a mountain of consumer goods. . . . [Hence] fun is the American lotus, the food of forgetfulness. . . . Where does American education fit here? The American system is torn between the old ideals of self-denial and achievement, and the new impulse toward permissiveness and toward ministering to the inner needs of the young child, who is really but the embodiment of our buried selves.[13]

Henry's comments might well warn us that the youth's recreational interests may be poorly guided. Suffice it to say that the school, through the curriculum, must provide for the establishment of desirable psychological sets (or plan to break old sets). It may well be that most Americans today no longer can readily appreciate that which they do not enjoy—but what they have learned to "enjoy" may not be really satisfying their need for recreation.

The social studies program, then, can make an important contribution by helping pupils to realize that recreation should be "building anew" rather than "escape." Hence, the study of recreation in the regions of nations might well seek to emphasize the root *creation* in recreation and emphasize the worthy use of leisure time. In modern technological societies, leisure time is becoming a social problem rather than a social blessing.

Of course recreation has natural appeal, to be capitalized upon in the social studies curriculum. Child and adult literature concerning peoples of other nations may provide much useful information, and pupils may enjoy playing detective in an effort to build a body of information concerning the leisure activities among the world's diverse cultures.

Basic Human Activity: Providing Recreation

OBJECTIVES

1. *Ability to reorganize data gathered from firsthand and vicarious experiences and represent them on maps with appropriate symbols.*

Develop knowledge of how man's values are reflected in his concept of recreation. While providing recreation is one of the basic human activities at all community levels, the ways of carrying out these activities and the values each culture places on them vary from one culture to the next.

Develop knowledge of how industrialization has led to mass forms of recreation. In many pre-industrial and transitional cultures providing recreation is centered in the home and the local community in contrast to mass commercialized types of entertainment appearing commonly in urban industrial cultures.

Develop knowledge of how man's creative and recreational activities may foster new feelings of belonging to a larger community. The cultural activities of all peoples provide colorful recreational outlets that often attract tourists from other parts of the world. The individual may discover shared recreational interests with peoples of distant nations, which in turn lead to other

TEACHING-LEARNING EXPERIENCES

1. *Mapping activities.*

Inter-American Community. Several members of the class may have had firsthand experiences in visiting places in either Canada or Mexico that have assumed international characteristics because people from all parts of the inter-American community visit and use them for recreation. Ask these pupils to describe the recreational facilities, both cultural and natural, and their distribution. Travel brochures, pictures, maps, etc., may be shown to the class and discussed.

Contrast these facilities with the state and national facilities in the United States as to form, function, and distribution. What opportunities for sports do these places provide? Are the activities related to the weather of the region? Are the facilities used by the people of the particular locality? If so, what segment of the population?

What holidays and festivals do the various nations celebrate that attract international visitors, and in which ones do all the people of the nation take part? Suppose one were interested in seeing native Indian dances; on a map place symbols to show the locations where they take place throughout the

awarenesses of commonalities.

Learn to translate and interpret map, geographic, and social science data related to providing recreational opportunities for the world's exploding populations. Maps come into a variety of natural uses in any consideration of or planning for recreational experiences. The pupil may gain new perspectives on social problems as he is guided to think critically about providing for as well as enjoyment of recreational opportunities.

Americas. What is the pattern of distribution? Help the class to understand that large segments of the populations of many nations in the inter-American community do not have incomes large enough to permit spending money on golfing, skiing, seeing a variety of Indian dances, etc.

Make a class map of recreational facilities that tourists from all parts of the inter-American community use. Make another map showing the cultural and recreational activities that involve all the people of the nation. Give these maps appropriate titles. In the map key explain the symbols used. Work on a globe and assume it is January. On the globe place the resorts or places you might ski.

Atlantic Community. Assign the production of large-scale sketch maps of famous recreation spots in Europe. Reinforce skills by requiring pupils to develop their own appropriate symbols, scale, orientations and grid systems. These maps should report accurately such facts as terrain, climatic features, location of sports areas, art centers, commercial entertainment "spots," scenic tours, zoos, etc. Ask several pupils to combine their sketch maps to produce a large bulletin-board-size small-scale map of Europe showing the spatial locations or distributions of their several findings.

Pacific Community. Have interested pupils plan a summer tour of selected "places of interest" in the Pacific region of nations. Help them gather data, make inferences, and then, using maps, compute such pre-trip information as: how many miles will be traveled by air?

by train? by auto? by boat? Map the trip choosing appropriate symbols, legends, scale, and comparative sequences. How is such a tour considered to be recreation? Direct pupils' attention to the fact that seeing and learning about new things can be recreation.

World Community. In order to enhance "research" skills as well as to produce more useful data concerning travel, recreation, and map utilization, assign pupils the task of planning a tour with a fixed budget. Establish a number of hypothetical one-month tours. Organize the class into competing teams whose task it is to preplan trips so as to "get the most" out of of both the time and money available. Consult travel agencies. Find as resource people those who have recently made trips abroad. Gather data on travel costs, medical and political screening, etc. Some pupils may be interested in setting up a full schedule of arrival and departure times for the complete itinerary of their group's selected tour. Others may be interested in planning suitable clothing for both the climatic conditions and the places they wish to visit (sports, museums, theaters, etc.). Have each team collect maps, pictures, and verbal materials which explain and/or justify their plans. When the plans are completed have class discussions to point out the strengths and weaknesses of proposals.

2. *Ability to read data recorded on maps and globes.*

Develop skills in identifying symbols portraying recreational phenomena. These symbols include point symbols for parks, stadiums, playgrounds, polo grounds, race

2. *Map-reading activities.*

Inter-American Community. In learning to read maps portraying recreational features and activities pupils should understand the meaning of the concepts symbolized. Have class discussions, dramatiza-

car speedway, skating rinks, curling rinks, Olympic Games, etc.; line symbols for boundaries of national parks, recreational districts, ski trails, boat cruises, etc.; area symbols for sandy beaches, state and national parks, hunting areas, fishing areas, lake regions, etc. Develop the ability to translate these symbols into meaningful imagery.

Become familiar with maps showing recreational features including international public recreational areas and institutions, international commercial recreational areas and institutions, national parks and monuments, sport fishing and hunting, winter sports, spectator sports, cultural features such as cities, fair or exhibition grounds, etc.

Develop the ability to interpret the patterns of distribution and relative locations of the recreational phenomena in any of the world regions of nations.

tions, and other activities to help develop and extend meanings of various kinds of recreational phenomena characterizing the inter-American community. For instance, have two committees plan make-believe recreational trips, one group to make use of natural recreational areas and the other to visit commercial recreational establishments. Where are the commercial facilities located? How prominent are they in the landscape? Who participates? In what sports, for example? Are there spectators? Are recreational activities all healthful? How do large-scale maps of recreational areas suggest answers to these questions?

Atlantic Community. Discuss pictures showing the famous auto races in Europe. Obtain maps of the racecourses. Can the class determine the special driving problems posed by different tracks and courses by study of large-scale maps? What kinds of maps would be useful in addition to the course layout description? What kinds of pictures or verbal descriptions are necessary to visualize reality? Find out what kinds of maps racers use in preplanning long-distance bicycle marathons. Can maps help the spectator decide where to position himself? Where will TV cameras be placed? Show on maps the areas of the world which will receive broadcasts of special sports events from Europe or the Americas.

Pacific Community. Compare the use of the symbols listed in the adjacent objectives column on small-scale maps and large-scale maps. Read patterns of distributions.

What additional symbols must be used (or created) in order to map the recreational activities of peoples among countries of the Pacific region of nations? Where will large-scale maps be helpful in a study of recreation? Small-scale? What kinds of small-scale map bases would be most useful for comparative studies? What kinds of symbols will be used to report a variety of activities in a restricted physical area? Have pupils prepare maps following research activities and then exchange with other pupils to criticize readability and appropriateness of selected map devices.

World Community. Gather information about the Olympic Games. Where have these events been held in the past? Prepare maps showing the participant nations in any given year. Read commercial maps and advertisements to help choose appropriate means for representing the features and activities on maps. Plan appropriate map-reading activities for review of the symbols listed in the adjacent objectives column. What U.N. agencies take an active interest in this basic human activity? Locate on maps where the headquarters of these agencies are located. Were these cities selected for advantages of communication? Transportation? Education? Organizing and governing?

3. *Ability to interpret distribution and location on maps and to reason geographically.*

Analyze relative location in terms of population. What is the nature of this population? Are there restrictions on where the people may live?

Interpret relative distance. How

3. *Map-reading activities.*
(Refer to "Aids for Teaching," Appendix A.)

Inter-American Community. Relate to population distributions. Are the transportation facilities of a region a factor in producing recreational areas? Is there any pattern for the provision of recreational fa-

far to get to areas of recreation in the various regions of the world?

Reason geographically concerning recreational phenomena characteristic of various physical and cultural environmental settings. How are physical and cultural factors such as weather, terrain, or customs and holidays taken into account in recreational planning?

Develop the ability to make inferences from maps. The "thinking out" of sources and the active search for data are key learning opportunities from which the pupil should profit. In the junior high school, pupils who have developed useful skills and understandings generally should be given opportunities to put this knowledge into practice in order to solve their own research and reporting problems.

cilities by governmental agencies? Commercial agencies? What are the future developments in providing recreation for people? Will there be more outdoor facilities for people who live in metropolitan areas? Where would you believe the next Pan-American games can be held? Why?

Atlantic Community. Interpret the patterns of distribution of cultural recreation features and natural recreation features. Do specific combinations of environmental conditions produce recreational areas? Reason about the great tourist attractions of large cities. Pupils have already considered recreational activities in their study of lesser communities. They also are becoming familiar with the many activities and customs of Americans which were borrowed from other nations and particularly from the Atlantic community. The teacher might encourage pupils to study the leisure-time activities of various nations; compare and map their findings with what they know about recreation in the United States.

Pacific Community. Are natural recreation areas located in rural areas? What kinds of recreational phenomena characterize mountainous regions? Coastal regions? Plains areas? Use climate maps of the regions to interpret your answers.

The findings of the class may be pooled and reported on a bulletin-board-size map. Effective displays might be developed of pictures and realia gathered by people in the school district who have visited nations in this part of the world. Travel magazines and especially the *National Geographic* are a rich source of pictures and information. The school librarian should be consulted. Certainly travel agencies should be queried, and "pen pals" may provide much interesting information.

World Community. "Recreational activities around the world" may be the theme for a teaching-learning experience which can employ all of the child's developing map skills and understandings. The following questions may suggest activities:

(1) What is the correlation between latitude and sports?

(2) What is the correlation between altitude and sports?

(3) What is the correlation between terrain and sports?

(4) What are the recreational activities having to do with rivers? With mountains? With oceans? With the skies? In the open country? In the cities? In homes?

(5) What are the recreational activities which stress the intellect? The muscles? Individual effort? Teamwork? Competition?

(6) What are the recreational activities of children? Of adults? Of the elderly?

(7) What are the game fish and animals of the world?

(8) What were the recreational activities of 1000 years ago? of 500 years ago? Of 100 years ago?

(9) What are common hobbies around the world?

(10) What are the favorite musical instruments around the world? The favorite musical forms? The favorite dances?

(11) Who are the authors most read around the world?
This list will naturally be expanded according to the interests of the pupils. All findings may be reported on various types of maps using a variety of reporting systems.

Basic Human Activity: Organizing and Governing

PROLOGUE

A useful conceptual grasp of organizing and governing should yield the generalization that every basic human activity must to some degree and in some form be organized and governed. Organizing and governing, then, must be considered briefly as each of the basic human activities is studied in each nation and region of nations. Regardless of the subject matter emphasis in the social studies, a desirable outcome is the achievement of a sense of involvement and purpose, and the acceptance of personal responsibility to see that good government under law prevails.

Knowledge of civics and the constitutional history of the United States is important, but of no less importance are learning to solve problems, developing positive attitudes, and mastering intellectual skills requisite to the assumption of citizenship responsibilities in each of the expanding communities of men. Map work directly and indirectly can help build the necessary knowledge and the intellectual skills.

Many ways of stressing the functional and interactional aspects of organizing and governing must be pursued. Geography as merely name and location of capital city, seat of government, political division and subdivisions (denoted by point, line, and area map symbol) can be "learned" without meaningful outcomes and without intellectual growth. The geographic questions of *what, where, how* and *why* must be asked again and again about aspects of organizing and governing and the other basic human activities to the full limit that the maturity and interest of the learners permit.

Teachers at each grade level must work to structure the scope and sequence of representative nations and specific subject matter content in order to construct the most effective teaching-learning experiences. There are more meaningful teaching-learning contexts for organizing and governing than are offered by "pure" political science and history; every effort must be made to enrich the social studies.

Previous social studies experiences in the middle school grades will have helped pupils become familiar with the functions and roles of a nation's political organizations. Now the concept will be developed that peoples in other nations hold many different expectations and criteria concerning "good" government. Social studies activities should help classes to appreciate how political differences and commonalities evolve in response to changes in the meaning to men of their physical and cultural environments. While maps are useful for describing the relative and exact location and areal extent of nations and communities of nations, they cannot indicate the nature or quality of experienced human interrelationships. Hence, social studies teaching-learning activities must strive to build broad knowledge and intellectual skills so that maps will be read meaningfully, thoughtful inferences can be generated, and comparative studies can prove profitable. Reading maps calls for more than use of map symbols; out of their studies and discussions pupils should become more aware of the relative meanings of barriers, corridors, and political boundaries.

Sooner or later as pupils study political maps a question will arise concerning why certain locations in the world have produced a number of small countries crowded together. Perhaps the teacher deliberately will draw attention to this fact in order to encourage pupils to apply their powers of interpretation.

The teacher should direct pupils to study maps of the "cockpit of Europe," i.e., the lowland countries through which flow the Rhine, Meuse, and Scheldt rivers. Maps used should include those describing the distribution of physical and cultural phenomena of those countries in particular and of western Europe in general. Once the class is aware that this area is a trade and communications center of great importance, the teacher must ask, "Why have the powerful nations not taken over these lands?" Whether or not the pupils "guess" the correct answer, the teacher should direct them to investigate the history of the "balance of power" concept. The difference between "buffer states" and the strategy of turning over geographically important locations to the control of weak states so that powerful rivals could avoid the direct competition which breeds war should be studied through maps and reference materials. Where empires and colonizing powers found competition costly, the result was fragmented countries and distorted boundaries such as those found between India and China, southeastern Europe and Asia Minor, and the so-called Pamir Knot where Russia, China, Afghanistan, Pakistan, and Kashmir all come together in an area of almost impassable mountains. The teacher might raise the question whether this trend of splintering may be reversed by new technology in the future. What are the advantages and disadvantages of consolidation? Of fragmentation?

As pupils come to appreciate the nature of political boundaries after having learned of the various physical, historical, social, and psychological causes for their existence, they will read maps more effectively and will be better able to attempt interpretations.

Basic Human Activity: Organizing and Governing

OBJECTIVES

TEACHING-LEARNING ACTIVITIES

1. *Ability to reorganize data gathered from firsthand and vicarious experiences and represent them on maps with appropriate symbols.*

Develop knowledge of forms of organizing and governing for political reasons. In the region-of-nations communities there are many independent political subdivisions illustrating the full range of political institutions created to conduct the processes of organizing and governing.

Develop knowledge of forms of organizing and governing for non-political reasons. Among examples of international arrangements established by private enterprise are the corporations devoted to obtaining foodstuffs and industrial raw materials for distant markets. There are also international educational organizations, architectural associations, medical societies, scientific institutes for exchanging information, International Boy and Girl Scouts.

Develop knowledge of forms of organizing and governing for international cooperation. Selected studies of such organizations as the OAS in the inter-American sub-community, NATO in the Atlantic, SEATO in the Pacific, and the U.N. in the world communities provide pupils opportunities to become knowledgeable of the means national communities are employing to solve mutual political, social, and economic problems through joint planning.

Learn to translate and interpret map, geographic, and social science

1. *Mapping activities.*

Inter-American Community. Discuss ways in which several nations can work together to solve common problems. For example, Canada and the United States have worked very closely together in solving a common transportation problem along the St. Lawrence River. Other nations have entered into agreements to work on health, education, and housing problems. Read accounts of the Organization of American States. What nations are members of this organization? Does it include the entire Western Hemisphere? Find where its activities are centralized. Get a picture of the headquarters building and the beautiful gardens that surround it. Discuss some of the work of its agencies. For example, the Institute of Agricultural Sciences promotes soil conservation, production methods, and technical education in three centers: Havana, Cuba; Lima, Peru; and Montevideo, Uruguay. On a large base map of the Western Hemisphere show the member nations of the OAS. Locate the regional centers that have been established to provide various kinds of education designed to improve agricultural production, health practices, and rural life. Locate the Pan American Union building in Washington, D.C. Choose appropriate point symbols to show the locations of these various functions. Explain the symbols in the key. Use this map in your class discussions of the work of the OAS. Make a

data related to organizing and governing. Include study of directly and indirectly related topics which require the child to build functional concepts and the ability to visualize the physical and human characteristics of institutionalized organizing and governing activities, both formal and informal.

map showing the activities of a private corporation that is organized throughout the inter-American community.

Atlantic Community. Help students select appropriate symbols, bases, and cartographic techniques to map inter- (and intra-) national frictions, groupings, neutrals, and activists in terms of site and situation as well as areal extent and distribution. Have the class prepare a series of areal interaction maps to illustrate how technological changes have altered trade-flow patterns (both internal and external) in the nations selected for study and among nations in the Atlantic community. Use maps to indicate the continued holdings and activities of European nations in this world region of nations.

Pacific Community. Build concepts concerning organizing and governing through study of the history of movements across the Pacific and of political struggles between peoples and dynasties of island and mainland cultures. In the subsequent studies use current events to emphasize political and economic problems and comparative aspects of selected Pacific nations. Study former colonies and emerging nations which are making the transitional leap into the twentieth century. Discuss the technologically caused changes in economic needs, social beliefs, and behavior standards.

World Community. Make a study of the organizational patterns of family and local community life in the Western and non-Western worlds. Discuss contrasting concepts of authority and social philosophy compared with practices in the pupils' more immediate experiences.

Encourage the invention of symbol systems and cartographic devices where conventional symbols are not available to depict and report the distributions of life styles and philosophies around the world. Encourage the use of sketch maps of areal extent, association, and interaction to accompany pictures, prepared graphs and written materials used in culminating reports. The United Nations and its various agencies furnish a wealth of material on world efforts in this basic human activity of organizing and governing.

2. *Ability to read data recorded on maps and globes.*

Develop skills in identifying symbols portraying organizing and governing functions. Develop the ability to translate these symbols into meaningful imagery. Maps pertaining to organizing and governing functions include:

(1) nations, colonies, territories and other dependencies;

(2) lesser political divisions: provinces, states, counties, precincts, etc.;

(3) metropolitan areas, cities, towns, villages;

(4) centers of government: capitals of nations, states, provinces, counties;

(5) nations at war, war allies;

(6) international agreements, political, social, economic, or educational;

(7) historical aspects of these political organizations.

Develop the ability to read areal

2. *Map-reading activities.*

Inter-American Community. Help pupils to develop meanings for the symbols used on maps that portray organizing and governing features. Have class discussions and dramatizations, and show motion pictures along with photographs to extend concepts introduced previously.

For example, the concept of boundaries may be discussed. Disputes over the location of international boundaries have resulted in wars in South America. Develop an understanding that the boundaries between nations are not visible landscape features. In some cases a river serves as the boundary line. However, when the river shifts its course, where is the boundary? Since many areas in South America have not been surveyed, they are open to dispute. Study rough survey maps. See if a local surveyor can take the class on a field trip. Visualize the diffi-

distributions, relative locations, and relative distance along with reading directions, scale, location, and simple map projections. Learn to use point symbols for the centers of volunteer agencies, international cooperative agencies, schools, health centers, etc.; line symbols to show international boundaries, areas of cooperative action, lines of communication, routes of travel, etc.; areal symbols for political divisions, cooperating nations, distribution of activities, etc.

Evaluate the graphic devices employed on maps to determine why certain symbols, bases, legends, titles, lettering, and sketching techniques were more effective than others.

Develop standards of accuracy. Seek to improve the use of maps and to demonstrate, locate, and report. Give attention to using several maps concurrently for comparative purposes in support of social science principles and methods.

culties in mountainous or jungle terrain.

Atlantic Community. Select a European nation for study. Read a relief map which also shows the political divisions. Where would the terrain present problems in determining or maintaining boundaries? See if photographs of these regions are available. Have pupils trace international boundaries of Africa and Europe on wall maps and the globe. Study sets of maps which record the changing political boundaries in this region of nations during the past century. Make an organizing and governing map of Europe employing the cartographic devices listed in the adjacent objectives column.

Pacific Community. Read about and locate the areal extent of the African-Asian "Bandung" states and the remaining European colonies and dependencies. Use the globe to locate world tension spots. Trace the frontiers of the communist bloc, which constitutes a generally unbroken line of upheavals caused by expansionist activities. Discuss and locate places in Africa, India, and Indonesia, and in the United States, where tensions are rising from efforts of "disadvantaged" citizens (racial and religious groups) to obtain political equality and/or nationhood. Through guided map reading help pupils to see the world scope of political problems and to appreciate that racial and religious political discriminations are not "cured" by simple legislation.

World Community. Study the United Nations. Use maps to trace the developmental history of the

U.N. which began in 1945 with 51 nations, doubled in size in 17 years, and reached a membership of 115 by 1965. Which nations now seek admission? Which have chosen to remain neutral? Why? For geographic reasons? Which newly formed nations are now being admitted? Do not use verbalized material when the same may be read from maps. Use maps to gather data, to compute and translate the information into new graphic form, and then report key facts in a new statement on a prepared outline map or with a freehand sketch map. Utilize the globe or polar projection frequently in order that relative locations are properly visualized and conceptualized and interpretations can be soundly based.

3. *Ability to interpret location and distribution on maps and globes and to reason about them geographically.*

Reason geographically about the location and distribution of the organizing and governing activities people carry on in the several region-of-nations communities.

Guide the development of the ability to understand and apply these generalizations by Kenworthy:
(1) Many of our ideas of government were obtained from people in other countries and several nations have adopted aspects of our government in their countries.
(2) There are many forms of government in the world today, including monarchies, constitutional monarchies, social democracies, capitalistic democracies, fascist regimes, and Communist governments.
(3) The form of government in any country is determined by

3. *Map interpretation activities.*

Inter-American Community. Discuss the location of the Institute of Agricultural Science's technical training centers:
(1) relative location of these centers: What are they near? Population centers? Rural areas? What geographical considerations determined their locations?
(2) relative direction: How large an area is served? Is it in mountainous regions?
(3) relative distances: What are the landforms of the regions? How are distances to centers influenced by these landforms?
Interpret the geographical location of the headquarters of the OAS. Compute the distance from the capitals of the member nations. Are there any drawbacks because of the location?

Atlantic Community. Use Kenworthy's concepts in the adjacent

many factors, among which are its economic status, its religion or religions, and its history.

(4) Several nations have recently won their independence and have set up their own governments. Others are still demanding a chance to form their own independent regimes.

(5) There is a great deal of competition around the world today between the various forms of government. This competition has caused "cold wars" and actual warfare.

(6) All governments have problems to solve and will continue to have problems in the future. Governments, however, do solve some problems.

(7) Over the centuries governments have been organized for larger and larger groups of people, ranging in size from clans and tribes to whole nations.

(8) There are some regional governmental organizations in the world today, plus the United Nations and its agencies.[14]

Keep in mind the broad ability and skill objectives which may be achieved. The above concepts (1), (2), (4), (7), and (8) all call for exact location reading skills. Some interesting aspects of relative location may be explored as pupils pose hypotheses concerning observed correlations and cause and effect. Concepts (3), (5), and (6) demand that pupils "dig into" facts and concepts from the several social sciences as well as undertaking some geographic thinking.

objectives column to begin the study of a selected emerging nation in Africa. Discuss its cultural traditions, mercantilism, industrialism, and nationalism. Use maps to trace the diffusion and distribution of ethnic groups, resources, economic development, political patterns, physical regions, and climatic regions in order to make generalizations concerning the nation's past and present problems of organizing and governing. Use "then and now" comparative maps and charts to help pupils visualize how modern technology is altering the patterns and meanings of political boundaries and associations.

Pacific Community. World War II drastically changed the relationships between the United States and the nations of the emerging Pacific community. Pupils may be helped to visualize and conceptualize the nature of these new commitments and their related responsibilities by interpreting "before and after" comparative maps of:

(1) nations with which we have defense agreements (Australia, East New Guinea, British Borneo, Malaya, South Vietnam, Siam, Formosa, Philippines, South Korea, Japan, and Canada);

(2) islands controlled by the United States (Aleutians, Midway, Marshalls, Carolines, Wake, Marianas, Bonins, and Ryukyus);

(3) the vast area of the world under communism;

(4) the areas and nations which are "neutral" or uncommitted.

Use pictures, movies, records, and textual materials as well as maps to introduce pupils to the lands and nations of the Pacific community. Help classes to become aware of their own indirect personal involvement and interest in the problems of these peoples.

The historic political connections between English-speaking nations (the United States, Australia, and New Zealand) resulted in the 1951 Anzus treaty (Pacific Security Treaty). Use this fact to explore political concepts underlying this question: Which seems to have more influence in determining political alliances: similar physical environments or similar cultural traditions? Might this change? How? Study terrain maps to see if there was physical "causality" behind observed international cooperation. Study trade-flow pattern maps to clarify why the Anzus group included New Zealand but not Java, British Borneo, or Malaya.

The modern history of China might be reviewed in conjunction with the formation of the South-East Asia Collective Defense Treaty (SEATO), which saw the Anzus group joined by Britain, France, Pakistan, Siam, and the Philippines. Inferences about the reasons for joining SEATO would help students appreciate the ties between the Western and non-Western communities.

World Community. On a broader level, study of the Western world's long history of political transition will disclose constant shifting of national boundaries and the formation and disappearance of many states. Attempting to interpret a series of historical physical-political maps will help pupils realize that knowledge of exact location and areal extent, while useful, is only the beginning. Teach, through illustration, the principle that maps and geography measure the meaning and significance of things by the *area* they take up on the map and by the intensity of the development of an area (i.e., *distance* and *density* describe the *significance* of mapped phenomena). Make comparative map studies of selected countries to answer these questions: Did the industrial revolution change the meanings of observed distances and densities in the Western world? Does physical size denote importance? Does population density denote political strength or effective government?

Generally, all nations claim exclusive sovereignty over the air space above their territories. Is this an appropriate "right" in an air age? Current events provide ample sources for the study of the consequences of this national political claim. Patrol planes get off course and are shot down. Disputes over territorial waters might be considered and mapped. "Spy in the sky" problems abound (whether camera-carrying "U-2" planes or television-carrying rocket satellites). Even the "race for space" has major political implications.

Trace world international flight patterns and flight patterns between major world capitals. Use polar projections and great-circle routes to illustrate what the flight patterns could be if roundabout "politically necessary" routes were not requisite.

Help pupils to realize by study of terrain maps that physical barriers to travel have been significantly reduced. Point out that political barriers cause more trouble today than physical ones. Might this change too? How?

Basic Human Activity: Expressing and Satisfying Aesthetic and Spiritual Needs

PROLOGUE

This basic human activity is one of the most difficult to adapt to teaching-learning experiences outside of specialized courses in art, philosophy, and religion. Teachers may find it rather hard to help pupils separate and categorize all of the ideas and feelings which are slowly coming into their awareness.

Typically, the background of the social studies teacher prepares him primarily to "talk about" or to "study about" things that are spiritual and aesthetic. For this reason he should draw upon the services of specialists if fruitful teaching-learning experiences are to be provided. The social studies teacher should be prepared to guide pupils in their thinking about and search for information concerning the where, when, and who aspects of the basic human activities but should not be expected to be proficient in establishing criteria for judging artistic merits (the what, how, and why) or ultimate values.

What is involved in this basic human activity?

The spiritual refers to the non-visible realm of phenomena influencing man's behavior—to the intellectual and the moral. Aesthetic refers to "taste" in identifying the beautiful—to discovering a "good" in something that does not include its utility. These are rather nebulous ideas and are difficult to convey to others, for "beauty lies in the eye of the beholder." People with absolute notions of the good, true, and beautiful may have no reservations about imposing their prejudices upon pupils concerning the world's "artless" or "non-spiritual" peoples or nations, but such "teaching" has no rightful place in the American public schools. However, it may be assumed that there are resource people who can help the social studies teacher provide pupils with experiences which will help them better understand and appreciate the social implications of spiritual and aesthetic impulses.

The following guidelines by Peck help us select concepts and generalizations concerning aesthetics.

> In this context generalizations about man as he seeks to satisfy his esthetic needs and impulses become eligible for inclusion if they are about:
> (1) Man in the production and use of art objects or objects which are produced or used for the pleasure they give.
> (2) Man in participation in the activities of the arts.
> (3) Man as he is affected by the emotional or sense qualities of his environment.[15]

Pupils probably will need help in reviewing all of their previous studies, and, again, an art specialist may be of great assistance. Classes should be encouraged to observe their own community and society in light of what they have discovered about other peoples in other nations. Do people everywhere "love" nature—flowers, animals, the mountains, the seashore, the colors and movement in the skies during the day and night, etc.? Do all people sing, draw, make up poems? Are all people concerned with the "style" of their clothing, tools, buildings, etc.? Does graceful movement and form bring admiration from observers whether exhibited in dance, bullfighting, or baseball's "perfect" double play? Are honesty, good will, respect, responsibility, integrity, etc., appreciated by all people?

Are aesthetic and spiritual elements mappable? Can pupils demonstrate their growth in and awareness of aesthetics through the quality of exactness, harmony, and creativeness revealed in their maps and other social studies projects? Do good maps illustrate beauty of line, form, color, and honesty?

Basic Human Activity: Expressing and Satisfying Aesthetic and Spiritual Needs

OBJECTIVES	TEACHING-LEARNING EXPERIENCES
1. *Ability to reorganize data gathered from firsthand and vicarious experiences and represent them on maps with appropriate symbols.* Develop knowledge of mankind's aesthetic and spiritual riches. Study of any nation reveals examples of these needs and values shared by its people. Each newly studied culture should help the pupil become more aware of this basic human activity in his life. Develop knowledge of how cultural borrowing enriches human life. Pupils should be aware of the sources of their own values and of the music, art, literary forms, and spiritual activities which they are learning to appreciate and enjoy. Develop knowledge of how traditions of spiritual and aesthetic expressions shape and constitute supranational communities. Our	1. *Mapping activities.* *Inter-American Community.* Begin with a discussion of the many ways people in the United States express aesthetic and spiritual impulses and note how the various forms of expression vary from one region of our national community to another. Would we expect to find this range of expression in the nations of the inter-American region? Read books and other printed material about and collect pictures of the activities of people in the various parts of the inter-American community that have assumed international characteristics: religious festivals in the Central and South American nations, like the pilgrimage to the shrine at Copacabana on the shore of Lake Titicaca; the handicraft arts of the artisans who live in Taxco, Mexico; the ballet activities of the Royal Winnipeg

art museums, beautiful gardens and architecture, orchestras, opera companies, ballet troupes, theaters, and other such forms of expression constitute facets of what we term the tradition of the Western world. In addition, the pupil must be guided to learn to respect and appreciate the modes of expression of other great cultural traditions.

Learn to translate and interpret map, geographic, and social science data related to tracing the geographic distribution of cultural influences, and to appreciate the aesthetic in the preparation of maps. Experiences in the employment of maps as investigative tools may be combined with experiences to achieve a fine blending of the useful and the aesthetic.

Be able to answer the following: How do we express ratios on maps? How do we indicate several distributions for the same area? Different symbols? Separate maps? Different color or shading intensities? How do we indicate the source of our data when mapping distributional data? Is it acceptable to prepare maps without such information? How do we verify the accuracy of prepared maps, charts, and graphs?

Ballet Company or the theater at Stratford, Ontario; the opera season in the winter months of July and August in the famous National Opera House in Buenos Aires; the beautiful floating gardens of Xochimilco, Mexico; the "City of Gardens," São Paulo, Brazil; and the like.

On a large bulletin-board-size map of the Western Hemisphere these features and activities may be represented with the use of appropriate symbols. Suitable pictures and drawings may be used to decorate the map and to make it an aesthetic product. The class may dramatize some of these events and activities and learn songs, etc., to help them feel some of the emotional reactions and motives of these people.

Atlantic Community. The following activities may guide teaching-learning experiences which combine aesthetics and map making. Provide prepared outline maps for those who do not need additional practice in developing base data. Review computational skills first so full attention may be given to graphic presentation. Review conventions for denoting locations, distributions, and areal differentiations and for labeling and titling maps and globes.

Select a topic such as "Folksongs of peoples and nations in the Atlantic Community." After gathering the raw data, guide the class toward answering one or more questions in the adjacent objectives column. A host of cartographic problems may emerge. (Refer to "Aids for Teaching," Appendix A.)

Pacific Community. Discuss "taste." Find examples of similarities and differences in taste among peoples and nations of the Pacific region of nations. Before having pupils attempt to map these areal differentiations, discuss possible solutions to the following "problems": Are there conventional map symbols for "taste" or "life styles"? If not, how do we inform our readers about the meaning of our map? Are there recognized principles (or correlations) concerning the presence or absence of certain cultural phenomena (e.g., aesthetic impulses) and the resultant "life styles" which may be plotted as areal association or interaction? Are there psychological and cartographic principles to guide us when we "invent" symbols or devices to report discovered relationships, associations, and interactions? Are there effective verbal forms of guidance to the map reader which should accompany our maps? Extensive legend? Brief marginal notes distributed in strategic locations on the map? An attached "guide and information sheet"? Transparent overlays?

World Community. Can we produce a world map showing patterns of spiritual impulses? What kind of projection should we choose? What scale would we need to best report the range of cultural expressions uncovered? Should our base data show terrain to better guide the reader? Might our use of color be useful or misleading? Would political-physical maps be adequate base data upon which to add our special symbols? If political boundaries do not differentiate life styles, how shall we orient the map reader as to relative and/or exact locations of the phenomena we wish to report? Discuss with the class the various social studies, geographic, and map skills and abilities requisite to making a "world taste map." If maps alone will not tell the story, what other media are available and functional?

2. *Ability to read data recorded on maps and globes.*

Develop the skills needed to identify symbols portraying spiritual and aesthetic phenomena. Develop the ability to translate these symbols into meaningful imagery and conceptual patterns of landscape. Maps portraying symbols pertaining to spiritual and aesthetic impulses include:

(1) churches, temples, shrines, cathedrals, synagogues, monasteries;

(2) museums: art, painting, sculpture, historical;

(3) structures of architectural interest;

(4) location of musical organizations, ballet schools and companies, theatrical groups;

(5) locale of artists, artisans, musicians, writers, composers;

(6) gardens, parks, plazas, and other man-made places of beauty;

(7) places of natural beauty.

Develop the ability to read the patterns of distribution of the above features and activities of people. Review the following: ability to read the relative locations, relative distances, and relative directions; ability to use a map grid to describe locations; ability to read several map projections.

2. *Map-reading activities.*

Inter-American Community. Begin with a review of the symbols introduced in previous communities emphasized. Have the pupils distinguish the spiritual and aesthetic formations and features from other configurations as they are symbolized on maps, both large and small scale. Discuss the essential characteristics of these various features within the context of the inter-American community. For example, are there any significant differences in the physical structure of a church located in South America and of a church of the same religion in the local community? The state community? Use appropriate pictures in your discussions and investigations. How do the sites and situations of the churches compare in the cities of various nations? What conclusions may be reached concerning observed differences in location? What conclusions are reached concerning the value of reading both large- and small-scale projections when reading to learn from maps?

Atlantic Community. Do the religious activities of the people and their ministers, clergy, or rabbis differ from those of the local community or nation? In reading maps portraying spiritual impulses the pupil should have an understanding of concepts symbolized. Plan several comparative teaching-learning experiences for reading the various symbols related to this basic human activity.

Read the location of outstanding gardens and parks that have unusual beauty and are internationally known. Read their locations in terms of the distance north or south of the equator, the elevation of the land, their relative location in terms of large bodies of water such as lakes and oceans. Read climate maps of the regions involved and maps showing the prevailing winds at various seasons of the year. Read climate maps of the Western Hemisphere to select regions for the location of exotic gardens and parks. Read tourist maps of the same region to check your answers.

Pacific Community. Place before the class the following quotation from Hoebel as a guide to the class's observations, research, map study, and discussions:

"By art we mean the overt expressions of impulses in line, form, color, rhythm, and word as drawing, painting, sculpturing, dance, tone, poetry, and literature. The feeling tone predominates over thought. . . . Art is . . . inevitably a part of culture . . . and serves . . . social as well as individual interests and needs. Art is inextricably tied to religion and magic . . . and to politics."[16]

Noted "centers" for the production of various art forms may be located on the map of this region of nations. Areal distributions may be plotted and compared to national boundaries and the distributions of ethnic groups, religious beliefs, and social philosophies. Examples of art forms may be exhibited upon a large sketched base of the Pacific region of nations. Noted works of architecture, beauty spots, etc., may be located.

Famous contributors to the arts and humanities may be studied through their biographies, and the sites of their professional activities noted. The centers of certain styles of music, painting, or writing may be located and then, with a series of historical maps, the spread of these artistic modes may be traced. Some pupils may enjoy mapping the history of various musical instruments by tracing their travels and evolution into modern form and recording the story upon appropriate map bases.

World Community. The junior high school social studies program introduces classes to basic concepts about religion and religious beliefs in the world. Pupils may be interested in attempting to map key events from the Old and New Testament upon a base outline map of the Middle East. Again, they may wish to trace with a series of maps the spread of Mohammedanism or other major world religion. The great world religions may be spatially located on maps and facts about them recorded on distribution maps. Teachers should strive to enhance the formation of positive attitudes concerning the world's rich range of religious orientations; maps provide an effective objective starting point to this end.

3. *Ability to interpret distribution and location on maps and to reason geographically.*

Use maps to reason geographically about the location and areal distribution of spiritual and aes-

3. *Map interpretation activities.*

Inter-American Community. Reason about the location of certain cultural features in remote regions. Note and explain any correlations of various religious groups and ac-

thetic phenomena. Analyze the geographic location and distribution of these phenomena as to
(1) relative location;
(2) relative distance;
(3) relative direction;
(4) spatial distribution;
(5) areal interaction.
Correlate the location and distribution of spiritual and aesthetic phenomena with other cultural features and physical features.

Continue to develop the ability to make inferences about data from two or more maps.

Review Peck's suggested guide for formulating generalizations about aesthetic and spiritual phenomena (see prologue). Discuss how the schools might better teach for appreciation of the spiritual and aesthetic contributions of all mankind.

tivities of people within the inter-American community. Compare the national origins of the people. Have the pupils read a map showing the locations and distributions of various religious groups and make inferences about the activities of the people during the various seasons of the year. Do common religious beliefs result in common cultures? Do people holding common religious beliefs seek similar physical environments for their homes?

Atlantic Community. Have the pupils compare a map showing the locations and distributions of cultural organizations such as the ballet, opera, and symphony in one section of the Atlantic community with those of another—for example northern and southern Europe. Have the pupils note the locations of musical organizations, ballet companies, theatrical groups, and symphony orchestras throughout this region of nations. What other cultural phenomena tend to correlate with these aesthetic elements? Reason about the variations in the distribution patterns, their concentration in particular regions and their absence in others. What inferences might you make about the particular locations and activities? Now compare this map with one showing the various national origins of people. Also use a population map. What inferences might be made from these data about the nations that border the Atlantic Ocean on the east and west?

Pacific Community. Many of the map interpretation activities suggested for lesser communities remain relevant and now may be taken up in greater depth. Go on to a study of how the people of India express their spiritual and aesthetic impulses. Make a study of the ritual and ceremony connected with the great world religions to which these people adhere. Identify appropriate cartographic symbols for the faiths of the non-Western world.

World Community. Collect pictures, art work, and written material to accompany the construction of a map of the world's major faiths. Collect similar materials to help pupils visualize the realities depicted on a map of "the world's architectural wonders." Review all of the basic human activities and analyze them for evidence of their association and interaction with spiritual and aesthetic phenomena. Make inferences concerning the roles of U.N. agencies in this area. Prepare distributional maps of several international associations devoted to the arts. Shape pupil growth in attitudes and continuing interests.

Basic Human Activity: Creating Tools, Technics, and Institutions

PROLOGUE

There is always the temptation to turn to the spectacular to "capture" students' interest, but such an approach is not without dangers. Social studies "units" in "Atomic Geography" or "Sputniks, Rockets, and Testing" may not tie in realistically with the pupil's experiences and thus fail to help guide his development of useful social concepts and generalizations. More mundane themes seem more appropriate for studying and mapping the significant aspects of this basic human activity.

Again, the effect of technological changes is reflected in the character of every basic human activity to some extent. "Then and now" comparative studies of the curriculum in a nation's schools before and after the industrial revolution may help pupils appreciate how much their daily lives and thoughts reflect the needs and demands of mass-scale production and consumption and of automation. Face the future and ask what changes in technology nuclear energy may bring.

Technologically based national economies depend upon exchange of raw materials, readily available resources and power, modern transportation systems and equipment, skilled labor forces, and effective communication and mutual understanding among nations which exchange scientific, technological, and cultural information. All of these phenomena demand new tools, technics, and institutions, and all can be mapped readily. To understand this modern age, pupils must give careful and serious attention to the interdependence of nations and to the role of our own nation as a member of the world community of nations. Geographic reasoning based upon study of areal association and areal interaction related to economic resources and their utilization should greatly help the pupil appreciate the importance of international and regional cooperation. From such studies he may be led to conclude inductively that today and tomorrow the United States does not and cannot live in isolation, nor can we turn back the tide of change. We must constantly engage in innovation and creative effort to direct and control this tide of change.

Basic Human Activity: Creating Tools, Technics, and Institutions

OBJECTIVES

1. *Ability to reorganize data gathered from firsthand and vicarious experiences and represent them on maps with appropriate symbols.*

    Develop knowledge of man's orientation to traditional tools, technics, and institutions. At every level of human community people spend much of their time using tools and technics developed by their ancestors. New tools, technics, and institutions grow out of the lifestyles shaped by the past.

    Develop knowledge of how man implements newly created tools, technics, and institutions. People today at all community levels realize the need for increased productivity and more effective implemen-

TEACHING-LEARNING EXPERIENCES

1. *Mapping activities.*

    Inter-American Community. Contrast and compare the tools and technics used by Canadian farmers in the prairie provinces with those used by farmers in various sections of South America. Read accounts and collect pictures of time-saving equipment used by Canadian farmers in preparing the soil for seeding and in harvesting the crops. Read accounts and collect pictures of farmers in South America using primitive methods to prepare the soil, seed the crops, and harvest them. Most of these tools and technics depend on manpower to do much of the work.

    Help the students to develop the

tation of all basic human activities. Industrial nations have turned to research and development to the extent that the "invention of invention" is becoming institutionalized as an important human activity.

Develop knowledge of how man strives to take advantage of new tools, technics, and institutions. People must be introduced to new ways of doing things. Educational programs are fostered at all community levels; our international aid programs and the Peace Corps are examples of American activities in this area at the international community level.

Learn to translate and interpret map, geographic, and social science data related to changes resulting from the use of new tools, technics, and institutions. Technological and social change affect the economic and social life of all communities. These changes can be described with maps. The pupil may develop an appreciation of the significance of newly created tools and technics through participation in such teaching-learning experiences as observation, investigation, comparative studies, discussion, and mapping activities.

Learn how maps help to present statistical data in an understandable and interesting manner. Dots may be used to symbolize the number of tractors per unit of farm workers, for example. Decide on how many tractors each dot will represent. Include this information in the map's legend.

generalization that machines increase production, machines work faster, and machines can do more work. Gather statistical data for making distribution maps showing the variations in the number of machines such as tractors in selected countries. When the map is completed, have the class observe and describe the distribution which is shown on the map. Relate data with the production of grain or other agricultural products for each of the countries. The same may be done for other tools and technics. In some statistical manner, present the data to show ratios per thousand farm workers.

Atlantic Community. Tools and technics as adaptive devices might be introduced with the generalization: Every nation represents the organized efforts of its inhabitants to adapt their activities, political and otherwise, to their environmental conditions. Switzerland provides an excellent national example of man's inventiveness and adaptability. Make a study of Switzerland's natural and cultural resources. Ask pupils to study the map of Europe and interpret the significance of Switzerland's relative location and situation. Use political, cultural, and raised physical relief maps to identify the kinds of problems and opportunities the Swiss experience and the kinds of tools and technics and institutions they have adopted. In discussions bring out the idea that all basic human activities are carried on with ever changing tools and technics.

Point out the economic value of the skills and talents of a nation's population. Suggest that industrialization has given many people in the world leisure time and more money than they need for simple subsistence. What tools and technics have the Swiss employed to take advantage of this fact? Ask pupils to interpret the map of Europe and explain how the Swiss policy of political neutrality may also be considered important. What institutions has neutrality enhanced? Summarize the study of Switzerland by asking the class to "prove" the generalization that the history of a region is intimately connected with the changes in land and resource utilization.

Pacific Community. Help students realize that a "resource" is only a resource when its value is recognized and employed. New tools and technics frequently are requisite to making use of previously merely latent resources.

Obtain for comparative study historical and present-day maps showing land use in selected Pacific nations so that pupils may gather data concerning changing technology, population patterns, economic activities, and social customs. How have these changes altered the "value" of natural resources? A study of changes in communication and transportation may be subtitled "Bringing the farm, forest and mine closer to the marketplace." Data on the technological removal of physical barriers and the social establishment of political barriers reflect changing technics and institutions. How may molded relief and physical-political maps be utilized in such studies? Comparative study of Atlantic and Pacific nations can sharpen understandings. For example, study "England from farm to factory" and its counterpart in the transition that has shaped modern Japan.

World Community. Call attention to the fact that nations vary in extent of mechanization in agriculture. Be sure pupils have an adequate visual image of the contrast between small and large scale farming and between modern and pre-industrial agricultural technology by utilizing maps, pictures and textual materials concurrently. If possible obtain large scale maps and aerial photographs of the same areas. Note the different kinds and degrees of supportive transportation and industrial activities common to various kinds of farming. How do institutionalized regional and international regulatory activities serve the farmer and all citizens? What has kept some nations from becoming more industrialized?

Historical perspective may be gained by gathering data for sketch maps of the medieval manor system and the land holding practices of the "landed aristocracy" of past and present. When pupils have studied the industrial revolution and mapped its changes upon the face of the earth, discuss the future changes facing the emerging primitive areas of the world.

2. *Ability to read data recorded on maps and globes.*

Develop skills in identifying symbols representing tools, technics, and institutions people are using to carry on the basic human activities. Develop the ability to translate these symbols into meaningful imagery and conceptual patterns of landscape. Maps with symbols showing tools and technics include:
(1) research and development facilities;

2. *Map-reading activities.*

Inter-American Community. Prior map-reading experiences have helped pupils to build a systematic understanding and imagery of the tools and technics symbolized on maps. Continue to use photographs wherever possible to help them to develop mental images of the relevant characteristics of the items being symbolized on maps. For example, they should understand the processes and machines used by

(2) areas served by these facilities;

(3) experimental farms and stations;

(4) pilot plants and facilities for new processes;

(5) use of specific tools and technics in such areas as agriculture, transportation, communication, producing, distributing, protecting, governing, and the like.

Further extend the ability to read the relative locations and distances of these features and activities within the various region-of-nations communities and the ability to read symbols on maps showing the areal distribution of these features and activities.

Develop the map-reading ability of being able to read area symbols which differentiate the kind of tools and technics used and the symbols which show variations in the number of tools per capita from place to place. The number and distribution of these man-made features may be shown on maps by dots. Number or amounts may be shown by varying the number or density of dots for a given area or by shading from a darker to a lighter color. Have pupils develop the habit of reading the legend, since dots represent different quantities on different maps. The visual values of shaded areas also vary from one map to another. Have the pupils become aware that these quantitative maps fall into two classes. Some show the actual number of things whereas others show averages or percentages. For example, some maps may show the percentage of tractors to total number of farms; others show the number of tractors for a given region.

farmers to produce grain in the prairie provinces of Canada. They also should have clearly in mind the tools and methods used by farmers in various countries of South America. How are the crops stored? Moved to market? Sold? Have the pupils prepare sketch maps to trace these events in both modern and primitive settings. Refer to the adjacent objectives column for guidance in reading and making maps showing comparative classes of data.

Atlantic Community. Have students produce sketch maps of the Atlantic coastal areas showing latitude and relative location of all nations which have developed their economies around seafaring activities. Correlate with sketch maps of the region's climatic patterns, its basic landform and physical relief, and the profile of its coastlines. Collect several sets of these comparisons for different nations in the Atlantic region of nations and have the class seek to discover common physical and/or cultural features. Which of these physical features might be most significant in leading to the adoption of certain tools, technics, and institutions? Compare the land of the Vikings, Greece, Portugal, and Great Britain. Does map study help show which countries have turned to industry, fishing, and shipping? Help the class prepare small-scale maps of the coastlines of these nations and the adjacent ocean depths in order to identify fishing areas, important water currents, and relative location to major world trade routes and population centers.

Pacific Community. Discuss "key" inventions in light of physical and cultural changes (problems) faced by peoples of Pacific nations as they relate to various basic human activities. A general map-reading problem related to adopting new tools and technics might be introduced with the generalization: Where topography and climate near a coast are inhospitable to economic activities on land, the inhabitants may turn to fishing and commerce for support. Japan offers a limited example for this study. Maps of the great rivers of China combined with maps showing population densities should help pupils understand the way of life of the riverboat people. Read maps and other social studies materials to discover which other peoples and nations have "turned to the sea" because of geographic, demographic, or economic necessity. Do maps show the changes these nations have experienced in recent years?

World Community. Discuss new inventions and try to identify nations which are in the process of shifting to new forms of economic activity as a result of new tools, technics, and institutions. What kinds of maps are useful for determining which new inventions are most directly competing with the world's merchant fleets? Use polar projections to show the growing networks of airlines, pipelines, highways, railroads, and other surface conveyor systems.

Discuss the problems of new conflicts between nations caused by new technics of commercial fishing and of "harvesting" mineral and oil wealth from beneath the seas. Make a study of the effects upon regions and nations of new synthetic products which replace plant and mineral resources. Do new maps show these changes? What new map symbols appear to tell the story of new tools, technics, and institutions?

3. *Ability to interpret distribution and location represented on maps and to reason geographically.*

Interpret the significance of the location and distribution of tools, technics, and institutions among the regions of nations.

Reason geographically about the presence or absence of specific tools and technics; look for associations of specific tools, technics, and institutions with other man-made features and natural features.

Develop the ability to make inferences about the location and distribution of tools, technics, and institutions and the character of the regions in which they are found. Continue to develop the ability to make inferences about data gathered from two or more maps.

Analyze the geographical location and areal distribution of tools and technics as to relative location, relative distance, and relative direction.

Evaluate outcomes in terms of the ability of the pupil to select maps and map data appropriate to their need for meaning. Through group evaluation strive to correct misconceptions and faulty map-reading technics and inferences. Such problems posed in areas new to the pupil make it possible to identify individual and group needs for reteaching or extending and re-fining of skills and abilities.

3. *Map interpretation activities.*

Inter-American Community. Plan teaching-learning activities to help pupils interpret the presence or absence of tools and technics in various regions of the inter-American community. For example, make inferences about the agricultural production of a region or country where the percentage of tractors to the total number of farms is small and where the percentage is large. What inferences might be made about the use of many tools and technics in the production of particular goods and services? Compare the location and distribution of factories that manufacture machine tools in such countries as Canada, Brazil, Chile, Peru, and the U.S. Compare data on the import and export of machinery for various nations and interpret the resulting balance-of-trade problems and the nation's degree of dependence upon its neighbors. What inferences would it be possible to make about the character of the region or nations from the presence or absence of symbols representing heavy and light industry? Map the ownership of various industries in these countries and interpret these facts in terms of future changes in tools, technics, and institutions.

Atlantic Community. Reason about the geographical locations of experimental farms and stations in several countries. Compare the distributions of these features in Europe with those of several nations in Africa. Read and interpret maps which have symbols showing the location and number of research and development centers. Help the pupils draw inferences from this information such as the character of the tools and technics being used as compared to those being used in the United States. Use the globe with the maps when comparing widely separated geographical areas in the Western Hemisphere.

Reason about the future of such new institutions as the European Common Market. What nations in Africa might profit from similar new institutions?

Pacific Community. Assign pupils to both independent and group studies in map research on "The land, cultural patterns, and economy of India past and present." Help them locate useful data concerning tools and technics old and new. Have them locate maps and map data to illustrate relationships. The value of such a "problems" approach rests in gains in mastery of process. India's population pressures on resources, arable land, transportation facilities, food processing, storage, and marketing represent cultural phenomena which may be described in terms of areal extent, distribution, and interaction. Interpret and analyze findings. Urge pupils to observe such activities in their immediate community and compare local problems with those found among nations in the Pacific region. Employ computational skills. Prepare maps, charts, and graphs to describe findings.

World Community. Make a comparative study of the world's west coast dry subtropical climate regions (Mediterranean climate). Ask pupils to collect maps and data necessary to identify the common physical characteristics of five world areas having this particular climate. Read from maps the precipitation (15–20 inches), the temperature (mild to hot temperature), seasonal changes (mild winter and dry summer), and infer what kind of vegetation is normal (dry brush, grains). Ask the class to explain why citrus fruits, peaches, cotton, etc., are grown in these areas today by reading topography maps (irrigation supplied by runoff from mountains to the east).

Discuss the tools, technics, and institutions related to irrigation in these areas. Obtain maps showing soils in the areas and seek to explain by use of relief maps what is discovered (soil is alluvium; valleys made up of alluvial fans deposited by many rivers flowing from mountains). Study maps showing problems of irrigating such regions (slope and drainage to combat salinity, leaching, drowning, etc.). Prepare sketch maps or models to describe findings, and chart the tools and technics important to these regions (include commercial fertilizers, methods of reducing frost damage, and food-preserving processes). Make inferences about the future of such world regions.

REFERENCES

1. B. S. Bloom (ed.), *Taxonomy of Educational Objectives: Handbook I, Cognitive Domain* (New York: David McKay Co., Inc., 1956).
2. UNESCO, "World Health, Ten Years of Progress," *Courier* (UNESCO Publication Center, 801 Third Avenue, New York), May, 1958, p. 13.
3. *Ibid.*, p. 12.
4. Ben W. Lewis, "Economics," *The Social Studies and the Social Sciences* (New York: Harcourt, Brace & World, Inc.), p. 123.

5. Alfred H. Meyer, "Geography in the Teacher Education Program," *Geographic Approaches to Social Education,* Nineteenth Yearbook, National Council for the Social Studies (Washington: NCSS, 1949), p. 284.
6. Malcolm P. Douglass, "Interrelationships Between Man and the Natural Environment for Use in the Geographic Strand of the Social Studies Curriculum," unpublished doctoral dissertation, School of Education, Stanford University, 1954.
7. *Ibid.*
8. *Ibid.*
9. Ralph Linton, *The Study of Man* (New York: Appleton-Century-Crofts, Inc., 1936), pp. 325–327.
10. Douglass, *op. cit.*
11. *Ibid.*
12. *Ibid.*
13. Jules Henry, "An Anthropologist's View of Curriculum Change," *Teachers College Record,* 62:543 (April, 1961).
14. Leonard S. Kenworthy, *Introducing Children to the World* (New York: Harper & Row, Publishers, 1956), pp. 160–161.
15. Albert D. Peck, "Social Science Generalizations for Use in the Social Studies Curriculum: Expressing and Satisfying Esthetic Needs and Impulses," unpublished doctoral dissertation, School of Education, Stanford University, 1959, p. 38.
16. Edward A. Hoebel, *Man in the Primitive World* (New York: McGraw-Hill Book Co., Inc., 1949), p. 572.

chapter eleven

THE JUNIOR HIGH SCHOOL

EMPHASES

Illustrative Pupil Experiences for Emphases 8–11

Geography and the social studies present a systematic way of looking at the adaptive activities of man in his several physical and cultural worlds. Opportunities to practice newly learned map skills and geographic understandings are introduced so that habits and attitudes of map employment and geographic reasoning are fostered. Skills, habits, and attitudes tend to become fixed through reinforcements of repeated rewarding utilization.

The more significant skills and understandings generally do not evolve incidentally; hence it is important that they be conceptualized and planned prior to establishing practice experiences.

These map skills are identified in Chapter One, and proposals in Chapter Ten coordinate the scope and sequence through which their development is guided through the larger-than-national communities. The present chapter suggests "problems" and activities which may be adapted to the particular needs and interests of any junior high school classroom. In most cases these activities need not be isolated from the ongoing social studies focus upon any region of nations or the world community.

Map-Reading Skills and Understanding

The following descriptions of map *projections* point up the student's need for constant guidance and encouragement in map vocabulary and reading skills growth. How might students react to the terms and meanings in these statements?

A homolosine projection such as Goode's Equal Area Interrupted projection is useful for a distributional map of the world community.

A cylindrical projection, the Mercator, for example, is useful for air and sea nagivational purposes.

A conical projection, the Albers or Lambert with two standard parallels, is especially recommended for countries or continents having a large east-west dimension but a relatively small north-south dimension.

These facts are useful to "know," of course, but mere memorization does not produce understanding or the ability to apply the knowledge. Effective teaching-learning experiences should lead to the discovery of the properties of various projections and to the forming of generalizations about various projection properties.*

Generalizations about projections will lead into problems of application and expose the need for more knowledge and understanding. Map vocabulary building should be a natural by-product of growth in understanding rather than merely a product of isolated drill sessions.

Should pupils attempt to compare distributions, they need to become aware that comparative studies of different nations or regions of nations call for selection not only of the most appropriate projection but also of similar projections, bases, and scales for areas compared. They might be helped to grasp the reason through comparing the relative areas of South America and Greenland in the Atlantic community on Mercator and Goode's Interrupted Homolosine projections of the same scale.

Another useful understanding is the fact that all maps of large areas distort something, and the sophisticated map reader selects the map which least distorts the phenomenon in which he is interested. If we want to show the transcontinental railroad network of the USSR, we use a projection which provides us with a reasonably accurate scale of the entire land area. In this case a conical projection with two standard parallels would be a good choice.

Again, if pupils are interested in transportation and the shipping of goods over long distances by sea or air, the Mercator projection is an appropriate map for plotting the route. Of course (as will be later explained), a globe should be consulted concurrently to properly visualize the route. While taking advantage of the "good points" of a Mercator or homolosine projection, a class may need constant guidance to keep from being "fooled" by the peripheral areas of such maps. A developmental lesson for this understanding might consist in comparing Sweden and Morocco as they appear on different projections or different areas within a projection. While both are approximately the same size, the

---

* The Study Guide prepared by Waldo R. Tobler for the *Map Projection Model* by Hubbard should be an invaluable reference source. See Appendix A, p. 465.

projection distortions may cause one or the other to appear as much as twice as large in area as the other.

Should the teacher's observation of the pupils' map skills and understandings indicate need for much review and/or basic training, it may be worthwhile to bring into the classroom prepared supplementary developmental map-reading lessons and spend a few days developing facility with these basic tools of geography.[1] Probably all junior high school classes could profit at some time from a week devoted to systematic review of the concepts of longitude and latitude, great circles, scale, and the most common azimuthal (polar), cylindrical, and conic projections. Pupils who show greater capability and those who have previously experienced a systematic educational program in map skills and understandings could use developmental lessons as a starting point for moving into interpretive studies and map computational and cartographic experiences. Certainly, no reasonably capable pupil should leave the junior high school without experiencing some basic training and enjoying the opportunity to put these learned skills and understandings into practice in his study of emerging communities in the global setting. Pupils, for example, may become interested in such map-reading activities following consideration of the movement of the Polynesians in the early history of the Pacific community.

Should the teacher choose to introduce a selected "representative nation" or a region-of-nations area making up part of an emerging global community through use of physical terrain maps, relevant lessons in "scientific reading" of terrain maps should be provided. Reading "between the lines" of terrain symbols in order to draw inferences and identify probable causes of observed phenomena can be an interesting and challenging undertaking. An excellent source of lessons and explanations of this type of geographic thinking and map reading has been compiled by Lobeck in his book *Things Maps Don't Tell Us.*[2]

Geographic materials such as Lobeck's book offer extensive material on coastlines which will tell the more sophisticated map reader much about the nature of the land, its resources and problems as well as its geological past. For example, when introduced to northern Europe in the Atlantic community, classes should note the effect of glaciers in shaping the land and water areas, and the flow patterns of rivers. Becoming aware of such physical realities may contribute a great deal to later understandings of agricultural production and trade problems. River deltas and the manner in which rivers alter coastlines become obvious to pupils who have learned to visualize the nature of the physical environment suggested by a few marks on a map.

Pupils can bring greater insight to their study of the Pacific regions if they have spent some time in considering the formation of islands (chains, volcanic, various shapes, etc.) and the nature of the surrounding water's currents, depths, plant and fish life, etc., and what such geo-graphic facts suggest about the basic human activities of yesteryear and today.

Man's activities have always been related to the nature of the various rivers that drain the land areas of the world. The "why" of where rivers are located will help classes to "read" unreported elevations, soil types, etc. The patterns of rivers will help them "read" the nature of the land surface and underground water tables, of runoff problems (slope of the land), of swamp lands and deserts along rivers as well as giving clues to where major cities might evolve when rivers can provide transporta-tion as well as life-giving water. Likewise, noting the relation of water drainage to the formation and nature of lakes can add real understanding to map reading.

Even the shape of cities (large-scale maps) is worth special attention, for the contour of cultural features can suggest to the social studies pupil something of historical as well as present and future problems.[3] When studying the cultural phenomena of Europe, for instance, consideration could be given to the circular defense patterns of earlier times and the progressive layers added to such cities as Paris which made her circular in shape as the city filled in on both sides of a bend in the Seine River. While studying the Atlantic community nations pupils may profit from comparisons of modern city plans for traffic flow and orderly expansion with those of the defensively oriented street patterns of old European cities, the plaza of a Spanish city, or the location of the commons in an Anglo-Saxon town.

Using maps to introduce a nation or emerging world community de-mands special planning. Generally, the first step is to employ the globe in order to provide the pupils with a general world orientation followed by more specific attention to the physical and cultural settings. Because much of the cultural environment tends to be understandable mainly in terms of human adjustments to physical environment, the first maps to be studied might be directionally oriented small-scale terrain and cli-matic descriptions of the community as a whole. Such an orientation might stress the relative locations of populated areas and the character and distribution of land and water bodies which are significant in under-standing the adjustment problems of the inhabitants.

Next, to this base might be added the parallels of latitude so that tenta-tive inferences as to seasons and climates may be elicited. Effective understanding of earth-sun global phenomena and interrelationships is requisite to this phase of geographic analysis. (For a detailed list of specific source materials in earth-sun relationships see "Aids for Teach-ing," Appendix A.) Climatic maps would further understandings of tem-perature and rainfall ranges, which are resultants of prevailing winds caused by high and low pressures of world thermal patterns, and/or by local wind barriers, and/or by proximity to warming or cooling bodies of land and water.

Now vegetation maps might confirm inferences concerning the expected plant-life responses to elevations, temperatures, precipitation, and growing seasons. For some regions it will be necessary to add maps of soils and/or drainage patterns for pupils to appreciate why vegetation patterns vary from the expected.

Through use of physical-political maps pupils could be aided to hypothesize about available resources and possible economic activities and interdependence of men in selected national settings. Maps reporting the distributions of mineral and power resources (developed and latent) will be necessary to undertake further analysis when the community of nations under study enjoys modern technological development.

By this time pupils may be well aware of the necessity of consulting maps for locating and describing past and present cultural features and conditions and of turning to the story of the developmental progress (history) of the inhabitants. Physical-political maps, population maps, land-use maps, transportation and communication maps, etc. (cartographic reporting of all the basic human activities), all become relevant to meaningful social studies undertakings.

Finally, the pupils become ready to build further concepts concerning the social problems of these vast regions of nations. Maps and other data sources will be used to facilitate grasping the implications and interrelationships of each newly studied national or region-of-nations community to the problems of the United States and ultimately to the problems of the emerging world community. Map studies that introduce a national community, then, must help distinguish the basic commonalities of man-land adaptations as well as identify its unique physical-cultural frame of reference and thus give rational perspective to the particular forms in which the basic human activities are manifested in this or any other sub-component of a selected expanding community of men. Awareness of each community's place and world significance, then, blends into the pupil's total "picture" of the world to add new meanings, appreciations, and understandings.

Developmental lessons related to current events items of import to the world community such as newly orbiting weather and communication satellites could provide effective opportunities for classes to make inferences concerning future levels of safety and efficiency in communication and travel as well as to conceptualize more easily the obvious implications of the world's apparent relative reduction in size. Reading about, computing, and plotting the reported data of space flights (which have numerous geographical as well as world political aspects) offer a multitude of opportunities to think scientifically and to explore causality (perceived and actual). Further expansion of the developmental lesson could consider the problems of technological change in the various lesser communities studied as classes explore implications of mankind's constant reduction of the limitations placed upon him by the physical environment and his biotic nature.

Map-Making Experiences

Most young adolescents should be able to express observations and data collections in the form of rough sketch maps. Cartographic additions to history reports and summaries make real contributions to the social studies program. A few of the more capable pupils who are interested in and challenged by mathematical accuracy could have the opportunity to produce field sketches which indicate exact location, direction, scale, and distributions upon appropriate large-scale bases of their own design. Care should be taken that such activities do not become ends in and of themselves but rather are undertaken in conjunction with study of the basic human activities and refinement of basic concepts of geography.

Discussion of the complexity of making maps may aid pupils to appreciate the inaccuracies of early explorers' maps and to realize that nations today are still improving the accuracy of the maps in use. Cause-effect correlational thinking may be introduced rather simply by review of an earlier concept-building experience. For instance, peeling an orange and attempting to spread it out flat and then seeing that the solution of cutting the peel into many slender gores (in fact, the identical means whereby the printed flat paper map is mounted on a globe) suggests that often a "solution" may not be useful. Attempting to read the world map presented as a long string of gores may dramatically remind pupils of the necessity of sometimes accepting "solutions" that have certain "errors."

Obviously, only rarely will teachers and pupils be able to make field trips into the world communities from which surveying experiences, sketch maps, and notes may be derived. However, useful vicarious experiences are available through motion pictures, photographs, and verbal descriptions, provided pupils have developed the requisite techniques and understandings. Continued firsthand field experiences focused upon comparative analysis can help broaden geographic understandings.

If classes are to appreciate better the value of maps to geographers and other people who make scientific or systematic use of man-land interrelationships, they will need to use field mapping and sketch work to solve some problems of meaning in their own lives. The general grows out of the specific. Here again is an example of the need for developmental lessons which stem from or anticipate the content of the total social studies program. It is appropriate that the need for skills and understandings emerge from within the context of the basic subject matter and pupil's social problems. It should not be arbitrarily assigned.

Teachers must expect a range of experiential backgrounds and maturity levels. Some pupils may be ready to do simple field survey work of physical or cultural features and record their data upon bases of their own devising. Many students have to be supplied with prepared outline maps upon which they may attempt to note the relative locations, distributions, and interrelationships among observed physical and cultural phenomena. Here the teacher's guideline concerning how much depth and breadth of field work will be appropriate must be a determination not of whether pupils can "do" something but of whether worthwhile use of the skills and understandings may be anticipated in the study of emerging communities. There is always the danger of getting carried away in activities to the detriment of the basic program of essential social skills and understandings requisite to adequate citizenship.

Sketch maps must be conceived of as ways by which to express geographic ideas and interrelationships in conjunction with pictures and verbal accounts. Many of these will be simple freehand drawings, for their purpose is to express geographic ideas rather than to exemplify cartographic excellence. Hence, developmental lessons and applicational experiences should not be distorted into "art experiences" which largely emphasize neatness, beauty, or creativeness. Of course, effective sketch maps, like any other form of communication, will be improved with due aesthetic attention as well as careful scientific accuracy. The major stress, however, should be upon the clarity with which the map-sketch relays its message.

Developmental lessons in map-sketching could consist of experiences in arriving at common symbols, learning cartographic standards, and studying psychological factors relevant to making key ideas visually effective on maps.[4] Standard cartographic symbol charts could be reviewed. Lettering standards and conventions should be emphasized. Techniques for indicating point, line, and area distributions may be augmented by some simple forms for indicating terrain features (hachures and shading) as well as work with contour lines. Grid systems might receive attention in terms of the types of geographic statements which call for exact location compared to those needing only indications of relative location. Some standards should be established for including landmarks or other reference points for the reader's general and directional orientation. Likewise, attention might be given to minimal standards for legends, especially the scale, direction, and the meaning of colors if they are to be employed.

Color introduces major perceptual and conceptual problems. Pupils ask, "Teacher, what color should I make my map?" Color is an abstract symbol which may help the map reader better visualize reality or give false cues and impressions. It has appeal and the power to highlight dramatically or emphasize certain facts at the expense of other ideas. Propaganda maps frequently resort to use of color to distort, cover up, or distract the reader from seeing important interrelationships and facts.

A search of the literature indicates that some educators suggest more or less rote teaching of commonly accepted conventional cartographic color schemes such as altitude tints. The value of teaching conventions is doubtful as they apply to only certain types of maps. There is a recent trend among cartographers to use the true colors of the physical environment. It is probably better to develop the habit of reading the map legend for the meaning of colors. A few educators have even suggested that the use of color can introduce so many misconceptions that it is better to avoid color in elementary school maps[5] if they are meant to be clear and meaningful statements[6] rather than just "pretty."

Obviously, here is a problem area. If color can be confusing to map readers, a sound approach to map use seems to suggest that pupils find out why. Commercially prepared maps for schools today use a combination of color, hill shading, and pictorial relief to portray surface characteristics of land and thus try to prevent misinterpretations. Pupils should have the opportunity to discover why cartographers have gone to so much trouble to use color symbols and shading techniques to express themselves. Problem-solving questions and topics for investigation might include the following:

1. What season of the year should we show on our maps? How might it be done? Should it be done? Why?

2. How shall we show the altitude of the land if we use color for vegetation?

3. If we make a molded raised relief map (see "Aids for Teaching," page 466), which should be our vertical scale? Should it be the same as our horizontal scale? Examine a commercially prepared raised relief map and note the amount of vertical exaggeration in comparison to the horizontal scale.

4. Should our map be a "picture" or an abstract symbol system? How might a map be more useful than a picture? Large scale? Small scale? What are the difficulties of interpreting aerial photographs? Are color pictures or black and white easier to read? Why?

5. Should snow-covered peaks be shown in the brown color convention of altitude tints? Why? When?

6. Are colors more important on small- or large-scale maps? What are the various common uses for color on small-scale maps?

7. What purpose does color serve on a two-dimensional wall relief map? In areas of mixed land use or vegetation, how do cartographers decide which color to use?

8. From our study of maps employing color and our investigation into the psychological responses of people to colors, which colors should we

be most cautious about using? Which colors are often used to mean many things? Which colors are generally consistent in referent from map to map?

9. What is meant by color connotations? Do such connotations make a difference in the meanings we get from maps?

10. Should a map be "pleasing to the eye"? Why? What does "color harmony" have to do with cartography? Is there a relation between "neatness" and thoughtful choice of color?

Computational Aspects of Using Maps

Map interpretation and expression should maintain focus on the primary geographic concerns of areal extent, areal association, and spatial interaction. As pupils investigate the various manifestations of the basic human activities throughout the world, they are of necessity going to have to deal with masses of facts. In junior high school pupils should begin to consider the implications of the facts of what and where, i.e., *so what?* and *where* in relation to what? If pupils have matured to this extent, it is possible they will also recognize the need for accuracy and legibility in their cartographic expression of social studies findings. With problems of factual descriptions of areal extent (size, shape, diffusion, and concentrations) there will be need for accuracy in scale and shape projection in the base data as well as thoughtful selection of ratio to denote the distribution. Value is thus placed upon computational abilities as well as research techniques and cartographic execution.

Basic map scale concepts should be generally familiar to those students who have gone through a developmental map skills program, but because the latter is far from common or uniformly effective many young adolescents will need extensive additional training.

All pupils should be helped to visualize and compute the unit-to-unit ratio (scale) of the globe or map to the actual phenomena mapped. The ratio is frequently provided in the legend verbally, graphically, or by a representative fraction (RF).[7] As a review of previous learning and as an opportunity to reinforce knowledge with a mathematical approach, classes could be encouraged to go through the classroom atlas and be sure they can convert and conceptualize the various standard ratios used in the many projections. It is important that scale be reviewed following study of the distortions in various projections so that pupils may understand that it is accurate for only the parts of the map that were not altered in order to accomplish the "flattening out." A Mercator projection uses a number of scales.

To help students check their map scale understanding they might be asked to evaluate the use of a map ratio of 1:1, or to explain their choice of an appropriate scale for a world community communications map base upon which they would note the distribution of telephones. Continued attention to scale is important because previous work with maps could possibly have failed to explain satisfactorily the basic reason for devising maps, namely, to condense vast areas into perceptually manageable wholes wherein spatial and locational distributions of phenomena might be expressed. Hence, as classes work with various maps there should be constant attention given to the selection of the most appropriate scale by which to express clearly geographic ideas and observations.

The pupil's understanding of the following measurement facts and relationships[8] seems to be requisite to skillful selection and utilization of map projections and their grid systems.

THE GRID SYSTEM

The map grid system requires that meridians and parallels intersect at right angles everywhere; not only can pupils learn to measure angles, but they might thus conceptualize the inherent precision of areal and distance measurement and point location based upon a system of accurate perpendiculars and tangents, parallels, and equal units.

On the globe or on equal-areal projections the meridians at 60° latitude are about half as far apart as they are at the equator. Pupils probably will better recognize the distortion in the Mercator projection if they have computed and measured the gradual convergence of meridians on a globe and thus come to realize that in the Pacific community, for example, Alaska at 60° latitude on the Mercator projection is distorted to four times larger than actual size if it were located on the equator.

When international scientists plan projects for improving maps and gaining more knowledge about the earth (IGY, for example) they have to take stations at exact locations for making and recording useful observations. The following data would help pupils conceptualize such problems. The intersection of the prime meridian and the equator in the Gulf of Guinea is the "point of origin" of the earth's coordinate grid. Degrees of longitude and latitude are divided into 60 minutes and subdivided again into 60 seconds. A minute of latitude has an average length of 6,080 feet (a nautical mile)* or about 1.15 statute miles. A second of latitude is about 101 feet.

Another related computational challenge is posed by the fact that the length of a degree of longitude is approximately the same as that of

---

* In the United States and other nations using the English system of measures, the international nautical mile equals 6,076.115 feet. A degree of latitude is about 70 statute miles.

a degree of latitude at the equator but, of course, it reduces to zero at the poles. Care must be taken that pupils do not confuse longitude and latitude properties. More capable pupils may enjoy the challenge of exactly locating (in terms of degrees, minutes, and seconds) a remote village in Alaska where a degree of longitude has been reduced to 34.6 miles in length (at 60° N. Latitude). Certainly more advanced study of the basic human activities related to transporting goods and people sooner or later will draw upon knowledge of these computational aspects of employing the world's grid system.

Students undertaking systematic work in cartography must have mastery of the mathematics of computing areas of all types of geometric figures. Of course, advanced proficiency is not necessary for all students, and the teacher must guard against their straying from the basic social studies program. Nevertheless, some pupils may readily attain the ability to compute the area of triangles and parallelograms and employ this knowledge in checking the distortions in peripheral areas of projections or in planning for more accurate base statements for their distributional maps. To the enrichment of their social studies experiences, a few pupils may enjoy checking various map projections against the principle that an area included between any two parallels, and measuring a given longitude in extent, will be the same anywhere between those two parallels.

Following measuring and computing such "facts," the pupil may grow to understand inductively the deductively presented fact that the scale upon a globe is everywhere the same regardless of direction while this cannot be the case for any global map projection. With such activities, pupils may come to appreciate the importance of mathematical analysis in modern technological communities as they realize that cartographers compute their projections and that even the apparently simple conic projection, which they may have made in class, is far too inaccurate for the cartographer's use and thus cartographers do not trace maps but derive them mathematically.

Time and Movement

Developmental lessons should continue throughout the study of emerging communities as needs arise. Probably a series of learning experiences would be useful in order to build an effective level of understanding concerning the relationships between latitude and climate, or longitude and time. Such understanding could then be employed more effectively in comparative studies of selected nations.

Specially planned lessons on the sun-earth relationships generally are needed to lend meaning to apparent correlations between latitude and climate. Review work and additional attention may be necessary in the vocabulary concepts of earth movement: angle, orbit, rotation, perpendicular, solstice, equinox, Tropics of Cancer and Capricorn, Arctic Circle, inclination, etc. Computational activities may include the earth's revolving speed (day and night), its orbiting speed (seasons and year), the distances involved, and the angle of tilt. Clarifications of correlations as opposed to cause and effect are exemplified in such problems.

Computation tasks may also serve to enhance other geographic skills and understandings. Computing the relationship of longitude to time would include the simple geometry problems of degrees of angles of longitude, degrees in a full circle, and conversion problems of degrees into miles and miles into hours and minutes, etc. Along with this approach, the conventions of date lines, time zones, east and west longitude, etc., are learned as pupils become aware of the need for established reference points from which to base various computations.

A WORKSHEET . . .

There are 360 degrees in a circle.

North-South lines divide the equator into 360 meridians.

The earth's equatorial circumference is 24,902 miles.

Thus, at the equator, each meridian equals $360/\overline{24,902}$ or 69.1 miles in length. In 24 hours the earth turns 360 degrees and the sun crosses $24/\overline{360} - 15$ meridians or 15 degrees of longitude every hour.

Studies of communication, navigation, and related basic human activities of protecting and conserving life, property, and resources will naturally become more meaningful once pupils can confidently attack simple problems of exact and relative location. The foregoing skills and understandings would seem to be most appropriate to include with the pupil's study of the history and development in recent times of the world's emerging communities. For example, during study of the Atlantic community, "then and now" comparisons of historic and modern maps as used in navigation and exploration might help many pupils far more than extensive verbalization.

NAVIGATION

Repeated reference has been made to computational problems related to navigation. A project in navigation developed by one or more able pupils might be most appropriate for the individual's growth and also serve to help the class appreciate the value of mathematics. Certainly, as man prepares for space flight, navigation problems come more and more into the realm of social studies topics.

Among the less informed there seems to be widespread belief that polar projection maps have more or less relegated the Mercator projections to the museum. That this is not so can be quickly appreciated when classes are asked to estimate the compass headings for ships or planes following great-circle routes that do not follow along meridians or the equator.

For those pupils who might wish to "solve" such a problem the following facts and concepts may be developed. Pupils may be introduced to the study of maps showing magnetic declination (isogonic lines) and thus learn why the invention of the gyrocompass was such an important breakthrough for modern navigation. It then becomes apparent that geographic (true) north may be maintained at all times while traveling. With the use of the Mercator projection, which, while distorting land areas, gives true direction via its grid system, the navigator may draw the route to be followed with a straight line (loxodrome or rhumb line) cutting all meridians on the Mercator at the same angle. Each degree line on a polar projection is cut at a different angle by a straight line—and the great-circle route is a straight line when viewed perpendicularly. Classes will be quick to see that major difficulties arise when attempting to plot or maintain a course when compass heading must be continuously adjusted. The solution by navigators is to plot their course by approximating it with a series of short rhumb lines drawn upon a Mercator projection. Pupils thus might appreciate how a polar projection helps one visualize relative locations and directions without the use of a globe, but they also may become aware of its limitations as a navigational aid.

Another computational problem in navigation may improve pupils' understanding of the placing and numbering of parallels of latitude. Pupils may be led to see that degrees of latitude are not arbitrarily assigned but may be computed by "shooting" the North Star (Polaris). Thus, if they have learned to measure and understand degrees of angles between the horizontal and the perpendicular, they will recognize that 0 degree latitude indicates that Polaris appears on the horizontal while 90 degrees latitude indicates that Polaris is on the perpendicular from the sighting position. One result of this study might be that the pupils will also come to understand that since the earth is not a perfect sphere the distance between degrees of latitude increases near the flattened poles and decreases near the bulged equator. For example, at the equator the length of one degree of latitude is approximately 68.7 miles; at the North Pole it is approximately 69.4 miles. Some work in construction of geometrical figures and in erecting perpendiculars and tangents seems necessary if angular relation (azimuth) to grid direction is to be conceptualized effectively.

Finding of exact location also calls for more work in longitudinal reading. Experiences may be provided to familiarize classes with the idea that meridians are "hour markers." Problems may be set up for computing longitude with chronometers and local noon sun (sun at zenith), which again may help pupils to appreciate how the earth's grid system was devised to take advantage of mathematical ways of expressing time and movement relationships. After they have computed local sun time, discussions should clarify why men find it convenient to adopt the conventions of standard time. Generally, junior high school pupils should be able to grasp the basic conventions of standard time and the international date line and use these "facts" in thinking through such geographically related problems as transportation and communication schedule coordination in the world.

Practice in Visualizing Reality Through Use of Supplementary Materials

Because of the almost unlimited variability in the responses of people to newly presented facts, concepts, and generalizations, it is difficult to anticipate what practice activities will be most productive. The teacher must look for clues to emerge from the teaching-learning situation in order to select the most fruitful applicational experiences. Of course, the basic "things to be learned" will be identified by educators prior to meeting with classes, and, in general, developmental lessons may be preplanned because of their inherent relationship to the selected curricular objectives. However, identification of appropriate applicational activities will depend upon the unique strengths and weaknesses of any given pupil or group of pupils which become evident as class work progresses.

Hence, the following practice activities are not prescriptive but, rather, descriptive of the type of teaching-learning activities which tend to follow logically from analysis of the nature of young adolescents, of the nature of the typical junior high school total curriculum, and of the requisites of thinking geographically and of the selected ability objectives in map skills and understandings. The particular nation chosen for study will also in part shape choices of activities.

Among the more effective aids to the teacher of the social studies and particularly to a program of practice activities to extend and refine map skills and understandings in the context of an emerging World Community is a readily available collection of *National Geographic Magazines*. Probably the foremost requirement of using a map with understanding is the mental ability to translate abstract symbols into visualizations of landscape reality. As classroom studies move to more and more remote arenas of the physical and cultural worlds, new phenomena are encountered constantly which tend to prove the truism that "a picture is worth a thousand words." We tend to have difficulty with new forms and variations of known phenomena because of the interference of our established response patterns. Adolescents, like all the rest of us, generally need much help to break away from egocentric and provincial concepts of the basic human activities and stereotypical responses to alien life styles.

The following example of how skills and understandings introduced in developmental lessons may be applied in practice activities is only suggestive of what the inventive teacher can do with a group of learners who have been freed to think, explore, and solve problems.

Our example is drawn from a map of Algeria which appeared on page 722 in the June, 1960, issue of *National Geographic Magazine*. This map has only a scale of miles and an explanation of some of the terms used on the map—i.e., Erg, sand dune region; Tassili, rocky plateau; etc. However, the map has an insert which establishes Algeria's location in relation to the western Mediterranean Sea, Europe, and France. A shading system indicates terrain, and the elevations of peaks are given in numbers. Color is not used to suggest vegetation or political distinction other than Algeria's relationship to France. By comparing this map to other maps of the area, worthwhile discussions of the problems of using color and shading systems could be conducted. Through use of other maps the pupils could add isolines to indicate slope away from the various high points, the relationship between altitude and temperature, etc.

All cities are indicated by the same size dot. Here classes could explore the cartographer's purpose with this map and come to understand that a map should be designed to tell selected things to be effective. Frequently a crowded "all purpose" map fails to convey much meaning because it does not call attention to any special relationships. Here the cartographer wished to stress the relationship between Algeria and France as a meaningful background to the prolonged Algerian-French internal warfare.

Further, this map supplies certain key orientations and some vital data, i.e., French atomic test site; new oil fields and pipelines (road and railroads must be inferred and/or checked with other maps for no legend explains the symbols provided). A brief paragraph near the center of the map tells of the man-to-man problem, which apparently could be illustrated on the map base in no other manner. Classes may wish to use such a technique with their sketch maps, i.e., using cartographic conventions to explain land-to-land and man-to-land relationships and brief verbal text to state a basic geographic interrelationship of man to man which is an outgrowth of man-land interactions.

The verbal message appearing on the map is reproduced here because it introduces several computational concepts of fractions and percentage and area as well as some words which must elicit conceptual responses if the reader is to interpret the writer's message.

LAND OF CONFLICT AND NEW RICHES, FOUR TIMES THE SIZE OF FRANCE—vineyard and wasteland, minaret and movie theater, tranquil plain and garrisoned town give Algeria a split personality. Only three per cent of its 920,000 square miles grows crops; a mere sixth pastures livestock. But new oil wells and iron deposits in the Sahara and recent finds of diamonds, nickel, and copper in the Hoggar give significance to the six-year-old war between French Army and Algerian nationalists.

The story of rising nationalism and dwindling colonialism in Africa could well be introduced by this one map and the discussions and problems for exploration which it might generate.

The map showing Algeria as five-sixths desert may call for a review of the climatic effects of the earth-sun relationships and the movement of the winds and ocean currents upon the surface of the earth. Since this map has no grid system, it would seem useful to affix lines of latitude in order to help draw attention to a possible relationship between latitude and climate.

A further "problem" study with this map which would tend to foster geographic and map skills and understandings would be the comparative study of the land at the same latitude on east and west coasts of continents or in the rain shadows of great mountains both north and south of the equator so that false generalizations about latitude and rainfall do not tie in with latitude and heat. Comparative study of maps and climatic data should result in the classes' inductively finding that "torrid" and "temperate" zone labels of yesteryear's geography, based upon logic instead of investigation, were seriously inaccurate generalizations.

Mapping Procedures Used to Investigate Recreational Activities

We suggest again a detailed developmental sequence of mapping procedures and activities employing a single basic human need—providing recreation through outdoor activities.

Travels of people across international boundaries within the Western Hemisphere to resort areas such as the Canadian Rockies, the lake regions of Chile, or the West Indies in the Caribbean highlight the recreational dimensions of the inter-American community. Recreational areas like these and many others in Europe or the South Seas have assumed international characteristics because people from all parts of the inter-American community and the world visit and use their facilities.

Teaching-learning experiences should direct the class to investigate ways the basic human activity of recreation is met through the use of many kinds of natural features and climatic conditions. The pupils may continue to explore the ways topography, vegetation, and climatic conditions influence recreational structures and activities. A workable sequence of mapping experiences provides another avenue of acquiring well-organized and accurate information about the areal distribution and growth patterns of recreational phenomena within, for instance, the Western Hemisphere. Skills and understandings learned in previous grades are maintained, reinforced, and extended within this larger community focus. More difficult and abstract aspects of previously acquired skills and understandings are initiated and developed.

Direct observations through field trips to see these international structures and natural features are not often possible. Few pupils will have had the opportunity to engage in such activities as boating on the famous man-made canals of Xochimilco in Mexico, swimming and playing along the sandy beaches of the Rio de la Plata in Uruguay during its summer months of January and February, or big-game-hunting in the wilderness areas of the high plateaus of Africa. The learning experiences, however, should be organized carefully so that the pupils do not transfer their visual images of well-known recreational features in the local or state community to these resorts situated in countries outside our national boundaries. Colored photographs, motion pictures, and filmstrips of various recreational phenomena should be used extensively along with the verbal explanations and descriptions in their social studies textbooks. The man-made recreational structures particularly will differ in many instances from those commonly found in the local, county, or state communities. Unfamiliar landscape features will need to be introduced. Here again, as in the previous grades, their introduction should be accompanied by the use of pictures, including aerial obliques, to help pupils build vivid mental images of the surrounding landforms and water bodies. A study of these pictures will allow them to perceive the spatial relationships of man-made structures and activities and the natural features of any given region. They should not be asked to depict any recreational phenomena on maps without the appropriate mental imagery.

Students at this age level are interested in faraway places and events. Maps continue to have a strong appeal. Likewise, they are capable of gathering data from a variety of sources and can classify and organize them into reports for further study and analysis. Reorganizing data gathered from vicarious experiences and representing them on various kinds of maps are both challenging and helpful especially when done as a regular part of the social studies program. One of the prime functions of maps is "to visualize what is abstract, as well as what is too immense or distant to see."[9]

The developmental sequence of mapping experiences within the emphasis of the United States and inter-American community or the Pacific community, for example, should begin with teaching-learning activities to extend the ability to observe carefully and accurately. Pictures, filmstrips, and motion pictures are a vital part of the teaching-learning experiences. Allocate class time to the study of these materials so that pupils can form visual images of the wide variety of recreational phenomena, both natural and man-made, being studied. Make certain that picture content is associated with the written content of the social studies textbooks. Continue to use the high oblique aerial photographs.

Introduce the reading of vertical aerial photographs of such cultural features as cities and their surrounding environs, resort areas, and so on. Such photographs are not easy to read and should be introduced with great care. Raisz analyzes the aerial photograph in this way:

> A vertical airplane photograph is a direct map picture of the earth; yet it is surprisingly difficult to read. . . . It is no surprise that beginners can read an oblique picture easily while a vertical picture often has no meaning for them. The ability to read vertical pictures, like the ability to read a foreign language, is the result of systematic study.[10]

He goes on to say:

> In a vertical photograph. . . . we see a strange world; the very place where we live looks unfamiliar. We see the earth as an eagle does, because usually we are unable to look straight down, even from an airplane. Mountains and hills are "flattened," river patterns stand out clearly, and variations in the soil and vegetation are most outstanding. The absence of color makes the country even more unfamiliar. The reading of vertical photographs requires special study.[11]

The beginning reading activities should be focused on the shapes of the objects since these are some of the most obvious features in the photograph. Man-made features with their regular geometric shapes are readily identifiable while natural features have irregular shapes.

The teacher should:

1. Continue to take the class on directed field trips to study landform features. Provide opportunities to extend observational skills such as: selecting and classifying data; noting configuration of physical features such as hills, mountains, canyons, and so on. Assist children in developing

techniques for drawing landscape sketches showing both the natural and man-made features. Sketch the outlines of prominent features first, then add the details.

2. Have a number of pictures for the class to read. (See page 466 for sources of large pictures.) These pictures make faraway places come alive. Identify significant aspects of recreational phenomena located in widely separated geographic regions. For example, contrast mountain scenery of the Canadian Rockies with the Andes Mountains or the Alps in Europe. Look for evidences of eroded and glaciated mountain surfaces. Note the ruggedness of the ranges, the sharp-edged pinnacles, the steep slopes. Contrast the Andes with the Appalachian Mountains in eastern Canada and the eastern United States. Note the rounded peaks, the gentle slopes, the broad sweeping valleys of this latter range. Relate these features to recreational activities such as skiing in the winter and hiking in the summer.

3. Show filmstrips and motion pictures of recreational phenomena. These visual aids should include such well-known resort areas as Banff and Jasper in the Canadian Rockies, the famous winter facilities of the Appalachian Mountains in the province of Quebec, the Caribbean resorts, the lake region of Chile, the cities of Buenos Aires and Rio de Janeiro. Keep records of data gathered from these sources.

4. Read a vertical aerial photograph of the local community and one of a large metropolitan area such as Buenos Aires or Rio de Janeiro. Note the various regular geometric shapes such as small squares for houses, larger rectangular figures for manufacturing plants, railroad terminals, etc. Note how the streets and roads appear as ribbon-like lines. Water bodies such as lakes and rivers appear as dark objects. The mottled features on these photographs may be wooded parks. Note the location of these recreational features.

It is suggested that the concept of contour lines for representing elevations now be introduced as a map-making exercise. The representation of the exact height or elevation of hills, mountains, and other elevated features of the earth's surface is one of the most difficult problems confronting cartographers. The raised plastic relief maps use the third dimension of height to show these features, but teachers should be aware of the fact that the vertical elements are exaggerated on them. The shaded merged relief map gives only approximate elevations and shapes. The use of a contour line is the only accurate cartographic method of showing the height and shape of the terrain features. Contour-line maps, unfortunately, are hard to make and to read.

Thus there is a need for planning carefully a series of teaching-learning experiences designed to help classes acquire the ability to understand and to visualize the landscapes represented by contour-line maps. The map-making activities which follow are proposed as a readiness stage prior to a detailed program of reading and interpreting contour-line maps later in the secondary school. To develop the concept of contour lines, the teacher may:

1. Have several groups of pupils plan mountain-climbing expeditions to explore the Andes Mountains. Discuss the kinds of information a climber needs: how steep the trails are, how high the peaks are, where the steep slopes are, where the gentle slopes are, and so on. Read aerial photographs (obliques) of the mountains noting these details as well as the configurations of the various faces of the mountains.
2. Have the class construct two identical models of each mountain from modeling clay. Decide on an appropriate scale. Use the models to discuss possible routes for climbing expeditions. Mark these routes on the models. Now slice one model of each mountain into layers of the same thickness, making each slice parallel to the base. Make contour-line maps of each mountain on separate sheets of paper by drawing a line around each of the layers. Place a small triangular symbol within the inner contour line to indicate the location of each mountain's peak. Add the approximate elevations for each of the contours and indicate the cardinal directions. Give the maps titles.
3. Have the class read their contour maps to find the steep slopes (the lines are closely spaced) and the gentle slopes (the lines are spaced farther apart). Use the model in conjunction with the map to note how each contour line connects points of equal elevation. Discuss why this kind of information is invaluable to the mountain climber. His contour-line map will tell him ahead of time how much uphill climbing he will have to do and how much of the climbing will be on the level or downhill.

Besides introducing the concept of the contour line such activities help learners to expand and extend their concept of elevation or altitude.

In developing the ability to read maps, the teacher should continue to provide map-reading activities aimed to help the pupil translate the symbolic representations on maps into conceptual patterns of landscape imagery. Each pupil should have the opportunity to read maps prepared by other members of the class, maps found in textbooks and reference books, and the specially prepared commercial maps for classroom use. Unfamiliar natural features associated with outdoor recreational structures and activities should first be introduced in photographs or any other appropriate visual aid before the student is asked to read them on a map. Teaching-learning experiences should be directed toward helping him develop meanings for the concepts symbolized. Oblique aerial photographs provide visual images of the appearance of the resort area along the La Plata River in Uruguay or the ski trails in the Laurentian Mountains of Quebec during the months of January through March. It is activities such as these that enable learners "to see through the symbols on a map and thereby read the map before them."[12] The teacher should:

1. Read and use the raised plastic relief maps (raised plastic relief maps of Canada, North America, and South America are available—see "Aids for Teaching") of North and South America as well as several maps of individual countries. These maps enable classes to feel as well as to see the landform features of the Western Hemisphere. Note the distribution patterns of mountains in the two continents of North and South America. Compare and contrast the terrain characteristics of the mountain ranges. Collect oblique aerial photographs and mount them alongside the maps.
2. Continue to review and teach the map symbols and terms used on physical-political maps which show the distribution of natural features and conditions in these two continents, as, for example, the major landforms and water bodies, the vegetation, elevation, and so on. Continue to teach and review the symbols which show the distribution of cultural features such as cities, highways, playgrounds, parks, beaches, etc., on both large-scale maps and small-scale maps. Note the use of certain conventional symbols such as colors for showing natural features and cultural features. Generally, blue represents bodies of water and black represents man-made objects.
3. Compare a map of the Western Hemisphere with the globe. Note the shape and area of the two large continental masses on a map and on a large globe. Read the map's key for the projection used. On an equal-area projection, for example, have the class note places on the map where the shape of the land has been twisted or distorted. What parts of the map have little distortion? Help them to become aware of the problem of expressing the spherical surface on a flat map surface. Discuss reasons for this. Keeping the properties of shape and area is not a major problem on a continental map, however. Make measurements on the globe and on a flat map and note any differences.

Continue to develop the ability to interpret the distributions and locations represented on maps and to reason geographically. Map interpretation activities should be directed toward helping pupils discover correlations between the natural features in an area and the many ways people may use these features for recreational purposes. Maps are basic tools in the study of the geographic aspects of recreational phenomena. The teaching-learning experiences should be arranged to help students make inferences about relationships between particular patterns of cultural features and natural features in any given arena. An invaluable method of becoming aware of these various elements is to examine several kinds of maps of the same area—a landform map, a transportation map showing the roads, railroads, and airports, a population map, and a climate map showing both rainfall and temperature. From an analysis of these several maps it should be possible to make inferences about the pattern of distribution of symbols portraying recreational phenomena within the Western Hemisphere. There is a concentration of recreational resort areas along the southeast coastal regions of Brazil and Uruguay and the central coastal region of Chile. The symbols representing Canadian resorts, golf courses, and so on are clustered along a narrow band of land adjacent to the international boundary between Canada and the United States. Have the class make inferences about the absence of resort areas in such regions as the sheltered Lake Maracaibo region of Venezuela, Lake Titicaca, one of the world's largest lakes high in the Andes Mountains, the coastal sections of Peru and northern Chile, the Hudson Bay region of Canada, the many thousands of lakes in Canada's Northwest Territories, and so on. Contrast these areas with the West Indies in the Caribbean. In the latter area we find a concentration of recreational phenomena where the relief and climatic conditions are favorable for such activities as swimming, boating, fishing, and golfing. One caution, however, is necessary as classes interpret the distributions and locations of recreational features on maps: "Area relations of many items may imply, but not necessarily denote, causal relations. Cause and effect relations should be definitely proved before the child draws any such conclusions from coincidence in distributions."[13]

In addition, the generalization that "recreation is so largely personal and subjective that it is to be sought wherever one finds it rather than in any specific combinations of environmental conditions"[14] should be introduced and discussed. Also, new locations in the world are becoming favorite recreational spots because jet transportation opens them up to easy travel. Do the pupils know of such areas in the South Pacific? in Alaska? in the wildlife preserves of Africa? The learning activities at this level should be directed toward helping students grow in their ability to think critically and creatively about formulating generalizations about recreational phenomena. They will discover that the major recreational foci in South America at present are found in the large centers of population—the cities of Rio de Janeiro in Brazil, Montevideo in Uruguay, Buenos Aires in Argentina, and so on.

In providing teaching-learning activities to develop relational thinking, teachers are aiding classes to see a series of relationships within each of the expanding communities in ways people engage in one of the basic human activities. The emphasis in this suggested series of teaching procedures and mapping activities has been on the spatial dimensions of a basic human activity within a number of communities of men. Through this curriculum organization of the expanding communities "students add to their understandings of a wide array of human activities in space with generalizations developed during the previous grade modified, changed, restated in light of additional information gained or new areas studied."[15]

A summary of the geographic concepts and map skills suggested for the developmental sequence of teaching procedures and mapping activities analyzed in relation to the three major map objectives. The map skills and understandings that have been selected for the illustrative developmental sequence for the three region-of-nations communities and the world community may be summarized as follows:

1. Ability to reorganize data gathered from firsthand and vicarious experiences and to represent them on maps with appropriate symbols.

Ability to observe accurately and note locations and distributions of natural and man-made features. Activities include field trips to make firsthand observations, and viewing motion pictures, filmstrips, and photographs.

Ability to plan and make three-dimensional models to represent terrain features and man-made features.

Ability to use pictorial and conventional symbols to represent natural and man-made features on base maps both large scale and small scale.

Ability to make both large-scale and small-scale maps using conventional symbols to represent natural and man-made features.

Ability to represent a single elevated feature such as a mountain through the use of contour lines.

2. Ability to read data recorded on maps. Initial map-reading skills developed through the map-making activities described above.

Ability to read the pictorial symbols on the class-made maps and visualize the natural and made-made features that these symbols represent.

Ability to read raised plastic relief maps and visualize the land forms and water bodies that are represented.

Ability to read physical-political maps with point, line, and area symbols that represent natural and man-made features along with their patterns of distribution.

Ability to read and use the small-scale landform maps with pictorial relief symbols.

Ability to read special-purpose maps with abstract conventional symbols to represent quantity or amount, as, for example, population density, average number of items in a given area, and so on.

Ability to read a contour-line map made in the class and visualize the shape and relief of the elevated feature being represented.

3. Ability to interpret location and distribution on maps and to reason geographically. Pupils develop initial ability to interpret maps by comparing and making inferences about things they have symbolized on maps made in the classroom.

Ability to perceive and express relative location and distribution of natural and man-made features within a given community emphasis.

Ability to compare maps and make inferences about the location and distribution of one kind of natural feature compared with the location and distribution of another.

Ability to compare and make inferences about the location and distribution of one kind of man-made feature compared with location and distribution of another.

Ability to compare maps and make inferences about the location and distribution of one kind of man-made feature compared with the location and distribution of one kind of natural feature.

Ability to analyze the geographical location and areal distribution of features, both man-made and natural, as to relative location, relative distance, and relative direction.

REFERENCES

1. Elaine Forsyth, *Map Reading*, Geographic Education Series No. 1 (Norman, Okla.: National Council for Geographic Education, n. d.). This is a series of lessons developing the necessary understandings of scale, network, and symbols. Also, the programmed text *Understanding Maps*, by Beulah Tannenbaum and Myra Stillman (New York: McGraw-Hill Book Co., Inc., 1957), may either be used in the classroom or assigned as home study wherever an understanding or review of map skills is needed. See also Mamie L. Anderzhon, *Steps in Map Reading* (Chicago: Rand McNally & Co., 1955).

2. Armin K. Lobeck, *Things Maps Don't Tell Us* (New York: The Macmillan Co., 1956).

3. See the large-scale maps of major world cities in *World Book Atlas* (Chicago: Field Enterprises Educational Corporation, 1964).

4. Excellent examples of simple sketch maps may be found in David Greenhood, *Mapping* (Chicago: University of Chicago Press, 1964).

5. Edward B. Espenshade, Jr., "Cartographic Developments and New Maps," *New Viewpoints in Geography*, Twenty-ninth Yearbook, National Council for the Social Studies (Washington: NCSS, 1959), p. 101.

6. Preston E. James, "New Viewpoints in Geography," *New Viewpoints in the Social Sciences*, Twenty-eighth Yearbook, National Council for the Social Sciences (Washington: NCSS, 1958), p. 49.

7. Refer to pp. 241–243, on scale.

8. V. C. Finch *et al.*, *Elements of Geography* (New York: McGraw-Hill Book Co., Inc., 4th ed., 1957), Chapter 1 and Appendix B.

9. Greenhood, *op. cit.*

10. Erwin Raisz, *General Cartography* (New York: McGraw-Hill Book Co., Inc., 1948), p. 196.

11. *Ibid.*, p. 186.

12. Clyde Kohn, "Interpreting Maps and Globes," *Skills in Social Studies*, Twenty-fourth Yearbook, National Council for the Social Studies (Washington: NCSS, 1953), p. 168.

13. *Ibid.*, p. 172.

14. Preston E. James and Clarence F. Jones (eds.), *American Geography Inventory and Prospect* (Syracuse, N.Y.: Syracuse University Press, 1954), p. 225.

15. Clyde Kohn, "Spatial Dimensions of Human Activities: Significance for Geographic Education," *Journal of Geography*, 58:125 (March, 1959).

APPENDIXES

appendix A

AIDS FOR TEACHING

Map Projection Teaching Aids To Demonstrate Map and Globe Relationships

Several practical map projection devices for classroom demonstrations to show how flat maps are made from globes are now available. The *Map Projection Device* by Farquhar Transparent Globes consists of one 10-inch-diameter transparent projection globe, a dual-unit projection lamp assembly and cord, and four translucent polyethylene overlays that are markable. The overlays consist of two cones, one cylinder, and one disk for demonstrating conic, cylindrical, and azimuthal map projections. By the shadow-casting method, the map on the surface of the globe is projected upon the surface of a cylinder, cone, or plane. A teacher's manual accompanies the device.

A *Map Projection Model* by Hubbard consists of an 8-inch-diameter globe and three transparent maps (cylindrical, conical, and azimuthal) that may be formed about the globe. The cylindrical and conical maps may be unsnapped to be seen as flat maps. A detailed teacher's study guide is included.

Wall maps for teaching projections are available from Denoyer-Geppert. There are three maps in this series: (1) hemisphere projections, (2) world projections, and (3) conic projections, each 44" by 58".

An invaluable teacher reference is Wellman Chamberlin, *The Round Earth on Flat Paper* (Washington: National Geographic Society, 1947).

Geography Pictures

Teachers find still pictures invaluable teaching aids for geographic study. There are many sources of pictorial material—magazines, travel brochures, publications of industrial firms, calendars, and advertising circulars. Picture-story sets may be purchased from a number of sources. Most of these pictures are suited to small-group study. A recommended reference that contains a listing of primary sources of instructional materials is Catharine M. Williams, *Learning*

465

from Pictures, NEA Department of Audio-Visual Instruction (Washington: National Education Association, 1963).

A picture-story study print, *Land Forms of Running Water,* Set Sp-118, is available from Society for Visual Education (SVE). Set consists of 8 prints, size 18″ by 13″ and in full color. On the back of each picture is lesson material for the teacher. The set is suitable for the middle grades.

Now available from Nystrom is a series of geography pictures highly appropriate for large-group instructional purposes. These pictures, 30″ by 21″, are full-color enlargements from photographic transparencies. Set titles include: *North America*—12 pictures; *Africa*—12 pictures; and *Europe*—14 pictures.

Aerial photographs may be purchased from several government sources. For information and ordering instructions, direct inquiries to the following agencies:

U.S. Geological Survey—Map Information Office, U.S. Geological Survey, Washington, D.C. 20242

U.S. Department of Agriculture: for eastern half of the U.S.—Eastern Laboratory, Compliance and Aerial Photography Division, U.S. Department of Agriculture, Washington, D.C.; for western half of the U.S.—Western Laboratory, Compliance and Aerial Photography Division, U.S. Department of Agriculture, 2505 Parley's Way, Salt Lake City, Utah.

Aero Service Corporation, 210 East Courtland Street, Philadelphia, Pa., is a basic source of aerial photos, the company being one of the largest aerial mapping concerns in the world.

Raised Relief Maps and Globes

Three-dimensional relief maps and globes are indispensable geographic teaching aids for developing concepts of the earth's physical features. Mountains, plateaus, plains, and valleys can be actually felt as well as seen. These raised relief map models, formed in sturdy lightweight vinyl plastic which is markable and washable, show the earth's physical features in accurate scaled proportions. (A caution: always check the amount of vertical exaggeration.)

Raised relief maps are fundamental teaching tools in a developmental program for teaching landform symbols such as contour lines on topographic maps and the significance of color-layer systems on physical-political maps.

A raised relief *Geographic Terms* map (Nystrom) 42″ by 46″ depicting and naming 116 geographic concepts is recommended for each elementary and junior high school. The map set includes 35 paper map reproductions for student desk use, plus a 44-page teacher's manual.

Titles now available in the Aero relief series (Nystrom) include the *United States, World, Europe, Asia, Africa, North America, South America,* and *Canada.* Denoyer-Geppert publishes maps of the *United States, Europe,* and *France.* Maps of individual states include *California, Wisconsin, Pennsylvania, New Jersey,* and *New York* (Nystrom), and *Ohio* (Denoyer-Geppert).

Desk-size relief maps of the U.S. for student use in sizes ranging from 19″ by 12″ to 27″ by 20″ are published by both Nystrom and Hammond.

For detailed study of physical and cultural features of selected regions of the United States, U.S. Geological Survey quadrangles in three-dimensional relief are now available from two sources: Nystrom and the Army Map Service, Corps of Engineers. Further information and prices available from these sources on request.

Globes showing the earth in raised relief both colored and uncolored are now available from most school map and globe outlets. The uncolored 12-inch globe manufactured by Panoramic Studios and by Hubbard can be used for student project activities. Hubbard has a 12-inch hydrographic relief globe. Earth-curved relief maps, actual segments of a 30-inch raised relief globe, are available from Panoramic Studios or from the map outlet firm of Denoyer-Geppert. Titles in this series include *North America, South America, Europe, Asia, Africa, Australia,* and *North Polar Area.*

An exciting 30-inch deluxe globe with the earth's surface in color and full relief with a vertical exaggeration of 30:1 is made by Panoramic Studios.

Inexpensive relief rubber molds for making small-scale relief models are made by Art Chemical Products, Huntington, Ind. (46750). Mold titles include *North America, South America* (approximate scale 1 inch to 400 miles), *United States* (scale of 1 inch to 200 miles), and *Palestine.* A special map mix is available.

Two suggested teacher references are:

Preston E. James and Shirley Hess, *Better Teaching with Relief Maps* (Philadelphia: Aero Service Corporation, 1962). A teacher's manual for the raised relief map of the U.S. is included.

Walter W. Ristow, *Three-Dimensional Maps: Annotated List of References Relating to Construction and Use of Terrain Models* (Washington: Library of Congress, 2nd ed., 1964).

Overhead Projection Transparencies

Transparency overhead projectors are now available in most elementary and junior high schools for classroom use. The projector can be used in lighted rooms. The teacher can write directly on the transparency and use overlays to help students reason about relationships between two or more sets of data.

A number of publishing firms now have transparencies for sale. A representative sampling of materials available includes:

Alpha Map Transparencies, Henry J. Warman, consulting geographer (Boston: Allyn and Bacon, Inc. 1964). Mid-continental United States. Set of 3 base maps and 30 overlays. Middle and upper grades.

Ginn Map Transparencies (Boston: Ginn & Company, 1965). A series of 30 transparencies using the Harrison relief maps for the background. Overlays add basic data on temperature, rainfall, and population distribution. Geographic areas include North America, United States, Canada, South America, Mexico, Eurasia, Europe, Africa, and Australia.

Nystrom Map Transparencies (Chicago: A. J. Nystrom and Co.). Titles available in various series include *Geography of the United States*. Outline maps with over 100 titles (*U.S., World, Continent*), physical-political maps in sculptural relief.

Language of Maps (Encyclopaedia Britannica Films, 1963).
A set of 4 units of transparencies: Unit I—Parallels and Meridians; Unit II—Reading Topographic Symbols; Unit III—Identifying Cultural Features; and Unit IV—Mapping a Small Area. Recommended for middle grades.

Recommended Materials for an Elementary School Building

Map and Globe Skills Kit. Developed by Robert A. Naslund and Charles M. Brown. Published by Science Research Associates, Inc., 259 East Erie Street, Chicago, Illinois (60611), 1964. The learning materials in the kit are organized into the following units: Introduction to Map Reading, Learning to Read Street and Highway Maps, Learning to Read Globes and Projections, Learning to Read Many Kinds of Maps, and Interpreting Maps. The kit contains skill cards, study cards, key cards, and pupil booklets. Designed for use in Grades 4–6. Teacher's handbook.

Graph and Picture Study Skills Kit. Developed by Robert A. Naslund and Jack McClellan. Published by Science Research Associates, 1961. The learning materials in the kit are divided into the following units: Graphic Forms, Charts and Diagrams, Cartoons, and Photographs. The kit contains sets of skill cards, key cards, study cards, and pupil booklets. Pupil booklet contains activity projects for each unit. Detailed teacher's handbook suggests ways of using kit. Designed for Grades 4–6.

Map Symbols and Geographic Terms Charts. Zoe Thralls and Frances M. Hansen. Published by A. J. Nystrom & Co., 1964. The set of charts contains 46 charts 18½" by 24". Photographs, in full color, diagrams, and symbols are paired on individual charts. For example, a photograph of a coastline is shown on the same chart with a diagram that illustrates how a coastline appears on a map. Charts cover such geographic concepts as a dry plain and a humid plain, plateau, tundra, pipeline routes, alluvial fan, delta, river confluence, latitude and longitude. Use of charts may be adapted to the primary and middle grades. Teacher's manual accompanies the set of charts.

Slated "Project" or "Activity" Globe. Available from map and globe suppliers such as Denoyer-Geppert and A. J. Nystrom. Land masses and water areas shown. Slated surface of the globe makes for an excellent chalk-writing surface for many student activities. The 20-inch globe (scale of 400 miles to 1 inch) or larger is recommended for use in both the primary and middle school grades.

Directory of Map and Globe Producers

A listing of major publishers and sources of geographic teaching aids for schools follows. These firms offer a variety of maps, atlases, charts, models, and globes. Catalogs published regularly are available to interested persons. The catalogs are usually well illustrated and provide valuable information about map and globe programs.

The George F. Cram Company, Inc.
730 E. Washington Street
Indianapolis, Indiana

Denoyer-Geppert Company
5235 Ravenswood Avenue
Chicago, Illinois

C. S. Hammond & Co., Inc.
515 Valley Street
Maplewood, New Jersey

A. J. Nystrom & Co.
3333 Elston Avenue
Chicago, Illinois

Rand McNally & Company
P.O. Box 7600
Chicago, Illinois

Weber Costello
1900 N. Narragansett
Chicago, Illinois

Additional sources:

Aero Service Corporation. Raised Relief Map Division of Aero Service is now a part of A. J. Nystrom & Company.

American Geographical Society
Broadway at 156th Street
New York, New York
Maps and specialized atlases.

Farquhar Transparent Globes
5007 Warrington Avenue
Philadelphia, Pennsylvania
Transparent globes and projection devices.

John W. Gunter, Inc.
1027 South Claremont
San Mateo, California
Maps of California a specialty.

Hagstrom Company Inc.
311 Broadway
New York, New York
Decorative and historical maps.

Hubbard Scientific Company
P.O. Box 105
Northbrook, Illinois
Models for laboratory activities and teaching aids.

Jeppesen & Co.
8025 East 40th Avenue
Denver, Colorado
Natural color relief maps.

National Geographic Society
16th and M Streets, N.W.
Washington, D.C.
Atlases, maps, globes, and geographic publications.

Panoramic Studios Inc.
179 West Berks Street
Philadelphia, Pennsylvania
Raised relief maps and globes.

Replogle Globes, Inc.
1901 N. Narragansett Avenue
Chicago, Illinois
Geographic globes.

Ward's Natural Science Establishment, Inc.
P.O. Box 1712
Rochester, New York
also
P.O. Box 1749
Monterey, California
Earth science filmstrips and transparencies.

Programmed Instructional Materials

A number of programmed geographic instructional materials are being published for classroom use. These programs lend themselves to a variety of uses.

They may be used as an independent teaching device for advanced students or as supplemental exercises for students who need additional work in specific fundamentals. They may serve as the basic program of instruction in a selected area for the entire class. The listings below represent a sampling of programs currently on the market.

China: A Programmed Unit in Geography. T. C. Soens and others. New York: Holt, Rinehart & Winston, Inc., 1963. Programmed text, 575 frames, paperback. Average time, 6 to 7 hours. Teacher's manual. Junior high school.

Earth in Orbit. (Geography, Part I) San Francisco: Fearon Publishers, Inc. Programmed text, 327 frames, paperback. Average time, 4 hours. Junior high school.

Latitude and Longitude. Learning Inc. Chicago: Coronet Instructional Films, 1962. Programmed text, 379 frames, paperback. Average time, 2 to 5 hours. Contains 10 sets of exercises. Program explains fundamental concepts of latitude and longitude with practice frames which build skill in finding locations. Middle grades and junior high school.

Maps: How We Read Them. Learning Inc. Chicago: Coronet Instructional Films, 1963. Programmed text, 315 frames, paperback. Average time, 2 to 4 hours. Twelve types of maps are presented. Teacher's manual. Middle grades.

A Program on Earth-Sun Relationships. Robert Saveland. Boston: Ginn & Company, 1962. Programmed text, 213 frames, paperback. Separate answer sheets. Two standardized tests and teacher's guide accompany program. Junior high school.

Programmed Geography. Sullivan Associates; written by Cynthia Buchanan. New York: The Macmillan Co., 1963. Three programmed textbooks, 1150 frames, paperbacks. Program consists of three separate courses in physical geography. Book I—*The Earth in Space*; Book II—*Continents and Oceans*; Book III—*Latitudes and Climates*. Progress tests accompany each book. Middle grades.

Reading Latitude from Maps and *Reading Longitude from Maps.* G. D. Koehrer, D. Peterson, and R. Paul. St. Louis: Webster Publishing Division, McGraw-Hill Book Co., Inc., 1964. Programmed textbooks, paperback. Middle grades and junior high school.

Understanding Maps. General Education, Inc. Boston: Allyn and Bacon, Inc., 1964. Programmed text, 249 frames, paperback. Organized in five sections, each independent of others. Topics include: kinds of maps, use of symbols, map projection, directions, and scale. Average time, 3 to 5 hours. Middle grades.

Research Aids and Materials: Periodicals and Publications of Geographical Associations

A number of organizations publish a variety of outstanding materials and studies of geographical interest to teachers. Descriptions and addresses are listed below.

Annals. A quarterly geographic journal of the Association of American Geographers, 1785 Massachusetts Avenue, N.W., Washington, D.C. Map supplements are of interest. The association also publishes the periodical *Professional Geographer.*

Canadian Geographical Journal. Published by the Royal Canadian Geographical Society, 488 Wilbrod Street, Ottawa, Ontario. Monthly; $6.00 per year.

The Geographical Journal. Official publication of the Royal Geographical Society. Subscriptions to the *Journal* are available to the public. Address: Kensington Gore, London, S.W. 7, Great Britain. Quarterly.

The Geographical Magazine. London. U.S. subscription office: The Times (London) Inc., 25 East 54th Street, New York. Monthly; subscription rate $7.50 yearly.

The Geographical Review. The scientific quarterly of the American Geographical Society, Broadway at 156th St., New York, N.Y. The society publishes many excellent maps and the periodical *Focus.* The publication *Current Geographical Publications* lists accessions of the society.

The Journal of Geography. The official publication of the National Council for Geographic Education, published by A. J. Nystrom & Company. Contains articles on teaching methods and techniques of particular interest to elementary and junior high school teachers. Monthly, except June, July, August; $7.00 per year.

Map Collectors' Circle. The series consists of pamphlets on all aspects of cartography—bibliographical, historical, and aesthetic. Durant House, Chiswell Street, London, E.C.I. Annual subscription $15.00. Publication titles to date have included among others *California as an Island, Maps of Antarctica,* and *Maps of the Yorktown Campaign.*

National Council for Geographic Education. Publications Center, Illinois State University, Normal, Ill. Inexpensive publications for teachers of geography and social studies at all levels of instruction. Items include *"Do It This Way" Series, Geographic Education Series, Inventory of Source Materials,* and *Leaflets.*

National Geographic Magazine. A publication of the National Geographic Society, Washington, D.C. Monthly; $6.50 per year.

Special Libraries Association, Geographical and Map Division Bulletin. The association, at 31 East 10th Street, New York, N.Y., publishes a list of new books and maps.

Surveying and Mapping. A quarterly journal of the American Congress on Surveying and Mapping, 733 - 15th Street, N.W., Washington, D.C.

The following publications are of particular value to both teachers and students. They should be included in the middle and junior high school classroom libraries.

The Cram Spotlight. A geographical leaflet. Published irregularly, each issue features a country or region. Illustrated with maps. No charge. The George F. Cram Co., Inc., 730 E. Washington Street, Indianapolis, Ind.

Cartocraft Teaching Aids. A periodical publication designed for teacher and student. Various topics of interest to teachers of geography, history, and social studies. A sampling of topics in series have included "How Many Miles in a Degree?" "First Voyage of Columbus," "Physical Framework of Africa." Subscription is $1.00 for each school year series. Back issues are available. Send for price list to Geographic Research Institute, Denoyer-Geppert Co.

Focus. A geographical leaflet, each issue dealing with an area or subject of current world interest, illustrated with appropriate maps. Monthly except July and August; subscription $1.25 for one year; $3.00 for three years; reduced rates for bulk orders. Recommended for junior high school students and teachers. Published by American Geographic Society.

Geographic School Bulletin. A full-color bulletin for elementary school children. Each issue features a country or area along with articles pertaining to geography, natural history, and science. Weekly, October to May; subscription one year $2.00, three years $5.00. School Service, National Geographic Society.

Selected References for Teachers' Professional Libraries in Elementary and Junior High Schools

The books and references mentioned in this list have been cited as examples of titles in the field of geographic content and methodological procedures which should be readily available to classroom social studies teachers.

Bloom, Benjamin S. (ed.). *Taxonomy of Educational Objectives.* New York: David McKay Co., Inc., 1956. *Handbook I, Cognitive Domain* contains a classification of educational goals with illustrative objectives and test items.

Brown, James W., Lewis, Richard B., and Harcleroad, Fred F. *A-V Instruction: Materials and Methods.* New York: McGraw-Hill Book Co., Inc., 2nd ed., 1964. Specific examples of teaching materials and their uses in the classroom.

Goode's World Atlas. Edited by Edward B. Espenshade, Jr. Chicago: Rand McNally & Co., 12th ed., 1964.

Harris, Ruby M. *The Rand McNally Handbook of Map and Globe Usage.* Chicago: Rand McNally & Co., 1959.

Hill, Wilhelmina (ed.). *Curriculum Guide to Geographic Education.* Normal, Ill.: National Council for Geographic Education, 1964.

Hoyt, Joseph B. *Man and the Earth.* Englewood Cliffs, N.J.: Prentice-Hall, Inc., 1962. Introductory college level text. Describes the land masses and oceanic configurations of the earth. Shows how geographic processes are related to man in his various cultures.

James, Preston E. *A Geography of Man.* Boston: Ginn & Company, 3rd ed., 1966. Presents basic geographic concepts and illustrates methods of geographic analysis.

James, Preston E. (ed.). *New Viewpoints in Geography.* Washington, D.C.: National Council for Social Studies, 1959.

Moore, W. G. *A Dictionary of Geography.* Baltimore: Penguin Books, 1962. Definitions and explanations of terms used in physical geography.

Oxford Economic Atlas of the World. New York: Oxford University Press, 2nd ed., 1959. Arranged in two parts: (1) world commodity maps grouped in ten sections and (2) an index arranged country by country.

Philbrick, Allen K. *This Human World.* New York: John Wiley & Sons, Inc., 1963. A world regional geography at the introductory college level. Emphasis on the arrangement of physical, cultural, and organizational elements of geography.

Raisz, Erwin. *Principles of Cartography.* New York: McGraw-Hill Book Co., Inc., 1962. Best single introductory college level textbook covering the principles and procedures to use in making and understanding maps.

Schultz, Morton J. *The Teacher and Overhead Projection.* Englewood Cliffs, N.J.: Prentice-Hall, Inc., 1965. A practical guide for the teacher with many useful examples for the classroom.

Stamp, L. Dudley (ed.). *A Glossary of Geographical Terms.* New York: John Wiley & Sons, Inc., 1961.

Warman, Henry J. *Geography—Background, Techniques and Prospects.* Worcester, Mass.: Clark University Press, 1954. A highly recommended source of information about the field of geography and its techniques, written for teachers.

Webster's Geographical Dictionary. Springfield, Mass.: G. & C. Merriam Co., 1964. A dictionary of names of places with pronunciations. Geographical and historical information included.

Basic Reference Atlases for Elementary and Junior High School Libraries

Ambassador World Atlas. Maplewood, N.J.: C. S. Hammond & Co., Inc. Contains 326 maps and an index of 100,000 entries.

Atlas of the Arab World and Middle East. New York: St Martin's Press, Inc., 1960. Maps by Djambatan of Amsterdam. Text and photographs. Exceptional cartographic work.

Atlas of European History. Edited by Edward W. Fox. New York: Oxford University Press, 1959. Contains 64 pages of maps and a gazetteer section.

Atlas of Florida. Compiled by Erwin Raisz and Associates with text by John R. Dunkle. Gainesville: University of Florida Press, 1964.

Atlas of the Pacific Northwest. Edited by Richard M. Highsmith. Corvallis: Oregon State University Press, 3rd ed., 1962.

Atlas of South-East Asia. New York: St Martin's Press, Inc., 1964. Contains 64 pages of colored maps including large-scale town plans of major cities. Brief text and photographs. Outstanding cartographic work by Djambatan of Amsterdam.

Atlas of Western Civilization. Frederic Van Der Meer. Princeton, N.J.: D. Van Nostrand Co., Inc., 2nd ed., 1960.

Bartholomew's Advance Atlas of Modern Geography. John Bartholomew. New York: McGraw-Hill Book Co., Inc., 5th ed., 1960.

Britannica World Atlas. Chicago: Encyclopaedia Britannica, Inc., 1965. Included in the atlas is a 64-page world scene section showing the world's population distribution, languages, soils, drainage regions, trades, and 22 maps and text of the national and international political structures.

Cram Modern World Atlas. Indianapolis, Ind.: The George F. Cram Co., Inc. Three sections: U.S. and World; World History; and Earth Sciences and Outer Space.

Economic Atlas of the Soviet Union. George Kish. Ann Arbor: University of Michigan Press, 1960.

A Historical Atlas of Canada. Edited by D. G. G. Kerr. Toronto: Thomas Nelson & Sons, 1960. A well-illustrated atlas. Excellent text accompanies maps. Highly recommended.

Life Pictorial Atlas of the World. By the editors of *Life* and Rand McNally. New York: Time Incorporated, 1961. In addition to the excellent sculptured terrain and political maps, the atlas contains many drawings, graphs, charts, and full-color photographs of landscapes around the world. Comprehensive index, unfortunately, does not contain a guide to pronunciations.

National Geographic Atlas of the World. Edited by Melville Bell Grosvenor. Washington: National Geographic Society, 1963. A standard reference atlas in two editions, the Standard and the Deluxe.

Philips' Library Atlas. Edited by Harold Fullard and H. C. Darby. London: George Philip and Son, Ltd., 7th ed., 1962. (Available from Denoyer-Geppert.) Two sections: first part has relief, climate, vegetation, population maps; second part has 32 pages of economic maps and diagrams.

Physical World Atlas. John Bartholomew, New York: American Map Co., 1964.

Prentice-Hall World Atlas. Edited by Joseph E. Williams. Englewood Cliffs, N.J.: Prentice-Hall, Inc., 2nd ed., 1963. Excellent portrayal of land forms. Recommended for student atlases.

Rand McNally Cosmopolitan World Atlas. Chicago: Rand McNally & Co., 1964. Good coverage for the Western Hemisphere.

The Reader's Digest Great World Atlas. Pleasantville, N.Y.: Reader's Digest Services, Inc., 1963.

The World Book Atlas. Chicago: Field Enterprises Educational Corporation, 1965. A general reference for school and home use.

Special Atlases Available for Reference Use at Most College and Local Public Libraries

Commercial Atlas and Marketing Guide. Chicago: Rand McNally & Co., 96th ed., 1965. All copies of this atlas remain property of Rand McNally. Complete data for each of the 50 states plus a world facts section and atlas.

The Times Atlas of the World. Edited by John Bartholomew. Mid-Century Edition. London: The Times. Available in the U.S. only through Houghton Mifflin Company, Boston. Published in five volumes: Vol. I, *The World;*

Vol. II, *Southwest Asia and Russia*; Vol. III, *Northern Europe*; Vol. IV, *Southern Europe and Africa*; and Vol. V, *The Americas*.

Student Atlases

Atlas of American History. Edited by Edward W. Fox. New York: Oxford University Press, 1964. Maps emphasize geographic features that have influenced settlements, migrations, and military movements. Junior high school.

Classroom Atlas. Chicago: Rand McNally & Co., 4th ed., 1963. Land forms shown through layer-tints and shading. All maps in full color. Middle grades.

Ginn World Atlas. Maps by Richard Edes Harrison. Boston: Ginn & Company, 1964. Topographic relief shown through a combination of layer-tints and hill shading. Contains 27 full-color maps and a phonetic pronunciation index. Middle grades.

Goode's World Atlas. Edited by E. B. Espenshade, Jr. Chicago: Rand McNally & Co., 12th ed., 1964. A standard reference for students and teachers. Middle grades and junior high school. Contains political, physical, and commodity maps. Index includes a guide to pronunciation.

Illustrated Atlas for Young America. Maplewood, N.J.: C. S. Hammond & Co., Inc., 1962. A guide to map reading supplemented by geographic sketches. Middle grades.

My First World Atlas. Maplewood, N.J.: C. S. Hammond & Co., Inc., 1963. A small introductory atlas with 30 maps in color. Middle grades.

Philips' New School Atlas. Edited by Harold Fullard. London: George Philip and Son, Ltd., 50th ed., 1961. (Available in U.S. from Denoyer-Geppert.) Contains over 100 maps, with a 10,000 name index. Junior high school.

Rand McNally Classroom Atlas. Chicago: Rand McNally & Co., 1950. Inexpensive paperback, useful in elementary grades.

Rand McNally Regional Atlas. Edited by E. B. Espenshade, Jr. Chicago: Rand McNally & Co., 3rd ed., 1964. An abridged edition of *Goode's World Atlas*. Contains 50 pages of maps in full color. Middle grades and junior high school.

The First Book Atlas. Maplewood, N.J.: C. S. Hammond & Co., Inc., 1960. A small introductory atlas. Lower elementary grades.

The Shorter Oxford Economic Atlas of the World. New York: Oxford University Press, 3rd ed., 1965. A recommended reference for student use at junior high school level.

The Teach Yourself Atlas of the World. Edited by Harold Fullard. London: English Universities Press, 1964. Useful student guide on how to use an atlas. Includes an atlas section of physical, political, and economic maps. Middle grades.

Westab World Atlas. Denver: Jeppesen & Co., 1962. Inexpensive 32-page student atlas with maps in natural color relief. A very limited index. Middle grades.

The World—Its Geography in Maps. Chicago: Denoyer-Geppert Co., 1965. A new 96-page atlas with 43 pages of full-color maps of the world, the continents, and regions. In four sections, atlas provides an introduction to map use. Text provides ready reference to basic geographic concepts. Middle grades and junior high school.

World Portrait Atlas. Chicago: Rand McNally & Co., 1963. A supplementary atlas for student use. Contains excellent landform illustrations. Junior high school.

Supplementary Book References for Pupils

PRIMARY

Estep, Irene. *Good Times with Maps.* Chicago: Melmont Publishers, Inc., 1962.
Jauss, Anne Marie. *The River's Journey.* Philadelphia: J. B. Lippincott Co., 1957.
Leaf, Munro. *Geography Can Be Fun.* Philadelphia: J. B. Lippincott Co., 1951.
Rinkoff, Barbara. *A Map Is a Picture.* New York: Thomas Y. Crowell Company, 1965.

MIDDLE GRADES AND JUNIOR HIGH SCHOOL

Arnow, Boris. *Oceans of the World.* Indianapolis, Ind.: The Bobbs-Merrill Company, Inc., 1962.
Asimov, Isaac. *Words on the Map.* Boston: Houghton Mifflin Company, 1962.
Ault, Phil. *This Is the Desert.* New York: Dodd, Mead & Co., 1959.
Bloch, Marie Halun. *Mountains on the Move.* New York: Coward-McCann, Inc., 1960.
Brown, Lloyd A. *Map Making: The Art That Became a Science.* Boston: Little, Brown & Company, 1960.
Chapman, Walker. *The Loneliest Continent: The Story of Antarctic Discovery.* New York: Graphic Books, 1964.
Epstein, Sam and Beryl. *The First Book of Maps and Globes.* New York: Franklin Watts, Inc., 1959.
Farb, Peter. *Face of North America.* (Young Reader's edition.) New York: Harper & Row, Publishers, 1964.
Farb, Peter. *Story of Dams.* Irvington-on-Hudson, N.Y.: Harvey House, Inc., Publishers, 1961.
Gamow, George. *A Planet Called Earth.* New York: The Viking Press, 1963.
Hackler, David. *How Maps and Globes Help Us.* Chicago: Benefic Press, New York: 1964.
Hagaman, Adaline P., and Durell, Thomas. *Basic Social Studies*, Book 4. Harper & Row, Publishers, 1964. Reference for geographic content.
Hathaway, James A. *The Story of Maps and Map-Making.* New York: Golden Press, Inc., 1960.
Hirsch, S. Carl. *The Globe for the Space Age.* New York: The Viking Press, 1963.
Life Magazine. *Ecology.* Peter Farb and the editors of *Life.* New York: Time Inc., 1964.

McFall, Christie. *Maps Mean Adventure.* New York: Dodd, Mead & Co., 1961.

Maloney, Terry. *The Story of Maps.* New York: Sterling Publishing Co., Inc., 1959.

Marsh, Susan. *All About Maps and Mapmaking.* New York: Random House, Inc., 1963.

Pond, Alonzo W. *Deserts: Silent Lands of the World.* New York: W. W. Norton & Company, Inc., 1965.

Raisz, Erwin. *Mapping the World: Portrait of Mother Earth.* New York: Abelard-Schuman Limited, 1956.

Tannenbaum, Beulah, and Stillman, Myra. *Understanding Maps.* New York: McGraw-Hill Book Co., Inc., 1957.

Classified Directory of Selected Sources of Government Maps

A number of U.S. government agencies publish maps and charts of particular interest and use to classroom teachers.

Superintendent of Documents, Government Printing Office, Washington, D.C. 20402. Price List 53, "Maps," describes available maps and related publications. Maps priced from 10¢ up. A sampling of publications: "Louisiana Purchase" contains 7 progress maps of the U.S., 15¢; "U.S. Wall Map," scale 1 inch to 50 miles, 65"×42", $2.00.

U.S. Department of Commerce, Director, Coast and Geodetic Survey, Washington, D.C. 20230. U.S. Coast and Geodetic Survey publishes many inexpensive maps and charts suitable for classroom use. Aeronautical charts, sectional and local, without aeronautical overprint, are available for 30¢ each. Large jet navigational charts of the U.S. in four sheets with a scale of 1:2,000,000 cost 50¢ for each sheet. Outline maps, both desk and wall size, are available. Indexes to the principal series and catalog pages sent on request. Remittance must accompany orders and should be made payable to C & G S, Department of Commerce. For information on nautical charts, tide tables, coast pilots, etc., send for the Coast and Geodetic Survey Catalog. Inexpensive U.S. outline maps are available in several scales. Chart No. 3093 outlines maps for construction of a model of the world (9-inch global) for 25¢.

Geography Division of the Census Bureau, Commerce Department, publishes maps of interest such as the United States Maps GE-50 series. Standard Metropolitan Statistical areas of the United States and Puerto Rico; population data from 1960 census of population, scale 500 miles to 6.2 inches. 1963, 50¢. For sale by Superintendent of Documents.

The Library of Congress, Reference Department, Map Division, Washington, D.C. 20540. Map Division makes available a number of publications and bibliographies. Library does not sell or distribute maps. Reproduction of items, not protected by copyright, may be ordered from Photoduplication Service. Publications available among others include *Facsimiles of Rare Historical Maps Available for Sale, Three-Dimensional Maps: an Annotated List of References,* and *New Government Maps for Everyone.* These publications are of high value to teachers.

Aeronautical Chart and Information Center, United States Air Force, St. Louis, Missouri 63118. Send for Aeronautical Chart and Information Center bulletin digest, new and revised editions of aeronautical charts.

Department of the Army, Army Map Service, Corps of Engineers, U.S. Army, Washington, D.C. 20315. Many maps approved for public sale by Army Map Service are suitable for classroom use. An example: Railroad Map of the U.S., Series 8204, four sheets assembled form one map 7' by 7' 4". The cost for the set is 60¢. Map Service also publishes molded plastic relief maps. Map indexes available at 5¢ each.

Department of the Interior, U.S. Geological Survey, Washington, D.C. 20242. Geological Survey publishes a number of maps including the National Topographic Maps Series, special-interest maps such as the national parks and monuments, base maps of each state. Aerial photographs available. Published quadrangle maps shown on index circulars available for each state. Descriptive folder and index circulars supplied free on request. A most valuable source of inexpensive maps.

Geographic Names Board, Interior Department, Washington, D.C. 20240. Board publishes its rulings covering place names. *Gazetteer* contains official standard names approved by the board. For information direct your inquiry to the Office of Geography, Department of Interior.

Maps of the Moon. For information about U.S. Air Force lunar charts, direct inquiries to the Superintendent of Documents, U.S. Government Printing Office. For example, the Ranger VII Lunar Charts RLC Series, compiled and published for the National Aeronautical Space Administration by the Aeronautical Chart and Information Center on Mercator projection is available for $3.00 per set of five charts from the Superintendent of Documents. Also, Lunar Charts and Mosaics Series, price $5.50; single copy, 50 cents. For another source of moon maps, write Geologic Moon Maps, U.S. Geological Survey, Washington, D.C. 20242.

United States Travel Service, Commerce Department, Washington, D.C. 20230, is a source for tour planner maps of the U.S. *Travel a New World, See U.S.A.* is a recent publication.

Maps and charts issued by other agencies of the U.S. government include:

Charts of Foreign Waters. U.S. Naval Oceanographic Office, Washington, D.C.

Charts of the Ohio River. U.S. Army Engineer Division, P.O. Box 1159, Cincinnati, Ohio.

Post Route Maps of States and Territories. Post Office Department, Washington, D.C.

Soil Maps in County Units. Division of Public Documents, Government Printing Office. Also, maps of the United States by the Bureau of Land Management are available from the Division of Public Documents.

Map Distribution Office, Surveys and Mapping Branch, Department of Mines and Technical Surveys, Geographical Branch, 601 Booth Street, Ottawa 4, Ontario. Individual sheets of the *Atlas of Canada* available at 50¢ each. Request latest List of Publications in which contents of the *Atlas* are listed. Maps of historical interest include "Routes of Explorers," "Mapping the

Coasts," and "Mapping the Interior." Desk version of the large *Atlas of Canada* scheduled for publication in 1967.

Films and Filmstrips

There are many excellent 16mm. sound motion pictures and filmstrips which deal with geography content, maps, and globes. These audio-visual aids have much to contribute to effective classroom teaching. Teachers should find the following list of films and filmstrips useful for planning purposes. Most of the films described may be rented at a nominal fee from the producers or local distributors. Also, many individual prints may be obtained on a rental basis from your local film library, public library, or nearest university extension division. Should additional information be needed, contact the district's audio-visual director or materials center.

Teachers should note that many geographical materials are now available for purchase under the National Defense Education Act. For eligibility of selected titles, check with appropriate authorities in your district or with your state NDEA Administrator, State Department of Education.

The grade level key for the films and filmstrips is: Primary, Grades K–3; Middle, Grades 4–6; Upper, junior high, Grades 7–9; Teacher Education, college, including in-service for teachers.

FILMS

All of the films listed are 16mm. Each entry provides information about length, sound, color, and film producer or distributor, and recommended grade levels. The addresses of producers or distributors are listed on pages 488–489.

Geography of Oceans and Seas

Beginnings: Dr. Roger Revelle, Oceanographer. 29 min., sound, B & W. (National Educational Television.) Indiana University. Upper. A discussion of what we know about the sea.

The Earth: Its Oceans. 13 min., sound, B & W or color. Coronet. Middle and Upper. An introduction to the study of the ocean.

Exploring the Ocean. 10 min., sound, color. Churchill. Primary and Middle. An introductory survey of the ocean.

The Last Continent, Antarctica: Oceanography. 29 min., sound, B & W. (National Educational Television.) Indiana University. Upper and Teacher Education. A detailed explanation of IGY program's study of Antarctic waters and the need for further knowledge of the sea.

Ocean Currents. 17 min., sound, color. McGraw-Hill. Upper-Middle and Upper. Describes the motions of the ocean.

Science of the Sea. 19 min., sound, color. Produced by Woods Hole Oceanographic Institution. International Film. Upper and Teacher Education. Presents the scope of oceanography and the importance of studying the sea and its usefulness to man.

Tides and Currents. 18 min., sound, color. Borrow from U.S. Coast and Geodetic Survey. Upper and Teacher Education. Defines tides and tidal cycles.

Tides of the Ocean. 16 min., sound, color. Academy. Middle and Upper. Explains tides and their effect on man.

The Geography of Soils

Birth of the Soil. 11 min., sound, color. Encyclopaedia Britannica. Upper. Explains the process of topsoil building.

Grass: The Big Story. 30 min., sound, color. Rent from U.S. Department of Agriculture. DuArt. Upper. Explains the characteristics and values of grassland farming.

Our Soil Resources: Formation and Conservation. 10 min., sound, B & W. Encyclopaedia Britannica. Upper. Analyzes soil groups, their location in the United States and need for soil conservation.

The Story of Soil. 11 min., sound, B & W or color. Coronet. Upper-Middle and Upper. Traces the story of soil and shows man's interference which has caused destruction.

Topsoil. 11 min., sound, B & W. U.S. Department of Agriculture. DuArt. Middle and Upper. Shows characteristics and importance of topsoil.

Understanding Our Earth: Soil. 11 min., sound, B & W or color. Coronet. Middle. Explains the soil profile (topsoil, subsoil, mantle rock, and bedrock), and soil types of the U.S.

What Is Soil? 12 min., sound, B & W. Encyclopaedia Britannica. Middle. Explains composition of soil and its effect on plant growth through a boy's experiment.

Globes

Globes: An Introduction. 10 min., sound, B & W or color. Indiana University. Primary and intermediate. Shows the globe as a model of the earth.

How We Know the Earth's Shape. 11 min., sound, B & W or color. Film Associates. Middle and Upper. Shows how man has changed his ideas about the earth's shape.

Introducing Globes. 10 min., sound, color. Bailey. Middle. Introduces global concepts of shape and size of the earth, distance and scale, rotation, parallels, and meridians.

Our Big, Round World. 11 min., sound, B & W and color. Coronet. Middle. Introduces basic geographical concepts such as size, shape, rotation, and temperature zones.

Maps, Map Making, Map Reading and Map Uses

Beginnings: Edward Espenshade, Jr., Cartographer. 29 min., sound, B & W. (National Educational Television.) Indiana University. Upper and Teacher Education. A discussion of maps and their uses.

Charts. 18 min., sound, B & W. U.S. Navy. Upper and Teacher Education. Explains map projection—Mercator, gnomonic, and Lambert.

The Compass. 12 min., sound, B & W. McGraw-Hill. Upper-Primary and Middle. Demonstrates the principle of a compass.

Finding Directions with a Map. 12 min., sound, B & W or color. Cenco. Primary. Shows elementary geographical concepts of direction and map orientation.

Global Concepts in Maps. 11 min., sound, B & W or color. Coronet. Upper-Middle and Upper. Shows basic principles of map projection and their practical applications.

How Far? 10 min., sound, B & W or color. Indiana University. Primary. Describes the meaning of distance by showing distance on ground and a map.

Impossible Map. 10 min., sound, color. National Film Board of Canada. Middle and Upper. Presents problems of projecting the earth's spherical surface.

Language of Maps. 11 min., sound, B & W or color. Encyclopaedia Britannica. Middle and Upper. Shows language of maps made up of symbols to represent physical and cultural features.

Let's Make a Map. 11 min., sound, B & W or color. Film Associates. Primary. Helps pupils learn how the world is represented on a map through the use of models.

Map Reading, Basic: Characteristics of Contour Lines. 6 min., sound, B & W. Borrow from U.S. Army. Upper and Teacher Education. Shows how to read contour lines on a topographic map.

Map Reading, Basic: Direction. 4 min., sound, B & W. Borrow from U.S. Army. Upper and Teacher Education. Defines true north, magnetic north, and grid north.

Map Reading, Basic: Elevation. 5 min., sound, B & W. Borrow from U.S. Army. Upper and Teacher Education. Shows methods used to indicate elevation.

Map Reading, Basic: Location. 4 min., sound, B & W. Borrow from U.S. Army. Middle and Upper. Gives instruction on the reading of grid line coordinates.

Map Reading, Basic: Scale and Distance. 5 min., sound, B & W. Borrow from U.S. Army. Upper-Middle and Upper. Describes how to determine scale.

Mapping the World. 26 min., sound, color. U.S. Army Engineers. Upper. Depicts making of maps and their uses by the Army.

Maps: An Introduction. 12 min., sound, B & W or color. Indiana University. Primary. Portrays the making of a map.

Maps Are Fun. (Second edition.) 11 min., sound, B & W or color. Coronet. Middle. Shows how a boy makes a map of his paper route with an explanation of the basic principles of a map.

Maps—Coastal Symbols and Terms. 14 min., sound, color. Academy Films. Middle and Upper. Third in a series, shows how U.S. coastline formations are represented on maps and how these formations actually appear from aerial photographic views.

Maps for a Changing World. 11 min., sound, B & W. Encyclopaedia Britannica. Upper. Map projections—their history and possible developments.

Maps—Land Symbols and Terms. 14 min., sound, color. Academy Films. Middle and Upper. An animated map and direct photographic description of cultural and physical features of the United States.

Maps of Our Locality. 13 min., sound, color. Bailey. Upper-Primary and Middle. A field trip and a photograph build meanings for maps and their use as reference material.

Maps of Our School. 11 min., sound, color. Bailey. Primary. Introduces three aspects in developing readiness for map-reading concepts: size relationship, symbolic representation, and direction.

Maps of Our World. 13 min., sound, color. Bailey. Middle. Uses scenes followed by models, contour maps, and conventional elevation maps to introduce three-dimensional map-reading skills.

Maps and Pioneers. 23 min., sound, color. Virginia State Board of Education. Upper-Middle and Upper. Maps and the early explorations of North America.

Maps and Their Meaning. 14½ min., sound, color. Academy Films, 1950. Middle and Upper. An animated map and direct photographic description of the meaning of a physical map of the United States.

Maps and Their Uses. 11 min., sound, B & W or color. Coronet. Middle. Shows how to read and use maps.

Principles of Scale Drawing. 11 min., sound, B & W or color. Coronet. Middle. Introduces basic principles and practical application to solve a problem.

Reading Maps. 11 min., sound, color. Encyclopaedia Britannica. Middle. Illustrates the skills needed to read a map.

Topographic Symbols. 18 min., sound, B & W. Borrow from U.S. Army. (Released for public educational use through U.S. Office of Education.) Middle and Upper. Shows how to read symbols and the meaning of color.

Which Way? 11 min., sound, B & W or color. Indiana University. Primary. Develops understanding of directions in space.

Physical Geography—Land Forms and Agents of Erosion and Deposition

Birth and Death of Mountains. 12½ min., sound, B & W or color. Film Associates. Middle and Upper. Shows the effects of tectonic and gradational forces on mountains.

The Earth: Changes in Its Surface. 11 min., sound, B & W or color. Coronet. Upper. Explains and demonstrates forces changing the surface of the earth.

The Earth in Change: The Earth's Crust. 16 min., sound, B & W or color. Encyclopaedia Britannica. Middle and Upper. Shows the action of forces that are changing the earth's surface.

Erosion—Leveling the Land. 14 min., sound, color or B & W. Encyclopaedia Britannica. Middle and Upper. Investigates the processes of weathering, erosion, and deposition and shows how movement of materials makes the land level.

Face of the Earth. 12 min., sound, color. Encyclopaedia Britannica. Upper.

Shows the forces that have shaped the earth's surface.

Geography of the United States—An Introduction. 13½ min., sound, B & W or color. Coronet. Middle. An overview of geographic features of the U.S.

Geography of Your Community. 11 min., sound, B & W or color. Coronet. Upper-Primary and Middle. Illustrates ways of studying a local community.

Lands and Waters of Our Earth. 11 min., sound, B & W or color. Coronet. Primary. Pictures a boy becoming aware of the many kinds of land and water forms.

Map of Hawaii—Hawaii's Land and Its Uses. 18 min., sound, color. Academy Films. Middle and Upper. Presents geography of the state, physical and cultural, including the variety of land uses.

Mountains. 11 min., sound, B & W or color. Indiana University. Elementary. Develops visual background for interpreting mountains on a map.

Our Earth. 12 min., sound, B & W or color. Cenco. Middle. Surveys the earth's major physical features.

Our Earth. 11 min., sound, B & W. Encyclopaedia Britannica. Upper. Describes principal physical aspects of the earth's surface including the influence of oceans and ocean currents.

Our Shrinking World. 11 min., sound, B & W. McGraw-Hill. Middle and Upper. Developments in communication and transportation bring the world closer together.

Understanding Our Earth: How Its Surface Changes. 11 min., sound, B & W and color. Coronet. Middle. Illustrates the forces which build up and wear away the earth's surface.

Why Do We Still Have Mountains? 20 min., sound, color or B & W. Encyclopaedia Britannica. Middle and Upper. Explores the formation of mountains and examines the evidence associated with the uplift of earth's crust.

Rivers and Water Resources

Albeni Fall Dam. 28 min., sound, color. Borrow from Corps of Engineers. Upper. A documentary film of the completed project on the Pend Oreille River, Idaho.

Dams (Primary Civilization Series). 10 min., sound, color. (John Griswell.) Gateway. Middle. Types of dams; why they are built and their construction.

Great River. 28 min., sound, color. (U.S. Bureau of Reclamation.) Frederick K. Rockett. Upper. Portrays the Pacific Northwest and the Columbia River system.

Rivers. 11 min., sound, B & W or color. Indiana University. Elementary. Develops understanding of rivers in the landscape and on a map.

The River. 32 min., sound, B & W. (U.S. Department of Agriculture.) DuArt. Upper and Teacher Education. A dramatic documentary of the history of the Mississippi River.

The River Valley. 11 min., sound, B & W or color. Encyclopaedia Britannica.

Middle and Upper. Explains formation of a river and its valley and shows the related activities of man.

Work of Rivers. 11 min., sound, B & W. Encyclopaedia Britannica. Upper-Middle and Upper. Shows running water at work including erosion and deposition.

Sun-Earth Relationships

The Big Sun and Our Earth. 11 min., sound, B & W or color. Coronet. Primary. Introduces concepts about the sun and its effect on the earth.

Earth and the Sun. 12 min., sound, B & W or color. Cenco. Upper-Primary and Middle. Presents concepts of earth-sun relationships.

Earth in Motion. 16 min., sound, B & W or color. Encyclopaedia Britannica. Upper. Spherical nature of the earth, orbit around the sun, rotation and revolution.

The Earth in Motion. 12 min., sound, B & W or color. Cenco. Middle and Upper. Basic presentation of the earth's movements—rotation, revolution, and inclination.

How We Know the Earth Moves. 11 min., sound, B & W or color. Film Associates. Middle and Upper. Demonstrates and explains the Foucault Pendulum including audience participation in an experiment that illustrates star shift.

Planet Earth: Shape of the Earth. 28 min., sound, color. (National Academy of Sciences.) McGraw-Hill. Upper. Detailed analysis of the earth's shape.

Shadows on Our Turning Earth. 10 min., sound, B & W or color. Film Associates. Middle. Illustrates how rotation causes shadows that produce day and night.

Weather and Climate

Climate and the World We Live In. 13 min., sound, B & W or color. Coronet. Middle and Upper. Climate and the factors which determine it—latitude, altitude, nearness to water, ocean currents, and mountain ranges.

The Climates of North America. 16 min., sound, color. National Film Board of Canada. Middle and Upper. Explains climate patterns with illustrations.

Origins of Weather. 13 min., sound, B & W or color. Encyclopaedia Britannica. Middle and Upper. Explains how the atmosphere, the sun's heat, and the moving masses of air produce changing weather conditions.

Reading Weather Maps. 13½ min., sound, B & W or color. Coronet. Middle and Upper. Shows how to identify and interpret symbols used on weather maps.

Water, Water, Everywhere. 11 min., sound, B & W or color. Coronet. Primary. Shows water evaporation and precipitation.

Water in the Weather. 16½ min., sound, B & W or color. Academy. Middle and Upper. Explains factors affecting the weather through the use of simple experiments and demonstrations.

FILMSTRIPS

All the filmstrips listed are 35mm. Each entry provides information about color, producer or distributor, and recommended grade levels. The addresses of producers or distributors are listed on pages 488–489.

Animal Geography Series. B & W. Hulton. Primary. *The Hot Lands, The Temperate Lands, The Cold Lands.*

Conservation Series. Color. SVE. Middle and Upper. *Soil Conservation Today, Forest Conservation Today, Water Conservation Today, Wildlife Conservation Today, Mineral Conservation Today, Urban Conservation, Land Conservation Today.* Teacher's manual and record for each filmstrip.

Conserving Resources Series. Color. Elkins. Middle and Upper. *Soil Resources, Forest Resources, Wildlife Resources, Water Resources, Mineral Resources, Human Resources, The Field Day.*

Earth, Home of Man Series. Color. Eye Gate. Middle and Upper. *This Earth of Ours, Where Man Lives, The Surface of the Land, Uplands and Plateaus, Coastal Lands, The Oceans, Islands, Mountains, Climate and Weather.* Includes teacher's manual.

The Earth and Its Moons. Color. McGraw-Hill. Upper. *The Earth's Shape and Size, Motions of the Earth in Space, The Earth as a Planet, Exploring the Space Around Earth, Information from Satellites, The Moon.*

Earth and Man Series. Color. Eye Gate. Middle and Upper. *South America—Physical Features and Natural Resources, South America—Climate and Vegetation, South America—Human Resources, Africa—Physical Features and Natural Resources, Africa—Climate and Vegetation, Africa—Human Resources, South Asia—Physical Features and Natural Resources, South Asia—Climate and Vegetation, South Asia—Human Resources.* Includes teacher's manual.

Earth Science Maps Series. Color. Jam Handy. Middle and Upper. *Meridians and Parallels, Flat Maps from Round Globe, Navigating the Globe, Topographical Maps, Weather Maps.*

Earth and Sky Series. Color. Elkins. Middle and Upper. *How Our Earth Began, About Our Earth, Our Earth Is Moving, Our Changing Earth.*

Essential Geography Set. B & W. Hulton. Middle. *Homes in Many Lands, Food in Many Lands, Clothes in Many Lands, Transport in Many Lands.*

Exploring Through Maps Series. B & W. McGraw-Hill. Middle. *Let's Read Our Maps* (color), *Maps and Men, Flat Maps of a Round World, Maps and Their Meanings, We Live on a Huge Ball.*

The Forest Community Series. Color. McGraw-Hill. Upper. *Building the Soil, Where Trees Grow, How Trees Grow, Forest Plants and Animal Relationships, Forests for the Future.*

Fundamental Elements of Weather Series. Color. Eye Gate. Middle and Upper. *Weather and Life, The Weather Powerhouse, Adventures of a Rain Drop, Our Ocean of Air, Whirling Winds, The World of Clouds, Weatherman at Work, Changing the Weather, Weather Folklore.* Includes teacher's manual.

The Fundamentals of Geography Series. Color. Eye Gate. Middle and Upper. *The Solar System and the Universe; The Earth on Which We Live; The Earth and Its Motions; Latitude, Longitude and Time; Maps, Globes and Graphs; Violent Forces of Nature; Air and the Weather; Land Areas and Land Formation; The Waters Around Us; What Do You Know?*

Gazetteers and Atlases (Library Tools Series). Color. McGraw-Hill. Upper.

How to Use Maps and Globe Series. Color. McGraw-Hill. Middle. *Maps: What They Are, Map Symbols and Terms, Globes: Our Most Accurate Maps, Latitude and Longitude—Finding Places and Directions, Latitude and Longitude—Time Zones and Climate.*

Introducing Map Scale. Color. Stanbow Productions. Middle and Upper.

Introducing the Topographical Map. Color. Stanbow Productions. Middle and Upper.

Introduction to the Globe Series. Color. Jam Handy. Middle. *Continents and Oceans; Up and Down; North, South, East and West; Night and Day; Hot and Cold Places.*

Introduction to Maps Series. Color. Jam Handy. Middle. *What Is a Map?; Coast Lines and Their Symbols; Land Forms and Their Symbols; Lakes, Rivers and Their Symbols; Towns, Cities and Their Symbols.*

Introduction to Our Earth and Sun Series. Color. SVE. Primary. *Our Earth: Land, Water and Air, Earth's Blanket of Air, How Earth's Movements Affect Us.* Teacher's guide and records.

Looking at the Earth We Live on Series. Color. McGraw-Hill. Middle. *Oceans and Coasts, Lakes and Rivers, High and Low Lands, Our Land and Its Waters, Weather and Seasons, Climate and Plants.*

Maps and How to Use Them Series. Color. (Produced with cooperation of American Geographical Society by Museum Extension Service.) Eye Gate. Middle. *What a Map Is, Elements of a Map, Using Common Maps, Maps of Physical Features, Maps for Special Purposes, The Globe, Using the Globe, Flat Maps Made Round, Maps for the Air Age, Maps Through the Ages.* 16-page teacher's manual available.

Nations of Today Series. Color. Filmstrip House. Upper. *France: Geography, Italy: Geography.* Includes teacher's guide and records.

The New Basic Weather Series. Color. SVE. Middle and Upper. *New—Why Does the Weather Change? New—Why the Seasons? New—Why Does It Rain, Snow, Hail and Sleet?*

Our Earth Series. Color. Jam Handy. Middle. *How We Think Our Earth Came to Be, Our Earth Is Changing, How Rocks Are Formed, The Story of the Earth We Find in Rocks, The Soil.*

Our Ever Changing Earth Series. Color. SVE. Middle and Upper. *Work of Running Water, Work of Wind, Work of Ground Water, Work of the Sea, Work of Snow and Ice, Work of Internal Forces.*

Outline Maps. B & W. McGraw-Hill. Middle and Upper. Suitable for projection on a chalkboard. *Asia and Australia* (19 maps), *The Americas* (21 maps), *Europe and Africa* (19 maps).

Physical Geography. B & W. Hulton. Upper. *The Work of the Sea—Waves and Destruction, The Work of the Sea—Constructive Processes, The Work of the Rivers, The Work of Ice, The Work of the Weather.*

Physical Geography Program. Programmed Instruction for Fourth Grade. Color. Eye Gate. Middle. A set of 39 filmstrips presents physical geography in programmed form. Contents: *The Desert* (5 filmstrips), *The Mediterranean Lands* (5 filmstrips), *The Mid-Latitude Grasslands* (6 filmstrips), *The Mid-Latitude Lands of Four Seasons* (6 filmstrips), *Northern Forest Lands* (5 filmstrips), *The Polar Lands of the Arctic* (5 filmstrips), *The Tropical Rain Forest* (6 filmstrips).

Physiographic Changes Series. Color. SVE. Middle and Upper. *Changing the Face of the Earth, Rivers of Water and Ice, Underground Water, Wind and Waves, Volcanoes and Earthquakes, Mountains.* With teacher's guide.

Reading Meaning into Maps Through the Camera Lens Series. Color. Elkins. Middle. *Mountains and Valleys, Rivers and Lakes, Features in the Landscape, Coastal Features, Cities and Highways, Boundary Lines, Relief and Elevation, Building a World in Your Classroom.*

Screenmaps. Color. Hulton. Physical and economic maps, each filmstrip containing about 16 maps. *Britain, North America, Europe, Africa, Asia, South America, Australia.*

Seasons and Weather Series. Color. McGraw-Hill. Primary. *All My Seasons, Daytime and Nighttime, A Foggy and a Windy Day, A Hot Day, A Rainy Day, A Short Day.*

Seasons, Weather and Climate Series. Color. Jam Handy. Middle. *Our Earth in Motion, The Sun and Our Seasons, What Is Weather, What Makes the Weather, Climate.*

Weather Series. Color. Filmstrip House. Middle. *Heat and the Atmosphere, Air Pressure, Wind, Moisture in the Atmosphere.*

World Geography Series. Color. McGraw-Hill. Upper. *Vegetation and Man, Landforms and Man, Maps and Map Projections, Climate and Man, World Trade and Trade Routes, Producing the World's Food, Producing the World's Goods, Village, Town and City.*

The World We Live In Series. Color. Life. Middle and Upper. *The Earth Is Born, The Miracle of the Sea, The Face of the Land, The Canopy of Air, The Desert, The Arctic Tundra, The Rain Forest.*

Your Home in the Americas Series. Color. SVE. Middle. *Green Lands; Using Maps and Globes; Map Symbols, Dots and Lines; Where People Live and Work.*

Instructional Aids for Teacher Education

Globes: Their Function in the Classroom. 16mm. film, 14 min., sound, color. Bailey. Shows types of globes, illustrating their specific uses from primary grades through high school.

Face of the World. 16mm. film, 29 min., sound, color. (National Educational Television.) Indiana University. Story of man's geographic knowledge of the planet earth. Illustrates the extent to which geography is significant in human affairs. Demonstrates use of the atlas.

Our World. 16mm. film, 18 min., sound, color. International Film. A middle grade school class builds a globe.

Relief Models. 16 mm. film, 10 min., sound, color. David Lipscomb College, Nashville, Tenn.

Starting with the Globe. 35 mm. filmstrip, color. Denoyer-Geppert. Illustrates how globes help children learn fundamental concepts of geography.

Teaching Map Reading Skills in Elementary Schools. 16mm. film, 22 min., sound, color. Bailey. Illustrates how to implement a program in map understandings through a series of classroom activities at primary, middle, and junior high levels.

Film and Filmstrip Directory

Academy Films
1145 N. Las Palmas Avenue
Hollywood, California

Bailey Films, Inc.
6509 De Longpre
Hollywood, California

Cenco Educational Films
1700 Irving Park Road
Chicago, Illinois

Churchill Films
662 North Robertson Boulevard
Los Angeles, California

Coronet Films
Coronet Building
Chicago, Illinois

Corps of Engineers
U.S. Army
Washington, D.C.

DuArt Film Laboratories, Inc.
245 West 55th Street
New York, New York

H. M. Elkins Co.
10031 Commerce Avenue
Tujunga, California

Encyclopaedia Britannica Films, Inc.
1150 Wilmette Avenue
Wilmette, Illinois

Eye Gate House, Inc.
146–01 Archer Avenue
Jamaica, New York

Frederick K. Rockett Co.
6063 Sunset Boulevard
Hollywood, California

Film Associates of California
11014 Santa Monica Boulevard
Los Angeles, California

Filmstrip House
432 Park Avenue South
New York, New York

Gateway Productions Inc.
1859 Powell Street
San Francisco, California

Hulton Educational Publications Ltd.
55 Saffron Hill
London E.C. 1

Indiana University
Audio-Visual Center
Bloomington, Indiana

International Film Bureau Inc.
332 South Michigan Avenue
Chicago, Illinois

The Jam Handy Organization
2821 East Grand Boulevard
Detroit, Michigan

Life Filmstrips
9 Rockefeller Plaza
New York, New York

McGraw-Hill Text-Films
330 West 42nd Street
New York, New York

National Film Board of Canada
680 Fifth Avenue
New York, New York

Society for Visual Education, Inc.
1345 Diversey Parkway
Chicago, Illinois

Stanbow Productions
12 Cleveland St.
Valhalla, New York

U.S. Army, Signal Officer at the following addresses:

First Army
Governors Island
New York, New York

Second Army
Fort George G. Meade, Maryland

Third Army
Fort McPherson, Georgia

Fourth Army
Fort Sam Houston
San Antonio, Texas

Fifth Army
1660 East Hyde Park Boulevard
Chicago, Illinois

Sixth Army
Presidio
San Francisco, California

U.S. Navy, Commandant at the following addresses:

3rd Naval District
90 Church Street
New York, New York

4th Naval District
Naval Base
Philadelphia, Pennsylvania

9th Naval District
Building 1
Great Lakes, Illinois

12th Naval District
Federal Office Building
San Francisco, California

(For addresses of other Naval Districts check local telephone directory.)

Virginia State Board of Education
Bureau of Teaching Materials
Richmond, Virginia

United World Films, Inc.
Educational Films Dept.
1445 Park Avenue
New York, New York

MAP AND GLOBE SYMBOLS

The following eight pages contain the symbols most useful for pupils in the elementary and junior high school grades.

The first five pages show symbols for important cultural features—those that man has added to the landscape. The last three pages show symbols for important natural features.

Elementary school children will probably encounter all of the cultural symbols on the first three pages on their maps before they leave the elementary grades. They will also encounter many of the point and line symbols. Junior high school pupils will probably encounter all of the cultural symbols shown. If pupils have gone through the steps suggested in this book—(1) observing the landscape, (2) mapping the landscape, and (3) interpreting the maps of others—they should have no difficulty in understanding all of the cultural features. If they have missed some of these necessary steps, they should be taken through all three with at least some of the cultural features to ensure that they understand the origin of map symbols as a way of representing something that relates to the real landscape.

On the first three pages of cultural symbols and on the three pages of natural symbols, for each feature a pictorial representation is given at the left, and then its abstract representation at the right. The pictorial representation is an important step between the real landscape and the abstract symbol. The class might find it very useful to make a large chart of each pair of symbols by projecting the pictorial and abstract representations with an opaque projector. It would be wise to make a given chart when that symbol appears on a map being studied.

Some of the natural feature symbols are quite difficult and should probably not be introduced until junior high school. These include the abstract representations of contour lines for elevation, abstract mountains, and the map showing grassland, forest, and wooded area. However, the pictorial representations of the natural features should be within the understanding of elementary school pupils.

Cultural Features

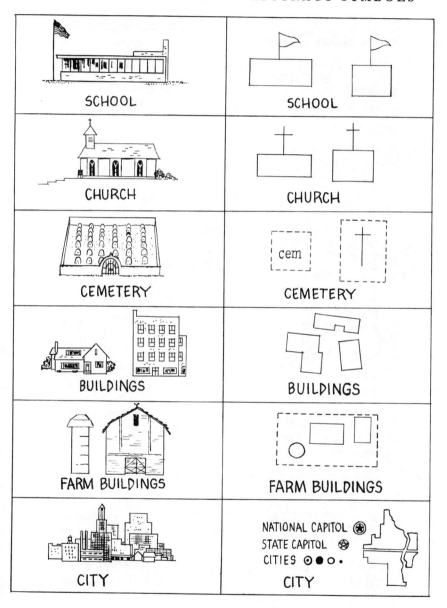

SCHOOL

SCHOOL

CHURCH

CHURCH

CEMETERY

cem

CEMETERY

BUILDINGS

BUILDINGS

FARM BUILDINGS

FARM BUILDINGS

CITY

NATIONAL CAPITOL ⊛
STATE CAPITOL ⊛
CITIES ⊙●○ ·

CITY

Cultural Features

HIGHWAY—FREEWAY / UNIMPROVED ROAD / **HIGHWAYS**	FREEWAY / PAVED / UNIMPROVED ROAD / **HIGHWAYS**
RAILROAD	RAILROAD
BRIDGE	BRIDGE
TUNNEL—RAILROAD	TUNNELS
AIRPORT	AIRPORT / HELIPORT
TELEPHONE OR TELEGRAPH LINE	TELEPHONE OR TELEGRAPH LINE

Cultural Features

PICTORIAL SYMBOLS	ABSTRACT SYMBOLS
DOCK	DOCK
DAM	DAM
PIPELINE	PIPELINE
CANAL	CANAL
ORCHARD	ORCHARD
CULTIVATED FIELDS	CULTIVATED FIELDS

Specialized Point Symbols

MOUNTAIN PEAK WITH ELEVATION IN FEET △ 2362	COAST GUARD STATION; ANCHORAGE ⚓
POINT OF INTEREST ■	LOOKOUT STATION ▽
LANDMARK ⊙	BUOY OR BEACON
CAMPSITE △	LIGHT BUOY
BASEBALL FIELD	MOORING MAST
HISTORICAL MONUMENT 🔔	BREAKWATER
OPEN-AIR THEATRE	LOCK (POINT UPSTREAM) ⇉

EXPERIMENTAL FARM ▬	CHURCH; CATHEDRAL; CHAPEL ▪ ✝
MINE, QUARRY	SPIRE; STEEPLE
FISH HATCHERY ⟨⟩	CHRISTIAN SHRINE
FISHERIES ⊔⊔⊔⊔⊔	SHINTO SHRINE
GRAVEL PIT	TEMPLE; PAGODA; BUDDHIST TEMPLE; JOSS HOUSE
OIL WELL ●	
OIL TANK ⊕ ·	MOSQUE; MINARET; MARABOUT
GAS WELL ⌀	MOSLEM SHRINE

POWER PLANT	TV TOWER ⊙ TV TR
RADIO STATION ⊙R. TR	RADAR STATION ◎ Ra

494

Specialized Line Symbols

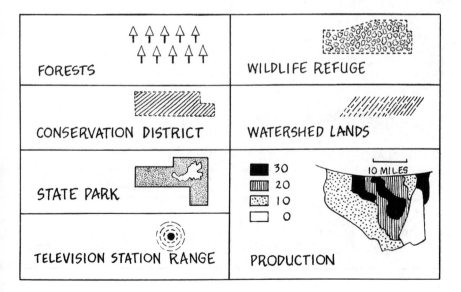

BOUNDARIES	**POWER TRANSMISSION**
INTERNATIONAL — ·· — ·· —	
STATE · — · — · — ·	**STREAM**
COUNTY – – – – – – –	
MILITARY STATION	**FERRY**
AIR ROUTES	**DISTRIBUTION**
SCENIC ROUTES	**WEATHER FRONT**
HIKING TRAIL	**TIME ZONE** X–X–X–X–X–X

Specialized Area Symbols

FORESTS	**WILDLIFE REFUGE**
CONSERVATION DISTRICT	**WATERSHED LANDS**
STATE PARK	**PRODUCTION** 30 20 10 0 10 MILES
TELEVISION STATION RANGE	

Natural Features

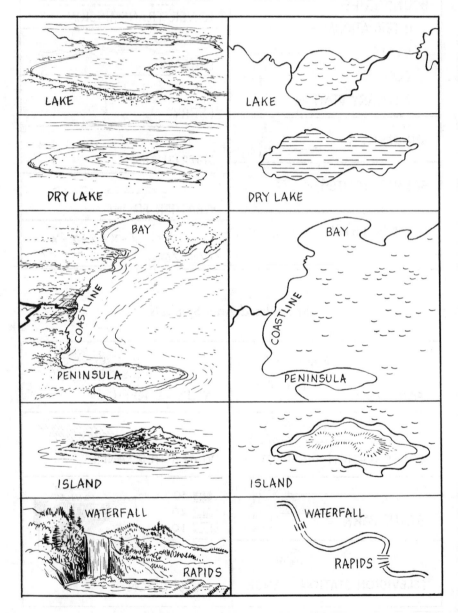

Natural Features

497

Natural Features

PICTORIAL SYMBOLS ABSTRACT SYMBOLS

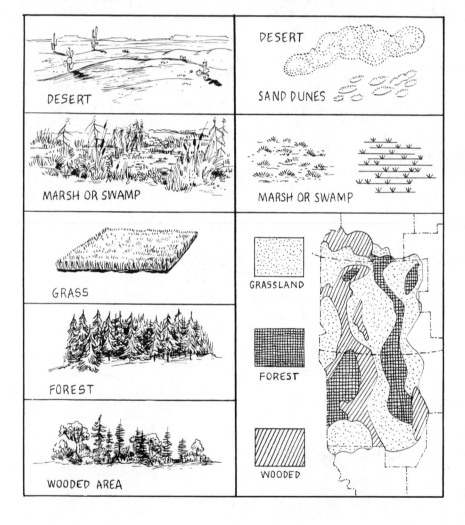

DESERT

SAND DUNES

DESERT

MARSH OR SWAMP

MARSH OR SWAMP

GRASS

GRASSLAND

FOREST

FOREST

WOODED AREA

WOODED

INDEX